NON-HUMANS IN AMERINDIAN
SOUTH AMERICA

EASA Series

Published in association with the European Association of Social Anthropologists (EASA)

Series Editor: Aleksandar Bošković, University of Belgrade

Social anthropology in Europe is growing, and the variety of work being done is expanding. This series is intended to present the best of the work produced by members of the EASA, both in monographs and in edited collections. The studies in this series describe societies, processes and institutions around the world, and are intended for both scholarly and student readership.

For a full volume listing, please see back matter.

NON-HUMANS IN AMERINDIAN SOUTH AMERICA

Ethnographies of Indigenous Cosmologies, Rituals and Songs

Edited by
Juan Javier Rivera Andía

berghahn
NEW YORK · OXFORD
www.berghahnbooks.com

First published in 2019 by
Berghahn Books
www.berghahnbooks.com

© 2019, 2022 Juan Javier Rivera Andía
First paperback edition published in 2022

Library of Congress Cataloging-in-Publication Data
A C.I.P. cataloging record is available from the Library of Congress
Library of Congress Cataloging in Publication Control Number: 2018026304

British Library Cataloguing in Publication Data
A catalogue record for this book is available from the British Library

ISBN 978-1-78920-097-3 hardback
ISBN 978-1-80073-445-6 paperback
ISBN 978-1-78920-098-0 ebook
https://doi.org/10.3167/9781789200973

Contents

Illustrations

Maps, Tables and Figures

Maps

Tables

Figures

Acknowledgements

I am grateful to the European Network of Social Anthropologists (EASA) for funding the one-week workshop attended by most of the contributors of this book, and also to the Netherlands Institute of Advance Studies (NIAS), who hosted us at their idyllic campus in Wassenaar, near the dunes of South Holland. Most of the volume consists of ethnographic case studies from South America, but these were informed by the theoretical conversations of the week we spent there. Although they could not join us until its final stage, I would like to mention Camilla Morelli, Harry Walker, María Antonieta Guzmán-Gallegos, Christopher Ball and Aristóteles Barcelos-Neto for their interest in this project. This project is also particularly indebted to Ramón Sarro and Simon Coleman, both coordinators of the EASA Religion Network, Eeva Berglund, former EASA book series editor, and Aleksandar Bošković, his successor, and to Aafke Hulk and Paul Emmelkamp, consecutive rectors of NIAS, where I could stay – this was also thanks to the support of the European Institutes for Advanced Study (EURIAS) Fellowship Programme. Informal conversations at the NIAS campus and 'blue room' with fellows Verena Berger, Natalie Scholz, Anne Gerritsen, Sharada Srinivasan, Marcelo Borges, Raphael Golosetti, Jürgen Jaspers, Teresa Proto, André Motingea, Florence Bernault and Carel Smith were also very useful. I am particularly indebted to Kathryn Woolard and Sander Adelaar for their insights on former drafts of the Introduction. This book also inherited some of its topics from the discussions held with Olivia Angé, Margarita Valdovinos, Dimitri Karadimas, Francis Ferrié, María Susana Cipolletti, Helmut Schindler, Diana Socoliuc, Ariane Monnier-Zographos and Fabiana Maizza at the symposia hosted in the 6. Treffen deutschsprachiger Südamerika-, Mesoamerika- und KaribikforscherInnen, organized by Karoline Noack, Nikolai Grube, Antje Gunsenheimer, Franziska Galinski and

Oliver Fritz in the Abteilung für Altamerikanistik und Ethnologie at the University of Bonn, where my research stay would not have been possible without the continuous support of the Alexander von Humboldt Stiftung. I also would like to thank Jonathan Devore from Yale University, Sofia Venturoli and Zelda Alice Franceschi from the Università di Bologna, and last but not least the Marie Curie Alumni Association for their support on specific phases of the production of this compilation. I thank the reviewers of the manuscript for their extraordinarily encouraging insights, and the contributors for tolerating my questions and those of the review process. Finally, all my gratitude to Margaux Majewska for her love.

Juan Javier Rivera Andía

Introduction

Towards Engaged Ontographies of Animist Developments in Amerindian South America

Juan Javier Rivera Andía

In memory of Dimitri Karadimas's *poursuite*

Nowadays we are prone to be less certain about the distinction between man and animal as well as finding ourselves with increasing frequency wondering whether things have souls, and what it means to call a thing a thing? We ask pointedly, What is an Animal? What is a Man? What is Life? … It is as if our humming is a conversation with the hummings of the world at large.

—M. Taussig, *The Corn Wolf*

How do the different norms, various moments, and diverse contexts found among South Amerindian peoples affect the principles around which indigenous daily interactions with non-humans occur? How do these interactions intersect with the human ability to give them multiple meanings, and what could be learned from it in the particular cases of South America? Which kinds of elements of the South American environments are considered to have human-like qualities, and for what reasons? How much productivity is left for categories such as 'culture' and 'nature' (and its various versions) in understanding a set of features considered as cross-species shared?

This volume offers bottom-up approaches – in the sense of a symmetric openness to the inflection of the ethnographer's concepts with the concepts of the field that he or she is confronted to – to relationships between human and non-human subjects among South American Amerindian peoples, illustrating both their spatial variations and temporal transformations. Following the evidence of their own fieldwork findings, the authors have compiled here work from ethnographic phenomena to theoretical frames, and their texts intend to stand in contrast to projects that are apparently mostly concerned with locating examples of more or less fixed typologies (Laugrand and Oosten 2007; Wardle and Schaffner 2017). Using different frameworks of interpretation and offering a series of mutually illuminating ethnographically focused studies, we would like this compilation to modestly contribute to a possible cross-fertilisation of current debates on non-humans in South America covering diverse groups (twelve in total, representing seven different language families), and contrasted – and usually opposed – geographical areas (those regions of the Chaco, the Andes and the Amazonia included in the territories of Peru, Chile, Paraguay, Brazil and Venezuela – see Map 0.1 of indigenous groups studied in this book).

Bringing together researchers from various institutions working in their different manners and from different angles, and in diverse ethnographic areas, this compilation engages with debates over the practical, symbolic and transformative aspects of human versus non-human interactions in the lowlands and highlands of South America. Although it would be impossible here to situate this volume in the long tradition of relevant South American ethnography, previous similar efforts include Claude Lévi-Strauss's fundamental *Mythologiques* (and the so-called *petites mythologiques*), later followed by compilations like those of Gary Urton (1985), Lawrence E. Sullivan (1988), Alejandro Ortiz Rescaniere (2006), Laugrand and Oosten (2007), and more recently Halbmayer (2012b) and Brightman, Grotti and Ulturgasheva (2012).[1]

The chapters joined here highlight the ethnographic complexities that allow 'the apprehension of more differentiated semiotic regimes' (Stolze Lima 2000: 51) linked to the relationships between humans and non-humans (like the souls of the dead, Incas, members of previous humanities, clans' properties, place-based beings, ritual offerings, plants, animals and artefacts). Themes explored include the relationships between Amerindian groups and 'natural' resources, and peasants or rural proletarians trying to make a living in the context of an extractive and exploitative economy that involves sociopolitical elites, communities, outsiders, and community members with differing opinions. Authors consider topics such as the subjectivity and agency of non-human beings, humans taking on non-human subjectivities, production and reproduction, continuity and change, and the situated context of time and symbolic landscapes. These topics are illustrated through their rituals, dances, musical expressions, narratives, material cultures, economic exchanges, and contemporary political vindications. They are addressed searching for 'ethnographic sites to conceptualise otherwise' (de la Cadena 2014) and for alternative forms of composing specific Amerindian worlds (Alberti et al. 2011). Seeking needed and practicable 'potential actions of other collectives' (Skafish 2016a: 79), this compilation aims to 'provide resonance to those other worlds that interrupt the one-world story' (Escobar 2016: 22). Avoiding both naturalist reductionisms and semiologist idealisms, every chapter intends to leave 'a way out for the people' who are described (Holbraad, Pedersen and Viveiros de

Map 0.1 Indigenous groups studied in this book. Map created by the author.

Castro 2014) producing 'non-existence points at the non-existence worlds' (Escobar 2016: 15).

A 'Bizarre Scandal' and an Ante-predicative Movement

Before describing and contextualising the contents of this book, I will offer a brief preliminary description of two key categories: 'non-human' and 'animism', both of which will be problematised and discussed in the following pages. The 'conceptual fuzziness' of the category of 'non-human' or 'other-than-human' has been justified considering its usefulness to 'recruit scores of new actants so as to render the theater of worldly interactions more complex' (Descola 2014a: 271–72). I intend to use this concept in a merely descriptive form and mainly as an alternative to 'nature', to 'supernatural beings' (which clearly mirrors the Western idea of nature) and also to 'spirits' (which evokes the spirit/body dualism of the modernist person concept) (Bird-David 1999: 71).[2]

It is important to highlight two aspects here. The first is that we are dealing with a 'contextual' non-human. It means that this category here 'has no overarching, common substantive (even if privative) definition' and therefore 'each non-human species is as different from all the others as it is from humans' (Viveiros de Castro 2015a: 226). The second aspect is that when these 'entities that are in constant interactions with us' (Descola 2014b: 281) are personified, they are given the capacities of conscious intentionality and social agency that define the position of the subject. In other words, non-humans are personified '*as*, *when*, and *because*' (Bird-David 1999: 78, emphasis in original) they are subjects and we socialise with them, rather than the other way around (Viveiros de Castro 2004a: 467. See also Venkatesan et al. 2013). Here, thus, personification is a *consequence* (Keane 2013: 189).

> *culture is the subject's nature*; it is the form in which every subject experiences its own nature. Animism is not a projection of substantive human qualities … but rather expresses the logical equivalence of the reflexive relations that humans and animals each have for themselves … 'humanity' is the name for the general form taken by the subject. (Viveiros de Castro 2015a: 245, emphasis in original)

The second concept that I wish to address is 'animism', 'the label traditionally applied to those ontological regimes in which … things and people assume the social form of persons' (Viveiros de

Castro 2015a: 149). Recently, the relations between humans and non-humans, both in South America and elsewhere, have been precisely considered through a redefined concept of 'animism' (Vilaça 1992; Århem 1996; Stolze Lima 1996, 1999; Howel 1996; Bird-David 1999; Stringer 1999; Morrison 2000; Pedersen 2001; Surrallés and García Hierro 2004; Descola 2005; Harvey 2005; Brightman, Grotti and Ulturgasheva 2012; Stengers 2012). Ethnographic peoples' postulation of 'ontological continuities … where the analyst's "common sense"… posits ontological separations' (Holbraad 2009: 431) has led to analytical considerations of an '[a]nimism's enigma of subverting same into other' (Willerslev 2013: 43).

As is well known, animism is one of the oldest concepts in anthropology, representing the 'century-old problem [of] why people animate what we regard as inanimate objects' (Bird-David 1999: 70). In fact, ethnologists' efforts to understand this 'bizarre scandal' (Kohn 2009: 136. See also Charbonnier, Salmon and Skafish 2017a: 9) could be traced at least to the very foundation of British social anthropology. Seminal work by Edward B. Tylor (1871) explained 'animism' in accordance with David Hume's thesis in *Natural History of Religion* (1757), taking the label from his 'contemporary spiritualists' (Brightman, Grotti and Ulturgasheva 2012: 3) and the German 'proto-vitalist' Ernst Stahl (Halbmayer 2012b: 9). After more than a century (Dransart 2013: 6), this attribution of a social character to relations between humans and non-humans is traditionally understood as configuring a world in which the default form of interaction between beings is modelled on that that occurs between subjects (Costa and Fausto 2010: 94).[3]

Some of the most important current theories dealing with animism have been primarily promoted by Viveiros de Castro (1998, 2004a, 2004b, 2009, 2012, 2015a) and Descola (2006, 2011), who are 'the main figureheads and provocateurs' (Wardle and Schaffner 2017: 11) of the so-called 'ontological turn'[4] in anthropology. This introduction will address the ontological turn only as a means of presenting the most recent contemporary debates concerning how Amerindians construct relations with non-humans (and in particular those discussions that have renovated the study of animism among various forms of otherness objectifications). Neither this Introduction nor this volume as a whole is interested in weighing or critiquing any of the diverse and still evolving perspectives that the ontological turn harbours today (Charbonnier, Salmon and Skafish 2017a: 19). In short, ontology is not used here as a strict method of investigation, but merely as an inspirational descriptive frame for recent studies closely linked to contemporary indigenous South America to which this volume contributes new material.[5]

The category of 'ontology' has been used as 'a concrete expression of how a particular world is composed, of what kind of furniture it is made, according to the general layout specified by a mode of identification' (Descola 2014d: 437). An ontology is based on something more general or 'more elementary' (Descola 2014b: 239) than, for instance, a cosmology: it is based on 'systems of properties that humans ascribe to beings' (Descola 2006: 139). These properties are censed to deal with 'generative patterns of inferences and actions, modes of worlds' composition and use that follow analogous principles and that, for this reason, can spread out in very similar forms in very diverse historical contexts' (Descola 2014b: 112, and 236–37. See also Skafish 2016b: 395). In contrast, for instance, a cosmology would be defined as something more specific: 'the form of distribution in space of the components of an ontology and the kind of relations that conjoin them' (Descola 2014d: 437. See also Law and Lien 2012; Jensen 2017: 530). Therefore, it has been suggested that in the Andes, for instance, 'certain landscapes' components [a lake, a mountain, a river, a cave, a slope] play an essential role in people's conception of social membership, they are full-fledged components of a collective much wider than human community' (Descola 2014b: 324).[6]

In short, as Pedersen (2012) puts it, ontology becomes 'anthropologically meaningful ... as "composition"'. Nevertheless, this composition takes different inflections. On the one hand, according to Descola, '[t]o compose a world is a form of perception, actualisation and detection (or non-detection) of our environment's qualities and of the relationships established at it' (Descola and Ingold 2014: 30). On the other hand, Tim Ingold has stressed the processual dimension of this notion of composition: 'a continuous process ... a perpetual development ... to compose the world is not to represent life as if it existed beforehand, but to make life come out as it grows' (ibid.: 37–38). In sum, while Descola considers the so-called composition of the worlds as a form of perception, actualisation and detection of certain qualities, Ingold thinks of it more as a construction, a development, a sort of instigation of life growth.

I will come back to this contrast later. For now, let us note that in both cases, ontology would open the field to explore the 'more fundamental intuitions [,] ... basic inferences' (Descola 2014b: 239–40) or, put more simply, some kind of 'reality' (Kohn 2015). It envisages a 'science of beings and of relationships yet to come' (Descola 2014b: 245) that could 'highlight the elemental components of the syntax of worlds and the rules of their combination' (ibid.: 265). In an ontologically inflected anthropology, animism has been redefined as an ontology concerned much more with 'being' than with *how* we come to know it, or if being is knowable at all (i.e. via epistemology). This has been recurrently used by many scholars as an argument for a critique of a 'Western European mononaturalist-multiculturalist ideology' based on a (particular) nature–culture binary (Latour 2009). They assert that 'the space between nature and society is itself social' (Viveiros de Castro 2004a: 481; 2015a: 232). In consequence, in order to truly understand the environment, we need to ignore or overcome the dualism that opposes nature to society. We must deny the existence of one unifying nature '[distilled] into its material properties alone, uncontaminated by symbolic meanings or social relations' (Hornborg 2006: 21; see also Hornborg 2013). We need to abandon the intellectualist perspective (Bird-David 1999: 83) that stabilises universality 'too fast' and accepts plurality 'too lightly' (Latour 2014b: 302). Finally, we might also need to recognise that '"what exists" is always in between the subject–object divide that is central to the modern ontology and [that] ... "what exists" is always the ongoing effect of practices or performances' (Blaser 2009: 11).[7] With this proposal and the consideration that 'objectivity and subjectivity, as well as morality and politics, are indissolubly entangled' (ibid.: 14), Blaser responds to a persistent 'factual' critique. This assessment of the ontological turn is concerned with an 'absence of objectivity' (Karadimas 2012: 28–29) and issues that produce questions such as the following: '[O]n what grounds can we make such a claim that it is the world and not our construal of it that differs?' (Keane 2013: 187. See also Wardle and Schaffner 2017: 10–23).

Thus, the distinction between some things of the world that would fall within the jurisdiction of human intentionality, and others that would obey to the universal laws of the material (Descola 2011: 34), would neither be universal nor demonstrable. It would merely be a conventional form 'of carving ontological domains in the texture of things' (Descola 2014c: 271). In fact, we would be facing an 'infernal' or 'nasty' dichotomy (Course 2010: 253; Viveiros de Castro 2015a), a contingent dualism that is 'historically situated and just one of many other possible and indeed empirically existing modes of understanding relations' (Brightman, Grotti and Ulturgasheva 2012: 1. See also Kapfhammer 2012: 152).

The following section will summarise two main well-known approaches that have emerged from both anti-dualist approaches and South American ethnography: Descola's new animism and Viveiros de Castro's perspectivism. It will highlight the continuities rather than the differences between them, as that has been stressed before (Karadimas 2012).

From Cosmochemistry to Bomb

Descola's fourfold typology of ontologies and six modes of identification – called cosmochemistry by Scott (2014) – follow his interest in actions and processes of knowledge that have already been accomplished.[8] According to him, what should be analysed is the institutional manifestation of these changing relationships between human and non-human entities (Descola 2011: 13, 76):

> the solidification, the actualisation, the objectification of those schemes in institutions … the stabilisation of worlds' compositions in devices whose power and duration persist beyond any individual existence.[9]

According to some scholars, this interest would overshadow the fact that 'these ontologies–worlds are not pregiven entities but rather the product of historically situated practices' (Blaser 2009: 11). Closer to Tim Ingold's proposal (see below), Blaser adds that 'the borders that delineate them [these ontologies–worlds] have to be traced constantly for they are in a constant state of becoming, not least through their ongoing interactions' (ibid.: 16. See also Medrano and Tola 2016).[10]

It is worth noticing, nevertheless, that this recognition could be implied in Descola's consideration of its typology as 'a kind of experimental machine' (Descola 2014b: 224; see also Kohn 2009: 143). Similar to Holbraad's 'analytical artifices' (2012: 255) and to Pedersen's 'open-ended and creative technology of ethnographic description' (2014: 5), this 'heuristic device' of Descola would allow us to identify how the inference of animism is being favoured or inhibited (Kohn 2009: 144). It would allow us, consequently, to recognise the frequent possibility of finding different degrees of prominence of modes of identification within the same society.

These 'degrees' take us to the issue of 'ontological hybridity' (Descola 2014d: 442. See also Scott 2014). Probably one of the most elegantly simple forms to deal with this problem has been proposed by Marshal Sahlins, who has rebaptised Descola's ontological grid or quartet (Skafish 2016a: 73) as composed of 'communal', 'segmentary' and 'hierarchical' forms of animism.[11] In the same vein as Descola takes Viveiros de Castro's 'perspectivism' as a particular elaboration of an animist ontology, Sahlins includes the former's animism within 'one overall human ontology' (Kelly 2014: 358). This 'animic ground' would be a form of anthropomorphism writ large (Karadimas 2012). As its 'closest systematization' (Descola 2014e: 295), this amplified animism would include naturalism (Sahlins 2014: 282) as one expression, though to a lower degree, of the same 'animic subjectivity'. Thus, although the degree of personhood is recognised as more present in animism – inasmuch as it implies the attribution of (human-like) subjectivity, agency and emotion – it would not be completely absent in naturalism. In any case, it becomes clear that animism cannot be isolated from its contexts, circumstances or relative positions in any given ontology or system of knowledge: the 'degree of subjectivity attributed to objects' are 'open to negotiation and debate ... [and] perceived by ... different categories of people in very different ways' (Santos-Granero 2009: 10). This position in which animism is neither fully present nor fully absent in any given group, in fact advocates that, at least apparently, the most common case could be that of hybridity or complex combinations (Dransart 2013: 7; Sahlins 2014: 282; Descola 2014c: 277; Bartolomé 2015; Wardle and Schaffer 2017: 29).

Among others, Lucas Bessire (2014: 19) has expressed his scepticism towards the supposition that Amerindian multinaturalism is external to modernity's predominant naturalism. This reservation is mainly directed towards what Michael Scott has described as

> [T]he chief distinction between ... Cartesian dualists [who] see things ... as discrete entities, [and] relational non-dualists [who] see things as relations, both internally and externally, [and for whom] ... there are no pure unmixed things or essences, only the web of relations which inhere in things and in which things inhere (Scott 2013: 867).

In consequence, the field is opened to subtler and more particular hierarchies between modes of identifications.[12] Descola himself has recently recognised that a 'hierarchical encompassment' would not be completely satisfying if the articulation of the ontologies were to be 'accidental' instead of 'built as potentialities into the very structure of the initial set of contrasts' (Descola 2014d: 441). Still, in another work, he has used the concept of 'permeability' (*perméabilité*) between different modes of identification (Scott 2014), but always pointing out its limitation to two final options: either an absorption or a radical change (Descola 2014b: 303–4).[13]

Besides the consideration of perspectivism as a type or as an extension of animism (Kohn 2009: 139; Karadimas 2012: 25–26; Halbmayer 2012b: 7, 12), some scholars have taken seriously the former's potential to provoke a crisis (Charbonnier, Salmon and Skafish 2017a: 1), to constitute a 'bomb' destroying a 'whole implicit philosophy' (Latour 2009: 2) of the interpretations ethnographers make of their material. In a recent interview, Viveiros de Castro stated: 'On the basis of perspectivism, it was easy to imagine a counteranthropology that could redescribe Western or modern anthropology ... a political object, a very handy political weapon against ... the "colonization of thought"' (Skafish 2016b: 410).

Furthermore, they justify this bomb as an 'end of the "Internal Great Divide" between culture and nature, and therefore of the fundamental characteristic that differentiates (and supposedly makes superior) the moderns in relation to the "others"' (Blaser 2009: 17). Always in the case of Amerindian societies, thanks to its 'collapse' of the 'modern constitution' (ibid.: 11), the multinaturalist approach would allow us to accept the existence of multiple ontologies or worlds, and to focus 'on what kinds of worlds are there and how they come into being' (ibid.: 18).

The elaborations of perspectivism on the physical discontinuity between the beings of the cosmos – the counterpart of the metaphysical continuity implied in animism – have lead it to define the body as 'the great arena' (Seeger, DaMatta and Viveiros de Castro 1979: 14), the 'assemblage of affects or ways of being that constitute a habitus' (Viveiros de Castro 2015a: 257).

The importance of the 'body' in perspectivism is such that it, for instance, defines nature as 'being the form of the other as body' (Viveiros de Castro 2015a: 273). Also, it creates a point of divergence from Descola's animism. As Viveiros de Castro said to Peter Skafish: 'Philippe had stopped at the realization that Indians think that everything in the universe has a soul – that's animism. But as to where the differences between things with souls come from, he had no answer to that question. My answer ... [is] that the difference comes from the body' (Skafish 2016b: 406). In fact, in the case of Descola, 'bodies are necessary paradoxes: they are both excessively effective barriers and eminently malleable means of intersubjective relations' (Scott 2014).

The theoretical consequences of considering the body as the 'site and instrument of ontological differentiation and referential disjunction' (Viveiros de Castro 2004b: 4) are clear in the definition itself of perspectivism as a set of ideas and practices that 'imagines a universe peopled by different types of subjective agencies, human as well as non-human, each endowed with the same generic type of soul, ... which determine that all subjects see things in the same way' (ibid.).

As Karadimas has rightly noticed, '[t]here seem to be no stable identities in the world view of the "perspectivist subject", as identity depends on the subject and that subject's point of view' (Karadimas 2012: 27). He was in fact only echoing one of the fundamental postulates of Perspectivism: '[This] representational or phenomenological unity … is purely pronominal or deictic, indifferently applied to a radically objective diversity. One culture, multiple natures – one epistemology, multiple ontologies' (Viveiros de Castro 2004a: 474).

Viveiros de Castro himself stresses this issue: 'Same representations, different objects; same meaning, different reference. This is perspectivism … A perspective is not a representation because representations are a property of the mind or spirit, whereas the point of view is located in the body' (2015a: 256). Taking Amazonian mythologies as an example, he makes explicit that '[b]lood is to humans as manioc beer to jaguars, in exactly the same way as a sister to me is a wife to my brother-in-law' (ibid.: 254). What the study of 'Amerindian souls' as indexical categories or 'cosmological deictics' would need is then 'a theory of the sign or a perspectival pragmatics' (ibid.: 244):

> The human bodily form and human culture … are deictics, pronominal markers … They are reflexive or apperceptive schematisms … by which all subjects apprehend themselves, and not literal and constitutive human predicates projected metaphorically … onto non-humans. Such deictic 'attributes' are immanent in the viewpoint, and move with it. (ibid.: 245)

In perspectivism, then, 'body and soul, just like nature and culture, do not correspond to substantives, self-subsistent entities or ontological provinces, but rather to pronouns or phenomenological perspectives' (ibid.: 268). It might not be useless to insist that, in concordance, here the categories of nature and culture 'refer to exchangeable perspectives and relational-positional contexts; in brief, points of view' (ibid.: 197).

It might also be worth noticing that perspectivism not only stresses (as animism) a certain porosity between the ontological status given to humans and non-humans (Césard, Deturche and Erikson 2003). Instead of the mere collecting of data about indigenous peoples for Western theoretical elaboration, perspectivism would also privilege the exploration of 'indigenous anthropologies' (Brightman, Grotti and Ulturgasheva 2012: 13; Charbonnier, Salmon and Skafish 2017: 7–14). Furthermore, it would stress an equivalence between academic and indigenous epistemologies, as has long been demanded by some anthropologists (Narotzky 2010). Therefore, perspectivism could be considered as a 'potentially generatively comparative' (Kohn 2015) Amerindian theory[14] of the subject (Tola, Medrano and Cardin 2013: 29). Nevertheless, we should keep in mind that it would be so not in the sense of

> a systematic, exhaustive native model without internal contradiction that applies deductively to the facts, but ... [only as] a set of interconnected assumptions, which inform and are informed by social practice, and which present a reasonable degree of internal coherence and interpretative flexibility. (Fausto 2012: 189)

In sum, perspectivism as a modality of Amerindian cosmology 'not only offers resources for thinking about alter-modernities but is itself just such a site of alter-modernity' (Scott 2013: 867. See also Salmon 2017: 55; Candea 2017: 85).[15]

At this point, it is important to remember that both Descola's new animism and Viveiros de Castro's perspectivism not only reject the dualism between nature and culture, but also rely on another fundamental dual distinction: that between interiority and physicality (Keane 2013: 187; Tola 2015; Skafish 2016a: 66,76). The epistemic opposition between interiority and physicality (*physicalité*) is key for the arguments of the ontological turn. It is a sort of 'hypothetical invariant' (*invariant hypothétique*) (Descola 2014b: 124) with the ambition to 'exploit universal mental constrains' (Salmon and Charbonnier 2014: 568). Interiority (sometimes called 'spirit' or 'soul') involves an intentionality, a subjectivity, a 'reflexive form', and a certain awareness that one is animated by an immaterial inner flow (but not necessarily by an immaterial inner substance). Physicality (sometimes called 'body') has been described as 'affectual dispositions', a system of physiological, perceptual, sensory-motor and intensive affects, as the awareness that one is embedded in systematic material constraints, but not necessarily an extended material organism or a substance (Halbmayer 2012b: 13; Kohn 2015; Viveiros de Castro 2015a: 260, 273). While interiority integrates, physicality differentiates (Viveiros de Castro 2004a: 475; Descola 2011: 94). Additionally, they are useful to contrast perspectivism and animism. If the definition of interiority mentioned above has been deemed the 'principle tenet of animism', the concept of physicality would be 'the minimum condition' for perspectivism (Costa and Fausto 2010: 94).[16] While in animism what matters is metaphysical continuity, what is at stake in perspectivism is the physical discontinuity between the beings of the cosmos (Viveiros de Castro 2015a: 260). '[I]f salmon look to salmon as humans to humans – and this is 'animism' – salmon do not look human to humans and neither do humans to salmon – and this is 'perspectivism' (ibid.: 247).

It is also important to notice that, if according to animism all creatures possess a kind of interiority, in the case of perspectivism they are all human in so far as they share a human culture (Course 2010: 250) or subjectivity (Sztutman 2008: 6). In short, metaphysical continuity seems to be present in Descola's animism in a more restricted form than in Viveiros de Castro's perspectivism.

In the case of Descola (2014d: 440), he has recently recognised his 'esthetic addiction to symmetry' and the 'irony' of taking as a universal or a pan-human cognitive propensity (Kohn 2009: 138) the awareness of a Husserlian distinction between material processes and mental states (Descola [2005] 2006: 138; Skafish 2016a: 90).[17] In the case of Viveiros de Castro, the following lines might illustrate what happens in perspectivism:

> The 'human mode' can be imagined, then, as the fundamental frequency of this animic field we can call meta-human ... every entity situated in a subject position perceives itself *sub specie humanitatis* – living species and other natural kinds (including our own species) can be imagined to inhabit this field's domain of visibility. (Viveiros de Castro 2007: 161)

To what extent does the equivalence between interiority and human qualities permeate or charge Descola's animism and Viveiros de Castro's perspectivism? Is the above-mentioned definition of interiority actually humanising all actants (Kelly 2014: 358)? According to some authors, in perspectivism 'the sharing of spirit by animals and plants comes down to a sharing of humanity' (Turner 2009: 17). Furthermore, Turner (ibid.: 37) states that, at least in Amazonian animism, the possession of a subjectivity 'does not in and of itself indicate that an animal or plant therefore identifies itself as human'. He has also found either untenable or contradictory 'the mutual dissociation and irrelevance of external bodily (natural, affective) form and internal spiritual (cultural, cognitive) content' (ibid.: 25–26). Moreover, Turner disputes perspectivism's conception of the body – 'this complex entity, comprised of the physiological body as mediated by the social body' (ibid.: 29) – as an external 'envelope' (ibid.: 31). In sum, 'granting ... to non-humans of an interiority identical to' humans (Rival 2012a: 70) seems to strongly contradict 'the ethnographic evidence ... consistent with a non-anthropocentric version of animism' (Dransart 2013: 20). According to other authors (Descola 2014b: 296), it would simply be enough to consider animism as 'anthropogenic'. Instead of anthropomorphism (deemed as a cognitive tendency to assign human personhood to other-than-humans), all that is needed to treat non-humans as humans would be derived from the interactions among the latter (Scott 2014).

The frequently advanced hypothesis that indigenous peoples call upon social relationships to shape their entanglements with the environment[18] faces the issue of agency (and intentionality) in the 'natural' world. The next section will deal with this and other issues related to the relationship between agency and animism – about which there is still not really a complete synthesis. This will lead us to what could be called eco-phenomenological perspectives on animism.

From Agency to Pan-semiotics?

Recent debates about the 'ontological turn' have evolved – sometimes violently (Jensen 2017: 535) – into various inquiries.[19] Here I will just point out one which appears as a more or less direct product of the above-mentioned anti-dualist proposals. I am referring to a group of questions that focus on the nature of the relationships between non-human beings and particular forms of perceiving the environment.

One possible answer to those questions acknowledges that if everyday life is the key foundation upon which the conceptualisation of non-human beings is built, then they should be viewed as agents in interaction with humans in concrete situations (Descola 2011: 100). In consequence, animism should be restricted to specific positions or contexts (Kapfhammer 2012: 162).[20] Also, the variation of these 'circumstances' (Descola 2014c: 277) would produce an oscillation of the ontological status and capacity of reaction of human and non-human entities. As Alf Hornborg wrote some years before,

> what distinguishes us from the animists … [may be our] incapacity to exercise such 'relatedness' within the discursive and technical constraints of the professional subcultures [that] organize the most significant share of our social agency. (Hornborg 2006: 24)

Various scholars follow this consideration of Amerindian cosmologies as inextricably linked to (or even produced by) their practices and everyday engagement with the environment. This could be illustrated by the use of the concept of 'worlding' to denote the particular daily assemblages that constitute the perceived environment (Descola 2014c: 272. See also Descola 2011).[21] Another example could be found in Tim Ingold,[22] who has characterised animism as a form of being (rather than a set of beliefs) and has also proposed to substitute the former with 'animist process' (*processus animique*), and ontology with ontogeny (*ontogénie*). Both substitutions are a consequence of Ingold's emphasis on the unavoidable temporality of constant human becoming:

> It is an historical process. Focusing on the study of processes, I was interested in distinguishing ontogenies (meaning the different paths of development) rather than ontologies ... I am trying to stop thinking in terms of animism ... and instead in terms of animist (or non-animist) processes in development ... I do not consider humans as human beings ... but as human becomings ... because we never cease building ourselves and contributing to build others in the same way [that] others build us. It is an uninterrupted process. (Descola and Ingold 2014: 37)[23]

Paul Kockelman summarises this tendency, pointing out that in fact 'ontologies are concomitant with ontogenies; that is, the latter describe how the former develop – either in history (as the conditions and consequences of their coming-to-be) or in practice (as the processes, practices and relations through which their being is constituted)' (Kockelman 2016: 61).

The problems of agency and intentionality in the natural world and of the 'symbol-induced passivity' (Descola 2014a: 269) of non-humans, have led some to consider the concept of agency dubious, inaccurate or even useless (Long and Moore 2013: 6). Holbraad (2009: 433) illustrates this point with a somehow sharp assertion: 'Whatever the "things" of animism might be, they are certainly not material objects (nor, by the same token, are they "imbued" with "non-material properties")'. It might be worth citing Ingold's argument on this issue at length:

> [E]ngaging directly with the materials themselves ... [w]e discover [they] ... are active. Only by putting them inside closed-up objects are they reduced to dead or inert matter. It is this attempted enclosure that has given rise to the so-called 'problem of agency' ... How is it, we wonder, that humans can act? If we were mere lumps of matter, we could do nothing. So we think that some extra ingredient needs to be added to liven up our lumpen bodies. And if ... objects can 'act back', then this ingredient must be attributed to them as well. We give the name 'agency' to this ingredient ... But if we follow active materials ... then we do not have to invoke an extraneous 'agency' to liven them up again. (Ingold 2011: 16–17)

It has been conventional to describe animism as a system of belief that imputes life to inert objects. But ... such imputation is more typical of people in Western societies who dream of finding life on other planets than of indigenous peoples to whom the label of animism has generally been applied.[24] These peoples are united ... in a way of being that is alive and open to a world in continuous birth. In this animic ontology, beings ... issue forth through a world-in-formation. (ibid.: 63)

Preceding Bruno Latour's insistence in that 'animation is the essential phenomenon' (2014a: 7), here Ingold is substituting a cognitive understanding of agency with a phenomenological account of the world as immanent and emergent. His dismissal of the concept of agency – still disguised in, for example, some authors' notions such as 'co-activity' (Pitrou 2016) – follows the idea that animism raises more questions about ourselves than about the so called 'animists' (Hornborg 2006: 22. See also Holbraad 2004). As Hornborg (ibid.: 25–26), Ingold draws from Jakob von Uexküll's account of *Umwelt*, a term that denotes a system in which the world is constituted within an animal's circuit of perception and action. For this German-speaking ethologist, meaning is bestowed by the organism on its environment, located in the immediate coupling of perception and action (Ingold 2011: 64). This form of approaching meaning makes Ingold (ibid.: 77) not only view von Uexküll as a 'pioneer of bio-semiotics', but also allows him to fight the usual idea that meaning is related to the correspondence between an external world and its interior representation (Ingold 2013: 107).

A similar concern to that of Ingold has recently been expressed in the perspectives of Eduardo Kohn. Although more explicitly grounded in ethnography, his recent elaborations not only pay similar attention to the ideas developed by von Uexküll during the 1940s, but similarly contest the boundary between humans and their environment. For instance, whether or not Ingold's work maintains humans–environment relations at the centre of his concerns, he is no less interested than Kohn in what the latter called an 'anthropology of life',[25] and, more recently, an 'anthropology beyond the human' (or the post-human). In a short commentary on Bird-David's well-known article, Ingold describes a 'system of perception and action constituted by the co-presence' of humans and non-humans:

Responsiveness, in this view, amounts to a kind of sensory participation, a coupling of the movement of one's attention to the movement of aspects of the world. If there is intelligence at work here, it does not lie inside the head of the human actor, let alone inside the fabric of the tree. Rather, it is immanent in the total system of perception and action constituted by the co-presence of the human and the tree within a wider environment. (Bird-David 1999: 82)

This 'intelligence at work' could be paralleled with Kohn's understanding of knowing: 'Humans are not the only knowers, and knowing (i.e. intention and representation) exists in the world as an other than human, embodied phenomenon that has tangible effects' (Kohn 2007: 17).

If significance is not exclusive to humans, and all living beings have semiotic dimensions, then we need to consider all organisms as selves and biotic life as a (non-symbolic and highly embodied) sign process (Long and Moore 2013: 16–19): '*As long as they act, agents have meaning*' (Latour 2014a: 12, emphasis in the original). How could we consider the forms in which non-humans represent themselves to humans? Based on the works of Terrence Deacon (2011) and Charles S. Pierce, Kohn considers the ecological relations of the Ecuadorian Runa as essentially constituted by two orders of things. In the first place, by the ways in which human and non-human beings perceive and represent their environment. Secondly, the Runa's forest would also be constituted by the interactions of phenomenal worlds that are specific to their respective perceptual and bodily dispositions, motivations and intentions (Kohn 2007: 5, 2014a).[26]

It has been suggested that 'a real investigation of how non-human forms *actually* deal with iconic and indexical signs' (Descola 2014a: 272, emphasis in original) would have at least two closely related consequences. First, the assertion that semiosis is intrinsic to life (Kohn 2007: 6) would rescue the question of being 'from its eclipse by concerns with epistemology' (Alberti et al. 2011: 900), concerns that sometimes persist under labels as extravagant as '*weak* ontology' (Keane 2013: 186–88. See also Viveiros de Castro 2015b; Escobar 2016: 22; Lebner 2017: 224).[27] In second place, and more importantly, this claim would ultimately collapse the distinction between epistemology and ontology (Costa and Fausto 2010: 98; Halbmayer 2012b: 18). In terms of his critique of the notion of language in primatology, David Cockburn has similarly stated:

> The point is, further, that in speaking of 'our' language we … will no longer be speaking of the language of a particular group of human beings. 'Our' vocabulary … will no longer be simply that of a human community; the standards embodied in it … will no longer be specifically human ones; or, better, those to whom we must answer in our use of that language is not restricted to other human beings. (Cockburn 2013: 178)

Nevertheless, it is important to recall that overcoming the conceptions embedded in a naturalist ideology does not appear to be a simple task (Descola and Ingold 2014). For instance, even if nature is no longer 'monolithic' – and culture is no longer the variable (Kohn 2009: 142) – the stability of the former might still persist. How should we then consider 'the Nature of Nature'? How could we overcome a merely negative account such as 'all sorts of not-necessarily human dynamics and entities' (Kohn 2014c)?

The perspectives of 'Kohn's pansemiotic approach' (Descola 2014a: 272) are not only in dialogue with Ingold's, but also (among other Americanists) with Descola's recent elaborations on 'collectives'. With this concept (along with that of 'associations') the latter defines 'hybrid multispecies groupings wherein humans strive, through complex rituals, to disentangle themselves from the mass of beings with whom they share an origin and an identity, and to carve out some functional mechanisms for their specifically human life concerns' (Descola 2014e: 296–97).

In general, these approaches that are borne from the study of indigenous South America could also be considered as following a tradition that dates back at least to Marcel Mauss's (1938) classic work on personhood. Viveiros de Castro's perspectivism, Kohn's 'sylvan thinking' and Descola's animistic 'collectives', for instance, not only raise doubts about the universality of the category of 'nature'. All of them, in fact, aim to re-establish the very object of the study of anthropology, by taking 'culture' and 'social' away from what we used to call 'human societies' (Viveiros de Castro 2015a: 16, 43. See also Salmon and Charbonnier 2014: 567; Salmon 2017: 55).[28]

The following subsection includes some definitions and critiques of the 'ontological turn' from another perspective, a political one. It summarises a broad range of critical approaches of ontology: both external (where cosmologies are seen as primarily resulting from practical engagements with the environment) and internal (where the concern is with the plurality, coexistence or hybridisation of ontologies and with the potential anthropomorphism vitiating the usefulness of the concept). Nevertheless, it does so only to the extent that the present state of temporary, unstable and emerging positions and paradigms of the current intellectual landscape of anthropological research on animism allows for it.

Is the 'Ontological Wolf' Afraid of Turbulences?

Taking into account its current relevance in mainstream anthropology, the concept of ontology has also been viewed as a sort of 'epidemic' (Halbmayer 2012b: 11) 'buzzword' giving a 'sense of déjà vu' (Pedersen 2014).[29] Popularised at least since the publication of *Thinking Through Things* (Henare, Holbraad and Wastell 2007), this so-called turn is seen today as not 'particularly new anymore, let alone that it will last forever' (Pedersen 2014). Authors working on different ethnographic regions around the world have, if not directly criticised this approach, at least recognised that 'we don't know what it [the 'ontological turn'] means yet' (Kelly 2014: 264) or even that 'what's good about the turn isn't new, and what's new isn't good' (Jensen 2017: 535).

Among the scholars who have developed a critique of certain aspects of it (Halbmayer 2012b; Pazos 2006, 2007), some focus on, for instance, its flaws regarding the ontological hybridations or ontodiversity, the possible internal differences within ontologies, or the ponderability of ontological classifications (Ingold 2000; Willerslev 2007; Piette 2012; Kohn 2013; Scott 2013; Descola 2014c: 298; Neurath 2015: 59–60). Others ask whether anthropologists are taking indigenous animism too seriously (Willerslev 2013: 49) or too literally (Keane 2013: 189. See also Killick 2015: 4). Is this seriousness in fact failing to recognise the ability of indigenous people to distance themselves from their official rhetoric? A reply to this question has asserted that what distinguishes the ontological turn is not an assumption of seriousness but a proposal of 'deliberate and reflexive' misunderstandings in ethnography, a proposal to 'pass through what we study ... as when an artist elicits a new form from the affordances her material allows her to set free' (Holbraad, Pedersen and Viveiros de Castro 2014).[30]

> [T]o take seriously does not mean to believe ... to be in awe of what people tell you, to take them literally when they do not mean ... to take it as a profound dogma of sacred lore or anything of the sort. It means to learn to be able to speak well to the people you study ... to speak about them to them in ways they do not find offensive or ridiculous. (Viveiros de Castro 2015b)

Other authors focus on a 'level of abstraction [in the ontological turn] that rarely deals with ethnographic material' (Fischer 2014: 348). In fact, some of them have compared it with a 'dogma' (Ramos 2012: 489) and an 'orthodoxy' (Course 2010: 249). The image of a 'doctrinaire' (Franklin 2017: 229) 'fundamentalism' (Oyuela-Caycedo 2014) that advocates a sort of 'conversion' (Scott 2013: 861), or that requires, in a moderated version, a sort of problematic 'faith' (Killick 2015) among its 'devotees' (Ramos 2017) has also been frequent: '[in the] discussion of the typology of animism and the variation of a society's perspectives of the body, the soul and non-humans ... we thus end up with this fundamentalist view of what an ideal ethnic group thinks, through the filters of the anthropologists' (Oyuela-Caycedo 2014: 53–54).[31]

Still other authors raise doubts about the indifference of the ontological turn to indigenous political concerns, adversities, and its 'disquieting potential to add to indigenous political difficulties and intellectual fragility' (Ramos 2012: 483–84). Following previous critiques of the representation of Western modern thought as an integral, homogeneous system of abstract type-concepts (Douglas 1989; Turner 2009: 16), Lucas Bessire and David Bond have suggested that the ontological turn involves an 'easy dismissal of modernity'. They also have questioned the conditions under which ontologies are 'made amenable to ethnographic analysis' (Bessire and Bond 2014a: 443. See also Heywood 2012: 146 and Gordillo 2014: 185–90). In his detailed review of Martin Holbraad's study on Cuban divination, Evan Killick has pointed out as well

> a particular trend in some current anthropological work in which the complex ideas, practices and social processes of everyday life are overlooked in the intellectual pursuit of radical alterity ... this proposed methodological emphasis on alterity ... [has] the danger both of over-interpreting, or perhaps over-intellectualising, alternative views and practices while also eclipsing a fuller and wider sense of the power of anthropological study itself ... the philosophical ideas become an end in themselves, not linked to raising further ethnographic questions or elucidating other social and cultural phenomenon but rather held up as precious jewels to be admired in isolation. (Killick 2014)

Bessire denounces a 'mystifying ethnographic project' based on the 'active omission of the conditions and relationships' that allow anthropological knowledge (Bessire 2014: 39). Furthermore, he advocates paying more attention to 'the palpable social presence of anthropological knowledge and the unequal forces that it conjures and exerts against human life' (ibid.: 26).[32] Addressing his own fieldwork among the Ayoreo, Bessire states that the search for

> an encounter with pure difference or an ontological alterity that exists external to the particular relationships between Ayoreo and outsiders ... the always-frustrated desires of ethnographers to gain access to a secret domain of true primitive difference is the key to understanding how the figure of that difference is reproduced and sustained by the same apparatus that consumes it and targets actual Ayoreo lives for extermination in the present. (Bessire 2014: 45. Cf. Killick 2015; Bartolomé 2015; Todd 2016)

The current restrictions of the 'often reactionary and romantic' (Kockelman 2016: 154) search for a 'primitive ontology' would actually domesticate alterity, making ontology 'available for governance' (Bessire 2014: 228. See also Skafish 2016a: 76). The ontological turn would also replicate 'the metanarrative that liberalism tells about itself and thus reanimates the colonial space of death for many people like the Ayoreo' (Bessire 2014: 192). This author echoes here those concerns about the reduction of the anthropological gaze to a 'citational' reproduction (Todd 2016: 13) and 'the class perspective of urban cosmopolitans making [a] career out of objectifying the rural and the local' (Bird-David 1999: 81), usually secluded in 'impoverished and formerly colonized' communities (Alberti et al. 2011: 907).

Furthermore, such liberal narrative may bear 'little relation to people's lives and deny their ability to interact with others' (Killick 2014), highlighting 'the dissonance between modernist and nonmodernist ontologies in localized case studies' (Alberti et al. 2011: 899). Bessire's severe critique also explicitly targets animism:

> Instead of animism, I found apocalypticism. Instead of jaguars who are humans, I found Indians who were animalized. Instead of wisely multinaturalist primitives crossing human/nonhuman divides at will, I found increasingly sharp and non-negotiable divides between nature and culture, primitive and human, past and future. (Bessire 2014: 15)

Bessire and Bond suggest that the restriction of 'Indigenous ontological legitimacy' to the terms of an 'orthodox dialectic of Otherness' might ethnographically erase those individuals who do not correspond to the mythology in which this dialectic is exclusively grounded (Bessire and Bond 2014a: 444. Cf. Killick 2015; Cepek 2016; Heywood 2017a: 227). They also urge us to inspect the 'hardening matrices' that select what must be safeguarded and what could be left, to explore the actually existing politics of nature and culture. We must pay attention to 'the more consequential makings' (Bessire and Bond 2014c) of an urgent present whose challenge lies precisely in 'devising ways to indefinitely sustain the possible' and in 'contributing to actualize some possibilities and not others' (Blaser 2014): the non-modern, the isolated field site, the 'colonizing binaries of structuralism' (Bessire and Bond 2014a: 442–49). What could be the relevance, they ask, of embracing an anachronistic hideaway towards these outdated topics (Scott 2013: 861; Bessire and Bond 2014b; Killick 2015)?

Among the answers to these questionings, the main two exponents of the ontological turn have both underlined the political dimension of their theoretical proposals. Descola (2014b: 348) asserts that ontology in fact amplifies the anthropological study of politics when it comes to indigenous movements that see non-humans as political subjects in their own 'collective' (*collectif*)

> to do away with those Eurocentric categories [class, race, gender] and with the colonial project of sucking into our own cosmology peoples who, having lost their lands, their dignity, and their work-force, face the added ignominy of having to translate their ways of life into our own way of life and of being grateful to us for providing them the tools to do so. (Descola 2014d: 436)

Viveiros de Castro makes a similar argument:

> [O]ntological questions are political questions insofar as they come into existence only in the context of friction and divergence between concepts, practices and experiences within or without culturally individuated collectives ... given the absolute absence of any exterior and superior arbiter. (Viveiros de Castro 2015b)

Certainly, the strength of a replica like this only holds if one considers that, for instance, Descola's distinction between interiority and physicality is neither one of those tools for which indigenous peoples should be 'grateful' nor operates an evolutionary 'absorption' disguised as translation (Haber 2009; Ramos 2012: 490 and Ramos 2017; Candea 2014; Tola 2015; Kohn 2015; Lebner 2017: 224). Is this the 'final act of colonization' (Kohn 2015)? To what extent could Descola's objectives be considered as a 'radically foreign conceptual dualism' (Skafish 2016a: 78) instead of the projection of a 'dialogic vacuum' (Bartolomé 2015) of 'disembodied representatives of an amorphous Indigeneity' (Todd 2016: 7)?

Tim Ingold has criticised what he considers the deep asymmetry of Descola's comparative project. On the one hand, it takes the peoples of the world as examples of the diverse modes of thinking. But on the other hand, it places the anthropologist as an emancipated observer, free to move around as he wishes in the domain of human diversity.

> [T]he observer has no place, he is nowhere, he does not recognise any ontology as his own ... he affirms that he is an ontological pluralist. One might say that he observes the world from a sort of ontological paradise from which we are all excluded, we who are imprisoned by our respective philosophies of being ... from his position of transcendental observer, he could thus affirm that there are different manners of composing a unique world. But this transcendental posture is in fact one of the bases of what he calls naturalist ontology ... whatever he might say, he adopts

as a neutral position a certain ontology: naturalism. (Descola and Ingold 2014: 54)[33]

In equally appealing terms, Severin Fowles has similarly argued that:

> the problem with going further and adopting ontological pluralization … is that this move ends up being so ironically, tragically, and embarrassingly modern … our modernist ontology is inseparable from what we might call the exceptional position of nonposition. Whatever the world is, there must always be some position of nonposition outside it for the Western liberal subject to occupy, as reason stands apart from emotion, mind from body, referee from players, scientist from experiments, anthropologist from natives. In this sense, there is nothing more profoundly modern than the effort to step outside modernity. And this is precisely what the advocates of the ontological turn claim to have accomplished twice over: first by standing in the position of nonposition vis-à-vis other people's worlds, and second by standing in the position of nonposition vis-à-vis the plurality of worlds itself. (Alberti et al. 2011: 907. See also Wright 2016)

In other words, 'how do we account for ontological encounters when any account presupposes an ontological grounding?' (Blaser 2009: 18). Is not an anthropologist such as Descola actually a 'masked moderniser who, under cover of pluralism, in fact restores anthropological science's guiding function and therefore reinforces the Western in its intellectual imperialism'[34] (Descola 2014b: 116)?[35]

The answers to these critiques are until now not many, and rather perform a sort of retreat. Pedersen, for instance, has argued that these scholars – who have been called 'default sceptics' (Pedersen 2014) and *ultras* (Descola 2014b)[36] – could also 'be criticized for a certain lack of reflexivity about their own theoretical grounds' (Pedersen 2014). He has also argued that the ontological turn might only take itself seriously to a limited degree and hence might not amount to a 'big theory' (ibid.). Additionally, this avoidance of the claim of a 'meta-ontology' echoes Holbraad's position on alterity as pertaining

> to the relationship between analysis and its objects (namely, anthropological concepts and the ethnographic … materials brought to bear on them) and not per se to how some bits of the world(s) relate (or not) to others, which I take to be a metaphysical issue best left to philosophers. (Alberti et al. 2011: 908)[37]

Besides pointing out a tendency to reify the nature–culture binary, and to treat it as 'on the same footing as ethnographic evidence' (Turner 2009: 7), some authors have described at least two consequences of the recurrent ontological turn's bemoaning of the dualism between nature and culture. One of them is a 'misrepresentation and mistrans-lation' (ibid.: 16) of Amerindian societies. Lowland South American ethnography shows that here culture 'neither excludes nor suppresses natural contents or qualities'. On the contrary, it 'rather retains and reproduces them through the employment of more abstract and generalized meta-forms' (ibid.: 22). Culture, in fact, would be under-stood as 'an incremental transformation of these natural elements', a sort of 'super-nature' (ibid.: 34). Based on a distinction between perspectivism and multinaturalism (a sort of metaphysical outcome of the former), Eduardo Kohn maintains that arguments as those illustrated here by Turner and Bessire would actually 'misunderstand the project' (Kohn 2015. See also Candea 2017: 100; Holbraad 2017: 142). According to Kohn, at least in the case of multinaturalism, it

> is not a description of how the world is, or how one kind of person thinks, but a call for a form of thinking, available to anyone, that is able to see possible ways of becoming otherwise ... It certainly grows out of certain styles of thinking that ethnography reveals, but it also grows out of the recursive nature of comparative ethnographic thinking itself, in which one's form of thinking is constantly being changed by one's object of thought. (Kohn 2015: 320. See also Alberti 2016 and Heywood 2017b)

Prefiguring the methodological version of the ontological turn that I will discuss in the next section, Salmond has also tried to clarify the problem, stating that alterity here points to 'relational contrasts produced in acts of comparing one set of purported commonalities with another ... Their "native thought" and "indigenous ontologies" are thus (for analytic purposes) artifacts of their own' (Salmond, in Boellstorff 2016: 402. See also Alberti 2016).

A second consequence of the ontological turn's 'radicalizing unfa-miliarity [or] alterity' (Alberti et al. 2011: 906) is its requirement of the most 'euro-centric' (Todd 2016: 9) and 'modern binary of all: the radical incommensurability of modern and non-modern worlds' (Bessire and Bond 2014a: 442).[38] Advocating incommensurable differences as an analytical point of departure might lend itself to potentially dangerous political constructions of Otherness that could actually be misused against marginalised groups (Rival 2012b: 138; Carstensen 2014: 26; Vigh and Sausdal 2014; Wright 2016: 10; Todd 2016: 10; Ramos 2017). According to Evan Killick 'the ontological position is now imposing a new stricture ... in placing too much emphasis on ... difference the ontological approach arguably over-emphasizes those aspects of these cultures and societies that are the most radically different' (Killick 2015).

Besides the issue of the problematic broadening of the scope of applicability of the ontological approach, Bessire affirms that it also 'standardizes multiplicity and fetishizes alterity' (Bessire and Bond 2014a: 449. See also Wardle and Schaffner 2017: 21; Todd 2016: 17). Ramos (2012: 483) echoes this concern, suggesting that 'to attribute so much uniformity to native thinking … is to flatten down (if not deny) their inventiveness and aesthetic sophistication, and to ignore their specific historical trajectories'.[39]

Among the arguments of the various authors described until here, two poles can be detected – a radicalisation and a questioning – and a sort of moderate position: a methodological one. On the one hand, some scholars have made remarkable efforts of generalisation of the perspectivist phenomenology. This amplification either heads towards a semiotics – in a phenomenology on the context-specific generation of the life process – (Kohn 2007, 2013), or the unpacking of the logical propositions that organise the relationship between beings (Holbraad 2009; Praet 2013; Viveiros de Castro 2015a: 219).

On the other hand, some authors denounce an unfortunate substitution of an urgently needed 'ethnography of the actual' in favour of a soteriological 'sociology of the possible' (Bessire and Bond 2014b: 449). Descola himself, for example, considers that exploring other possible metaphysical combinations, and other conceivable cohabitations of humans and non-humans (Kohn 2014b: 275; Holbraad, Pedersen and Viveiros de Castro 2014) becomes even more urgent in a planetary crisis he deems as a 'byproduct of naturalism' (Kohn 2009: 147). Almost simultaneously, Viveiros de Castro has resorted to the same argument:

> I am talking of the feeling that there is now one big, global, major problem that confronts 'all of us', nay, that conjures and at the same time utterly problematises this entity I am calling 'all of us' … the ecological catastrophe and its dialectical connection to the economic crisis … I am convinced that in the somber decades to come, the end of the world 'as we know it' is a distinct possibility. And when this time comes … we will have a lot to learn from people whose world has already ended a long time ago – think of … the Amerindians who, nonetheless, have managed to abide, and learned to live in a world [that] is no longer their world 'as they knew it'. We [will all] soon be Amerindians. Let's see what they can teach us in matters apocalyptic … Anthropology would be thus in a position to furnish the new metaphysics of the 'Anthropocene'. (Viveiros de Castro 2015b: 16. See also Brum 2014)

A similar allegation – in a more concise but also seemingly paradoxical form – could also be found in Kohn's suggestion that indigenous 'environmentalism' would be better understood, para-doxically, if we accepted that 'there's no nature [as a monolithic object opposed to a variable culture] to protect' (Kohn 2009: 147). In the next subsection, I wil describe in more detail what I have called the moderate or methodological position.

From Cartography to Engaged Recursivity

The issues related to hybridity that were summarised above prob-lematised the idea of a cosmochemistry transformed in a sober but rigid cartography – or 'fantastic geography' (Skafish 2016a: 88) – of different ontologies (Salmon and Charbonnier 2014: 568; Candea 2014). 'To what extent do we need to territorialize modes of knowing' (Rival 2012b: 129), and to commit to a notion of general ontology (specifiable through particular scientific concepts), which excludes the exploration of multiple natures that have different forms (Jensen 2017: 536)? Skafish (2016b: 397) reminds us that 'thinking is much more than a matter of classification. The whole point is to shift the focus of anthropology from classification to speculation' (See also Carstensen 2014: 27). The caution implied in the previous ques-tion and affirmation takes us to a somehow more productive aspect of the ontological turn: its methodological reconceptualisation, the production of 'genuinely alter concepts' (Kohn 2015) or 'the active transformation of anthropological concepts' (Rival 2012b: 129). This could be a form of evading the exercise of mere intellectual games and consolidating a useful tool for advancing comparative under-standings of indigenous South American collectives and practices (Devore 2017: 122).

Hornborg has asked how we could 'reintroduce morality into our dealings with our non-human environment' (2006: 25), with a nature that we have for centuries deprived of ethics (Callicot 1989; Berkes 2005; Harvey 2005; Kapfhammer 2012; Long and Moore 2013: 17; Latour 2014a: 13; Kohn 2015, 2017; Rees 2016)? Is the Other's suffering and devastation (Escobar 2016: 23) produced by the Anthropocene's geological agency of humans the high price we must pay for the pursuit of human 'freedom' (Chakrabarty 2009: 210)? Is 'this wonder-friendly ontology … with the potential to revolutionize anthropological practice and even save the planet from ecological apocalypse' (Scott 2013: 860) indeed hampering much needed situated analyses of afflictions, dominations and struggles? If so, those pro-posals in which 'indigenous people [are deemed] as an environmental antidote to the behavior of the West' (Killick 2015) would constitute nothing but a 'problematic form of speculative futurism' (Bessire and Bond 2014c). A 'revisionary futurism, in which some vertically ranked world- and life-making projects count more than others' (Bessire 2014: 228) does 'a disservice to the past, present and future complexity and diversity of Amerindian ways of living' (Killick 2015. See also Kapfhammer 2012: 149–52). Facing these issues, the works compiled in this book, as will be detailed below, aim to provide with (ontographic) descriptions of those dimensions of South American worlds that have usually been ignored (Schavelzon 2016; Todd 2016: 15) or 'actively produced as non-existent' (Escobar 2016: 15).[40]

Among those we have called above the 'moderates', some scholars have acknowledged that there is a diversity of animisms, each one with its local authority – which also foretells its own local exclusions – status, history and structure (Bird-David 1999: 79). Such a recognition is crucial for that group of works of 'relational ontology' that 'hardly accounts for the peculiar ways in which each of them [animist phenomena] may be analytically challenging' (Holbraad 2009: 436). It should be acknowledged that 'these worlds and the borders that delineate them have to be traced constantly, for they are in a constant state of becoming not least through their ongoing interactions' (Blaser 2009: 16). Killick has also advocated for 'a slightly more realistic, and yet still hopeful view of the future in which indigenous people are … [not] fixed in a particular worldview as the ontological approach sometimes appears to suggest' (Killick 2015).

Despite their differences, as radicals, and sceptics, moderates follow the claim that reality is constructed through the practices of human and non-human beings. They also seem to agree about the necessity of including in the description of animistic ontologies' sociality,[41] at least those non-human beings with whom human society, life and interactions are considered inextricably bound up. As any critical approaches of ontology, they could probably agree that there is still much to be known about, first, how indigenous groups detect and use particular properties of their environments and, second, how they change this environment 'by weaving with it and between themselves' diverse kinds of relations (Descola 2014c: 273). Despite these points in common, the moderates tend to restrict the ontological turn to a reasonable and productive methodology (such as, for instance, Holbraad's 'ontography'). More importantly, this restriction might be one of the reasons why these authors have not been so directly affected by the strong critics of the philosophical or metaphysical premises reviewed above (Salmon and Charbonnier 2014: 567;

Wardle and Schaffner 2017: 17–21; Charbonnier, Salmon and Skafish 2017a: 7; Jensen 2017: 530–31). Pedersen, for instance, considers the ontological turn as 'a strictly methodological proposal':

> Far from prescribing the horizon of anthropological inquiry in the name of an ultimate reality or essence that may ground it ... OT [the ontological turn] is the methodological injunction to keep this horizon perpetually open, including the question of what an object of ethnographic investigation might be and, therefore, how existing genres, concepts and theories have to be modulated the better to articulate it ... [T]he ontological turn is not concerned with the 'really real' nature of the world ... [but] is a methodological project that poses ontological questions in order to solve epistemological problems ... epistemology in anthropology has to be about ontology too. (Pedersen 2017: 229–30)

Stressing the ontological turn's 'commitment to recalibrate the level at which analysis takes place' (Course 2010: 248), Martin Holbraad has characterised it as a radicalisation of three anthropological basic requirements: reflexivity, conceptualisation and (empirical, methodological and theoretical) experimentation (Alberti et al. 2011). Holbraad insists on the need to reject any previous compromise concerning what type of phenomena could constitute an ethnographic discipline and how the anthropological concepts should be transformed in order to observe them. Instead of transformation, Kohn thinks in terms of 'deformation': 'anthropology's method of inquiry places our field in a position to deform it by being itself deformed by the different forms of thought it encounters' (Kohn 2015). Holbraad's radicalisation of reflexivity indeed gives conceptualisation a central place in the ontological turn, which aims to transform critical reflexivity into conceptual creativity (Holbraad 2014: 128–37). Consequently, he describes his ontographic approach as a 'break out of the circle of our conceptual repertoire' (Holbraad 2009: 433) using 'the extraordinary data to reconceptualize ordinary assumptions in extraordinary ways' (Holbraad 2009: 435). According to him, a 'copious effort' (Holbraad 2009: 434) or an 'extra care' (ibid.: 436) is needed 'to explore the enormous conceptual wealth of the Western intellectual tradition in order to find concepts that may ... be appropriate to the analysis of animism'. In other words: '[T]he task of conceptualization that any given set of animist phenomena may necessitate may certainly involve engaging with Western ontological revisions, but is most likely to require analytical labour that goes further than that, and often in different directions' (ibid.). A few years later, the same author added that 'the turn to ontology in anthropology is not about offering some suitably improved and ontically fortified replacement for culture. Rather, it is about offering a better way to address just one of the questions [that] "culture" was always supposed to absorb – namely, the analytical problem of how to make sense of things that seem to lack one' (Alberti et al. 2011: 902.[42] See also González-Abrisketa and Carro-Ripalda 2016: 119; Holbraad 2017; Kohn 2017; Laidlaw 2017; Lebner 2017: 225; Wardle and Schaffner 2017: 11).

A similar conviction lies behind the following statement: 'Anthropology's role, then, is not that of explaining the world of the other, but rather of multiplying our world' (Viveiros de Castro 2015b). In fact, there are multiple concordances between Holbraad's concept and the proposals of Viveiros de Castro – who has also written about what he calls 'speculative ontography' (Viveiros de Castro 2015a: 75) and declared that the most interesting thing in perspectivism is not that it illustrates an ethnographic phenomenon but that it illustrates a methodological imperative for anthropological thinking: to be able to exert radical reconceptualisations (ibid.). It echoes, for example, his notion of 'controlled equivocation', which has been profusely used by various ontologically inflected anthropologists (Blaser 2009; de la Cadena 2015; Vilaça 2016). The reflexivity implied in ontography also resonates in Strathern's well-known proposal: 'It matters what ideas we use to think other ideas', which some of her colleagues have amplified and updated to the point of saying, 'It matters what worlds world worlds' (Haraway 2016: 35).[43]

As already mentioned, the aim to rethink the object of anthropological studies by shifting from what we called 'human societies' to what we can provisionally name 'hybrid collectives' represents one of the main challenges (Ramos 2012: 485. See also Howe 2015) to scholars interested in the study of human/non-human interagentivity. 'The point of living in the epoch of the Anthropocene is that all agents share the same shape-changing destiny, a destiny that cannot be followed, documented, told [or] represented by using any of the older traits associated with subjectivity or objectivity' (Latour 2014a: 15). Kohn's proposal, for instance, is considered to lead 'away', 'underneath', 'elsewhere', and definitely 'without' (Latour 2014b: 305) what has been applied so far. Lucas Bessire puts it in terms of surplus:

> If there is any opening to a so-called alter-modernity to be located among those struggling to survive on the margins of low-land South America, it may well lie in the ways that Indigenous senses of being in the world always already exceed the terms of the radical imaginaries they ostensibly sustain. (Bessire 2014: 445. See also Povinelli 2016; Todd 2016; Goldstein 2016; Taguchi 2017)

In front of this challenge and between these paths, this volume is rather interested in underlining the prominence of ethnographic field studies for further theoretical development. We are willing to acknowledge that much detailed research is necessary to understand the multiplicity of conceptual and practical relationships that humans establish with their environment: '[I]t tends to be ethnography, the actual words, actions and ideas of other people, that generates alternative versions that are much more complex and novel than anything "we" can dream up' (Killick 2014).

Indeed, the present Introduction does not try to fix a particular methodological statement, just as it does not intend to sharply demarcate the position or theoretical lines of contrast among the arguments summarised above or to discuss in detail the adequacy of any of them. It rather aims to help to situate some issues at stake which are still growing in this rather bewildering intellectual landscape. It wants to facilitate, in the South American context, the use of anthropological imagination and the forging of new concepts and approaches that could help to release anthropology from the 'centrality and paradigmatic clout' of certain 'conventional tools' (Descola 2014c: 278–79). Recent calls have been made to re-establish ethnography as 'the prime heuristic in anthropology' and to return it to the foreground of its current conceptual developments in order to face 'the loss of the discipline's distinctive theoretical nerve'. We want to test this engagement with ethnography through the potency of detailed field studies that are not beholden to the most recent theoretical developments. We aim to overcome the latter and to advance towards new approaches derived from the former's 'translational inadequations and equivocations' (HAU n.d.).

The following three sections present ethnographic studies of South American indigenous worlds that aim to avoid 'idealized and nostalgic fantasies' (Shellenberger and Nordhaus 2011) and prophetic futurisms, and intend to pay attention to the coercion or punitive actions (Povinelli 2001; Scott 2014; Bessire 2014: 228; Carstensen 2014; Killick 2015; Lebner 2017: 225) related to their current political situations (Holbraad, Pedersen and Viveiros de Castro 2014). They intend to grasp the turbulences of unequal ontologies striving 'to sustain their own existence as they interact and mingle with each other … [in a context of] continuous enactment, stabilization, and protection of different and asymmetrically entangled ontologies or worlds (Blaser 2009: 11. See also Mol 1999: 75; Viveiros de Castro 2015a: 17; Blaser and de la Cadena 2017: 190).

This collection is divided into parts, each of which attempts to intensify the reflexivity, conceptualisation and experimentation of their ethnographic explorations of the diverse relationships between human and non-human beings in South America. The grouping of the chapters into parts does not privilege the materials from which the authors have reflected. For instance, the slight predominance of ritual songs and music as a point of departure in these chapters – an acknowledgement of the extensibility of the 'sonorism' proposed in South American lowlands (Brabec 2012; Lewy 2015) – is not taken as a main criterion. What is outlined here instead is the main Amerindian features the authors have chosen to examine from their fieldwork experiences.

Finally, while most of the authors provide descriptions focusing on only one group, two chapters in this book (those of Brabec de Mori and Sax) involve different groups. Marieka Sax, for instance, stresses a rather unusual (at least, for the area concerned)[44] synchronic comparison between the socialities regarding place-based beings in two distant Andean regions.

Part I. Securing Body and Wealth

The first part deals with local variations of sociality that certain relationships can afford. The works compiled here deal with what might be thought of as 'canonical' non-human beings, those that most ethnographic accounts on South America are usually prepared to deem as part of the 'traditional' cosmology under consideration. On the one hand, this part explores humans' need to permanently struggle in order to keep their condition as such (debated by Ventura I Oller, Ferrié and, in Part II, Otaegui). This requirement is examined through the study of indigenous categories of beings, the composition of personhood, attributes of humanness, and the therapeutic treatment of illness where the balance between human and non-human beings is based on the administration of a porous body. On the other hand, these chapters also show the partial reliance of securing crucial sources of wealth (for example, cattle fertility) upon obtaining resources from non-indigenous worlds. They analyse how these resources are distributed, circulated and displayed in order to exhibit humans' wealth, and to allow them to enter into a relationship of reciprocity with place-based beings (see Dransart, Sax and Ferrié). Additionally, another important topic emerging from this part is the relationship with place-based beings embedded in diverse

Andean regional traditions, in both rural and urban contexts (see Sax and, in Part III, Vindal Ødegaard).

Two chapters deal with the highlands and the other two with the lowlands. Penelope Dransart writes about the Aymara people of Isluga (Chile), Marieka Sax compares Quechua-speaking peoples from the southern and northern Peruvian Andes, Montserrat Ventura i Oller considers the case of the Tsachila, who dwell in the western lowlands of the Andes of Ecuador, and Francis Ferrié addresses the community of Apolo in the Bolivian piedmont.

Penelope Dransart studies a ritual performed by Aymara-speaking herders in the highland steppes of northern Chile, in which cattle become a locus of wealth and are morally appreciated and praised.[45] Dransart shows that securing the cattle's fertility depends as much on ensuring the creative and transformative capacities of their human owners as it does on obtaining resources from non-indigenous worlds (Ortiz Rescaniere 1999; Viveiros de Castro 2004a: 475). These resources are distributed, circulated and displayed in order to exhibit the owner's wealth (Dransart 2002 and this volume; Rivera Andía 2003, 2014) and to allow them access into a relationship of reciprocity with local place-based beings (described also by Sax, Ferrié and Ødegaard in this volume). Dransart draws on the concept of 'inspiration' to illuminate these ritual relationships between humans and cattle that are intended to transform the behaviour of the latter.[46] Finally, let us note that showing how ritual efficacy depends on a two-way relation between humans and non-humans, this chapter complements Otaegui's discussion of non-humans as operators of intra-human relations (through ritual practices).

The chapter by Marieka Sax develops a comparative framework in two different Andean regions, exploring the relationship with place-based beings[47] embedded in two different Quechua shamanic traditions. In southern Peru, place-based beings are intimately implicated in the fortunes of individuals and households. Andean people provide them with ritual offerings, and can expect agricultural fertility, prosperity and well-being in turn. Accordingly, place-based beings are named, individualised, assigned particular characteristics and preferences, and even arranged in a political hierarchy (Salas 2012). In contrast, in the northern Peruvian Andes, although place-based beings are also embodied in particular high-altitude lakes and mountains, they are not given ritual offerings, and only shamans can communicate with them in order to direct their power (Douglas and Joralemon 1993; Polia 1996). Additionally, they neither seem to have a 'contract' with human beings nor are they expected to care for the fate of humans. Contrasting the distinguishability of these different subject positions, this study of 'the kinds of things that are amenable to subjectivation' (Santos-Granero 2009: 13) suggests a link between the lack of moral responsibility of northern place-based beings' actions and a sort of disaffection towards their experientially real effects on people. Finally, thanks to her use of Amazonian data to triangulate her intra-Andean comparison, Sax is able to frame northern Andean sorcery as in between south-western Amazonian predation and southern Andean offerings (at least in what concerns to shamanism).

The chapter of Montserrat Ventura i Oller – in fact, the only author here explicitly dealing with debates on animism and the ontological turn – reminds us how Melanesian and Amazonian anthropologies' recognition of indigenous theories over the last two decades has revealed itself as a highly fertile ground for exploring notions of the individual, cosmological and ontological classification systems, and also the possible divisions (or rapprochements) between nature and culture. Ventura examines specific categories of being, components of the person, attributes that imply 'humanity', and forms of affliction of the Tsachila. Her comparative revision of the conceptualisations of human beings, and of the particular conditions under which the attribution of human qualities to non-humans is effected, makes her suggest that the Tsachila ethnographic information is compatible with those that prompted the so-called 'ontological turn'. According to Ventura i Oller, Tsachila ontology contains 'a logic of the continuum' that is common to societies classified as animist and in which humans need to permanently strive to identify themselves as such, and not lose their condition. Therefore, if the condition of being human is shared with other beings, the differences between humans and non-humans is one of degree: instead of an equal distribution of human features among living beings in the universe (and in contrast to the Ayoreo – who, like the Tsachila inhabit an area that is neither Andes nor Amazonia – studied by Otaegui in this volume), there is a rather complex scale of intensities. In consequence, despite Tsachila's human–non-human continuity, this collective would constantly need to seek mechanisms (mainly activated through ritual and body marks) to signal certain discontinuities.

In the final chapter of Part I, departing from an ethnographic account of a therapeutic treatment for a specific but broadly distributed illness called *susto* (fear) in the Apolo Bolivian foothills, Francis Ferrié reflects on the porosity of the human body, the danger of certain non-human entities and their specific eating habits. The author considers the healer's diagnosis, which comprises a highly detailed knowledge of the parts of the body through which the pathogen enters or an immaterial part of the sick person leaves; and the usual temporal and geographical sites within which predatory entities dwell. Ferrié shows how the therapeutic treatment intends to recover a lost immaterial part of the human being (called *ánimu*), usually in return for ritual offerings (called *mesas*). These *mesas* are composed of culinary elements that satisfy the hunger of the attacking non-humans (cf. Rösing 2013). The author suggests that the shamanic re-establishment of the balance between human and non-humans beings that he found in Apolo is based on the use of substances that open and seal the channels of communication between them, ultimately configuring a game of exorcism and endorcism.

Finally, let us note that what distinguishes these studies from those in the next two parts is their emphasis on the striving of humans to preserve themselves in their encounters with specific components of the environment (cattle, mountains, other fearful entities or some detachable components of the person). In the next part, this confrontation is substituted by another frequent modality of human–non-human relationship: conviviality.

Part II. Cohabitation and Sharing

In this part, Bernd Brabec de Mori investigates the Central Panoan (Kakataibo and Shipibo-Konibo) of Ucayali (Peruvian Amazonia); Guillermo Salas Carreño discusses about the Quechua people of Cuzco (Peru); Alfonso Otaegui deals with the Ayoreo of the Northern Chaco (Paraguay), which is one of the two case studies in the book that is neither Amazonian nor Andean; and Minna Opas writes about the Yine (also known as Piro), an Arawak-speaking people of the south-eastern Peruvian Amazonia (in the Madre de Dios region).

This part addresses the centrality of continuous cohabitation, food circulation, and sharing in the creation and maintenance of existing relationships with non-human beings (see Otaegui, Salas and Opas). Its authors explore ethnographic case studies of what has been called an 'ontological incubator' (*couveuse ontologique*) (Descola 2014b: 326). They deal with verbal arts addressed to non-human beings, rituals associated with death (see Otaegui, Brabec and Salas, along with Yvinec in Part III), and ontological realities performed by shamanism that allow humans to exert certain transformations in their world (see Brabec, along with Hill in Part III).

Bernd Brabec de Mori explores, in the first chapter of this part, the image of the Andes among the Central Panoan of Ucayali (Peruvian eastern lowlands) through what is probably its most widespread cultural hero (shared by cosmologies of the highlands and the western Amazonian rainforest): the 'Incas'. The author considers the ontological level on which these non-human beings are located – an 'Inca timescape' removed from everyday experience – as paradigmatic of the different realities that are performed by shamanic narratives and songs. In line with Hill's proposals (this volume), Brabec shows how these verbal arts referring to the Inca among the Shipibo-Konibo allow them to bring about changes in their environment.

Guillermo Salas Carreño's chapter explores the forms by which Quechua-speaking indigenous groups in the Peruvian southern highlands around Cuzco relate to the dead. Considering Quechua sociality as constructed through implicit notions of continuous cohabitation and food circulation and sharing (Bird-David 1999: 73; Sax 2012), Salas shows how both of these components shape the relationship with the dead and other non-human beings. Illustrating these relationships through concrete rituals and narratives, he proposes a reassessment of notions of ancestry and descent in current Andean studies using kinship analogies. In contrast to Brabec, who discussed a relationship shaped as 'filiation' in an Amazonian context where consanguine kinship ties are frequently seen as more or less peripheral, Salas discusses the subsuming of descent to commensal ties in an Andean context where descent is usually considered as a key social and cosmological axis. Furthermore, taken together, both chapters state that while filiation is not insignificant in Amazonia as an operator, in the Andes descent does not totally determine sociality. In consequence, as suggested by one wise reviewer, it appears as if here the domain of the dead (as considered in the cases observed by Brabec and Salas) would be simultaneously increasing the flexibility of the Amazonian conceptualisation of the ancestors and also moderating the existence of Andean descent ties. Finally, as Salas himself suggests in his conclusions, these contrasts seem to provide a good example of the fictional and inert aspects of the frontier between the Andes and Amazonia.

Alfonso Otaegui's chapter also deals with cultural manifestations related to death (as does Salas') and verbal arts (as the studies of Yvinec and Brabec, this volume), but in an ethnographic area that is as relatively little studied as it is particularly interesting.[48] In fact, addressing a society that is neither from the Andes nor Amazonia, Otaegui's chapter (along with Ventura's) can provide a strategic triangulation of the issues sketched by this book's other chapters. Otaegui explores how the belonging of non-human beings to different clans produces a mutual interdependence – both affective and economic – between their members. And, at the same time, these clans' relationships are addressed through ritual songs[49] and food sharing that do not relegate humans and non-human beings to different realms.

'What object was this that allowed all other objects to be obtained, but which was never in a fixed relation with a determined quantity or quality for objects?' (Fausto 2012: 309). This question could illustrate the issues that run through the chapter by Minna Opas, which examines the conceptions surrounding a non-human being called *Kaxpomyolutu* or Hand-whistler among the Yine. In so far as Opas deals with an 'owner-master' figure, it pairs with and complements Brabec de Mori's study on the Shipibo-Konibo (neighbours of the Yine), and Sax's chapter on owner spirits (of Andean mountains and lakes). The author suggests that, contrary to previous studies, indigenous understandings of late capitalism and monetary economy (as they are highlighted by the notions around the Hand-whistler) should be considered not just as 'reactions' to a shifting economic scene, but also as 'pro-actions' simultaneously directed towards guarding the integrity of their community and embracing a controlled change. The Other here is both required and generative to the extent that, for instance, dangerous relationships linked to the production and circulation of money are at least welcomed, if not sought out. In short, Amerindian understandings of capitalism and the monetary economy, according to Opas, actually comprise moral actions that simultaneously embrace otherness and safeguard the integrity of their community.

In sum, the second part of this book describes responses to a continuously changing scene, attempts to secure indigenous' collectives and to incorporate externally driven transformations, daily reinventions and new understandings of the relations between humans and non-humans, and also new ontologies developed through an active engagement with material surroundings. These creative processes are subject to variation and negotiation in everyday life and are certainly open to failure, which could, for instance, switch the socialities between human and non-human beings into an extreme form of predatory alterity (Salas and Otaegui, this part, along with Ødegaard in Part III).

Finally, let us note that what distinguishes these first two parts from the chapters of the last one is the weight put on certain balance in the relationship between humans and particular components of the environment (cattle, mountains, Hand-whistler, death, Incas, clan's possessions and diverse components of the person). In the next part, the locus of this persistence is replaced by transformation.

Part III. Transformations and Slow Turbulences

The third part includes ethnographically tailored studies of the strategies performed to face the transformations – usually attached to the 'slow violence' (Nixon 2013) or the turbulences mentioned by Bessire (2014) – undergone by human/non-human relationships (Long and Moore 2013: 13). The chapters in this part test and discuss developments related to some of the most significant processes of continuity and discontinuity experienced by contemporary South American indigenous collectives. The possibilities for socialities between humans and non-humans to allow the enactment of different types of current and historical adaptations to new components of the environments (associated, for example, with migration, late capitalism or monetary economy) become visible in various forms in this part. Some of them are the 'naturalized social space' in which human interactions are interwoven with the sounds and behaviours of non-humans (Hill, this volume), particular grammatical procedures and rhetorical patterns (Yvinec, this volume), and the re-signification of conceptions of well-being and prosperity (Ødegaard, this volume, and also Opas as mentioned in Part II).

As a whole, these contributions engage with those incessant transformations that emerge at the interface of indigenous understandings of historical dynamics and current intercultural relations and expectations (High 2015: 74). Stressing either national or international dimensions, or internal structures observed during fieldwork, the authors deal with one particularly recurrent figure in debates on 'cultural changes' within indigenous peoples: the adoption and incorporation of foreign powers and wealth. One chapter is concerned with the Andes (Ødegaard), and two with South American lowlands in the Amazonian region – the Wakuénai of Venezuela (Hill) and the Suruí in Brazil (Yvinec). While Hill provides a comparative framework for examining social transformation, Yvinec explores the Amerindian logics of religious conversion. Yvinec studies the forms in which 'outside' urban worlds are read by non-urban societies (as Opas, who in the previous part examined the inner mechanism of incorporation of late liberalism). Their chapters are at the same time complementary to, and the inverse of, Ødegaard's exploration of the forms in which an Andean indigenous society's worldings are challenged by urbanisation and the impact of migration to the cities. Additionally, as will be detailed below, Ødegaard's chapter addresses aspects that have so far received little attention from scholars interested in the relationships between human and non-human beings.

Following previously proposed itineraries (Blaser 2009; Costa and Fausto 2010: 100; Brightman, Grotti and Ulturgasheva 2012: 19; Bessire 2014: 221–29), this part deals with transformations in people's symbolic engagements with non-humans in the context of a conversion to particular forms of Christianity (Yvinec, this volume) and a practical involvement with ecosystems in urban contexts (Ødegaard, this volume) (additionally, let us remember that in Part II Opas discussed the insertion in a monetary economy and state systems).

The first chapter of Part III, by Jonathan Hill, is about constructing landscapes through discourse, music and ritual among the Arawak-speaking Wakuénai of the Venezuelan Amazon. This chapter provides a framework for understanding socialities between humans and non-humans and their potential for facilitating social transformation and adaptation within new environments (Hill and Chaumeil 2011; Bessire 2014: 110–93; High 2015: 50–97). Following his previous work of this concept, 'musicalisation' is here understood as a process of creating a 'naturalised social space' in which human interactions are interwoven with the sounds and behaviours of non-human animals. This semiotic use of sound might allow the enactment of different types of transformations (for instance, from life-cycle transitions, to politico-economic resistance), as is suggested also by Yvinec's study of Suruí evangelical singing in this book. This opening to transformation may be found not only in contemporary ethnographies, but also in comparative approaches to Amazonian cultural creativity across diverse historical periods. Showing how human and non-human relations are crystallised in ritual through attention to their aural aspects, the notion of 'musicalisation' suggests a critique of perspectivism contextualising its overemphasis on vision, as Brabec (2012) and Lewy (2015) have also proposed.

Cédric Yvinec's linguistic-anthropological approach to Amazonian ritual songs as a window into human/non-human relationships highlights the forms in which certain grammatical procedures of Amerindian languages contribute to the expression of a specific type of personhood, ontological set and epistemological choice. Yvinec analyses the recent religious conversion of the Suruí (a Tupi-Mondé-speaking population of Brazilian southern Amazonia) to Protestantism in terms of the invention of 'a new system of ritual speech'. Suggesting that among the Suruí 'before turning into "beliefs" and representation, Christianity first appears as a set of discursive and ritual practices', the author focuses on the role played by verbal arts[50] in their conversion. He proposes that the 'success' of the new verbal arts lies in their interaction with performative properties and symbolic values implicit in the kind of authorship used in previous indigenous songs. In the case of the Suruí, and in contrast to previous approaches indebted to visual metaphors, Yvinec explores shamanic singing (and its ambiguous subject position between human and non-human) through its specific authorship. Spirits sing their own songs, and are the 'official authors', whereas trans-specific beings, such as shamans, merely execute or 'perform' them to ordinary humans, for whom they stay largely incomprehensible and radically different from everyday songs. Describing the rhetorical patterns shared by evangelical and previous Suruí songs, Yvinec shows how they maintain an elusive authorship, and an ambivalence in its authoring pattern, which allows the advantages of older genres to be retained. In resonance with what has been stated by other studies of Christian conversion (Vilaça 2016), Yvinec finally suggests that it is this indigenous pragmatic issue (the avoidance of 'witnessed evidentiality' that lies behind the introduction of 'co-speakers'), rather than beliefs or stylistic devices, that constitute a dynamic aspect in the renewal of verbal arts.[51]

How are relationships to beings linked to the environment reproduced or discontinued among indigenous peoples who have radically changed their environments? Recent developments of cosmological understandings across rural–urban differences are explored by Cecilie Ødegaard through the resignification of non-human beings in contexts of displacement to urban contexts, rather than in terms of loss, alienation or even infection (as noted also by Yvinec, this volume). Always with a comparative attention, Ødegaard analyses the meanings of Andean forms of communication with place-based beings (called *apus*, and examined in this volume also by Sax, Dransart and Salas) in specific processes of mobility: indigenous experiences of leaving their rural communities for the city. The main forms of communication in this context are now ritual offerings related to the creation and maintenance of well-being and prosperity in urban forms (such as money and business). As Minna Opas (this volume) and other ethnographies of the lowlands point out, these interactions with place-based beings are subject to variation and negotiation in everyday life. For instance, the *apus* in the city may have different desires compared to those in the highlands. The transformative capacities of a relationship of reciprocity and sharing – studied also by Salas and Otaegui (this volume) – become visible when humans fail to give a ritual offering to the *apus* (who see it as human food). According to the author, this failure might involve not only an omission, but also an active refusal that could switch the socialities between human and non-human beings into an extreme form of predatory alterity.

The studies joined in this part all account for transformations by paying attention to inner dynamics, rather than by focusing exclusively on exogenous (either regional or national) conditions (Bessire 2014; High 2015) or in terms of loss or infection. This is particularly the case of religious conversion, in which cultural changes are considered in terms of practices that follow previously established and functional features of the composition of ritual songs (Yvinec). The influence of previous analyses of Amerindian socialities – where humans establish relations of exchange with a multiplicity of worlds inhabited by ontologically diverse beings in order to appropriate their forces and resources – is also visible in the relationship between Amerindian groups and external power structures (Ødergaard, and also Opas in the previous part).

Right after this third part, the book finishes with an epilogue by Mark Münzel, who pinpoints some wider issues that have started to be discussed only recently (Candea 2017; Holbraad 2017). Münzel regrets how a sort of excessive interest to enter into dialogue with Western metaphysics might have suffocated indigenous philosophies in recent writings on Amerindian ontologies. As suggested by some of the authors grouped in this Introduction under the label of 'sceptics', Münzel is actually pointing out precisely what the chapters of this book have aimed to avoid through their different ethnographic engagements.

Some Final Remarks

Other issues arise when considering Amerindian collectives in the context of the so-called 'Anthropocene'[52] (Kohn 2014c), globalisation, and the world ecological crisis that exacerbates 'the translation of nature into resources' (de la Cadena 2014). One of these is 'the ecologically destructive and socially disruptive forces' (High 2015: 101) that continue to pressurise those indigenous people who are nowadays struggling 'to engage these processes on their own terms' (ibid.: 170). This compilation aims to explore those aspects of indigenous cosmologies that express particular strategies linked to the incorporation of what is recognised by many indigenous community members as external and new.

Nowadays Amerindian collectives of South America are facing remarkable dilemmas associated with ideologies and processes characteristic of globalisation. In this context, on the one hand, some scholars have shown ethnographically how 'the modern world or ontology sustains itself through performances that tend to suppress and or contain the enactment of other possible worlds' (Blaser 2009: 16). These aims to subject (Escobar 2016: 15) – but also to collaborate or depend on one another (Mol 1999: 83. See also Kohn 2015) – are implicit in the imposition described as part of a 'war of worlds': 'the world ("as we know it") is imposed in myriad ways on other peoples' worlds (as they know them), even as this hegemonic world seems to be on the brink of a slow, painful and ugly ending' (Viveiros de Castro 2015b. See also Kohn 2015, Schavelzon 2016 and Escobar 2016).[53]

On the other hand, most of the ontologically inflected authors mentioned in this Introduction persistently stress that 'culture', as opposed to nature, would not be sufficient to understand the challenge that represents indigenous politics and its quest to promote their rights (Blaser 2009; de la Cadena 2010, 2015). This challenge concerns an ontological politics, a so-called 'cosmopolitics', by which different possible entanglements between humans and non-humans become occasions for ethical controversy (Latour 2014a: 14–15; Wardle and Schaffner 2017: 9–24). One example would be contemporary indigenous movements that fight nowadays not only against the predatory politics of multinationals, but also against the great infrastructure building projects of the developmentalist Left. Some authors discern in these protests what they call 'a third suggestive path that re-establishes the long distended links between humans and nonhumans in what concerns the forms of sovereignty that each of them exercises over themselves' (Descola 2014b: 55).[54]

Previous approaches to the conceptualisation of these processes among contemporary Amerindian collectives have tended to focus on the relationship between ethnic groups and external capitalist agents, or upon questions of individualism, monetisation and inequalities between indigenous peoples and capitalist modes of production.[55] Instead, this book examines the relationship between the individual and his or her own group, asking how Amerindian groups can maintain their ability to be part of a localised (place-based) community (in a socially legitimate manner) while simultaneously facing, for example, the forceful expansion of a monetary economy and wage labour. Taking into account this encounter between different perspectives, ideologies and praxes – by no means new, but in many cases with 'a new rhythm' (Brightman, Fausto and Grotti

2016: 2) – scholars concerned with indigenous societies have had to broaden the scope of their reflections and adopt new analytical tools.

Before ending this rather long Introduction, I would like to stress that these chapters neither intend to deny the depth of the transformation, nor assert its ineluctability or radicalness – both options typically employed, for instance, in the study of Andean 'syncretism' (Marzal, Romero and Sánchez 2004). Instead, they try to test how turbulences and changes in Amerindian collectives could be explained by indigenous patterns that have been called 'constitutive alterity' (Erikson 1986), 'cosmopolitanism' (Ortiz Rescaniere 1999), 'infidelity' (Pitarch 2003), or 'inconstancy' (Viveiros de Castro 2004a, 2011) across diverse Amerindian regions (Erikson 1999; Fausto [2001] 2012; Gutiérrez 2001; Rivera Andía 2008; Santos-Granero 2009). Despite their differences, all these terms try to summarise the strategies used in the incorporation of the Other as an indispensable feature of the making of the self (High 2015). 'In Amerindian mythology, the origin of cultural implements or institutions is canonically explained as a borrowing, a transfer … of prototypes already possessed by animals, spirits, or enemies. The origin and essence of culture is acculturation' (Viveiros de Castro 2004a: 475).

But is not the ostensible consideration of what is own as foreign originated (Coelho de Souza 2016) logically linked to the 'capacity of self-transformation' detected, for instance, by Lucas Bessire (2014: 228)? Furthermore, one of the latter's requirements to understand an indigenous 'project of rupturing-becoming' (ibid.) might be found in those 'more sophisticated and appropriate' (Escobar 2016: 14) knowledges linked to that persistent Amerindian borrowing, as the model of 'familiarising predation' (Fausto 2012 [2001]) shows. Is the 'anthropology of unauthorized becomings' (Bessire 2014: 229) not at the basis of the 'permanent decolonization of thought' (Viveiros de Castro 2015a: 75)? As we can see, despite their explicit differences, Bessire and Viveiros de Castro are not so far apart as they might at first seem: the same ethnographically inspired question is actually behind their apparently dissimilar projects.

Nowadays, 'rights of the earth' (in Bolivia) or 'rights of the nature' (in Ecuador) are becoming part of national agendas and policies in South America (and beyond). In a region that includes many of the few remaining 'wilderness' areas of the world, some think they could constitute 'a movement for the right to exist differently' (Escobar 2016: 26). Instead of allowing them to be 'swallowed' by modern politics (de la Cadena 2014), indigenous social movements – in a context considered as threatening for environmental and land defenders

(Álvarez-Berrios and Aide 2015) – have invoked non-human beings linked to the landscape (mountains, water and soil) as 'actors' in the political arena. These invocations that apparently oppose local populations to states and multinationals stress divergences of basic ontological interpretations concerning what the world is made of, what is valuable within or about it, and why. Whichever value one allocates to these movements, it is clear that if we want to escape the catastrophic world scenario in which we seem to be caught nowadays (Alberti et al. 2011: 898), it is important to enter into a dialogue with these concrete differences. In other words, we need to overcome that form of 'autism' (Cockburn 2013: 170) – and maybe also the search for a 'cosmopolitan human reason' (Rival 2012b: 140) – that is suffered by many of us today, and to consider the idea of a 'world not predicated on the essential difference of Indigenous peoples but on our shared capacity to transform ourselves' (Bessire 2014: 227). Or, in a less dramatic form, as depicted by Evan Killick:

> [N]o single ontology offers any hope of remedy in any simple manner … the focus must turn precisely to ways in which such ontologies transform, interact and blend over time and the everyday practices and encounters in which this occurs … [T]he anthropological imperative, rather than focusing on alterity and purity, should *be to focus on the encounters and collaborations* that emerge in the real and everyday world, and the manner in which new ways of living and interacting are produced. (Killick 2015, emphasis added)

Juan Javier Rivera Andía is former director of cultural patrimony at the Ministry of Culture and director of the National Museum of Peruvian Culture in his homeland. He has published widely on contemporary Andean Quechua indigenous worlds in various books, articles and chapters. His publications include the following books: *La fiesta del Ganado en el valle del Chancay* (2003), *La Vaquerita y su Canto* (2017) and *Indigenous Life-Making Projects and Extractivism* (co-edited with C. Ødegaard, forthcoming). His researches have obtained the support of UNESCO, the Smithsonian Institution, the Alexander von Humboldt Foundation and the Marie S. Curie Fellowship Program, among others.

Notes

1. Important differences between these compilations and the present one should be mentioned. First of all, this volume differs from Urton's landmark compilation in that it does not restrict the study of non-human beings to animals; and it differs from Ortiz Rescaniere's in that it is not restricted to oral traditions. Secondly, the present compilation deals with theoretical perspectives that have been developed after the late 1980s, and therefore after both Urton's anthropological collective approach and Sullivan's comprehensive study on history of religions had been published. Thirdly, another important difference between these two remarkable works and the present volume is that the former do not directly address transformations among indigenous peoples. Fourthly, in contrast to Brightman, Grotti, and Ulturgasheva's (2012) and Laugrand and Oosten's (2007) encompassment of apparently distant geographical contexts (such as Amazonia and Siberia, or South and North America), this present book intends to cover areas (Amazonia, the Andes and the Chaco) that, while quite distinct from one another, maintain strong historical, cultural and geographic continuities. Finally, and also regarding the areas covered in South America, both Laugrand and Oosten (2007) and Brightman, Grotti and Ulturgasheva (2012) leave unaddressed the Chaco region (not to speak of intermediate zones between the Andes and Amazonia) and – in contrast to Urton (1985) and Ortiz Rescaniere (2006) – also the Andes. Sullivan's ambitious study does address all the main areas of South America, but is not primarily based (as this compilation and the other ones mentioned here) in any specific anthropological fieldwork. Although it is not aimed to be a review essay, this introduction is profusely citational in order to honour the insights of the authors who inspire it and to show that it represents their arguments accurately. Previous versions of a few sections of this Introduction have been published in Rivera Andía (2015) and in Rivera Andía and Ødegaard (forthcoming).

2. Although the images of non-humans can usually be linked to what is construed as 'asocial ... and certainly amoral ... as negative examples of just what sociality should not be' (Overing and Passes 2000: 6), it is not a priori taken as such by these contributions. See Münzel, this volume. On the term 'sociality', see endnote 41.

3. See Hornborg (2006: 29) for a restricted or 'more strictly defined category of animism ... reserved for ... *all living things*'. Here the attribution of agency and subjectivity to inert objects (as stones) would rather be a form of fetishism. In a similar vein, but in an opposite direction, Laura Rival has argued the need to 'renew' an ontological animism based on 'symbolic ecological data, mainly derived from the treatment of animals ... by refocusing the analytical lens on representations involving plants' (Rival 2012a: 70. See also Hill 2011). Finally, Istvan Praet defines 'animist' societies in the following terms, which may not be so far from those suggested for the Andean region by Ortiz Rescaniere

(1995): 'Animists propose metamorphosis instead of evolution, catastrophe instead of permanence, and regular extinction instead of perpetual continuity. However, this alternative is never taken entirely seriously' (Praet 2013: 138). For a rather simplistic application of the concept of animism to the Andes, see (Di Salvia 2016).

4. Still an unstable term (Pedersen 2017: 229) and movement (Kohn 2015), the label of the ontological turn is sometimes replaced by others such as relationalism, non-dualism, phenomenological anthropology, new animism, post-humanism, speculative realism, speculative turn, political ontology, symmetrical anthropology and perspectival anthropology. Some of its proponents have defined ontology as the 'comparative, ethnographically grounded transcendental deduction of Being ... as that which differs from itself" (Holbraad, Pedersen and Viveiros de Castro 2014; see also Lebner 2017: 223). In this Introduction, I will not describe in detail the fundaments or developments of Viveiros's perspectivism or of Descola's animism. I will restrict the debate here to the relevant methodological aspects of what I call an 'ante-predicative movement' as it appears in those authors with a strong ethnographic interest in South America.

5. Issues, for instance, like the distinction between ontology and culture could certainly be relevant, but only in so far as it allows us to rethink ethnographic work on how non-humans and animism are being treated today, and not as a specific problem to which this volume contributes possible solutions (Carrithers et al. 2010; Kohn 2015).

6. Author's translation of 'ces composantes du paysage jouent un role essential dans la coneption que se font les gens de l'appartenance sociale; ce sont des composantes à part entière d'un collectif beaucoup plus large que la communauté humaine' (Descola 2014b: 324).

7. Furthermore, Law and Lien state that 'if ontological matters emerge locally, then the cosmos as a whole (except that there is no whole) is no longer endowed with any specific form. It becomes vague, fluid, indeterminate, multiple, and contextual ... there is no cosmos ... the world is acosmotic' (2012: 14. See also Alberti 2016). It is worth noticing that, according to Holbraad and Pedersen, the proposers of this kind of approach (such as Mario Blaser and Marisol de la Cadena) are still (sometimes implicitly) 'grounding the possibility of political difference in a prior story of how the world(s) must work' (Holbraad and Pedersen 2017: 54).

8. The modes of relations are exchange, predation, gift, production, protection and transmission (see also Ventura i Oller's and Otaegui's chapters in this book). For a genealogy of the definitions of the four modes of identification, 'animism', 'naturalism', 'analogism' and 'totemism', see Descola (2014b: 198–217). For an exhaustive explanation of some of its logical implications and some of its most salient problems and ambiguities (in particular with analogism and history), see Howell (1996), Stengers (2012), Scott (2014), Kohn (2015), Millán (2015), Viveiros de Castro (2015a), Tola (2015), Dos Santos and Tola (2016) and Skafish (2016a: 69–70, 75). Descola's schemas have been applied in quite diverse

fields (Serres 2009; Baschet, Bonne and Dittmar 2012; Wengrow 2014; Tournay 2014; Rochabrún 2014; and Carstensen 2014).

9. Author's translation of 'la solidification, l'actualisation, l'objetivation de ces schèmes dans des institutions ... la stabilisation des compositions des mondes dans des dispositifs dont la puissance et la durée persistent audelà de l'existence individuelle' (Descola and Ingold 2014: 44).

10. Additionally, this might constitute a path towards the inclusion of ritual in debates whose 'privileging of the order of concepts over the order of practice' has already been pointed out by other authors (Costa and Fausto 2010: 95–96. See also Neurath 2015: 59; Alberti et al. 2011: 898). On the emergence of perspectivism from the analysis of the concepts of ritual songs, see Viveiros de Castro (2015a: 185) and Skafish (2016b: 403).

11. Sahlins' rearrangement of Descola's proposal in terms of anthropomorphism – the 'default scheme of things' (Sahlins 2014: 281) – seems in fact prefigured in previous works of Karadimas (2012: 49) and Halbmayer (2012b: 14). Bartolomé (2015) makes a proposal similar to Sahlins', but replacing anthropomorphism by analogism.

12. A recent compilation (Brightman, Fausto and Grotti 2016) focusing on Amazonian cases provides various illustrations of these hybrid combinations when discussing indigenous notions related to ownership.

13. Descola has also considered indigenous visual worlds as 'an effect of the inflection that the terms receive when they are displaced in a different pragmatic setting' (Descola 2014d: 442). Thus, the problem of 'ontological hybridity' is also at the base of current analyses of the ontological predication of indigenous images as 'un révélateur d'un régime hybride' (Descola 2014b: 262).

14. As with academics, we could also ask who, among their indigenous interlocutors, are those who are being institutionally authorised to illustrate such theories (I thank to J. Devore for calling my attention to this issue).

15. Perspectivism has been characterised as lacking a point of view on the 'whole' (Stolze Lima 2000: 50) – crucial, as will be explained later regarding Ingold's response to Descola's model (see also endnote 35), for the flourishing of 'an ontology of many worlds' (Strathern 2011: 92) – and for too quickly dismissing objective associationism as the determining constituent of the 'spiritual' identities of all creatures (Turner 2009: 11).

16. The literature on perspectivism as part of the 'ontological turn' (Martínez 2007; Luciani 2010; Rocha 2012; Martins 2012; Halbmayer 2012a, 2012b; Kohn 2015; González Varela 2015; González-Abrisketa and Carro-Ripalda 2016; Wright 2016; Jensen 2017) and its ethnographic applications (Vilaça 1992, 2006; Stolze Lima 1996, 1999; Teixeira-Pinto 1997; Fausto 2001; Gonçalves 2001; Lasmar 2005; Gordon 2006; Andrello 2006; Calavia Sáez 2006; Lagrou 2007; Pissolato 2007; Cesarino 2011; Pacini 2012; Pansica 2012; Citro and Gómez 2013; Bacigalupo 2016: 55–67; Brightman 2016: 13–16) has been constantly increasing in recent years. Although most of this literature is based on ethnography from the

lowlands, a few authors have began to apply this theoretical frame to the Andes (Allen 2015, Ødegaard 2016). On perspectivism's antecedents as 'perspectival quality' or 'perspectival relativity', see Århem (1993) and Gray (1996).

17. Furthermore, other scholars have asked whether nature would here be 'reduced to a ward of humanity ... [to the extent that] what might appear as the recognition of non-human beings may quickly slip into instrumentality' (Devore 2016: 202).

18. A statement that, in fact, could be considered as a variant of a more widespread anthropological perspective, which can be illustrated, for instance, by this well-known quote from Edmund Leach: 'Nats [spirits] are ... nothing more than ways of describing the formal relationships that exist between real persons and real groups in ordinary Kachin society' (Leach 1965: 182).

19. As Bessire and Bond (2014b) note (and perhaps inaugurating real time online anthropological academic debates), mainly on websites hosted by Savage Minds, Somatosphere, Cultural Anthropology and HAU.

20. Therefore, depending on the context in which it is experienced, a stone in the Andes, for example, could be either just that, or a person with its own intentionality and agency, i.e. a *wak'a*. The same goes for the mountain, whose personhood in the Andes is usually called *apu*, as described in this volume by Salas, Dransart and Sax.

21. The concept of 'worlding' has certainly been used by many other scholars, some of them beyond indigenous ethnology (Long and Moore 2013) but still relevant for anthropological debates on the relationship between ontologies, social changes, colonialism (Escobar 2016) and multispecies collaborations in the Anthropocene (Haraway 2016).

22. On how Ingold has helped crucial previous insights – as those of Irving Hallowell (1960) – to have an impact on anthropology, see Costa and Fausto (2010: 90). On a critique of Ingold's proposals, see Rival (2012a and 2012b) who consider that he, along with Descola and Viveiros de Castro, 'equally agree that whatever animism is, it is antithetical to modern scientific knowledge' (2012b: 138). Finally, on a strict application of Ingold's concepts linked to 'ontogenesis', see De Munter (2016).

23. Author's translation of: 'Il s'agit d'un processus historique. En me concentrant sur l'étude de ce processus, je me suis davantage intéressé à distinguer les ontogénies (c'est-à-dire les différents chemins de développement) que les ontologies... J'essaie de ne plus penser en termes d'animisme... mais plutôt en termes de processus animiques (ou non-animiques) en développment... je ne considère pas les humains comme des êtres humains... mais comme des êtres en devenir... car nous ne cessons jamais de nous construire, ni de contribuer à construire les autres de la même manière que les autres êtres nous construisent. Il s'agit d'un processus ininterrompu'.

24. On some of the consequences of this imputation of an 'allegedly wonder-sustaining relational non-dualism', see Scott (2013: 861).

25. The label of 'anthropology of life' has also been used, with different variations of Kohn's proposal, by other authors working on South American lowlands (Rival 2012a; Praet 2013) and more recently in its highlands (Arnold 2017).
26. The consideration of interactions between humans and non-human components of the environment with an emphasis on sensitivity and responsiveness has been labelled 'sentient ecology' (Anderson 2000). On studies of Amerindian cultures, the concept has been applied, for instance, among the Yoreme of north-west Mexico as a way of bringing humans into 'communicative relationships with the ecological world' and extending 'the concept of personhood ... to all ecological life' (Simonett 2014: 122). For a brief insight on Venezuelan cases, see Kapfhammer (2014).
27. For some authors, nevertheless, 'epistemology need not be derealization' (Boellstorff 2016: 397).
28. A couple of examples might illustrate how particular South American indigenous descriptions of an original common condition of both humans and non-humans could challenge our own assumptions about personhood. One could be the deduction that 'the self is always the gift of the other' (Viveiros de Castro 2004: 480). The other is the consideration that there are 'no pure species, but rather a variety of species manifesting the affects and capacities of a diversity of other living beings' (Santos-Granero 2009: 7). See also Rees (2016).
29. Those criticisms that stand out because of their rather unrestrained causticity or because of their pamphleteering style (Reynoso 2015; Morales 2015, 2016; Todd 2016) will not be discussed here. There is also a group of works that seem to miss the point about the ontological dimension of relationalism (Keane 2013; Bartolomé 2015; Boellstorff 2016; Wardle and Schaffner 2017). Regarding those critiques coming from within the field of cognitive sciences (Guthrie 1995; Gatewood 2011; Bloch 2012), I will not discuss them in detail for the sake of concision. I might only mention that, despite its importance, their role in the debates on the 'ontological turn' seems somewhat marginal. Some followers of the latter have proposed that animism as an 'innate' cognitive attitude (i.e. naturally selected for its attention-grabbing potential and its practical predictive value) could also be a completely cultural feature susceptible to 'systematic and deliberate use' (Viveiros de Castro 2004a: 469). Others have dismissed the relevance of cognitive anthropology for the ethnographic understanding of cosmologies (Willerslev 2013), declaring they had either little to say on its consideration about anthropomorphism (Descola 2014e: 295) or 'little to expect from, and little to contribute to, cognitivist theories and concerns' (Viveiros de Castro 2015a: 216).
30. In fact, a proposal that draws a parallel between the importance of humour – which has been stressed by different authors in various regions (Ortiz Rescaniere 2002; Overing and Passes 2000: 15–16) – and the 'cynical' attitude of the US administration (Willerslev 2013: 52), may raise further doubts. Does laughing at beliefs in certain contexts imply that they

are never intimately adopted? Does the acceptable 'ironic distance from its official rhetoric' reduce animism as practised to an 'illusion' (ibid.)? Could the issue of seriousness also be understood as an expression of certain gravitas that affects human sciences in general (Hobart 1995)? Finally, to what extent and in which terms is it possible to distinguish metaphor from reality, and how could the debates on the 'metaphors of daily life' be related to the discussions on animism? (Lakoff and Johnson 1980; Hesse 1988; Ortony 1993; Gibbs 2008; Sahlins 2014: 282, 288).

31. See also the accusation of a 'vile fundamentalism' (*vil fundamentalismo*) (Reynoso 2015: 192) and a 'militant methodology' (*metodología militante*) (Ramos 2017) 'verging on the prophetic and the messianic' (González Varela 2015: 41). It is not without interest to contrast these tacit comparisons with dogmatism and the allusions (linked to transgressors) used by the authors of an ontologically inflicted anthropology to describe themselves: 'delinquents' (Viveiros de Castro 2015b) and 'partner in crime' (Pedersen 2012).

32. On the public afterlife of ethnography (although in a completely different setting), see Fassin (2015).

33. Author's translation of 'l'observateur n'y occupe aucune place, il n'est nulle part, il ne reconnaît comme sienne aucune ontologie … il affirme être lui-même un pluraliste ontologique. On dirait qu'il observe le monde depuis un sorte de paradis ontologique dont nous serions tous exclus, nous qui sommes emprisonnés par nos philosophies de l'être respectives … depuis sa position d'observateur transcendentale, il pourrait affirmer qu'il y a ainsi différentes manières de composer un monde unique. Mais cette posture transcendentale est en fait l'un des fondements de ce qu'il appelle l'ontologie naturaliste … quoi qu'il dise, il adopte comme point neutre une certaine ontologie: le naturalisme'. A similar concern has been expressed by Salmon and Charbonnier (2014: 570–72), Bartolomé (2015) and Skafish (2016a: 70–71). See Karadimas (2012: 29), Charbonnier (2017: 169) and Descola (2017: 35) for an opposite consideration of the same feature of this proposal.

34. Author's translation of 'modernisateur masqué qui, sous couvert de pluralisme, restaure en fait la science anthropologique dans une fonction rectrice, et conforte ainsi l'Occident dans son impérialisme intellectuel' (Descola 2014b: 116).

35. Note that Viveiros de Castro does explicitly deny the existence of any figure similar to Descola's 'arbiter' (as Ingold critically assesses above): 'maintaining an Other's values implicit … amounts to refusing to actualise the possibilities expressed by indigenous thought – choosing to sustain them as possible indefinitely, [without] fantasising ourselves that they may gain their reality for us. (They will not. Not "as-such", at least; only "as-other". The self-determination of the other is the other-determination of the self.)' (Viveiros de Castro 2015b: 12). See endnote 15.

36. To the denominations of 'ultras' and 'default sceptics', it could be added that of 'indulged': 'to indulge in the heliocentric trick of making the

observed turn (ontologically) around the observer' (Viveiros de Castro 2015b).

37. For a recent summary of the arguments given by an opposite position, see Charbonnier, Salmon and Skafish (2017a).

38. It might be worth noticing that this search for a radical alterity has been illustrated, by some authors, with controversial works such as those of the Peruvian anthropologist Carlos Castañeda (Abramson and Holbraad 2014: 25; González-Abrisketa and Carro-Ripalda 2016: 117).

39. Nevertheless, at least in the case of perspectivism, it has been made explicit that 'the decision to concentrate on some similarities internal to (but not exclusive to) the Amerindian domain and on an overall contrast with the modern West is mostly a question of choice of level of generality; it has no "essentialist" value' (Viveiros de Castro 2015a: 211–12). Another counterargument can be found in Candea (2017).

40. Escobar has also proposed the concept of 'futurality' to describe the imagination and struggle for those conditions that would allow particular communities to 'persevere as a distinct world' (2016: 19. See also Salmond 2012).

41. The term 'sociality' is used here trying to avoid 'the objectifications and valuations of the modernist use of the term 'society'. Sociality denotes an 'abstract quality of the social in general, without determining the kind of relation involved' (Fausto 2012: 72), and also 'face-to-face relationships of a community', acknowledging that 'the social requires individual agency (acting, reflecting, moral agents) and thus the two [the society and the individual] are constitutive of one another' (Overing and Passes 2000: 14). See also Santos-Granero (2007), Long and Moore (2013: 8) and endnote 2.

42. Martin Holbraad is one of the authors participating in the debate surrounding this essay..

43. Still another example could be found in the concept of 'reversibility' proposed by Corsín Jiménez and Willerslev (2007). Recent review essays have highlighted the connections between Holbraad's proposal and those of authors such as Michael Lynch (Jensen 2017: 535), Roy Wagner, Graham Harman and Albert Piette (González-Abrisketa and Carro-Ripalda 2016: 111–14. See also González Varela 2015). Additionally, Paolo Heywood has highlighted that an '*a priori* commitment to the idea that we should have no prior commitments apart from the methodological injection to allow our empirical material to transform the concepts we use to analize it … may be seen as somewhat self-refuting' (2017: 5, emphasis in original).

44. The only exception I know to this pattern could be found in two recent works of Fernández Juárez (2010, 2012).

45. For examples of Amerindian groups where animals can be considered in much less favourable terms, see Londoño (2005: 15–16).

46. Further possibilities for a detailed comparison between specific Andean and Amazonian ideologies concerning non-human beings arise from

Dransart's chapter. The forms by which the behaviour of cattle is thought to be influenced by ritual suggests a predominance of vision in the Andes in contrast to the central importance of sound in Amazonia (Hill, Brabec de Mori, this volume) in at least two ways. First, the micro-aesthetic of the textile chromatic gradations (Cereceda 1987, 1990, 2010) used in the *herranza* (Rivera Andía 2003) seem to be analogous to that implicit in Hill's concept of aural 'microtonal rising' (Hill 1985). Secondly, the way in which Andean people reintroduce non-human behaviours (for example, reproductive ones) into the centre of visible human acts is also analogous, for example, to the case of the Wakuénai and their perception of the behaviour of spawning fish in terms of the sound it produces.

47. Andean place-based spirits are endowed with cognition, emotion and responsibility, and animate the world circulating a sort of force among themselves, the environment and people. Additionally, they seem to 'function as hypostases of the species with which they are associated, thereby creating an intersubjective field for human/nonhuman relations even where empirical nonhuman species are not spiritualized' (Viveiros de Castro 2004a: 470–71).

48. The Paraguayan Chaco has not only been considered as free from both the 'overwhelming weight of the Inca empire' and the 'blocking mythic figure of the Amazonian Indian safeguarding the forest' (Boidin 2011), but also as the place where current studies are 'producing an original synthesis of many of the long-standing concerns of Andeanist and Amazonianist scholarship' (Combès, Villar and Lowrey 2009).

49. Also, the Ayoreo songs studied by Otaegui illustrate the ways by which sound (or musicality, as understood by Hill in this volume) can bridge social and spatial distances in Amerindian cultures.

50. Whose relevance seems to be supported by recent studies of the 'acoustic iconicity' (Meyer and Moore 2013) in Suruí's neighbouring groups' languages.

51. A similar phenomenon – but in bodily terms – could be found among Quechua-speaking people in the Bolivian Andes, where Tristan Platt, studying a parallel between the early formation of the person and the mytho-historical origins of the society, suggests that 'a pre-Columbian pagan substance flows constantly' into a society of 'converts' (Platt 2001: 127).

52. I define here the concept of 'Anthropocene' simply as the term most commonly used to 'remark that humans are now the dominant environmental force on the Earth' (Caro et al. 2012: 185). Also considered as the consequence of a particular practice of worlding, in which the status of the planet becomes an object of human design (Chakrabarty 2009: 210), the Anthropocene has made the general public more receptive to alternative life projects, thus suggesting the possibility of 'redesigning' the planet consciously (Shellenberger and Nordhaus 2011; Kawa 2016). An alternative perspective on the Anthropocene is sceptical to 'design' responses involving a unified 'conscious agent', seeing

more promise in the aggregate result of the uncoordinated and more heterogeneous practices that can coexist, but might also interrupt each other (Latour 1999; Blaser, Feit and McRae 2004; Carstensen 2014). In this scenario, politics is about fraught and always-ongoing worldings, which, while thoroughly imbricated, are nevertheless different (Povinelli 2001). It becomes an ontological politics, or a 'cosmopolitics' (Stengers 1996), that questions taking human rights as the ultimate justification for claims mobilised through identity politics (Haraway 2008). For a critic of the term 'Anthropocene', see Chakrabarty (2009), Latour (2014a), Haraway et al. (2016) and Demos (2017). Most of these ideas were developed by Mario Blaser in a paper presented at a workshop that I co-organised with Cecilie Ødegaard in Bergen (Norway) in 2016: 'Indigenous Cosmologies and Politics of Extractivism in Latin America: Ethnographic Approaches'.

53. Compare with: 'No hay un "mundo común". La cuestión de los combustibles provenientes de fuentes vegetales es una guerra' (Latour 2015), or 'struggles for the defense of territories and difference' (Escobar 2016: 13).

54. Author's translation of: 'une troisième voie suggestive en ce qu'elle renoue les liens longtemps distendus entre humains et non-humains quant aux formes de souveraineté qu'ils exercent chacun sur eux-mêmes'.

55. A tendency evident, for example, in many Andean studies, where human subjectivity has sometimes been drastically opposed to objects, and an economy of reciprocity to a monetary one (Rivera Andía 2014). In general, current Andean ethnographic studies dealing with non-humans (cf. Bellenger 2007; Ricard 2007; Robin 2008; Strong 2012 – with a few exceptions (Abercrombie 1998; Karadimas 2012, 2015) – have not entered in a long or explicit dialogue with the recent perspectives developed in South American lowlands (Viveiros de Castro 2009; Karadimas and Goulard 2011; Halbmayer 2012b; Tola, Medrano and Cardin 2013; Descola 2014b). Despite the fact that Amerindian ontologies have become an important locus of debate in the anthropology of religion, the line dividing the Andes and Amazonia is still as strong as blurred, and permeates not only national and local imaginaries, but also scholarly efforts to understand the indigenous groups in both areas (Taylor, Renard-Casevitz and Saignes 1998; Chaumeil, Espinosa and Cornejo 2012), allowing a conspicuous lack of ethnographic comparisons of both areas.

References

Abercrombie, A. 1998. *Pathways of Memory and Power: Ethnography and History among an Andean People*. Madison: University of Wisconsin Press.

Abramson, A., and M. Holbraad. 2014. 'Introduction: The Cosmological Frame in Anthropology', in A. Abramson and M. Holbraad (eds), *Framing Cosmologies: The Anthropology of Worlds*. Manchester: Manchester University Press, pp. 1–28.

Alberti, B. 2016. 'Archaeologies of Ontology', *Annual Review of Anthropology* 45: 163–179.

Alberti, B., et al. 2011. '"Worlds Otherwise": Archaeology, Anthropology, and Ontological Difference', *Current Anthropology* 52(6): 896–912.

Allen, C. 2015. 'The Whole World is Watching: New Perspectives on Andean Animism', in T. Bray (ed.), *The Archaeology of Wak'as: Explorations of the Sacred in the Pre-Columbian Andes*. Boulder: University Press of Colorado, pp. 23–46.

Álvarez-Berrios, N., and M. Aide. 2015. 'Global Demand for Gold is Another Threat to Tropical Forests', *Environmental Research Letters* 10(1): 1–11.

Anderson, D. 2000. *Identity and Ecology in Arctic Siberia: The Number One Reindeer Brigade*. Oxford: Oxford University Press.

Andrello, G. 2006. *Cidade do Indio: Transformações e Cotidiano em Iauaretê*. São Paulo: Unesp.

Århem, K. 1993. 'Ecosofía makuna', in F. Correa (ed.), *La selva humanizada: Ecología alternativa en el trópico húmedo colombiano*. Bogotá: Instituto Colombiano de Antropología, pp. 109–26.

———. 1996. 'The Cosmic Food Web: Human–Nature relatedness in the Northwest Amazon', in Ph. Descola and G. Pálsson (eds), *Nature and Society: Anthropological Perspectives*. London: Routledge, pp. 185–204.

Arnold, D. 2017. 'Hacia una antropología de la vida en los Andes', in H. Galarza (ed.), *El desarrollo y lo sagrado en los Andes: Resignificaciones, interpretaciones y propuestas en la cosmo-praxis*. La Paz: ISEAT, pp. 11–40.

Bacigalupo, A. 2016. *Thunder Shaman: Making History with Mapuche Spirits in Chile and Patagonia*. Austin: University of Texas Press.

Bartolomé, M. 2015. 'El regreso de la barbarie: Una crítica etnográfica a las ontologías "premodernas"', *Trace* 67: 121–49.

Baschet, J., J.-C. Bonne and P.-O. Dittmar. 2012. *Le Monde Roman: Par delà le bien et le mal*. Lyon: Editions Arkhé.

Berkes, F. 2005. 'Traditional Ecological Knowledge', in B. Taylor (ed.), *Encyclopedia of Religion and Nature*. London: Thoemmes Continuum, pp. 1646–49.

Bellenger, X. 2007. *El Espacio Musical Andino: Modo Ritualizado de la Producción Musical en la Isla de Taquile y en la Región del Lago Titicaca*. Lima: IFEA.

Bessire, L. 2014. *Behold the Black Caiman: A Chronicle of Ayoreo Life*. Chicago, IL: University of Chicago Press.

Bessire, L., and D. Bond. 2014a. 'Ontological Anthropology and the Deferral of Critique', *American Ethnologist* 41: 440–56.

———. 2014b. 'Ontology: A Difficult Keyword', *Virtual issue, Ontology in American Ethnologist, 1980–2014*. Retrieved 19 March 2016 from https://anthrosource.onlinelibrary.wiley.com/doi/toc/10.1002/ (ISSN)1548-1425(CAT)VirtualIssues(VI)Ontology.

———. 2014c. 'The Ontological Spin', *Cultural Anthropology Online*. Retrieved 19 March 2016 from http://www.culanth.org/fieldsights/494-the-ontological-spin.

Bird-David, N. 1999. '"Animism" Revisited: Personhood, Environment, and Relational Epistemology', *Current Anthropology* 40(S1): S67–S91.

Blaser, M. 2009. 'The Threat of the Yrmo: The Political Ontology of a Sustainable Hunting Program', *American Anthropologist* 111(1): 10–20.

———. 2014. 'The Political Ontology of Doing Difference … and Sameness', *Cultural Anthropology Online*. Retrieved 19 March 2016 from http://www.culanth.org/fieldsights/474-the-political-ontology-of-doing-difference-and-sameness.

Blaser, M., and M. de la Cadena. 2017. 'The Uncommons: An Introduction', *Anthropologica* 59: 185–93.

Blaser, M., H. Feit and G. McRae. 2004. *In the Way of Development: Indigenous Peoples, Life Projects and Globalization*. New York: Zed.

Bloch, M. 2012. *Anthropology and the Cognitive Challenge*. Cambridge: Cambridge University Press.

Boellstorff, T. 2016. 'For Whom the Anthropology Turns: Theorizing the Digital Real', *Current Anthropology* 57(4): 387–407.

Boidin, C. 2011. 'Peoples Indigènes au Paraguay et Bicentenaire National: Perspectives Historiques et Anthropologiques', *Journal de la Société des Américanistes* 97(2): 137–52.

Brabec, B. 2012. 'About Magical Singing, Sonic Perspectives, Ambient Multinatures, and the Conscious Experience', *Indiana* 29: 73–101.

Brightman, M. 2016. *The Imbalance of Power: Leadership, Masculinity and Wealth in the Amazon*. New York and Oxford: Berghahn Books.

Brightman, M., V. Grotti and O. Ulturgasheva (eds). 2012. *Animism in Rainforest and Tundra: Personhood, Animals, Plants and Things in Contemporary Amazonia and Siberia*. New York and Oxford: Berghahn Books.

Brightman, M., C. Fausto and V. Grotti (eds). 2016. *Ownership and Nurture: Studies in Native Amazonian Property Relations*. New York and Oxford: Berghahn Books.

Brum, E. 2014. 'Diálogos sobre o fim do mundo', *El Pais*. Retrieved 19 March 2016 from https://brasil.elpais.com/brasil/2014/09/29/opinion/1412000283_365191.html.

Calavia Sáez, O. 2006. *O Nome e o Tempo dos Yaminawa*. São Paulo: Unesp.

Callicot, J. 1989. *In Defence of the Land Ethic: Essays in Environmental Philosophy*. Albany: State University of New York Press.

Candea, M. 2014. 'The Ontology of the Political Turn'. *Theorizing the Contemporary, Cultural Anthropology website*. Retrieved 22 June 2017 from https://culanth.org/fieldsights/469-the-ontology-of-the-political-turn.

———. 2017. 'We Have Never Been Pluralist: On Lateral and Frontal Comparisons in the Ontological Turn', in P. Charbonnier, G. Salmon and P. Skafish, *Comparative Metaphysics: Ontology After Anthropology*. London and New York: Rowman & Littlefield, pp. 85–105.

Caro, T., et al. 2012. 'Conservation in the Anthropocene', *Conservation Biology* 26(1): 185–88.

Carrithers, M., M. Candea, K. Sykes, M. Holbraad and S. Venkatesan. 2010. 'Ontology Is Just Another Word for Culture', *Critique of Anthropology* 30: 152–200.

Carstensen, J. 2014. 'Capturing The Anthropocene: Sensory Ethnography in Anthropogenic Biomes'. Master's dissertation. Lund: Lund University.

Cepek, M. 2016. 'There Might Be Blood: Oil, Humility, and the Cosmopolitics of a Cofán Petro-being', *American Ethnologist* 43(4): 623–35.

Cereceda, V. 1987. 'Aproximaciones a una Estética Andina: De la Belleza al *Tinku*', in T. Bouysse-Cassagne, O. Harris and T. Platt (eds), *Tres Reflexiones sobre el Pensamiento Andino*. La Paz: Hisbol, pp. 133–231.

———. 1990. 'A Partir de los Colores de un Pájaro ', *Boletín del Museo Chileno de Arte Precolombino* 4: 57–104.

———. 2010. 'Semiología de los Textiles Andinos: las Talegas de Isluga', in *Chungara. Revista de Antropología chilena* 42(1): 181–98.

Césard, N., J. Deturche and Ph. Erikson. 2003. 'L'utilisation des Insectes dans les Pratiques Médicinales et Rituelles d'Amazonie Indigène – Insects in Medicinal and Ritual Practices in the Indigenous Amazon', in F.. Motte-Florac and J. Thomas, *Les Insectes dans la Tradition Orale – Insects in Oral Litterature and Traditions.* Paris: Peeters-SELAF, pp. 395–406.

Cesarino, P. 2011. *Oniska: poética do xamanismo na Amazônia*. São Paulo: Perspectiva /Fapesp.

Chakrabarty, D. 2009. 'The Climate of History: Four Theses', *Critical Inquiry* 35(2): 197–222.

Charbonnier, P. 2017. 'Breaking Out of the Modern Circle: On Conceptual Issues of Critical Anthropology', in P. Charbonnier, G. Salmon and P. Skafish, *Comparative Metaphysics: Ontology After Anthropology*. London and New York: Rowman & Littlefield, pp. 157–67.

Charbonnier, P., G. Salmon and P. Skafish. 2017a. 'Introduction', in P. Charbonnier, G. Salmon and P. Skafish, *Comparative Metaphysics: Ontology After Anthropology*. London and New York: Rowman & Littlefield, pp. 1–23.

——— (eds). 2017b. *Comparative Metaphysics: Ontology After Anthropology*. London and New York: Rowman & Littlefield.

Chaumeil, J.-P., O. Espinosa and M. Cornejo. 2012. *Por donde Hay Soplo: Estudios Amazónicos en los Países Andinos*. Lima: IFEA, PUCP.

Citro, S., and M. Gómez. 2013. 'Perspectivismo, Fenomenología Cultural y Etnografías Poscoloniales: Intervenciones en un Diálogo sobre las Corporalidades', *Espaço Ameríndio* 7(1): 253–86.

Cockburn, D. 2013. '"Anthropomorphism", "Anthropocentrism" and the Study of Language in Primates', in P. Dransart (ed.), *Living Beings: Perspectives on Interspecies Engagements*. London: Bloomsbury, pp. 167–82.

Coelho de Souza, M. 2016. 'The Forgotten Pattern and the Stolen Design: Contract, Exchange and Creativity among the Kisêdjê', in M. Brightman, C. Fausto and V. Grotti (eds), *Ownership and Nurture: Studies in Native Amazonian Property Relations*. New York: Berghahn Books, pp. 156–85.

Combès, I., D. Villar and K. Lowrey. 2009. 'Comparative Studies and the South American Gran Chaco', *Tipití: Journal of the Society for the Anthropology of Lowland South America* 7(1): 69–102.

Corsín Jiménez, A., and R. Willerslev. 2007. '"An Anthropological Concept of the Concept": Reversibility among the Siberian Yukaghirs', *Journal of the Anthropological Institute* 13: 527–44.

Costa, L., and C. Fausto. 2010. 'The Return of the Animists: Recent Studies of Amazonian Ontologies', *Religion and Society: Advances in Research* 1(1): 89–109.

Course, M. 2010. 'Of Words and Fog: Linguistic Relativity and Amerindian Ontology', *Anthropological Theory* 10(3): 247–63.

Deacon, T. 2011. *Incomplete Nature: How Mind Emerged from Matter*. New York: W.W. Norton & Company.

De la Cadena, Marisol. 2010. 'Indigenous Cosmopolitics in the Andes: Conceptual Reflections Beyond "Politics"', *Cultural Anthropology* 25(2): 334–70.

———. 2014. 'The Politics of Modern Politics Meets Ethnographies of Excess Through Ontological Openings: Theorizing the Contemporary', *Cultural Anthropology Online*. Retrieved 19 March 2016 from http://www.culanth.org/fieldsights/471-the-politics-of-modern-politics-meets-ethnographies-of-excess-through-ontological-openings.

———. 2015. *Earth Beings: Ecologies of Practice across Andean Worlds*. Durham, NC: Duke University Press.

Demos, T.J. 2017. *Against the Anthropocene Visual Culture and Environment Today*. Berlin: Sternberg Press.

Descola, Ph. 2005. *Par-delà Nature et Culture*. Paris: Gallimard.

———. [2005] 2006. 'Beyond Nature and Culture. Radcliffe-Brown Lecture in Social Anthropology, 2005', *Proceedings of the British Academy* 139: 137–55.

———. 2011. *L'écologie des Autres: l'Anthropologie et la Question de la Nature*. Versailles: Quae.

———. 2014a. 'All Too Human (still). A Comment on Eduardo Kohn's How Forests Think', *HAU: Journal of Ethnographic Theory* 4(2): 267–73.

————. 2014b. *La Composition des Mondes: Entretiens avec Pierre Charbonnier*. Paris: Flammarion.

————. 2014c. 'Modes of Being and Forms of Predication', *HAU: Journal of Ethnographic Theory* 4(1): 271–80.

————. 2014d. 'The Difficult Art of Composing Worlds (and of Replying to Objections)', *HAU: Journal of Ethnographic Theory* 4(3): 431–43.

————. 2014e. 'The Grid and the Tree. Reply to Marshall Sahlins' Comment', *HAU: Journal of Ethnographic Theory* 4(1): 295–300.

————. 2017. 'Varieties of Ontological Pluralism', in P. Charbonnier, G. Salmon and P. Skafish, *Comparative Metaphysics: Ontology After Anthropology*. London and New York: Rowman & Littlefield, pp. 27–40.

Descola, Ph., and T. Ingold. 2014. *Être au Monde: Quelle Expérience Commune?* Lyon: Presses Universitaires de Lyon.

Devore, J. 2016. '[Review of] Environment and Citizenship in Latin America: Natures, Subjects and Struggles. Alex Latta and Hannah Wittman, eds. 2012', *American Ethnologist* 43(1): 201–3.

————. 2017. 'The Mind of the Copaibe Tree: Notes on Extractivism, Animism, and Ontology from Southern Bahia', *Ethnobiology Letters* 8(1): 115–24.

De Munter, K. 2016. 'Ontología relacional y cosmopraxis, desde los Andes: Visitar y conmemorar entre familias aymara', *Chungará: Revista de Antropología Chilena* 48 (4): 629–44.

Di Salvia, D. 2016. 'Contribución a la ontología animista andina: funciones, poderes y figuras en los cultos telúricos de los Andes sur-peruanos', *Revista Española de Antropología Americana* 46: 97–116.

Dos Santos, A. and F. Tola. 2016. 'Ontologías como modelo, método o política? Debates contemporáneos en antropología', *Avá* 29: 71--98.

Douglas, M. 1989. 'A Gentle Deconstruction', *London Review of Books* 11(9): 17–18. Retrieved 19 March 2016 from http://www.lrb.co.uk/v11/n09/mary-douglas/a-gentle-deconstruction.

Douglas, S., and D. Joralemon. 1993. *Sorcery and Shamanism: Curanderos and Clients in Northern Peru*. Salt Lake City: University of Utah Press.

Dransart, P. 2002. *Earth, Water, Fleece and Fabric: An Ethnography and Archaeology of Andean Camelid Herding*. London: Routledge.

———— (ed.). 2013. *Living Beings: Perspectives on Interspecies Engagements*. London: Bloomsbury.

Erikson, Ph. 1986. 'Altérité, tatouage et anthropophagie chez les Pano: la belliqueuse quête du soi', *Journal de la Société des Américanistes* 72: 185–210.

————. 1999. *El Sello de los Antepasados: Marcado del Cuerpo y Demarcación Étnica entre los Matis de la Amazonía*. Quito: ABYA-YALA, IFEA.

Escobar, A. 2016. 'Sentipensar con la Tierra: Las Luchas Territoriales y la Dimensión Ontológica de las Epistemologías del Sur', *AIBR, Revista de Antropología Iberoamericana* 11(1): 11–32.

Fassin, D. 'The Public Afterlife of Ethnography', *American Ethnologist* 42(4): 592–609.

Fausto, C. 2001. *Inimigos Fiéis: História, Guerra e Xamanismo na Amazônia*. São Paulo: Edusp.

———. 2012. *Warfare and Shamanism in Amazonia*. Cambridge: Cambridge University Press.

Fernández Juárez, G. 2010. '"Norte contra Sur": Análisis Comparativo sobre Ofrendas Rituales Andinas', *Revista Española de Antropología Americana* 40(1): 239–59.

———. 2012. *Hechiceros y Ministros del Diablo: Rituales, Prácticas Médicas y Patrimonio Inmaterial en los Andes (Siglos XVI–XXI)*. Quito: Abya-Yala.

Fischer, M. 2014. 'The Lightness of Existence and the Origami of "French" Anthropology: Latour, Descola, Viveiros de Castro, Meillassoux, and their So-called Ontological Turn', *Hau: Journal of Ethnographic Theory* 4(1): 331–55.

Franklin, S. 2017. 'Situated Apprehensions: A Comment on Ashley Lebner's "Interpreting Strathern's 'Unconscious' Critique of Ontology"', *Social Anthropology* 25(2): 228–29.

Gatewood, J. 2011. 'Personal Knowledge and Collective Representations', in D. Kronenfeld, G. Bennardo, V. de Munck and M. Fischer (eds), *A Companion to Cognitive Anthropology*. Malden, MA: Blackwell, pp. 102–114.

Gibbs, R. 2008. *The Cambridge Handbook of Metaphor and Thought*. Cambridge: Cambridge University Press.

Goldstein, D. 2016. *Owners of the Sidewalk: Security and Survival in the Informal City*. Durham, NC: Duke University Press.

Gonçalves, M. 2001. *Mundo Inacabado: Ação e Criação em uma Cosmologia Amazônica. Etnologia Pirahã*. Rio de Janeiro: UFRJ.

González-Abrisketa, O., and S. Carro-Ripalda. 2016. 'La apertura ontológica de la antropología contemporánea', *Revista de Dialectología y Tradiciones Populares* 71(1): 101–28.

González Varela, S. 2015. 'Antropología y el estudio de las ontologías a principios del siglo XXI: sus problemas y desafíos para el análisis de la cultura', *Estudios sobre las Culturas Contemporáneas* 21: 38–64.

Gordillo, G. 2014. *Rubble: The Afterlife of Destruction*. Durham, NC and London: Duke University Press.

Gordon, C. 2006. *Economia Selvagem: Ritual e Mercadoria entre os Indios Xikrin-Mebêngôkre*. São Paulo: Unesp.

Gray, A. 1996. *The Arakmbut of Amazonian Peru, vol. I: Mythology, Spirituality and History*. New York and Oxford: Berghahn Books.

Guthrie, S. 1995. *Faces in the Clouds: A New Theory of Religion*. Oxford: Oxford University Press.

Gutiérrez, M. 2001. 'La Perspectiva de los Súbditos Indios del Emperador', in E. Belenguer (ed.), *De la Unión de Coronas al Imperio de Carlos V*.

Madrid: Sociedad Estatal para la Conmemoración de los Centenarios de Felipe II y Carlos V, Volume II, pp. 497–515.

Haber, A. 2009. 'Animism, Relatedness, Life: Post-Westerm Perspectives', *Cambridge Archaeological Journal* 19(3): 418–30.

Halbmayer, E. 2012a. 'Amerindian Mereology: Animism, Analogy, and the Multiverse', *Indiana* 29: 103–25.

———. 2012b. 'Debating Animism, Perspectivism and the Construction of Ontologies (Dossier)', *Indiana* 29: 9–23.

Hallowell, I. 1960. 'Ojibwa Ontology, Behavior and World View', in S. Diamond (ed.), *Culture in History: Essays in Honor of Paul Radin.* New York: Columbia University Press, pp. 19–52.

Haraway, D. 2008. *When Species Meet.* Minneapolis: University of Minnesota Press.

———. 2016. *Staying with the Trouble: Making Kin in the Chthulucene.* Durham, NC: Duke University Press.

Haraway, D., et al. 2016. 'Anthropologists Are Talking – About the Anthropocene', *Ethnos* 81(3): 535–64.

Harvey, G. 2005. *Animism: Respecting the Living World.* New York: Columbia University Press.

HAU: Journal of Ethnographic Theory. n.d. *HAU: Journal of Ethnographic Theory [Presentation].* Retrieved 22 June 2017 from https://www.haujournal.org/index.php/hau/index.

Henare, A., M. Holbraad and S. Wastell (eds). 2007. *Thinking Through Things: Theorising Artefacts Ethnographically.* London: Routledge.

Hesse, M. 1988. 'The Cognitive Claims of Metaphor', *The Journal of Speculative Philosophy* 2(1): 1–16.

Heywood, P. 2012. 'Anthropology and What There Is: Reflections on "Ontology"', *The Cambridge Journal of Anthropology* 30(1): 143–51.

———. 2017a. 'Commentary on Ashley Lebner's "Interpreting Strathern's 'Unconscious' Critique of Ontology"', *Social Anthropology* 25(2): 227–28.

———. 2017b. 'Ontological Turn, the', in F. Stein, S. Lazar, M. Candea, H. Diemberger, J. Robbins, A. Sanchez and R. Stasch (eds). *The Cambridge Encyclopedia of Anthropology.* Retrieved 26 June 2018 from http://www.anthroencyclopedia.com/entry/ontological-turn.

High, C. 2015. *Victims and Warriors: Violence, History, and Memory in Amazonia.* Champaign: University of Illinois Press.

Hill, J. 1985. 'Myth, Spirit Naming, and the Art of Microtonal Rising: Childbirth Rituals of the Arawakan Wakuénai', *Latin American Music Review / Revista de Música Latinoamericana* 6(1): 1–30.

———. 2011. 'Fashioning Plants: An Amazonian Materiality in Three Movements', *TRANS-Transcultural Music Review* 15. Retrieved 19 March 2016 from http://www.sibetrans.com/trans/public/docs/trans_15_15_Hill.pdf.

Hill, J., and J.-P. Chaumeil (eds). 2011. *Burst of Breath: Indigenous Ritual Wind Instruments in Lowland South America.* Lincoln: University of Nebraska Press.

Hobart, M. 1995. 'As I Lay Laughing: Encountering Global Knowledge in Bali', in R. Fardon (ed.), *Counterworks: Managing the Diversity of Knowledge*. London and New York: Routledge, pp. 49–72.

Holbraad, M. 2004. 'Response to Bruno Latour's "Thou Shall Not Freeze-Frame"', *Núcleo de Antropologia Simétrica*. Retrieved 25 June 2018 from https://sites.google.com/a/abaetenet.net/nansi/abaetextos/response-to-bruno-latours-thou-shall-not-freeze-frame-martin-holbraad.

———. 2009. 'Ontology, Ethnography, Archaeology: An Afterword on the Ontography of Things', *Cambridge Archaeological Journal* 19(3): 431–41.

———. 2012. *Truth in Motion: The Recursive Anthropology of Cuban Divination*. Chicago, IL and London: The University of Chicago Press.

———. 2014. 'Tres Provocaciones Ontológicas', *Ankulegi* 18: 127–39.

———. 2017. 'The Contingency of Concepts: Transcendental Deduction and Ethnographic Expression in Anthropological Thinking', in P. Charbonnier, G. Salmon and P. Skafish (eds), *Comparative Metaphysics: Ontology After Anthropology*. London and New York: Rowman & Littlefield, pp. 133–58.

Holbraad, M., and M. Pedersen. 2017. *The Ontological Turn: An Anthropological Exposition*. Cambridge: Cambridge University Press.

Holbraad, M., M. Pedersen and E. Viveiros de Castro. 2014. 'The Politics of Ontology: Anthropological Positions', *Cultural Anthropology Online*. Retrieved 19 March 2016 from http://culanth.org/fieldsights/462-the-politics-of-ontology-anthropological-positions.

Hornborg, A. 2006. 'Knowledge of Persons, Knowledge of Things: Animism, Fetishism, and Objectivism as Strategies for Knowing (or not Knowing) the World', *Ethnos* 71(1): 21–32.

———. 2013. 'Submitting to Objects: Animism, Fetishism, and the Cultural Foundations of Capitalism', in G. Harvey (ed.), *The Handbook of Contemporary Animism*. London: Routledge, pp. 244–59.

Howe, C. 2015. 'Latin America in the Anthropocene: Energy Transitions and Climate Change Mitigations', *The Journal of Latin American and Caribbean Anthropology* 20(2): 231–41.

Howell, S. 1996. 'Nature in Culture or Culture in Nature? Chewong Ideas of "Humans" and Other Species', in Ph. Descola and G. Pálsson (eds), *Nature and Society: Anthropological Perspectives*. London: Routledge, pp. 127–44.

Ingold, T. 2000. *The Perception of the Environment: Essays on Livelihood, Dwelling and Skill*. London: Routledge.

———. 2011. *Being Alive: Essays on Movement, Knowledge and Description*. London: Routledge.

———. 2013. *Making: Anthropology, Archaeology, Art and Architecture*. London: Routledge.

Jensen, C. 2017. 'New Ontologies? Reflections on Some Recent "Turns" in STS, Anthropology and Philosophy', *Social Anthropology* 25(4): 525–45.

Kapfhammer, W. 2012. 'Amazonian Pain: Indigenous Ontologies and Western Eco-spirituality', *Indiana* 29: 145–69.

———. 2014. 'A Forest of Signs: Mindful Communication in Human–Nature Relations among an Indigenous Community in the Brazilian Rainforest', *Seeing the Woods. A Blog by the Rachel Carson Center*. Retrieved 19 March 2016 from http://seeingthewoods.org/2014/11/23/a-forest-of-signs-mindful-communication-in-human-nature-relations-among-an-indigenous-community-in-the-brazilian-rainforest/.

Karadimas, D. 2012. 'Animism and Perspectivism: Still Anthropomorphism? On the Problem of Perception in the Construction of Amerindian Ontologies', *Indiana* 29: 25–51.

———. 2015. 'The Nina-Nina, the Devil and Oruro: The Origins of a Diabolical Figure', *Indiana* 32: 23–45.

Karadimas, D., and J.-P. Goulard (eds). 2011. *Masques des Hommes, Visages des Dieux*. Paris: CNRS Éditions.

Kawa, N. 2016. *Amazonia in the Anthropocene*. Austin: University of Texas Press.

Keane, W. 2013. 'Ontologies, Anthropologies and Ethical Life. Comment on Lloyd, G.E.R., 2012. Being, Humanity, and Understanding. Oxford: Oxford University Press', *HAU: Journal of Ethnographic Theory* 3(1): 186–91.

Kelly, J. 2014. 'The Ontological Turn: Where Are We?', *HAU: Journal of Ethnographic Theory* 4(1): 357–60.

Killick, E. 2014. 'Whose Truth Is It Anyway? A Review of Truth in Motion: The Recursive Anthropology of Cuban Divination', *Anthropology of this Century* 9. Retrieved 19 March 2016 from http://aotcpress.com/articles/truth/.

———. 2015. 'Perspectives on Climate Change and its Mitigation: Ontological Wars in Amazonia'. Keynote paper given at the conference Trans-Environmental Dynamics: Understanding and Debating Ontologies, Politics and History in Latin America, LMU Munich, October 2015. Retrieved 19 March 2016 from https://www.academia.edu/20759277/Perspectives_on_Climate_Change_and_its_Mitigation_Ontological_Wars_in_Amazonia.

Kockelman, P. 2016. *The Chicken and the Quetzal: Incommensurate Ontologies and Portable Values in Guatemala's Cloud Forest*. Durham, NC and London: Duke University Press.

Kohn, E. 2007. 'How Dogs Dream: Amazonian Natures and the Politics of Transspecies Engagement', *American Ethnologist* 34(1): 3–24.

———. 2009. 'A Conversation with Philippe Descola', *Tipití: Journal of the Society for the Anthropology of Lowland South America* 7(2): 135–50.

———. 2013. *How Forests Think: Toward an Anthropology Beyond the Human*. Oakland: University of California Press.

———. 2014a. '"An Anti-nominalist Book": Eduardo Kohn on How Forests Think'. An interview with Alex Golub. Retrieved 19 March

2016 from http://savageminds.org/2014/06/02/an-anti-nominalist-book-eduardo-kohn-on-how-forests-think/.

———. 2014b. 'Further Thoughts on Sylvan Thinking', *HAU: Journal of Ethnographic Theory* 4(2): 275–88.

———. 2014c. 'What an Ontological Anthropology Might Mean', *Cultural Anthropology Online*. Retrieved 19 March 2016 from http://www.culanth.org/fieldsights/463-what-an-ontological-anthropology-might-mean.

———. 2015. 'Anthropology of Ontologies', *Annual Review of Anthropology* 44: 311–27.

———. 2017. 'Thinking with Thinking Forests', in P. Charbonnier, G. Salmon and P. Skafish (eds), *Comparative Metaphysics: Ontology After Anthropology*. London and New York: Rowman & Littlefield, pp. 181–200.

Lagrou, E. 2007. *A Fluidez da Forma: Arte, Alteridade e Agência em uma Sociedade Amazônica (Kaxinawa, Acre)*. Rio de Janeiro: Topbooks.

Laidlaw, J. 2017. 'Review Article. Holbraad, M. and Pedersen M.A. 2017. *The Ontological Turn: An Anthropological Exposition*. Cambridge: Cambridge University Press', *Social Anthropology* 25(3): 396–402.

Lakoff, G., and M. Johnson. 1980. *Metaphors We Live By*. Chicago, IL: University of Chicago Press.

Lasmar, C. 2005. *De Volta ao Lago do Leite: Gênero e Transformação no Alto Rio Negro*. São Paulo: Unesp.

Latour, B. 1999. *Pandora's Hope: Essays on the Reality of Science Studies*. Cambridge, MA: Harvard University Press.

———. 2009. 'Perspectivism: "Type" or "Bomb"?', *Anthropology Today* 25(2): 1–2.

———. 2014a. 'Agency at the Time of the Anthropocene', *New Literary History* 45: 1–18.

———. 2014b. 'Another Way to Compose the Common World', *HAU: Journal of Ethnographic Theory* 4(1): 301–7.

———. 2015. 'Los Modernos, Según la Antropología', *Ñ. Revista de Cultura (Clarín)*. Retrieved 19 March 2016 from http://www.revistaenie.clarin.com/ideas/Bruno-Latour-modernos-antropologia_0_1295270475.html.

Laugrand, F., and J. Oosten (eds). 2007. *La Nature des Esprits dans les Cosmologies Autochtones / Nature of Spirits in Aboriginal Cosmologies*. Québec: Presses de l'Université Laval.

Law, J., and M.E. Lien. 2012. 'Denaturalising Nature'. Public Inaugural Sawyer Seminar talk at University of California, Davis, on 29 October 2012. Retrieved 31 March 2018 from http://www.sv.uio.no/sai/english/research/projects/newcomers/publications/working-papers-web/denanturalisingnaturetalk2.pdf.

Leach, E. 1965. *Political Systems of Highland Burma: A Study of Katchin Social Structure*. London: Bell.

Lebner, A. 2017. 'Interpreting Strathern's "Unconscious" Critique of Ontology', *Social Anthropology* 25(2): 221–33.

Lewy, M. 2015. 'Más allá del "punto de vista": sonorismo amerindio y entidades de sonido antropomorfas y no-antropomorfas', in B. Brabec, M. Lewy and M. García (eds), *Sudamérica y sus mundos audibles*. Berlin: Indiana, pp. 83–98.

Londoño, C. 2005. 'Inhuman Beings: Morality and Perspectivism among Muinane People (Colombian Amazon)', *Ethnos: Journal of Anthropology* 70(1): 7–30.

Long, N., and H. Moore (eds). 2013. *Sociality: New Directions*. New York and Oxford: Berghahn Books.

Luciani, Jose Antonio Kelly. 2010. 'Perspectivismo Multinatural como Transformação Estrutural', *ILHA, Revista de Antropologia* 12(1): 137–60.

Martínez, I. 2007. 'Eduardo Viveiros de Castro: de Imaginación, Traducción y Traición', *Anales de Antropología* 41(2): 239–62.

Martins, H. 2012. 'Tradução e Perspectivismo', *Revista Letras* 85: 135–49.

Marzal, M., C. Romero and J. Sánchez (eds). 2004. *Para Entender la Religión en el Perú*. Lima: PUCP.

Mauss, M. 1938. 'Une Catégorie de l'Esprit Humain: la Notion de Personne celle de "Moi"', *The Journal of the Royal Anthropological Institute of Great Britain and Ireland* 68: 263–81.

Medrano, C. and F. Tola. 2016. 'Cuando humanos y no-humanos componen el pasado. Ontohistoria en el Chaco', *Avá* 29: 99–129.

Meyer, J., and D. Moore. 2013. 'Arte verbal é Música na Língua Gavião de Rondônia: Metodologia para Estudar e Documentar a Fala Tocada com Instrumentos Musicais', *Boletim do Museu Goeldi* 8(2): 52–70.

Millán, S. 2015. 'Ontologías en fuga: a propósito de un artículo de Miguel Bartolomé', *Trace* 67: 158–62.

Mol, A. 1999. 'Ontological Politics: A Word and Some Questions', *The Sociological Review* 47(S1): 74–89.

Morales, S. 2015. 'Sobre Objetos que Vuelan en el Cosmos: Crítica al Perspectivismo Amerindio de Eduardo Viveiros de Castro (parte I)', *Patio de Sociales*. Retrieved 19 March 2016 from http://patiodesociales. cei.org.pe/2015/09/sobre-objetos-que-flotan-en-el-cosmos.html.

———. 2016. 'Sobre Objetos que Vuelan en el Cosmos: Crítica al Perspectivismo Amerindio de Eduardo Viveiros de Castro (parte II)', *Patio de Sociales*. Retrieved 19 March 2016 from http://patiodesociales. cei.org.pe/2016/02/sobre-objetos-que-flotan-en-el-cosmos.html.

Morrison, K. 2000. 'The Cosmos as Intersubjective: Native American Other-than-Human Persons', in G. Harvey (ed.), *Indigenous Religions: A Companion*. London: Cassell, pp. 23–36.

Narotzky, S. 2010. 'Las antropologías hegemónicas y las antropologías del sur: el caso de España', *Antípoda* 11: 241–58.

Neurath, J. 2015. 'Shifting Ontologies in Huichol Ritual and Art', *Anthropology and Humanism* 40(1): 58–71.

Nixon, R. 2013. *Slow Violence and the Environmentalism of the Poor*. Cambridge, MA: Harvard University Press.

Ødegaard, C. 'Alterity, Predation, and Questions of Representation: The Problem of the *Kharisiri* in the Andes', in B. Bertelsen and S. Bendixsen (eds), *Engagements in Human Alterity and Difference*. New York: Palgrave Mcmillan, pp. 65–87.

Ortiz Rescaniere, A. 1995. 'Unas Imágenes del Tiempo', *Anthropologica* 13: 141–66.

———. 1999. 'El Individuo Andino, Autóctono y Cosmopolita', in C. Degregori et al. (eds), *Cultura y globalización*. Lima: PUCP, Universidad del Pacífico, IEP, pp. 129–38.

———. 2002. 'Carnaval y Humor Andinos', *Anthropologica* 20: 293–308.

——— (ed.). 2006. *Mitologías Amerindias*. Madrid: Trotta.

Ortony, A. 1993. *Methaphor and Thought*. Cambridge: Cambridge University Press.

Overing, J., and A. Passes (eds). 2000. *The Anthropology of Love and Anger: The Aesthetics of Conviviality in Native Amazonia*. London: Routledge.

Oyuela-Caycedo, A. 2014. 'Book review of Brigthman, M., Grotti, V.E., and Ulturgasheva, O. (2012) Animism in Rainforest and Tundra: Personhood, Animals, Plants and Things in Contemporary Amazonia and Siberia', *Bulletin of Latin American Research* 33(4): 536–37.

Pacini, A. 2012. 'Um Perspectivismo Ameríndio e a Cosmologia Anímica Chiquitana', *Espaço Ameríndio* 6(2): 137–77.

Pansica, R. 2012. 'Perspectivismo e relacionalismo estrutural ameríndios', *Revista de Antropologia da UFSCar* 4(2): 71–94.

Pazos, A. 2006. 'Recensión Crítica de Philippe Descola Par-delà Nature et Culture', *AIBR. Revista de Antropología Iberoamericana* 1(1): 186–94.

———. 2007. 'Recensión Crítica de Tierra Adentro: Territorio Indígena y Percepción del Entorno', *AIBR. Revista de Antropología Iberoamericana* 2(2): 369–77.

Pedersen, M. 2001. 'Totemism, Animism and North Asian Indigenous Ontologies', *Journal of the Royal Anthropological Institute* 7(3): 411–27.

———. 2012. 'Common Nonsense: A Review of Certain Recent Reviews of the "Ontological Turn"', *Anthropology of This Century* 5. Retrieved 19 March 2016 from http://aotcpress.com/articles/common_nonsense/.

———. 2014. 'A Reader's Guide to the "Ontological Turn" – Part 3', *Somatosphere*. Retrieved 19 March 2016 from http://somatosphere. net/2014/02/a-readers-guide-to-the-ontological-turn-part-3.html.

———. 2017. 'Strathern and Ontology: An Awkward Relationship. A Comment on Lebner', *Social Anthropology* 25(2): 229–30.

Piette, A. 2012. *De l'Ontologie en Anthropologie*. Paris: Berg International.

Pissolato, E. 2007. *A Duração da Pessoa: Mobilidade, Parentesco e Xamanismo Mbya (Guarani)*. São Paulo: Unesp.

Pitarch, P. 2003. 'Infidelidades indígenas', *Revista de Occidente* 269: 60–76.

Pitrou, P. 2016. 'Co-activity in Mesoamerica and in the Andes', *Journal of Anthropological Research* 72: 465–82.

Platt, T. 2001. 'El Feto Agresivo: Parto, Formación de la Persona y Mito-Historia en los Andes', *Anuario de Estudios Americanos* 58(2): 633–78.

Polia, M. 1996. *Despierta, Remedio, Cuenta: Adivinos y Médicos del Ande*. Lima: PUCP.

Povinelli, E. 2001. 'Radical Worlds: The Anthropology of Incommensurability and Inconceivability', *Annual Review of Anthropology* 30: 319–34.

———. 2016. *Geontologies: A Requiem to Late Liberalism*. Durham, NC: Duke University Press.

Praet, I. 2013. *Animism and the Question of Life*. New York and Abingdon-on-Thames: Routledge.

Ramos, A. 2012. 'The Politics of Perspectivism', *Annual Review of Anthropology* 41: 481–94.

———. 2017. 'El giro que no gira o esto no es una pipa'. Paper presented in IV Congreso de Antropología Latinoamericana. Retrieved 11 July 2016 from https://www.academia.edu/33392177/El_giro_que_no_gira_o_Esto_no_es_una_pipa.docx.

Rees, T. 2016. 'On Deanthropologizing Anthropology – An Essay on Tarek Elhaik's "The Incurable Image"', *Somatosphere. Science, Medicine and Anthropology*. Retrieved 11 July 2016 from http://somatosphere.net/2016/12/on-deanthropologizing-anthropology-an-essay-on-tarek-elhaiks-the-incurable-image.html.

Reynoso, C. 2015. *Crítica de la Antropología Perspectivista (Viveiros de Castro – Philippe Descola – Bruno Latour)*. Buenos Aires: SB editorial.

Ricard, X. 2007. *Ladrones de Sombra: El Universo Religioso de los Pastores del Ausangate (Andes surperuanos)*. Lima: IFEA.

Rival, L. 2012a. 'Animism and the Meanings of Life: Reflections from Amazonia', in M. Brightman, V. Grotti and O. Ulturgasheva (eds), *Animism in Rainforest and Tundra: Personhood, Animals, Plants and Things in Contemporary Amazonia and Siberia*. New York and Oxford: Berghahn Books, pp. 69–81.

———. 2012b. 'The Materiality of Life: Revisiting the Anthropology of Nature in Amazonia', *Indiana* 29: 127–43.

Rivera Andía, J. 2003. *La fiesta del Ganado en el Valle de Chancay*. Lima: PUCP.

———. 2008. 'Apuntes sobre la alteridad constituyente en los Andes: Ambivalencias Rituales y Lingüísticas sobre un Espacio Imaginario', *Revista Española de Antropología Americana* 38(1): 191–215.

———. 2014. *Comprender los Rituals Ganaderos en los Andes y más Allá: Etnografías de Lidias, Herranzas y Arrierías*. Aachen: Shaker Verlag.

———. 2015. 'Amerindian Misfortunes: Ethnographies of South American Rituals and Cosmologies on Danger, Illness, and Evil', *Indiana* 32: 9–22.

Rivera Andía, J., and C. Ødegaard. Forthcoming. 'Indigenous Peoples, Extractivism and Turbulences in South America', in C. Ødegaard and J. Rivera Andía (eds), *Indigenous Life Projects and Extactivism: Ethnographies from South America*. London: Palgrave, pp. 7–43.

Robin, V. 2008. *Miroirs de l'Autre Vie: Pratiques Rituelles et Discours sur les Morts dans les Andes de Cuzco (Pérou)*. Nanterre: Société d'ethnologie.

Rocha, R. 2012. 'Perspectivismo e Relacionalismo Estrutural Ameríndios', *R@u. Revista de Antropologia da UFSCar* 4(2): 71–94.

Rochabrún, G. 2014. 'Cuando Todos los Puntos de Apoyo se Mueven', *Revista Argumentos* 4(8). Retrieved 19 March 2016 from http://revistaargumentos.iep.org.pe/articulos/cuando-todos-los-puntos-de-apoyo-se-mueven/.

Rösing, I. 2013. *The Ten Genders of Amarete: Religion, Ritual and Everyday Life in the Andean Culture*. Madrid and Frankfurt: Iberoamericana / Vervuert.

Sahlins, M. 2014. 'On the Ontological Scheme of Beyond Nature and Culture', *HAU: Journal of Ethnographic Theory* 4(1): 281–90.

Salas, G. 2012. 'Entre les Mineurs, les Grands Propriétaires Terriens et l'État: les Allégeances des Montagnes dans le Sud des Andes Péruviennes (1930–2012)', *Recherches amérindiennes au Québec* 42(2–3): 25–37.

Salmon, G. 2017. 'On Ontological Delegation: The Birth of Neoclassical Anthropology', in P. Charbonnier, G. Salmon and P. Skafish, *Comparative Metaphysics: Ontology After Anthropology*. London and New York: Rowman & Littlefield, pp. 41–60.

Salmon, G., and P. Charbonnier. 2014. 'The Two Ontological Pluralisms of French Anthropology', *Journal of the Royal Anthropological Institute* (NS) 20: 567–73.

Salmond, A. 2012. 'Ontological Quarrels: Indigeneity, Exclusion and Citizenship in a Relational World', *Anthropological Theory* 12(2): 115–41.

Santos-Granero, F. 2007. 'Of Fear and Friendship: Amazonian Sociality beyond Kinship and Affinity', *Journal of the Royal Anthropological Institute* 13: 1–18.

———. 2009. 'Introduction. Amerindian Constructional Views of the World', in F. Santos-Granero (ed.), *The Occult Life of Things: Native Amazonian Theories of Materiality and Personhood*. Tucson: University of Arizona Press, pp. 1–29.

Sax, M. 2012. *An Ethnography of Feeding, Perception, and Place in the Peruvian Andes (Where Hungry Spirits Bring Illness and Wellbeing)*. New York: Edwin Mellen Press.

Schavelzon, S. 2016. 'Cosmopolíticas e ontologies relacionais entre povos indígenas e populaçoes tradicionais na América Latina. Apresenração', *Revista de antropologia* 59(3): 7–17.

Scott, M. 2013. 'The Anthropology of Ontology (Religious Science?)', *Journal of the Royal Anthropological Institute* 19(4): 859–72.

———. 2014. 'Book Review: Anthropological Cosmochemistry. "Beyond Nature and Culture" by Philippe Descola', *Anthropology of This Century* 11. October. Retrieved 6 June 2018 from http://aotcpress.com/articles/anthropological-cosmochemistry/.

Seeger, A., R. DaMatta and E. Viveiros de Castro. 1979. 'A Construção da Pessoa nas Sociedades Indígenas Brasileiras', *Boletim do Museu Nacional, Série Antropologia* 32: 2–19.

Serres, M. 2009. *Écrivains, Savants et Philosophes Font le Tour du Monde*. Paris: Le Pommier, Les Essais.

Shellenberger, M., and T. Nordhaus. 2011. 'The Long Death of Environmentalism', *The Breakthrough*. http://thebreakthrough.org/archive/the_long_death_of_environmenta.

Simonett, H. 2014. 'Envisioned, Ensounded, Enacted: Sacred Ecology and Indigenous Musical Experience in Yoreme Ceremonies of Northwest Mexico', *Ethnomusicology* 58(1): 110–32.

Skafish, P. 2016a. 'The Descola Variations: The Ontological Geography of *Beyond Nature and Culture*', *Qui parle: Critical Humanities and Social Sciences* 25(1–2): 65–93.

———. 2016b. 'The Metaphysics of Extra-moderns: On the Decolonization of Thought – A Conversation with Eduardo Viveiros de Castro', *Common Knowledge* 22(3): 393–414.

Stengers, I. 1996. *Cosmopolitiques 1. La guerre des sciences*. Paris: La Découverte.

———. 2012. 'Reclaiming Animism', *e-flux* 36. Retrieved 11 July 2016 from http://www.e-flux.com/journal/36/61245/reclaiming-animism/.

Stolze Lima, T. 1996. 'O Dois e Seu Múltiplo: Reflexões sobre o Perspectivismo em uma Cosmologia Tupi', *Mana* 2(2): 21–47.

———. 1999. 'Para uma teoria etnográfica da distinção natureza e cultura na cosmologia Juruna', *Revista Brasileira de Ciências Sociais* 14 (40): 43–52.

———. 2000. 'Towards an Ethnographic Theory of the Nature/Culture Distinction in Juruna Cosmology', *Revista Brasileira de Ciências Sociais* 1(1): 43–52.

Strathern, M. 2011. 'Binary License', *Common Knowledge* 17(1): 87–103.

Stringer, M. 1999. 'Rethinking Animism: Thoughts from the Infancy of Our Discipline', *The Journal of the Royal Anthropological Institute* 5(4): 541–55.

Strong, M. 2012. *Art, Nature, and Religion in the Central Andes: Themes and Variations from Prehistory to the Present*. Austin: University of Texas Press.

Sullivan, L. 1988. *Icanchu's Drum: An Orientation to Meaning in South American Religions*. New York: Macmillan Co.

Surrallés, A., and P. García Hierro (eds). 2004. *Tierra Adentro: Territorio Indígena y Percepción del Entorno*. Copenhagen: IWGIA.

Sztutman, R. 2008. *Encontros: Eduardo Viveiros de Castro*. Rio de Janeiro: Azougue Editorial.

Taguchi, Y. 2017. 'An Interview with Marisol de la Cadena', *NatureCulture*. Retrieved 26 June 2018 from http://natureculture.sakura.ne.jp/an-interview-with-marisol-de-la-cadena/.

Taussig, M. 2015. *The Corn Wolf*. Chicago, IL and London: The University of Chicago Press.

Taylor, A.C., F.M. Renard-Casevitz and Th. Saignes. 1998. *Relaciones entre las Sociedades Amazónicas y Andinas entre los Siglos XV y XVII*. Quito: Abya-Yala.

Teixeira-Pinto, M. 1997. *Ieipari: Sacrifício e Vida Social entre os Indios Arara (Caribe)*. São Paulo: Hucitec.

Todd, Z. 2016. 'An Indigenous Feminist's Take on the Ontological Turn: "Ontology" Is Just Another Word for Colonialism', *Journal of Historical Sociology* 29(1): 4–22.

Tola, F. 2015. Comentario a 'El regreso de la barbarie. Una crítica etnográfica a las ontologías "premodernas"', *Trace* 67: 150–57.

Tola, F., C. Medrano and L. Cardin (eds). 2013. *Gran Chaco: Ontologías, Poder, Afectividad*. Buenos Aires: Asociación Civil Rumbo Sur.

Tournay, V. 2014. *Penser le Changement Institutionnel*. Paris: Presses Universitaires de France.

Turner, T. 2009. 'The Crisis of Late Structuralism, Perspectivism and Animism: Rethinking Culture, Nature, Spirit and Bodiliness', *Tipití* 7(1): 3–42.

Tylor, E. 1871. *Primitive Culture: Researches into the Development of Mythology, Philosophy, Religion, Art, and Custom*. London: J. Murray.

Urton, G. (ed.). 1985. *Animal Myths and Metaphors in South America*. Salt Lake City: University of Utah Press.

Venkatesan, S., K. Martin, M. Scott, C. Pinney, N. Ssorin-Chaikov, J. Cook and M. Strathern. 2013. 'The Group for Debates in Anthropological Theory (GDAT), The University of Manchester: The 2011 Annual Debate – Non-dualism Is Philosophy not Ethnography', *Critique of Anthropology* 33(3): 300–60.

Vigh, H., and D. Sausdal. 2014. 'From Essence back to Existence: Anthropology beyond the Ontological Turn', *Anthropological Theory* 14(1): 49–73.

Vilaça, A. 1992. *Comendo como Gente: Formas do Canibalismo Wari' (Pakaa Nova)*. Rio de Janeiro: ANPOCS.

———. 2006. *Quem Somos Nós: Os Wari' Encontram os Brancos*. Rio de Janeiro: UFRJ.

———. 2016. *Praying and Preying: Christianity in Indigenous Amazonia*. Oakland: University of California Press.

Viveiros de Castro, E. 1998. 'Cosmological Deixis and Amerindian Perspectivism', *The Journal of the Royal Anthropological Institute* 4(3): 469–88.

———. 2004a. 'Exchanging Perspectives: The Transformation of Objects into Subjects in Amerindian Ontologies', *Common Knowledge* 10(3): 463–84.

———. 2004b. 'Perspectival Anthropology and the Method of Controlled Equivocation', *Tipití: Journal of the Society for the Anthropology of Lowland South America* 2(1): 3–22.

———. 2007. 'The Crystal Forest: Notes on the Ontology of Amazonian Spirits', *Inner Asia* 9(2): 153–72.

———. 2009. *Métaphysiques Cannibales: Lignes d'Anthropologie post-Structurale*. Paris: Presses Universitaires de France.

———. 2012. *Cosmological Perspectivism in Amazonia and Elsewhere*. Manchester: HAU Network of Ethnographic Theory.

———. 2015a. *The Relative Native: Essays on Indigenous Conceptual Worlds*. Chicago, IL: HAU Press.

———. 2015b. 'Who is Afraid of the Ontological Wolf? Some Comments on an Ongoing Anthropological Debate', *The Cambridge Journal of Anthropology* 33(1): 2–17.

Wardle, H., and J. Shaffner (eds). 2017. *Cosmopolitics: Collected Papers of the Open Anthropology Cooperative, Volume I*. St Andrews: Open Anthropology Cooperative Press.

Wengrow, D. 2014. *The Origins of Monsters: Image and Cognition in the First Age of Mechanical Reproduction*. Princeton, NJ: Princeton University Press.

Willerslev, Rane. 2007. *Soul Hunters: Hunting, Animism, and Personhood among the Siberian Yukaghirs*. Berkeley: University of California Press.

———. 2013. 'Taking Animism Seriously, but Perhaps Not Too Seriously?', *Religion and Society: Advances in Research* 4(1): 41–57.

Wright, P. 2016. 'Perspectivismo amerindio: notas antropológicas desde una crítica postcolonial', in J. Renold (ed.), *Religión, Ciencias Sociales y Humanidades*. Rosario: UNR, pp. 139–50.

Part I

Securing Body and Wealth

1

On the Wings of Inspiration

Ritual Efficacy, Dancing Flamingos and Divine Mediation among Pastoralists and Herd Animals in Isluga, Chile

Penelope Z. Dransart

At high altitude in northern Chile, the winds have sculpted the steppe-like terrain into a largely treeless scrub. Large expanses of wind-torn soil, scoured from rock formations, give way to swampy bottomlands where water sources sustain areas of continuous vegetation. At altitudes greater than 3,700 metres above sea level, land used for cultivating quinua becomes exhausted, turning it sterile and bereft of the dry shrubby vegetation and isolated grass tussocks that ought to cover it.

Isluga, in this highland zone in Tarapaca, which forms part of II Región of Chile, borders the international frontier with Bolivia. Herders here put a great deal of ritual effort into enhancing the vital strength of their llamas, alpacas and sheep, as well as of the land that nourishes them all. They recognise that the regeneration of fertility or potency in people, herds and the earth itself is a property of the *uywiris*, the divinities of the hills and water sources, who are powerful grantees or withholders of good fortune. People are reluctant, however, to leave matters of fertility to chance, and they direct much ritual effort to complement the daily and annual round of caring for their herd animals. They also seek to *dar fuerza* (give strength) to the land itself, whom they address as Wirjin Tayka (Virgin Mother), using a half-Aymarised Spanish, half-Aymara term of respect.

My aim in this chapter is to examine the notion of efficacy in connection with a ritual action involving the burning of feathers as part of a major ceremony called the *wayñu*, which is celebrated in Isluga by individual households in honour of the herd animals. Part of the effort that humans undertake is to co-opt herd animals as active ritual agents into the ceremonies. Elsewhere I have demonstrated that the *wayñu* brings to the fore a sense of parallelism between the lineages of llamas, alpacas and sheep and those of human beings (Dransart 2002a: 89, 95–98). Here I will argue that the co-option of the herd animals into ritual observances contributes to the idea that non-verbal communication between species is possible via the mediation of other-worldly beings. For the purposes of this discussion I extend the notion of the term 'species' to refer to mortal and divine beings as well as human and non-human species.[1] Among human participants, the motivation for undertaking the *wayñu* is to ensure the well-being of their llamas, alpacas and sheep. As the thread of my argument emerges below, another element comes into focus. It is based on a principle I call inspiration in reference to the divine influence that animates people *and* herd animals *with* feeling. In other words, inspiration infuses feeling *into* them. My exposition therefore differs from that of many authors who tend to concentrate on the interests of the human contributors in the performance of rituals.

In exploring such human interests, Humphrey and Laidlaw (1994) have suggested that participants may appeal to the authority of ancestors to disavow their own intentions in conducting the ritual. The title of their book, *The Archetypal Actions of Ritual*, drew attention to the prototypical qualities of such practices. In Isluga, people often defer to the concept of *costumbre* (custom) in order to explain their ritual actions. Yet it is their custom to avoid providing a verbal exegesis of what a *costumbre* might mean; as Marietta Ortega Perrier (1998: 92) observed, in Isluga *costumbre es* (custom is). Juan van Kessel (1989: 50) treated such a concept as a means of authentication, which also indicates that the rituals follow a standard model. Superficially, at least, the argument might be applied to the ritual actions of Isluga people: they engage in them because their ancestors did. Catherine Bell (1997: 150) argued that whether or not the ritualised practices are as authentic as the practitioners maintain, the appeal to a sense of tradition provides them with values that are coherent and have the potential to endure.

These authors therefore consider the events of a ritual to carry a strong charge derived from the perceived legacy of the participants' forebears. Humphrey and Laidlaw's argument additionally carries with it the notion that these human pursuits differ from those activated in other spheres of practice. They thought that a 'different standpoint, the ritual stance' transforms such acts (Humphrey and Laidlaw 1994: 121). But the correct performance of ritual action is insufficient for it to be efficacious; in their view, participants should be conscious agents in giving meaning to the archetypal actions of ritual practice because they share some meanings but not others (ibid.: 13). In particular, they thought that the devotees they studied developed their subjective experiences to the extent that their fervent devotions become 'the animating force of ritual efficacy' (ibid.: 42).

Johannes Quack and Paul Töbelmann (2010: 18, 24 n.17) approached the problem from a different angle in expressing the conviction that one cannot study ritual or ritualised practices in isolation, as though it were possible to separate them from other aspects of social life. They also drew attention to the effects that a certain ritual may have, depending on whether one assesses its efficaciousness from the perspective of a native practitioner or that of an analyst. Social actors have desires when they perform a ritual, and those desires provide sufficient grounds for undertaking it. Quack and Töbelmann argue that it can be difficult for academic observers to distinguish between intended and unintended consequences of ritual practice. Certain consequences may be incidental to the intended action, and they maintain that the explanations and intentions of the practitioners are privileged because 'only they can explain why the people performed the ritual action at all' (ibid.: 25, n.13).

In the ritual practice examined here, the purpose Isluga people give for burning flamingo feathers is to discourage their llamas, alpacas and sheep from wandering and to keep them together as a tightly formed herd. This small act constitutes a particular moment in a larger complex of events celebrating the coming into sexual maturity of the herd animals. In the Andes this ceremony is often called, in Spanish, the *floreo* (flowering) or *herranza* (branding), but in the Aymara of Isluga it is the *wayñu*, which is a type of dance (Mamani Mamani 2002: 169). There is a pronounced liturgical aspect to Isluga people's celebration of the *wayñu*, and they are scrupulously careful to observe its correct sequential performance despite the convention according to which the couple who host the event are expected to consume an excess of alcohol (Dransart 1997: 85; 2002b).

This chapter draws attention to the effects participants seek to accomplish in conducting such actions by exploring the motivation for undertaking particular ritual movements as well as considering potential founts of inspiration. A desire on the part of the herders to avoid spending time and energy looking for errant llamas supplies the motive for going in the dark of night on the eve of the *wayñu* ceremony to the pastures that their animals frequent during daylight hours. If motivation has to do with initiating movement or action – bearing in mind that the ceremony itself, significantly, is called a dance – then inspiration has to do with the drawing in of breath and the offering of smoke to divine beings. The animation of feeling that accompanies the ceremony as a whole springs from sources broader than the immediate cause of motivation, and is related to the notion that it is possible for divinities to communicate non-verbal incentives to herd animals.

Questioning 'Ritual Efficacy'

In a handbook published in 1621, the Jesuit Pablo de Arriaga entitled one of his chapters 'Que ofrecen en sus sacrificios, y como' (What they offer in their sacrifices, and how). The publication was intended to assist priests in campaigns to extirpate idolatry, and listed in the chapter were pink feathers from flamingos 'they call *pariuna*', which frequented highland lakes (Arriaga 1621: 26).[2] Despite the tenor of the language he used – Sabine MacCormack (1991: 406) called it a 'terminology of contempt' – his text injects a sense of curiosity and even wonderment into the inventory of sacred objects and ritual practices intended to assist priests to discover prior to destroying them. In a detailed study of the extirpation of idolatry during the mid-Colonial Period (1640–1750), Kenneth Mills (1997: 63) found that witness statements recorded in inquisition trials conveyed local people's sincerity in their commitment to ritual observance; indeed, one person spoke of his fear of the Catholic Church but also of his greater fear of Andean divinities, so much so that in his ritual practices he was unable to cease invoking them. Despite the efforts of the mid-colonial missionaries, people did not always find the Christian mass to be efficacious (ibid.: 185).

In the light of Stanley Tambiah's (1981: 128) comment that 'traffic with the supernatural [is] notoriously uncertain', it is important to take such historical circumstances into account. He relates how people used to venerate the Sri Lankan smallpox goddess until Western medicine succeeded in eradicating the disease and, as a result, the goddess's cult became almost obsolete (ibid.: 129). Andean rites to enhance the fertility of the crops and herd animals have followed a different historical trajectory. People continue to celebrate them, despite the severe punishment meted out by the authorities during the Colonial Period and the present-day disapproval emanating from evangelical protestant churches. Today, as Peter Gose (2014: 9) observes, countless herding rituals from many different

Andean communities feature on YouTube. Participants in these ritual performances use such media to present their 'interests and future identities' to 'publics' that are increasingly heterogeneous (Hughes-Freeland and Crain 1998: 1–3. See also Crain 1998). Some aspects of these rituals, however, are so highly charged that they are not deemed suitable for public exposure via electronic communication.

An awareness of changing historical circumstances alerts us, as researchers, to the consequences produced by the style of our questions. Note that Pablo de Arriaga used the relative pronoun 'what' in an interrogative manner. Perhaps he relied on information supplied by parish priests who had questioned people, asking them to identify selections from an indefinite number of things or values. For instance, in response to a question such as 'What do you offer to the deities?', someone could have replied, 'We offer the smoke of burnt *parina* feathers'.

In order to establish the subject of an enquiry, however, pronouns can be employed in a more elliptical fashion. Quack and Töbelmann (2010: 17) therefore proposed a strategy for examining the problem of ritual efficacy by recommending that researchers ask precisely: 'What or who affects what or whom, and according to whom?' This tripartite question rests on a distinction between the *efficiens* and the *efficiendum*. The *efficiens* is the element (somebody or something) who/that effects (or produces) a change to an extent that the participants/interpreters regard the ritual as having been worthwhile. The *efficiendum*, in contrast, is the person, body or thing upon which the ritual is enacted. An interpreter or interpreters comprise the third element in providing an assessment of the degree to which the ritual process results in an efficacious outcome.[3]

As a starting point, the herders might be regarded as the *efficiens* because they offer the smoke of the burnt feathers to the spirits of the hills and water sources. The llamas, alpacas and sheep constitute the *efficiendum*, and the herders evaluate the quality of the rite's efficacy on the extent of the walking they have to do to bring dispersed herd members back together in the course of their daily herding activities.

These distinctions only provide a baseline for the enquiry because, Quack and Töbelmann argued (2010: 17–18), people who agree on the efficaciousness of the outcome might disagree on how that successful outcome has been achieved. A healer who conducted a ritual, for example, might acknowledge the intervention of divine beings to whom he or she attributed the cure of a patient, but an outside observer might consider that the cure worked instead on the patient's psyche by removing the anxieties that had caused the problem. Quack and Töbelmann (2010: 17) observe that the efficacy is perceived from the perspective of 'different "spheres" or "levels"'. They also draw attention to possible alternative interpretations of the 'means' used to bring about the efficacious 'ends'; if participants use offerings to make contact with divinities, do the offerings cause the divinities to intervene positively, or do these offerings have a symbolic role? Finally, they observe that special conditions can serve as context-dependent variables impinging on how people regard the efficacy of a ritual. Admitting that such issues are not always mutually exclusive, they suggest that the analyst ask these questions:

1. Who or what is held to be efficacious in the ritual? (*efficiens*)
2. What is held to be affected in the ritual? (*efficiendum*)
3. In what sphere or on what level is the ritual efficacious?
4. By what means is the ritual efficacious?
5. Under which conditions is the ritual efficacious? (Quack and Töbelmann 2010: 18)

These questions will also serve as a reminder that the effects of ritual are achieved through an understanding of its interacting or contextual aspects rather than on just one of its constituent moments (a point also made by Endres 2008: 77). In this light, concerns about the efficacy of ritual action should be situated in the context of the value and worth of other sorts of activity. Peter Gose (1994: 6) regarded ritual 'as a moment of practice that is intrinsically incomplete and necessarily resolves itself into other moments, most notably labour'. This contextualisation of what comprises ritual provides a framework for a discussion of the feather-burning ritual in Isluga as an integral part of the work involved in the annual cycle of the herding year.

The exploration that follows, therefore, concerns the burning of *parina* feathers and is based on my fieldwork in Isluga. It is framed in a consideration of relevant comparative ethnographic and historic literature, tracking certain issues that operate on aesthetic and configurational levels. The discussion also takes into account some of the conditions under which participants might consider the ritual to be efficacious. It concludes with a reflection on what has been termed a 'ritual sense', as discussed by Quack (2010) and Quack and Töbelmann (2010). During the *wayñu* celebration the congregation assembled before the *uywiri* consists of both human and non-human beings (llamas, alpacas and sheep), which means that the ceremony is not just a matter of bringing about changes in the mental condition of the human participants, precisely because the ritual practices are intended to change the behaviour of the herd animals and to strengthen non-human fertility.

The Vigil

In Isluga, the caring for llamas, alpacas and sheep takes place in the context of cycles of dispersal to distant pasture grounds during the arid windy season and congregation in residential communities during the rainy season. An annual round of rituals also accompanies these centrifugal and centripetal forms of movement (Dransart 2002a: 56–58). Herders are deeply knowledgeable about the birds they encounter during these cycles. These include *parina*, which mediate between the watery, earthy and celestial realms of the steppe-like terrain and the skies above it. The act of burning *parina* feathers as part of ritual action among herders has received less attention than other birds featuring more widely in the ethnographic literature.[4]

The *wayñu* takes place during the rainy season, typically during the months of January to March. Whether celebrated in its full or a shorter version, known as the *ch'allta*, it is an elaborate event requiring considerable preparation (Dransart 2002b). It opens with an all-night vigil, followed by at least one full day of ritually 'dressing' the herd animals with ear ornaments, neck pieces and brightly dyed fleece, which is tied to their backs, and an evening meal in which the meat of a sacrificed animal is served (Dransart 1997, 2002a: 82–100, 2002b).

During the vigil held in the homestead of the host family, the couple at the head of the household leave the rest of the participants to go to a well-watered pasture ground that their herds frequent. There they burn *parina* feathers, offering the smoke to the divinities. When mating, flamingos perform a tightly choreographed dance in which the members of the flock act in close unison (Illustration 1.1). The request for divine assistance is meant to act on the behaviour of llamas, alpacas and sheep, to encourage them to act in their herd units. If individual llamas wander from their group, hours or even days can be spent looking for them.[5] The desire of the herders is that their llamas, alpacas and sheep behave like bunched *parinas*. Hence the message conveyed in the smoke produced by burning *parina* feathers is the product of what Emily Ahern (1979: 7–10) would have called an illocutionary act with strong intentions.[6]

Illustration 1.1 A group of puna flamingos in a mating dance. Photograph: Pedros Szekely, Creative Commons Attribution 2.0 Generic license.

To explore notions of ritual efficacy on which this practice is predicated, I appeal to a notion concerning the 'wings of inspiration', in an allusion to the kinds of inspiration that can take place between human, non-human and divine beings through ritual practice.[7] The ritual action of burning feathers is directed towards working on the behaviour of llamas and alpacas but, if the desired result does occur, an outside observer cannot be sure that the effort did indeed produce the intended outcome. A sceptic might say that when well-behaved herds remain together, the situation might have occurred without the assistance of the ritual practice, especially as herders take additional measures to encourage good discipline within the herd. In one *wayñu* I attended, the wife of the couple hosting the event lightly kicked one of her llamas, berating her for constantly wandering from the herd (Dransart 2002a: 92). Burning *parina* feathers is a ritual resolving itself into significant other moments, and the next two sections explore some of the qualities from which it might be said to be efficacious, according to the different perspectives involved. The first of these sections deals with aesthetic principles in chronological depth, bearing in mind that, as an adjective, the word 'aesthetic' originally referred to perception by the senses and is related to the notion of *feeling*. A subsequent section considers configurational principles concerning the offering of smoke to divine beings.

On What Sphere or Level Is the Burning of *Parina* Feathers an Efficacious Ritual?

Aesthetic Level

Flamingos (or *parina*) have not been as consistently present in Andean iconography and material culture as other birds such as condors, but they have occurred in visual images and ritual practice down the centuries. Some studies suggest that flamingo feathers were used over a long period of time in pre-Hispanic textiles and other artefacts. John O'Neill examined a set of ornaments now in The Textile Museum, Washington DC, dated to *c*.300–200 BC (Early Horizon 10). Because the feathers had been trimmed, the identification was not secure and he judged the feathers to be 'either scarlet macaw or Chilean Flamingo' (cited in Rowe 2012: 53–54). The wing feathers of Chilean flamingos, however, have been reported in plumes inserted into copper shafts accompanying the burial of the Lord of Sipán in the Lambayaque Valley of northern Peru (King 2012b: 23). The bird species whose feathers have been positively identified in the textiles studied by John O'Neill and Mark Robbins include cotinga, macaw, parrot, tanager, toucan and trogon from Amazonia, as well as Muscovy duck (Rowe 1984; Reina and Pressman 1991: 114). King (2012a: 128) thought a tabard with rows in alternation consisting of long green and pink feathers came, respectively, from Amazonian parrots and Chilean flamingos.

Feathers are what Alfred Gell (1998: 111–13) called an exuvial substance and, in an Andean context, his reasoning would also extend to camelid fleece and human hair, which both stand in a homologous relationship to *parina* feathers.[8] Indeed, Isluga herders describe a colour of fleece as *parina* if it is 'red' or *qhusi* (a type of beige) on top and white underneath (Dransart 2002a: 78). Analogous chains of associations can be seen at the end of the rainy season when men form groups to play *siku* (panpipes) in a kind of music called *sikura*, wearing red *parina* feathers standing proud in their hatbands.[9]

The conjunction of hair and feathers also occurred in the documentary records of the mid-Colonial Period idolatry trials. In San Pedro de Quipán, Province of Canta, Peru, the chief religious celebrant donned a finely woven black tunic to lead a procession in a dry season ritual on the 'night of the moon' falling after Corpus Christi, during which people made offerings of food and drink to a divinity. Noteworthy in this account is the brightness of the celebrant's coloured headdress, which incorporated flamingo feathers (Mills 1997: 39). In another instance, a native priest made a love talisman by plaiting hair of a would-be lover through a flamingo feather along with hair taken from a woman, whose affections he desired (ibid.: 115). The principle here is based on a desire to unite two people, as *parinas* form pairs after the mating dance.

A type of alpaca found in the Cuzco area of Peru provides yet another example of a homology between fleece and feathers because it is named *suri* in Quechua, after the Andean *avestruz* or rhea. The long fleece staples of the *suri* alpaca resemble the feathers of the bird. A particularly evocative example of the connection between fleece and feathers and the context of herd animal fertility occurs on a Wari tapestry (*c.*AD 500–800), now in the Brooklyn Museum. It shows a series of alpacas giving birth, and the staples of fleece hanging from the flanks of the mothers are stylised as feathers (Dedenbach-Salazar Sáenz 1990: illustration 7; Stone-Miller 1992: 341–42). Although far distant from Cuzco, María Ester Grebe Vicuña and Blas Hidalgo (1988: 86) noted that musicians in the communities west of the Salar de Atacama sometimes wore red-dyed *suri* feathers in their headdresses to replace those of *parina*.

Pre-Hispanic textiles present stylised birds, some of which may depict flamingos or *suris*, but they are not always clearly identifiable since both can have a pointed or humped back. The logic of this kind of stylisation also occurs in a belt woven by María Flores, an Isluga herder (Illustration 1.2). The prominent hooked beak in one of the motifs and the alternation of light pink and black in the main part of the belt indicate that the weaver depicted a *parina*. When tending her

Illustration 1.2 Detail of a belt of a type called *faja carnero*, woven by María Flores, of birds, including a *parina* (the left of the two birds), and an upside-down flower. Photograph: P. Dransart.

herds in the pasture grounds in Arabilla, her native community, she would see flamingos feeding in a small lake nearby.

At the top and bottom of each box containing the figurative motifs of her belt, but inside the zigzag border design, there are little narrow stripes, passing in alternation from dark brown to white (when edging the dark background) and from yellow, through orange, to dark red (when edging the pink background). Isluga weavers use the term *k'isa* for such configurations. Veronica Cereceda (1987) thought a *k'isa* in a textile serves as an indexical icon because it is a conventionalised likeness of a rainbow – while not being an exact copy – at the same time as being an existential expression of light in the textile on a cosmological level of reference. She framed her interpretation in reference to the work of Claude Lévi-Strauss ([1955] 1993: 137), from whom she borrowed the term *gamme* (gamut). In my experience of doing fieldwork in Isluga, however, weavers have told me that the tonal steps of a *k'isa* must 'sound out' (*sonar*) against the colour selected for the ground of a textile. As a consequence, I consider a *k'isa* to be a homologue of a 'microtonal rising' in the contrasts and transformations of making music (Hill 1985; Stobart 2006: 113; Dransart 2016).

The *wayñu* vigil is a time for singing sad-sounding songs, which also accompany the daytime events in the corral when people ritually dress llamas and alpacas with ear tassels and neckpieces consisting of yarns arranged in *k'isa*.[10] When the hosts penetrate the darkness during the vigil to burn *parina* feathers, they perform a ritual practice that does not just concern substance or symbolic expression, but also has to do with altering the behaviour of wayward herd animals throughout the annual cycle. People supplicate the *uywiri*, asking that llamas act together, like *parinas* in their mating dance when they form a congregation of tightly bunched birds. Maintaining good discipline forms part of the successful raising of herd animals. The multiplication of alpacas bearing different fleece colours, in particular, is important if a weaver is to have access to a good range of tones with which to create *k'isa* configurations in her textiles.

Is There a 'Configurational Totality'? (Tambiah 1981)

A configurational approach to the study of ethnographic data is grounded in a strategy of 'seeing how the whole is built up from, but is also greater than, the parts'. It demonstrates 'how lower level units build up into or fuse into higher-level units and processes, how different media are made to converge, and how total experiences are produced' (Tambiah 1981: 140). The previous section explored some of the salient aesthetic principles concerning feathers as a substance or coloured matter. This section, in contrast, considers comparative evidence for the burning of items, turning pungent-smelling matter into fine ash.

An extensive literature, based on ethnographic observations as well as colonial documentary sources, has considered the offering of burnt substances to divine beings. The act of burning is a significant one because it converts solid substances into smoke for conveyance to other-worldly beings. A funerary custom reported in the Andes concerns the actions taken by mourners who, in some communities, burn the deceased person's clothing for him or her to continue wearing in the afterlife (Duviols 1986: 170; MacCormack 1991: 428).[11]

Colonial Period documents provide evidence that the vital essence of substances might be transferred 'through the smoke of a burnt offering, on a breath of air, in a current of liquid, or through simple touch' (Dean 2010: 35). Hence textiles during Inka times were alternatively cast into water or into flames as offerings to divinities. In the great state-sponsored cycle of ritual performances, the *citua* was celebrated during Quyaraymi (the month of September in the Gregorian calendar) and priests consigned sacrificed llamas, along with brightly coloured clothing, coca leaves and flowers, to rivers in order to carry pestilence away from Cuzco. In contrast, royal family lineages marked the period of the summer solstice (December and January) by each sacrificing ten llamas and ten garments of very fine white and red cloth, burning them in offering to the celestial and terrestrial divinities, in order to preserve the health of the supreme Sapa Inka (Murra [1958] 1975: 161).

Some acts of burning, however, entail an element of extreme risk on an other-worldly level. Over a considerable period of time ethnographers have reported that to watch the flames consuming the offering is to place individuals in an extremely vulnerable situation (Lira 1953: 128). For this reason, only two or three people draw apart from the main group to the place where they make the offering to invite the attention of the divine beings (Cáceres Chalco 2014: 131). Not even the ritual specialist, the *paqu*, should see how the spirits of the hills eat the burnt offering, say Sylvia Mayorga, Félix Palacios and Ramiro Samaniego (1976: 231).

Inge Bolin (1998: 41–42) described how her research participants in Chillihuani, a high-altitude herding community in the Department of Cuzco, Peru, took offerings, including coca leaves, sprinkled them with alcohol and wrapped them in paper. They placed them in a carrying cloth, which was also given an alcohol libation. Two people (a niece and her uncle) then took the offering to burn in a niche in the rock face of a corral reserved for ritual use. Bolin was not present at that part of the ritual because, her research participants informed her, the ritual must be performed in silence, and to view the act would be highly dangerous. Having offered the little parcel to the spirits of the hills on behalf of the female alpacas, the same two people returned to make another offering in the name of the llamas and alpacas. They reported that that the first offering had been received by the divinities who evidently consumed it 'with pleasure' because it had been transmuted into ash 'as white as silver' (ibid.: 42). If dark lumps survive in the ash it is a worrying sign for the fate of the llamas and alpacas in the year to come. In contrast, if the ashes are found to be 'white like silver' the divinities have demonstrated their contentment with the offering (ibid.: 63). This concern not to expose individuals unnecessarily when making illocutionary performances with particularly strong intentions indicates the degree to which people believe in the ontological power of the divinities to grant their requests, should they be disposed so to do.

Reports from agro-pastoral communities situated in the inter-Andean valleys of northern Chile indicate that people clean canals before they plant the seeds. They perform ceremonies that include burning *parina* feathers then casting the remains into the water, which is made to course through the irrigation canals for the first time of the new season. According to María Ester Grebe Vicuña (2004: 152–53), people in Socoroma offered burnt flamingo feathers to the irrigation waters as a *pago* or 'payment'. Ricardo Moyano (2011) also considered a similar use of such feathers in Socaire, where the cleaning of canals takes place on 24–26 October each year. Citing the work of Barthel ([1957] 1986: 156–57), he stated that bottles of *aloja* adorned with flamingo feathers served as what I would call homologies *for* (rather than of) people – black for adult men, pink and red for adult women and small and white for children.[12]

Canal-cleaning rituals in agro-pastoral communities are intended to enhance the fertility of the crops. Isluga people, in contrast, use canals to irrigate unenclosed pasture rather than fields, and they do not make canal cleaning the focus of major celebration as they do with the *wayñu* of the herd animals. The place where they burn *parina* feathers is precisely one of the pasture grounds that they frequent with their llamas, alpacas and sheep during the annual herding cycle.

In other accounts feathers do not feature, as in Peter Gose's analysis of canal cleaning in Huaquirca, Department of Apurímac, Peru. This event takes place between 15 and 30 August, but he found it lacked the complexity of the symbolic content he detected in other ritual events in Huaquirca – perhaps, he thought, because people had more control over water distribution than elsewhere (Gose 1994: 99). Nonetheless the water judge elected to oversee the distribution of water for the coming wet season placed sprigs of wild plants in the hatbands of the other participants once the work party had finished its tasks. This action seems to parallel the red *parina* feathers placed in the hatbands of the *siku* players at the beginning of the dry season in Isluga; in these instances, both the plants and the feathers are associated with human hair. Although the context of the specific labour being undertaken differed from one community to another, Gose (1994: 101) observed that whether burnt, libated or interred, people performed the same sort of ritual practices for different instrumental ends.

A wide configurational field was sketched in this section, discussing how people in different Andean communities convey the substance of burnt offerings to the divinities through the medium of air or water. The concluding step in my argument considers some of the conditions that might apply when Isluga people perform the illocutionary act of burning *parina* feathers.

Under What Conditions Does the Burning of Feathers Become an Efficacious Ritual?

I started out by assuming that herders are the *efficiens* and llamas, alpacas and sheep are the *efficiendum*. From a human perspective it seems clear the *wayñu*'s primary beneficiaries are the llamas, alpacas and sheep. If they were to adopt the analytical language, however, Isluga people might regard the *uywiri* as being the *efficiens*, because they are the divine beings who produce the important changes for the ritual to make its effects, and they could say the *efficiendum* is the ritual sense of the human and herd animal participants, which is acted upon in the ceremony. This possession of something like a ritual sense or instinct becomes a significant condition for an efficacious outcome.[13] The important point here is that in Isluga not only human beings but also llamas, alpacas and sheep possess this ritual propensity.

In my introduction, I outlined two different anthropological approaches to the study of ritual efficacy. On the one hand,

Humphrey and Laidlaw (1994) argued that the ritual stance of the participants enabled them (the participants) to develop their subjective experiences in infusing their ritual actions with an animating force. For Quack and Töbelmann (2010), on the other hand, ritual practices are not separable from daily life, and they offer a series of questions for probing who affects what and from whose perspective the ritual might be judged to have an efficacious outcome. In this second approach, the 'ritual stance' of the human participants is not such a crucial factor as is their possession of a ritual 'feeling' to reconfigure their social practices, increasing the likelihood of a favourable outcome. By adapting their questioning approach, it becomes possible to investigate the different perspectives of the participants in a ritual, whether they be humans, herd animals or divinities. I therefore used their questions to develop a strategy for exploring the participants' motivation for performing the *wayñu* and the possible routes for receiving inspiration as a successful outcome.

Quack and Töbelmann devised their questions in a review of Catherine Bell's (1992) discussion of ritual efficacy. Bell argued that the ritual sense becomes a form of social action that works dialectically because it provides participants with the means to ritualise space and to deploy culturally appropriate strategies that lend themselves to ritualised practices (Quack and Töbelmann 2010: 21). But in her multilayered treatment of ritualisation, Quack and Tobelmann (ibid.: 23) thought that her use of Pierre Bourdieu's concepts of habitus and what she called 'schemes of ritualization' resulted in a deflection of the participants' point of view because her argument rested on an unacknowledged Durkheimian notion that people's ritual practice is 'embedded in a misrecognition of what it [ritualisation] is in fact doing' (Bell 1992: 81). Émile Durkheim ([1915] 1965: 373–74) argued that native ritual practitioners do not doubt the efficacy of rites performed to enhance fertility, and he considered the efficacious outcome of a ritual to be based on functions and reasons other than those provided by the participants.[14] For Quack and Töbelmann (2010: 23), however, the separation of the instrumental and symbolic aspects of ritual actions leads analysts to run the risk of ignoring the participants' intentions in performing the ritual.

They levelled a similar criticism against S.J. Tambiah (1981: 129), in spite of his urging of anthropologists to examine conventional acts as a logical social performance by taking into account people's 'canons for their validity from the actors' point of view'. Quack and Töbelmann (2010: 16) also detected a Durkheimian legacy in Tambiah's approach because they claim he gave too much emphasis to 'conventions' – which results in the analyst imposing an exogenous point of view on the ethnographic data – rather than paying proper attention to indigenous 'intentions'.

Johannes Quack (2010: 183) argued that the explanation for why people consider their ritual practices to have successful results is not amenable to a general theory of ritual because the efficacy may not be specific only to ritual practice. For Peter Gose, rituals cannot be divorced from the cycle of the working year. He urged us to consider the interconnections between labour and ritual because they stand in a complex relation to each other 'as means are to ends' (Gose 1994: 7). Bourdieu's (1991: 52) argument that people can effect a transformation 'on a habitus predisposed to respond to them' through the use of language and powers of suggestion does not carry much weight for Gose (1994: 7), because it does not take into account the 'instrumental intentions of ritual'.

This argument is related to Quack and Töbelmann's (2010: 23) concerns that the 'participants' perceptions of what they are doing' have been overlooked. Quack (2010: 170) has a different take on the relevance of Bourdieu's arguments compared with Gose, and he used them as a basis for understanding how the notion of a 'ritual instinct' (rather than a 'ritual sense') might be applied to ethnographic materials.

Based on Quack and Töbelmann's (2010: 18) questions, in this chapter I have explored specific perspectives concerning the efficacy of burning *parina* feathers during the *wayñu* ceremony. Participants' intentions in *wayñu* celebrations involve approaching the *uywiri*, requesting them to look favourably on their herd animals and to grant them an abundance of well-behaved llamas, alpacas and sheep. They do not automatically assume such a favourable result because the outcomes of their ritual intentions will be tempered by changing fortunes in the granting of *suerte* which, on the basis of fieldwork in Oruro, Bolivia, Gweneth Armstrong (1990: 7) defined as 'material fortune' and as 'personal well-being and harmony with the cosmos'. People attempt to cultivate *suerte* and to attract it through divine intervention, but they do not take it for granted (ibid.: 53–54, 65). In many parts of the Andes, Tuesdays and Fridays are days of the week not to be considered propitious for undertaking activities such as slaughtering a herd animal (Bugallo and Vilca 2011). Families in Isluga hold their *wayñu* either on Thursdays or Saturdays, which are the days on which the llama or alpaca sacrifice takes place (Dransart 2002a: 83). According to Armstrong (1990: 29–30), Tuesdays and Fridays are days when the 'balance of *suerte* is most vulnerable, but ... easiest to manipulate or cultivate for individual benefit'. The vigil of a *wayñu* ceremony therefore begins with a *víspera* (the eve) that falls on a day immediately after a vulnerable day (Wednesday evening) or with a *víspera* falling on the eve of a vulnerable day itself (Friday evening). These are calculations that the host couple must consider when deciding on which day to celebrate their *wayñu*.

In many anthropological accounts of ritual practice, the overwhelming tenor of the arguments seem to be predicated on the effectiveness of rituals for the human rather than the non-human participants. I have, instead, treated herd animals and divinities as other participants whose perspectives ought to be taken into account along with those of the humans celebrating the *wayñu* ceremony. Examples of human recognition of non-human perspectives do occur in anthropological accounts; to mention but one, María Guzmán-Gallegos (n.d.) describes how Amazonian Kichwa people in Ecuador throw cultivated garden products – maize and peanuts – in the Niñu Jista ritual. Their specific objective is to call together wild animals to be hunted by the human members of the community. The intention of the action is to effect changes of behaviour among wild animals, but because the growing of plant foods is a product of human labour, and hunting is another form of labour, following Gose (1994: 7), the ritual 'depends on, and interacts with, other kinds of purposive activity'.

To conclude, I have used an approach here that questions who is affecting whom in a specific type of regulative ritual in Isluga. It has enabled me to consider the perspectives of different categories of participants concerning whether or not the ritual's aim of instilling lasting behavioural changes in the llamas, alpacas and sheep has an efficacious outcome. Although individual participants may know little of the pre-Hispanic or colonial uses of *parina* feathers, I have considered this wider contextual dimension of such a ritual legacy. As celebrated in Isluga, the congregation that meets before the *uywiri* consists of llamas, alpacas, sheep and human beings. Both constituencies, human and non-human, stand in a spiritual relationship to the *uywiri*, and the human participants offer to the divinities the breath of the smoke from burnt *parina* feathers. As part of a larger annual round of other types of pastoral care, herders supplicate the *uywiri* with a request on a breath of smoke, asking the *uywiri* to mediate on their behalf and to inspire their herd animals to act as a well-behaved unit, like *parina* in their mating dances.

Penelope Z. Dransart is honorary reader in the School of Social Science, University of Aberdeen. Since 1986 she has been undertaking fieldwork in northern Chile. Her publications include *Earth, Water, Fleece and Fabric: An Ethnography and Archaeology of Andean Camelid Herding* (2002), and *Textiles from the Andes* (2011). She is editor and contributor to *Living Beings: Perspectives on Interspecies Engagements* (2013), *Kay Pacha: Cultivating Earth and Water in the Andes* (2006) and *Andean Art: Visual Expression and its Relation to Andean Beliefs and Values* (1995). A recent article is 'The curious case of Sir Henry Wellcome's wooden statuette clad in tie-dyed Wari cloth' in Pre-Columbian Textile Conference VII (2017). She is the recipient of a research grant from the Wenner-Gren Foundation, which has supported fieldwork in Isluga in 2017, investigating how herders are being challenged by changing weather conditions, especially rain, mist and wind.

Notes

1. For a further discussion of the term 'species', see Dransart 2013: 4–6.
2. In the Andes, flamingos are known as *parina* or *parihuana*, but Arriaga (1621) used the spelling *pariuna*. The flamingo with the most widespread distribution in Peru and Chile is the *Phoenicopterus chilensis*, but the species inhabiting the highlands are likely to be the *Phoenicoparrus jamesi* (puna flamingo) or *P. andinus* (Andean flamingo). In a survey of the birds' abundance and distribution, Caziani et al. (2007: 279) reported that puna flamingo numbers were high in Surire, which is at the northernmost extent of Isluga territory.
3. The sub-heading of this section is borrowed from the title of Quack and Töbelmann (2010).
4. For example, chullumpi ducks feature in ethnographies on Isluga (Martínez Soto-Aguilar 1976; Dransart 2002a), Qaqachaka, Bolivia (Arnold and Yapita 1998: 358–62), and Chillihuani, Peru (Bolin 1998: 39, 72), as well as the dancing partridge studied by Rivera Andía (2003, 2012).
5. In the festivities accompanying an annual rodeo of cattle every August in Viscas, in the Valley of Chancay, Peru, men and women used to form parallel lines in a dance imitating partridges (*kiwyu*). An explanation that this dance was performed because the community members 'go to the last hill of the territory to gather together the last of the cattle' (*se van hasta la última colina del territorio para juntar la última res*) provides an example of ritual action intended to bring herd animals together,

paralleling the motivation for performing the ritual considered in this chapter (Rivera Andía 2003: 141).

6. Ahern based her discussion on the work of J.L. Austin (1962), in which an illocution is an utterance intended to achieve something. The performance or practice of such an act has been considered by other authors, including Bourdieu (1977: 410), Tambiah (1981: 127) and Quack and Töbelmann (2010: 15).

7. This tripartite conformation of participants into two mortal (human and animal) categories plus one divine category is reminiscent of the ontological triad that Viveiros de Castro (1992: 29) called Nature/Society/Supernature in his discussion of Araweté eschatology. He argued that human beings are not the antithesis of animals, but of divine beings, who are eaters of raw flesh (ibid.: 22, 74). In Isluga, the uywiris are anthropophagic and they are gendered. They sometimes reveal themselves in human guise, but their human or non-human condition is not clearly articulated (Dransart 2002a: 59, 62).

8. Homology has to do with the perception of some kind of similarity between different organisms or parts of organisms. Veronica Strang (1999: 92, n.4) referred to homologues as 'strings of conceptual associations', seeing them as a means for human beings to 'project themselves' onto the surrounding environment in relation to the human body. For discussions of the cultural expression of homologous relationships in the South Central Andes between fleece, human hair and plant fibre, see Dransart 2002a: 146 and Dransart 2010: 85.

9. In an article published posthumously, Gabriel Martínez Soto-Aguilar (2009) observed a group of siku players performing a night-time ritual on Maundy Thursday. The calendrical timing of the ritual is significant, because sikura music belongs to the windy dry season, and by the time the moveable feast of Holy Week comes round, the rains have usually already but ceased. Siku are wind instruments, and some Isluga concepts concerning the animating properties of air have been discussed by Dransart (2010: 91).

10. Lévi-Strauss ([1964] 1970: 280–81) observed that South Americans considered microtonal phenomena to possess a 'primordial maleficence' associated with the giving of life as well as the giving of death.

11. In Isluga it seems that people burn the deceased person's garments. In other Andean communities, the relatives and friends wash the garments to avoid the risk of the deceased making a return to this world if any garment remains unwashed (Murra [1958] 1975: 153). For a finely detailed analysis of clothes washing in Huaquirca, Peru, see Gose 1994: 120–23, 138–40, 154. As Ina Rösing (1995: 74) observed, variations on the rules structuring ritual performances in the Andes may be based on the logical use of water, to avoid unwanted heat and drought, or of fire, to communicate with deities.

12. Grebe Vicuña and Hidalgo (1988: 86–88) also commented on this ethnographic information, in a discussion of people's views concerning the

mediation that took place between ritual specialists and divine beings in Socaire and other communities in the Atacama desert.

13. Not all people in Isluga share the same ritual sense, especially since the late 1980s when people in the community in which I have done my fieldwork started to become followers of an evangelical Protestant sect (Dransart 1997: 96; 2002b: 2–3, 16–17). Evangelicals, however, might still recognize *uywiri* as having an ontological existence, although it would be in a demonic guise. The coexistence of different forms of religious experience also makes it possible for sceptics to express their agnosticism or atheism (Dransart 2002a: 49). Sceptical responses in the face of questions concerning ritual efficacy have been discussed by Sax (2010).

14. As cited by Ahern (1979: 1).

References

Ahern, E.M. 1979. 'The Problem of Efficacy: Strong and Weak Illocutionary Acts', *Man* (NS) 14: 1–17.

Armstrong, G. 1990. 'Symbolic Arrangement and Communication in the *Despacho*'. PhD thesis. University of St Andrews.

Arnold, D.Y., and J. de D. Yapita. 1998. *Río de vellón, río de canto: Cantar a los animales, una poética andina de la creación*. La Paz: Universidad Mayor de San Andrés.

Arriaga, P.I. de. 1621. *Extirpacion de la idolatria del Piru*. Lima: Geronymo de Contreras.

Austin, J.L. 1962. *How To Do Things with Words*. New York: Oxford University Press.

Barthel, T. [1957] 1986. 'El agua y el festival de primavera entre los atacameños', *Allpanchis* 28 (año XVIII): 147–84.

Bell, C. 1992. *Ritual Theory, Ritual Practice*. New York: Oxford University Press.

———. 1997. *Ritual: Perspectives and Dimensions*. New York: Oxford University Press.

Bolin, I. 1998. *Rituals of Respect: The Secret of Survival in the High Peruvian Andes*. Austin: University of Texas Press.

Bourdieu, P. 1977. Sur le pouvoir symbolique, *Annales ESC* 32(3): 405–11.

———. 1991. *Language and Symbolic Power*. Cambridge, MA: Harvard University Press.

Bugallo, L., and M. Vilca. 2011. 'Cuidando el ánimu: salud y enfermedad en el mundo andino (puna y quebrada de Jujuy, Argentina)', *Nuevo Mundo Mundos Nuevos*. Retrieved 12 June 2018 from http://nuevomundo. revues.org/61781.

Cáceres Chalco, E. 2014. '*Uwya siñalakuy*: un rito para la reproducción de animals en el sur andino del Perú (Puno)', in J.J. Rivera Andía (ed.),

Comprender los rituales ganaderos en los Andes y más allá: etnografías de lidias, herranzas y arrierías. Bonn: Bonner Amerikanistische Studien BAS 51, pp. 123–44.

Caziani, S.M., O. Rocha Olivio, E. Rodríguez Ramírez, M. Romano, E.J. Derlindati, A. Tálamo, D. Ricalde, C. Quiroga, J.P. Contreras, M. Valqui, and H. y Sosa. 2007. 'Seasonal Distribution, Abundance, and Nesting of Puna, Andean, and Chilean Flamingos', *The Condor* 109(2): 276–87.

Cereceda, V. 1987. 'Aproximaciones a una estética andina: de la belleza al *tinku*', in Javier Medina (ed.), *Tres reflexiones sobre el pensamiento andino*. La Paz: Hisbol, pp. 133–231.

Crain, M. 1998. 'Reimagining Identity, Cultural Production and Locality under Transnationalism: Performances of San Juan in the Ecuadorean Andes', in Hughes-Freeland and Crain (eds), in F. Hughes-Freeland and M.M. Crain (eds), *Recasting Ritual: Performance, Media, Identity*. London: Routledge, pp. 135–60.

Dean, C. 2010. 'The After-Life of Inka Rulers: Andean Death before and after Spanish Colonization', *Hispanic Issues On Line* 7: 27–54.

Dedenbach-Salazar Sáenz, S. 1990. *Inka pachaq llamanpa willaynin: Uso y crianza de los camélidos en la epoca incaica*. Bonn: Bonner Amerikanistische Studien BAS 16.

Dransart, P.Z. 1997. 'Cultural Transpositions: Writing about Rites in the Llama Corral', in R. Howard-Malverde (ed.), *Creating Context in Andean Cultures*. New York: Oxford University Press (Oxford Studies in Anthropological Linguistics), pp. 85–98.

———. 2002a. *Earth, Water, Fleece and Fabric: An Ethnography and Archaeology of Andean Camelid Herding*. London: Routledge.

———. 2002b. 'Concepts of Spiritual Nourishment in the Andes and Europe: A Study of Rosaries in Cross-cultural Contexts', *Journal of the Royal Anthropological Institute* (NS) 8(1): 1–21.

———. 2010. 'Animals and their Possessions: Properties of Herd Animals in the Andes and Europe', in M. Bolton and C. Degnen (eds), *Animals and Science: Anthropological Approaches*. Newcastle: Cambridge Scholars Publishing, pp. 84–104.

———. 2013. 'Living Beings and Vital Powers: An Introduction', in P. Dransart (ed.), *Living Beings: Perspectives on Interspecies Engagements*. London: Bloomsbury, pp. 1–16.

———. 2016. 'The Sounds and Tastes of Colours: Hue and Saturation in Isluga Textiles'. *Nuevo Mundo Mundos Nuevos*, Symposia, posted online 7 July 2016, http://nuevomundo.revues.org/ 69188.

Durkheim, É. [1915] 1965. *The Elementary Forms of the Religious Life*, translated by J.W. Swain. New York: Free Press.

Duviols, P. (ed.). 1986. *Cultura andina y repression: procesos y visitas de idolatrías y hechicerías: Cajatambo, siglo XVII*. Cusco: Centro de Estudios Rurales Andinos Bartolome de las Casas.

Endres, K.W. 2008. 'Engaging the Spirits of the Dead: Soul-Calling Rituals and the Performative Construction of Efficacy', *Journal of the Royal Anthropological Institute* (NS) 14(4): 755–73.

Gell, A. 1998. *Art and Agency: An Anthropological Theory*. Oxford: Clarendon Press.

Gose, P. 1994. *Deathly Waters and Hungry Mountains: Agrarian Ritual and Class Formation in an Andean Town*. Toronto: University of Toronto Press.

———. 2014. 'Prefacio', in J.J. Rivera Andía (ed.), *Comprender los rituales ganaderos en los Andes y más allá: etnografías de lidias, herranzas y arrierías*. Bonn: Bonner Amerikanistische Studien BAS 51, pp. 9–11.

Grebe Vicuña, M.E. 2004. 'Amerindian Music of Chile', in M. Kuss (ed.), *Music in Latin America and the Caribbean: An Encyclopedic History*. Austin: University of Texas Press, pp. 145–62.

Grebe Vicuña, M.E., and B. Hidalgo. 1988. 'Simbolismo atacameño: un aporte etnológico a la comprehensión de significados culturales', *Revista Chilena de Antropología* 7: 75–97.

Guzmán-Gallegos, M.A. n.d. 'Fertility, Beauty and Money in an Amazonian Kichwa Ritual in Ecuador'. Paper presented at 'Amerindian Rites and Non-human Entities in South America: Reassessments and Comparisons', European Association of Social Anthropologists and Netherlands Institute of Advanced Study in the Humanities and Social Science, Wassenaar, The Netherlands, 2–6 December 2013.

Hill, J.D. 1985. 'Myth, Spirit Naming, and the Art of Microtonal Rising: Childbirth Rituals of the Arawakan Wakuénai', *Latin American Music Review / Revista de Música Latinoamericana* 6(1): 1–30.

Hughes-Freeland, F., and M.M. Crain (eds). 1998. 'Introduction', in F. Hughes-Freeland and M.M. Crain (eds), *Recasting Ritual: Performance, Media, Identity*. London: Routledge, pp. 1–20.

Humphrey, C., and J. Laidlaw. 1994. *The Archetypal Actions of Ritual: A Theory of Ritual Illustrated by the Jain Rite of Worship*. Oxford: Clarendon Press.

Kessel, J. van. 1989. 'Los Aymaras contemporáneas', in J. Hidalgo Lehuedé (ed.), *Las culturas de Chile*, Vol. I. Santiago: Andrés Bello, pp. 47–68.

King, H. (ed.). 2012a. *Peruvian Featherworks: Art of the Precolumbian Era*. New York: Metropolitan Museum of Art.

———. 2012b. 'Feather Arts in Ancient Peru', in H. King (ed.), *Peruvian Featherworks: Art of the Precolumbian Era*. New York: Metropolitan Museum of Art, pp. 9–43.

Lévi-Strauss, C. [1964] 1970. *The Raw and the Cooked: Introduction to a Science of Mythology, I*, translated by John and Doreen Wightman. London: Jonathan Cape.

———. [1955] 1993. *Tristes tropiques*. Paris: Plon.

Lira, Jorge. 1953. 'Puhllay, fiesta india', *Perú Indígena* 4(9): 125–34.

MacCormack, S. 1991. *Religion in the Andes: Vision and Imagination in Early Colonial Peru*. Princeton, NJ: Princeton University Press.

Mamani Mamani, M. 2002. *Diccionario práctico bilingüe Aymara-Castellano. Zona Norte de Chile. Suman chuymamp parlt'asiñi.* Antofagasta: EMELNOR NORprint.

Martínez Soto-Aguilar, G. 1976. 'El sistema de los uywiris en Isluga', *Anales de la Universidad del Norte (Homenaje al Dr Gustavo Le Paige S.J.)* 10: 255–327.

———. 2009. 'Humor y sacralidad en el mundo autóctono andino', *Chungara* 41(2): 275–86.

Mayorga, S., F. Palacios and R. Samaniego. 1976. 'El rito Aymara del "despacho"', *Allpanchis* 9: 225–41.

Mills, K. 1997. *Idolatry and Its Enemies: Colonial Andean Religion and Extirpation, 1640–1750.* Princeton, NJ: Princeton University Press.

Moyano, R. 2011. 'Sub-tropical Astronomy in the Southern Andes: The Ceque System in Socaire, Atacama, Northern Chile', *Proceedings of the International Astronomical Union* 7: 93–105.

Murra, J.V. [1958] 1975. 'La función del tejido en varios contextos sociales y políticos', in J.V. Murra, *Formaciones económicas y políticas del mundo andino.* Lima: Institute de Estudios Peruanos, pp. 145–70.

Ortega Perrier, M. 1998. '"By Reason or by Force": Islugueño Identity and Chilean Nationalism'. PhD thesis. University of Cambridge.

Quack, J. 2010. 'Bell, Bourdieu, and Wittgenstein on Ritual Sense', in W.S. Sax, J. Quack and J. Weinhold (eds), *The Problem of Ritual Efficacy.* Oxford: Oxford University Press, pp. 169–88.

Quack, J., and P. Töbelmann. 2010. 'Questioning "Ritual Efficacy"', *Journal of Ritual Studies* 24(1): 13–28.

Reina, R.E., and J.F. Pressman. 1991. 'Harvesting Feathers', in R.E. Reina and K.M. Kensinger (eds), *The Gift of Birds: Featherwork of Native South American Peoples.* University Museum Monograph, 75. Philadelphia: University of Pennsylvania, pp. 110–15.

Rivera Andía, J.J. 2003. *La fiesta del ganado en el valle de Chancay, 1962–2002: ritual, religón y ganadería en los Andes: etnografía, documentos inéditos e interpretación.* Lima: Pontificia Universidad del Perú Fondo Editorial.

———. 2012. 'A partir de los movimientos de un pájaro … La "danza de la perdiz" en los rituales ganaderos de los Andes peruanos', *Revista Española de Antropología Americana* 42(1): 169–85.

Rösing, I. 1995. 'Paraman Purina – Going for Rain. "Mute Anthropology" versus "Speaking Anthropology": Lessons from an Andean Collective Scarcity Ritual in the Quechua-speaking Kallyawaya and Aymara-speaking Altiplano Region (Andes, Bolivia)', *Anthropos* 90: 69–88.

Rowe, A.P. 1984. *Costumes and Featherwork of the Lords of Chimor: Textiles from Peru's North Coast.* Washington, DC: The Textile Museum.

———. 2012. 'Early Featherwork from Ocucaje', in H. King (ed.), *Peruvian Featherworks: Art of the Precolumbian Era.* New York: Metropolitan Museum of Art, pp. 45–54.

Sax, W.S. 2010. 'Ritual and the Problem of Efficacy', in W. Sax, J. Quack and J. Weinhold (eds), *The Problem of Ritual Efficacy*. Oxford: Oxford University Press, pp. 3–16.

Stobart, H. 2006. *Music and the Poetics of Production in the Bolivian Andes*. Aldershot, Hants: Ashgate, SOAS Musicology Series.

Stone-Miller, R. 1992. 'Camelids and Chaos in Huari and Tiwanaku Textiles', in R.F. Townsend (ed.), *The Ancient Americas: Art from Sacred Landscapes*. Chicago, IL and Munich: Art Institute of Chicago and Prestel Verlag, pp. 335–45.

Strang, V. 1999. 'Familiar Forms: Homologues, Culture and Gender in Northern Australia', *Journal of the Royal Anthropological Institute* (NS) 5(1): 75–95.

Tambiah, S.J. 1981. 'A Performative Approach to Ritual: Radcliffe-Brown Lecture, 1979', *Proceedings of the British Academy* LXV: 113–69.

Viveiros de Castro, E. 1992. *From the Enemy's Point of View: Humanity and Divinity in an Amazonian Society*, translated by C.V. Howard. Chicago, IL and London: The University of Chicago Press.

2

Southern Sacrifice and Northern Sorcery

Mountain Spirits and *Encantos* in the Peruvian Andes

Marieka Sax

The Andean landscape is animated by place-based spirits. Ethnographers in the highlands of Peru, Bolivia and Ecuador have documented local practices through which Quechua and Aymara-speaking peoples articulate a range of understandings of their lived worlds, in which powerful supernatural entities embodied in mountains and other prominent landforms have the potential to both help and harm people. In the southern Andes, people expect mountain spirits to provide agricultural fertility and prosperity. Andean peoples further understand these 'earth-beings'[1] to demand sacrificial offerings in return. In the northern Peruvian Andes, lay people do not have individual relationships with place-based spirits. Instead, people communicate with these entities through the mediation of a ritual specialist. Such specialists can perform ceremonies to increase an individual's productive capacities, but clients most commonly consult them to be healed of illnesses attributed to place-based spirits.

For my present purposes, I define the southern Andes as the highland region south of the Jequetepeque River valley, near the city of Cajamarca. I use this as a conceptual boundary because different ritual substances characterise the areas on each side of this valley: the cactus 'San Pedro' to the north, and coca leaves to the south (Juan Javier Rivera Andía, personal communication, January 2014).

While southern Peru and Bolivia are more commonly identified as the Central Andes, this word choice is intended to succinctly juxtapose the northern and southern Peruvian highlands. Commentators often think of the southern region of Cuzco as the classic Andean cultural area, but Quechua-speaking people in northern Peru also act according to a distinctly Andean understanding of the world. This includes a personified landscape, social emphasis on generalised reciprocity, and the common legacy of the Incan empire and Spanish colonialism.

In this chapter, I outline the 'mountain spirit complex' of the Andean cultural area. Throughout the Andes, mountains spirits bring life and death, health and illness, luck and misfortune. While place-based spirits in the southern and northern Peruvian highlands have similar capacities, people interact with these entities in distinct ways. In the south, illness attributed to mountain spirits is an outcome of a person's incorrect action or failure to fulfil obligations. People say the mountain spirit is either 'punishing' the victim or attempting to deepen a ritual relationship. In the north, similar classes of illness are a consequence of neither the person's inaction nor the spirit's intention. Instead, people say that a fellow community member envies the victim, and has contracted a ritual specialist to do witchcraft against this individual. While Andean peoples in southern and northern Peru attribute mountain spirits with individual identities, self-consciousness and the ability to act, the ways in which people assign responsibility for the outcomes of a spirit's action are significantly different.

Southern Mountain Spirits

'I didn't always live here', Rosa says. It is 2007, near the town of Paucará, in the region of Huancavelica.

> I lived in Lima for several years with my husband, Manuel. I had three children then. I had another little baby who died when she was three months old. She died from *chocando* when I brought her to visit [this is a condition explained as both a crash with a mountain spirit, and shock from the high-altitude climate] … We were doing well enough in the city, but Manuel got sick. We took him to the hospital and the doctors said he was malnourished. They gave him lots of injections and pills – I worked hard to buy all the medicines, selling food on the street with a baby at each breast – but still Manuel was sick. He had no strength; he couldn't even get out of bed. I thought he would die, so we returned here. We went to a *curandero* [a ritual healer] and he said that it was the *diablo chacho* making him sick. You see, when Manuel was younger, he had a bad father, a drunk, and he had spent many nights sleeping on the hillsides with his mother. Who knows how many years he had that devil inside him. We fed the devil and Manuel got better. Now you can see him, he's fine …

I believe in the *curanderos*. Doctors don't believe in them, so they can't know. That's why we couldn't cure him in the city. (Sax 2011: 122)

When Manuel became severely ill with a condition unresponsive to biomedicine, he visited a ritual healer from his natal community. After this consultation, Rosa came to understand that Manuel had become ill as a result of an encounter with a malicious spirit residing in hillsides her husband had slept on as a child. The 'devil' was hungry and was feeding on an immaterial part of Manuel's person, making him sicker as time passed. Rosa did not tell me what they had fed the spirit, but based on what other people in Huancavelica told me, it was likely to have been a ritual 'plate' of corn kernels, coca leaves and other consumables that had been burned close to the place where the spirit resided.

Rosa did not identify this particular devil as a mountain spirit. Outside the context of mining (e.g. Nash 1979; Platt 1983; Salazar-Soler 2006), Andean peoples never describe mountain spirits as 'devils'. In this cultural area, devils are spirits who reside in hillsides, gullies and pools of water. Unlike mountain spirits, these lesser devils only harm, 'frightening' and 'grabbing' the souls of vulnerable people such as children, which results in illness. Nevertheless, Rosa's story illustrates the basic logic regulating interactions between place-based spirits and people in the southern Andes. In this region, human and supernatural relations are mediated by the idioms of sacrifice, payment, hunger and feeding (Fernández Juárez 2004: 135; see also Crandon Malamud 1991: 124; Gose 1994: 223–24; Allen 2002: 127–35; Sax 2011: 83–84, 89–92).

In the highlands of southern Peru and Bolivia, householders make ritual offerings, payments and libations to tutelary divinities. These are the mountain spirits and 'earth mother' (*pachamama*), who ensure the productivity of crops and animals. People in Paucará referred to these entities with the Spanish term for 'mountain' (*cerro*). Ethnographers in other Andean communities note that people also call them by deferential Quechua terms such as 'lord' (*apu*), 'condor' (*mallku*), 'hawk' (*wamani*) and 'mummy' (*auquillo*) (Bastien 1978: 63; Isbell 1978: 59; Allen 2002: 26; Rivera Andía 2003: 457–70). Community members attribute local mountain spirits with individualised names and characteristics. For example, the most important mountain spirit in Paucará is Qapaq Santiago (also called Señor Wamani), who watches over the sheep and other herd animals who pasture on 'his' mountain, Cerro Calvario (Sax 2011: 41). People make offerings to this spirit on the Feast of Santiago, on 25

July – a time of animal fertility rites (Sax 2011: 39–52). Another local mountain spirit, Cerro Huallanca, is the 'god' of the Scissor Dancers, famous in Huancavelica for their acrobatic moves tapped out to a rhythm of shear-like scissors (Arce Sotelo 2006; Sax 2011: 53–56).

Anthropologist Catherine Allen argues that mountain spirits are repositories for a life-giving energy (*sami*) that fertilises and animates living things (Allen 2002: 33ff.; see also Gose 1994: 126–35, 203). Through water, mountain spirits direct this vital energy to the crops, animals and people under their care (Gose 1994: 126–35, 217; 2008: 314–19). Through ritual offerings such as coca leaves and corn beer, householders direct this energy back to the mountain spirits, maintaining the 'pump' of reciprocity that makes life in the highlands possible (Gose 1994: 194–254; Allen 2002: 73, 107–10).

Mountain spirits are also 'hungry', and householders are obligated to 'feed' and 'pay' them with ritual offerings (Allen 2002: 127–35; Bastien 1978: 65–67, 75–76, 136, 147; Crandon-Malamud 1991: 124; de la Cadena 2015: 94–95; Gose 1994: 222–24; Fernández Juárez 2004: 134–35). People make offerings to mountain spirits on ritual 'tables' (*mesas*),[2] which are then burned or buried (for a detailed description, see Gose 1994: 194–224). In the terms of anthropologist Gerardo Fernández Juárez, people make ritual offerings on a 'ceremonial banquet table', with each plate carefully constructed according to the preferences of particular spirits and desired goals of householders (Fernández Juárez 1997: 222; cf. Gose 1994: 215). Besides coca leaves, offerings include llama chest fat; metal figurines of humans, animals, farm tools, stars, the sun and the moon; hard sweets and sweet biscuits; coloured wool threads; small squares of shiny gold or silver paper; incense and aromatic resins; and sugar cane alcohol, wine and beer (Fernández Juárez 2004: 123–33). A particularly powerful offering is the dried foetus of a llama, alpaca or other animal (Gose 1994: 215; Fernández Juárez 2004: 126, 130). Once the practitioner has carefully assembled a selection of ceremonial ingredients, he wraps them in paper and burns it so that the plate can be 'tasted' by the mountain spirit (Fernández Juárez 2004: 134).

Andean peoples make consumable offerings at key moments in the agricultural year, including field preparation, sowing, harvest, and just after the harvest when animal fertility rites take place (Bastien 1978: 51–53, 61; Isbell 1978: 59, 151–55; Gose 1994: 110–14, 151–52, 156–57, 165–67, 174, 194–95; Allen 2002: 129–43; Fernández Juárez 2004: 134; Sax 2011: 39–49). People also make ritual offerings to place-based spirits during community-wide rituals, such as canal cleaning, the feast of the community's patron saint, Carnival, All

Illustration 2.1 Ritual table for an animal fertility rite (Paucará). 2009. Photograph: M. Sax.

Soul's Day, and other festivals that correspond to the Catholic calendar (Isbell 1978: 138–51; Gose 1994: 101, 141–43; Gelles 2000: 75–82; Allen 2002: 139–40, 150–71). Householders who neglect to make offerings can experience crop failure, animal loss, and the illness or death of family members because of the retribution of an angry mountain spirit (Crandon-Malamud 1991: 4–5; Gose 1994: 220, 222).

In the southern Andes, lay people communicate with mountain spirits through these ritual offerings. In addition, ritual specialists prepare more elaborate offerings during times of illness and exceptional need (Bastien 1978: 135ff.; Gelles 2000: 81–82; Allen 2002: 135–37). Such specialists include ritual healers called *curanderos*, *paqos* and *yatiris* (Crandon-Malamud 1991: 128–29; Gelles 2000: 82; Allen 2002: 23, 111–12; Fernández Juárez 2004: 19–20, 28; de la Cadena 2015: 164, 196). Ritual healers treat illnesses that biomedical doctors cannot – those conditions that affect the client's soul and social well-being – by making offerings to the spirit that has caused the illness (Fernández Juárez 2004: 112 n.105, 113 n.107, 134). Other, nefarious, specialists called sorcerers or *layqas* make ritual tables to cause illness and misfortune through witchcraft, although this is less commonly represented in the ethnographic literature than offerings for fertility and healing (Gose 1994: 186; Gelles 2000: 82; Allen 2002: 23; Fernández Juárez 2004: 40, 50 n.38).

Mountain spirits are tutelary divinities that look after the people under their care. As divine guardians, these entities are generally benevolent. The supernatural power of the mountain spirits gives life and vitality to plants and animals (Gose 1994: 126–35; Allen 2002: 33–37). But these place-based spirits are also occasionally capricious and retributive (Isbell 1978: 153–55). For example, a mountain spirit can punish householders, travellers and miners who have failed to approach the spirit with adequate deference and respect (Isbell 1978: 153–54; Crandon-Malamud 1991: 3–5; Salazar-Soler 2006: 163–69).

The generative and destructive modes of mountain spirits are clearly illustrated in relation to mining. Throughout the Andes, people call powerful spirits of mines 'uncles' (*tíos*), thereby evoking the assistance and patronage of a rich business associate, and 'devils' (Sp. *diablos*; Qu. *supay*), which, rather than indicating an opposition to all that is good, refers to the spirit's potential danger (Salazar-Soler 2006). Miners must regularly provide the uncle or devil of the mine with offerings such as coca leaves and cigarettes, for he is hungry, and if he is not fed, he will take a human life instead (Nash 1979: Chapters 5–6; Platt 1983; Salazar-Soler 2006: 137–42ff.).

Mountain spirits have the dual capacity to bring life and fertility, loss and death. A person who suffers serious misfortune or illness attributed to a mountain spirit has either offended the entity or is being drawn into a more intense ritual relationship. For example, anthropologist Peter Gose relates the story of an Andean farmer whose calf was killed by a bolt of lightning (Gose 1994: 220). When the man consulted an oracular medium, he was told that a mountain spirit named Phukawasi 'had "sold" the animal because the offerings he was receiving were inadequate' (ibid.). Phukawasi demanded more elaborate ritual payments, and the man complied, which eventually resulted in an increase in the farmer's animals.

The ritual offerings that indigenous peasants provide are both gifts to encourage the spirit's care, and compensation for using the spirit's resources. Throughout the Andes, people say mountain spirits are the 'owners' of the livestock and crops on 'their' lands. These same mountains house powerful owners or bosses (*dueños*), which are the spirits in human form. Inside the mountain there is a world that mirrors the external world, just richer. The inner world has prosperous fields and herds, hoards of gold and silver, and secret gardens with medicinal plants. People say the rich owner exits the mountain at night, riding a horse, wearing boots and a wide-brimmed hat, with a pale complexion and bearded face (Gose 2008: 297–98). In other words, he looks distinctly white or *mestizo* (of mixed descent), not like an indigenous peasant. The owner of the mountain is not a local, but a member of the ruling classes who long kept highland peoples in a subordinate position of indebted servitude.

This points to an additional attribute of mountain spirits in the southern Andes: their dual identity as both guardians that belong to Andean communities, and as hierarchically superior foreigners and racial others. Mountain spirits are autochthonous to Andean communities because only community members recognise and interact with them.[3] Mountain spirits do not 'belong' to other people in Peru, and non-Andean peoples do not usually find themselves interpolated by these place-based spirits. As divine sources of life and fertility, mountain spirits provide for the people under their care. People acknowledge their reciprocal obligations to mountain spirits who are the ultimate owners and providers of subsistence, and 'feed' the spirits in turn through ritual offerings and payments.

Yet even as mountain spirits are community insiders, in their human form they resemble quintessential outsiders. The human incarnation of a mountain spirit may be male or female, but it is always racially 'white', at least in all the stories I have heard. The mountain spirit looks and acts as if he were a large-scale foreign landowner (*hacendado*), the kind of person whom many Andean peasants were obligated to work for under highly exploitative conditions well into the twentieth century. Similarly, the spirit and 'owner' of the mountain is incredibly rich, with prosperous fields and precious metals housed within the inner, hidden world of their domain.

The Historical Roots of Mountain Spirits

Why are mountain spirits described by Andean peoples as at once tutelary divinities and powerful outsiders? This is not as straightforward as critically reading race and class into the historical experience of Spanish colonialism and Christian evangelisation would seem. Nor are mountain spirits simply a matter of cultural continuity with a primordial Andean past. An answer lies in the historical roots of mountain spirits, and the changes of their pre-Columbian and pre-Christian antecedents over time.

Peter Gose has done just this in his book, *Invaders as Ancestors: On the Intercultural Making and Unmaking of Spanish Colonialism in the Andes* (2008).[4] I follow Gose in arguing that contemporary mountain spirits are a product of pre-Columbian forms of social, political and spiritual orders on one hand, and the transformation of the lived Andean world through Spanish colonisation and Catholicization on the other. Prior to the arrival of the Spanish in the sixteenth century, Andean peoples venerated deified ancestors associated with particular places. In pre-Columbian myths recorded by Spanish chroniclers (e.g. Betanzos, Cieza de León, Molina, Sarmiento de Gamboa) and the first descendants of the Incan nobility and Spanish elite (e.g. Pachacuti Yampqui, Guaman Poma), communities were founded by ancestral beings who either rose up from deep within the earth or came down through lightening (Gose 2008: 18). The founding ancestors modified the landscape, domesticated uninhabited space, and expanded their territory by conquering other groups. After establishing the descent-based community or 'ancestor-worshipping polity' of the *ayllu*, the ancestor turned to stone, and thereafter remained in the place where they had emerged or touched down (ibid.). Andean communities venerated the stones of their founding ancestors, which they housed in shrines (*huacas*) at these 'dawning points' (*pacarinas*), located in a mountain or cave, or by a tree, spring or lake (Gose 1993: 489ff.; 2008: 18, 243).

The community's local leader was represented as a direct descendant of the founding ancestor, and when he died he was mummified and stored in the same shrine at the sacred place (Gose 2008: 16). The stones and mummies of the ancestors continued to be active participants in the well-being of their community by ensuring the agricultural fertility and prosperity of their people (ibid.: 14–18). People regularly provided their founding ancestors with sacrifices and libations of corn beer (Gose 1993: 486–87). As Gose contends, pre-Columbian Andean peoples venerated the ancestors housed in sacred places, not the places themselves (Gose 2008: 165–66, 239–44).

The Spanish were deeply disturbed by this ancestor worship, which so closely resembled their own adoration of Catholic saints as semi-divine intermediaries between people and God (Gose 2008: 21). The newcomers established an office of the Catholic Church to root out and destroy this indigenous practice. Under the Extirpation of Idolatries, the Spanish destroyed sacred stones and shrines, burned mummies, and erected crosses in their place (ibid.: 156–60, 274). Meanwhile, local elites and commoners each forwarded their own interests in the changed politico-economic context; some converted to Christianity and married Spaniards, some became colonial administrators, and others abandoned their natal communities to avoid burdensome labour tribute (ibid.: 136–37). By the end of the eighteenth century, a new ritual order had emerged in the Andes. Instead of the ancestors animating the land, now the landscape itself was personified (ibid.: 241). Andean peoples came to see particular mountains as tutelary divinities who mediated relations between the community and the state (ibid.: 11–12, 296–97).

Yet there is a further twist to this story. People in the Andes today do not simply consider mountain spirits to animate the land. They also say that the human incarnation of the spirit looks like a white foreigner or powerful overseer. Gose's ethnohistorical work is again enlightening. He argues that the idea of local divinities as rulers who originated elsewhere made sense in the pre-Columbian Andes. Empire and colonisation were 'fully developed' before the Spanish arrived, and the region had already undergone several waves of political 'expansion, contraction and subsumption' (Gose 2008: 17, 20). The Incan empire was only the most recent iteration of this indigenous form of intrusive conquest and foreign rule. The foreignness of local, divine rulers is also marked in Incan myths, in which founding ancestors 'conquered and partially displaced previous groups and their ancestors' (ibid.: 18). Newly conquered peoples were not exterminated or dispossessed, but instead obligated to share their 'agricultural resources and women with the conquerors' (ibid.: 19). Subjugated peoples had to provide tribute in the form of material and social resources that made the administration of the Incan empire possible (see Gose 2000).

The 'political script' following Andean conquest was for the two groups to coexist peacefully, with 'significant intergroup reciprocity and symmetry' (Gose 2008: 19, 20). For example, ruling and subjugated groups recognised they shared a common ancestor, or worshipped each other's ancestors (ibid.: 17). In each successive wave of conquest, the founding ancestors of the vanquished group continued to exist, only now in a relation of shared kinship to those of the hierarchically superior group. This mutual recognition of ancestral relation ritually legitimated the alliance and the peaceful coexistence between the usurpers and the subjugated. Conquered peoples retained a degree of local sovereignty, including the right to venerate the ancestor who had founded their local polity, who was represented by their local lord (*curaca*) (ibid.: 15–17). Gose argues that the pre-existing Andean order conventionalised the idea of intrusive conquest, and presumed that the ancestors had distant origins, distinct from the communities they founded (Gose 1993: 489ff.; Gose 2008: 20, 299).[5]

These pre-understandings played a critical role in how Andean peoples received the Spanish, first as potential allies against the Incan elites, and then as colonial rulers. Colonisers were people with whom subjugated groups expected to share common ancestors, and therefore common interests and reciprocal obligations (Gose 2008: 14–21, 64–66). For the first century, local lords played an important role in the 'indirect rule' of the Spanish colony of Peru (ibid.: 43–47, 81, 128–36). Archival documents indicate that throughout the sixteenth and seventeenth centuries, both local elites and Andean commoners continued to acknowledge their founding ancestors and ancestral mummies, albeit in constant negotiation with Spanish colonial administrators and representatives of the Catholic Church (ibid.: 155–60). By the late eighteenth century, however, the Spanish had stripped the lords of their privileges, and many of these local representatives had abandoned their offices (ibid.: 237–39, 277–79). At the same time, Andean commoners came to reject their hereditary leaders and ancestral rulers, whom they no longer considered to be their political representatives and sacred sources of fertility (ibid.). People came to regard the sacred stones and mummies as the remains of threatening pre-Christians and pagans, unrelated to them (ibid.: 283–94). Today, many Andean peoples consider pre-Columbian burial sites and artefacts to be the remains of these malicious 'non-Christian' spirits (*gentiles*).[6]

Yet ancestor worship persisted in another form. According to Gose, after the collapse of the indirect rule of local lords, 'localized divine kingship' became 'progressively more subaltern', defined by indigenous commoners who made the mountain spirits into their new tutelary divinities (Gose 2008: 322–24). Mountain spirits took on the roles of provision and mediation with higher levels of political administration, which the local lords and founding ancestors had fulfilled in pre-Columbian times. For example, lords gathered tribute on behalf of the Inca, and redistributed products and resources to commoners (Rostworowski 1999: Chapter 6; Gose 2000; Murra 2002: 47ff.). This continued through the indirect rule of local lords in the Spanish colony up to the eighteenth century (Gose 2008: 130–34). But as local lords 'systematically broke' the implicit Andean social duty for elites to protect the community and ensure prosperity, 'commoners stopped sacralizing them through ancestor worship and transferred their authority to mountain spirits, who personified the new community-based republicanism' (ibid.: 279). Instead of the founding ancestors, Incas, or local lords, Andean peoples now owed mountain spirits 'their fundamental social allegiance', organised through 'residence and affinity' rather than descent-based *ayllu* groups (ibid.: 241). Commoners came to demand 'protection and prosperity from such spirits and the republican states they came to represent' (ibid.: 280).

Gose suggests the emergence of place-based spirits was partly out of a culturally grounded habitus, namely the long-standing Andean practice of making sacrificial offerings in sacred places to 'ancestor-rulers' who animated the local landscape (Gose 2008: 322). More significantly, however, Andean commoners also took up an innovative 'egalitarian levelling' of the 'previous ancestral regime', in which local mountain spirits took on the '[p]olitico-ritual mediation' previously carried out by local lords and ancestral deities (ibid.: 322, 323). Gose argues that this 'conscious reform and reconstruction' of 'the ancestral past' was deployed by Andean commoners partly as a strategy to demand that colonial (and postcolonial) administrators continue to provide them with the means to support themselves (ibid.: 324ff.).

Following Gose, the whiteness and foreignness of mountain spirits is – or arguably was, at least until the rise of identity politics in the late twentieth century – about Andean commoners holding the state accountable, rather than symbolically appropriating the hierarchically superior racial, ethnic and class positions of the colonizers:

> Andean people repeatedly extended their ancestral relation with mountain spirits into political struggles over the land, using them to articulate successful alliances with the state and regain land lost to *hacendados* ... In these and more routine agrarian contexts, Andean people clearly relate to mountain spirits as ancestral advocates, and do not worship white domination through them. (Gose 2008: 298)

Through the mountain spirits, Andean peoples came to assert a shared genealogy with ruling groups, a long-standing cultural notion that draws elites and commoners into a relationship of reciprocal obligations. From this perspective, the state is morally obligated to provide indigenous peasants with the means to support themselves and achieve their own goals, such as agricultural livelihoods and meaningful political participation.

Place-based spirits in the Andes thus developed out of two processes. The first is the pre-Columbian practice of ancestor worship and divine kingship, in which Incan and other Andean peoples interred the sacred stones and mummies of their ancestors in prominent landforms such as mountains. The second process is the constraints Andean peoples faced and the strategic responses they employed in the context of Spanish colonialism and Christian evangelisation. In the centuries following the arrival of the Spanish and the demise of the Incan empire, Andean peoples moved away from their customary leaders and forms of worship. Eventually people came to understand the mountains themselves as embodiments of supernatural entities, who are repositories for a vitalising energy that makes crops and animals fertile.

Contemporary mountain spirits are at once tutelary divinities and foreign to the localities and polities they represent. This was also the function of their pre-Columbian antecedents. Mountain spirits are white outsiders not because these powerful foreigners are inherently threatening, or because the ruling elites have long had a control over wealth. The mountain spirits have to be white, because this symbolically articulates a kinship relation between the community and their political superiors, who are now representatives of the republican state instead of an invasive conquering group. Contemporary Andean peoples want to be related to these outside rulers, not because they wish to share the same racial or ethnic identity, but because this makes the state morally obligated to recognise their legitimate participation in the nation as modern citizens, and on their own terms.

Synthesis

Throughout the Andean cultural area, mountain spirits are place-based beings embodied in particular, named mountains. Mountain spirits are repositories for a life-giving and vitalising energy, and Andean peasants (particularly in the southern Andes) address these non-human entities to ensure the fertility of their crops and herds. The power of mountain spirits has the potential to bring life and prosperity, misfortune and death. In their benevolent form, mountain spirits are tutelary divinities who provide for the people under their care. But mountain spirits can also threaten by 'eating' a family's livelihood or 'grabbing' a person to demand more sacrificial payments.

The dualistic character of mountain spirits is further illustrated by the human form that Andean peoples say the spirits take, that of a rich white person, whose dress and comportment immediately marks him or her as not native to the community. Yet Andean peoples suggest they belong to the mountain spirits, and the spirits belong to them. Mountain spirits are sacred sources of fertility and prosperity, and their people should address them with deference and respect. These ultimate owners animate the local landscape and appear as powerful foreigners, because these were also key characteristics of localised divine rulers in the pre-Columbian Andes.[7]

In the southern Andes, ritual offerings mediate the undomesticated power of the mountain spirits, and direct this life-giving energy towards Andean peoples' desired goals. In the northern Andes, place-based spirits embodied in mountains, waterfalls and high-altitude lakes are also repositories for an invisible force that can both help and harm people. However, most people cannot communicate with these place-based spirits directly. Lay people do not have individualised relationships of obligation and reciprocity with these non-human entities, called 'enchantments' (*encantos*). Instead, householders and peasant farmers need the mediation of a ritual specialist in order to direct the power of the *encantos* to a desired goal. While ritual practices in the south indicate that mountain spirits have an essential role to play in agricultural production, powerful place-based spirits in the north are at the centre of a genre of ritual healing and malicious witchcraft for which northern Peru is famous: sorcery (*brujería*).

Northern *Encantos*

'There once were two brothers who were sorcerers', says Andrés. It is now 2011, in the town of Kañaris, in the northern Peruvian highlands of Lambayeque.[8]

> Their names were San Juan and San Cipriano. They fell in love with the same girl. Eventually their rivalry came to a battle of sorcery. San Juan, the elder and more experienced brother, sat in the west. San Cipriano chose to sit in the east, where he knew he would have the power of the rising sun behind him. San Cipriano had vision and knew how to take San Pedro [a plant]. With San Pedro, he saw all the moves of his opponent, who launched his attack from a great distance away. San Juan threw a dart at San Cipriano, but the younger one saw it coming and moved so that it crashed onto the wall behind him. Then San Cipriano threw a dart at San Juan and killed him.

Andrés heard this story from his father, who had heard it from a very old sorcerer. San Cipriano is closely associated with sorcery in northern Peru. Anthropologist Mario Polia describes him as the 'patron saint' of the ritual specialists interchangeably called 'masters' (*maestros*), 'healers' (*curanderos*) and 'sorcerers' (*brujos*) (Polia 1996: 202–3). The figure is based on Saint Cyprian of Antioch, a 'black magician' who converted to Christianity and was martyred in the fourth century (ibid.: 202; Sharon 1978: 63, 165). San Cipriano is compelling to practitioners because he can be called upon to do both curing and witchcraft. He is at once a pagan magician and a Christianised saint. As Polia argues, San Cipriano mediates the Catholic and indigenous evaluations of sorcery that coexist in the northern highlands (Polia 1996: 200–4).

Sorcery (*brujería, curanderismo*) is a genre of both ritual healing and malicious witchcraft practised throughout a large area of northern Peru. This includes the coastal cities of Trujillo, Chiclayo and Piura; Loja in southern Ecuador; Jaén and Chachapoyas on the eastern slopes of the Andes; and Cajamarca to the south (Camino 1992: 44, 54–55; Joralemon and Sharon 1993: 2–4; Glass-Coffin 1998; Bussmann and Sharon 2006). A key characteristic of this practice is that sorcerers call upon the power of spirits embodied in mountains and high-altitude lakes to cause and cure illness. Practitioners sometimes call these spirits 'mountains' (*cerros*), and other times 'enchantments' (*encantos*).

For the sake of clarity, I differentiate mountain spirits from *encantos* in Kañaris. In practice, however, the important distinction is what functions the place-based spirit is fulfilling in relation to people in a specific situation. In their occasional roles as tutelary divinities, northern *cerros* resemble the mountain spirits of the southern Andes. But when invoked by a sorcerer, these place-based spirits are *encantos*, and specific to the two-sided practice of ritual healing and witchcraft (*brujería*). Sorcerers in Kañaris call upon the *encantos* by their mountain names, such as Cerro Kutilla, Cerro Capitán, Cerro Zanawaka, Cerro Yanaqaqa, Cerro Campana and Cerro Ankash. *Encantos* are also embodied in prominent bodies of water, such as Lake Tembladera, Lake Shin Shin and the waterfall El Chorro. All of these spiritual entities and sacred places are repositories for the supernatural power the sorcerer directs to cure or cause illness, increase good luck, and cleanse bad luck.

Although people also practise ritual healing and witchcraft in the southern Andes, and to the east of the mountains in the 'eyebrow of the jungle', practitioners in those areas do not address *encantos* or use the psychotropic cactus San Pedro (*Trichocerus pachanoi*). In the southern Andes, ritual healers feed hungry mountain spirits with offerings of coca leaves and corn beer, paradigmatically Andean ritual substances absent in northern communities such as Kañaris. In western Amazonia, shamans call upon forest and river spirits to help to extract illness from the client's body with ayahuasca (*Banisteriopsis caapi* mixed with other psychotropic plants).

The differences and similarities in ritual performance and praxis are notable. In the jungle, shamans primarily treat illnesses attributed to witchcraft (i.e. ritual action intended to harm a specific individual). Anthropologist Peter Gow emphasises that people in the region do not seek the help of 'mother' or 'forest spirits' to increase production, money or luck (Gow 1994: 102). According to Gow, production in western Amazonia requires neither sacrifice, as in the southern Andes, nor hunting magic, as with Amazonian peoples in other areas (see Århem 1996; Viveiros de Castro 1998; but compare Brown 1986: 70–96). Ayahuasca shamans only cause or cure illness attributed to witchcraft. Moreover, shamans perpetrate witchcraft themselves by 'throwing' unseen sorcery objects such as darts, thorns and animal teeth into the victim's body (Harner 1972: 119, 157).

Sorcerers on the northern Peruvian coast also treat illnesses attributed to witchcraft. Although sorcerers call upon the supernatural power of place-based spirits to cure clients, God ultimately supersedes the *encantos*. As anthropologist Douglas Sharon notes, sorcery becomes more Catholicised as one moves from the highlands to the coast (Sharon 1978: 35). On the coast, *encantos* function like 'free-flowing forces of nature' (Joralemon and Sharon 1993: 150). The sorcerer directs the spirit's latent supernatural power to heal with the 'grace of God' (Glass-Coffin 1998: 54, 70, 77, 79). In this light, it makes sense for coastal practitioners to frame the healing ritual as a battle to balance the forces of good and evil (Sharon 1978).

In Andean communities such as Kañaris, however, God has a marginal role in sorcery, and the *encantos* are at once bewitching not-quite-human entities and dualistic mountain spirits. The precedence northern people give to the *encantos* has also been documented in the highlands of Piura, close to the Ecuadorian border (Camino 1992; Polia 1996). This includes Huancabamba and a series of high-altitude lakes called Las Huaringas (Sharon 1978: 123–27; Giese 1991; Camino 1992: 113; Polia 1996: 99; Arroyo Aguilar 2004). Both highland and coastal sorcerers call upon the famous *encantos* of Las Huaringas during their ritual healing sessions.

On the surface of ritual performance, sorcery practised throughout the northern Peruvian coast and highlands appears to be the same. However, the local understandings of the sorcerer's efficacy and the motivations of the clients are significantly different. In Kañaris, the sorcerer directs the generative force of the *encantos*, rather than the Christianized God. The power of the *encantos* has the potential to produce both helpful and harmful effects in a person's body and total situation. In its helpful mode, the power of the *encantos* bestows people with 'good luck'. In its harmful mode, this same power is evil (*mal*), and curses an individual with 'bad luck'. A person can 'cleanse' and 'raise' their luck by visiting a sorcerer. The sorcerer will call on the *encantos* to increase the client's productive success and mitigate the individual's vulnerability to future suffering.

Like mountain spirits, *encantos* are embodied in particular, named mountains, high-altitude lakes, and waterfalls. These non-human entities are also repositories for a sacred power that has the potential to bring prosperity, health and well-being on one hand, and illness, loss and misfortune on the other. However, unlike mountain spirits, lay people cannot direct the flow of the spirit's power through ritual offerings. Instead, sorcerers are the only people qualified to direct the power of place-based spirits towards people. By virtue of his innate ability, learned technique and sacred relationships, the sorcerer calls upon 'his' *encantos* to cure or cause illness, and to increase good luck or contaminate with bad luck. He does this during an all-night ritual event called the *mesa*.[9]

In his morally upright and discursively foregrounded role as a ritual healer, the sorcerer draws upon an established repertoire of ritual acts to cure and cleanse his client through the extraction of the invisible substance that is the power of the *encantos*. He 'refreshes' the sacred power-objects on his ritual table by blowing floral waters in a fine spray through his pursed lips. He shakes a rattle and murmurs secret songs to 'wake up' the presence of the *encantos* latent in the rocks, swords and staffs that are his power-objects. He then 'rubs' one or more of these objects over the client's body to 'extract' the invisible illness-causing substance that is the power of a given *encanto*. Through this physical contact, the invisible substance transfers from the client's body to the power-object, and the ritual specialist can 'dispatch' the substance to the high-altitude place where it originated. The sorcerer also places his lips on the region of the client's body where the sickening power of the *encanto* has become lodged, to 'suck out' any remaining substance. He does this, for example, on the crown of the head, nape of the neck, upper chest, stomach, hands or feet. To strengthen his client during this process, the sorcerer 'raises' tobacco, nasally ingesting a mixture of sugar cane alcohol and tobacco leaves.

Throughout the night, the sorcerer continues to sing to specific *encantos* and 'refresh' each spirit's power-object by blowing sugar cane alcohol over the ritual table. If the ritual specialist neglects to provide these offerings for the *encanto*, the spiritual entity will harm instead of help, by causing the sorcerer himself to become ill (Polia 1996: 98–99). Nonetheless, the sorcerer does not simply use the power of the *encantos* as one would use a tool. He is only able to direct the power of specific *encantos* who grant him permission to do so. The sorcerer communicates with 'his' *encantos* after drinking a cooked mixture of the mescaline-rich cactus San Pedro to detach his shadow-soul (*sombra*) from his body and enter the invisible, parallel spirit world.[10] By 'visioning' in this way, the sorcerer learns what caused his client's condition and what he must do to cure it.

The sorcerer also directs his client to 'raise' tobacco, drink San Pedro, and 'refresh' the ritual table throughout the night. At the end of the ritual session, the sorcerer and his client undertake a final blessing called the 'flowering', nasally ingesting sweet floral waters, and orally blowing more over the ritual table.

People in northern Peru consistently told me that witchcraft is perpetrated by one community member who envies another. One person desires the good fields, prosperous business or happy household of a neighbour, work partner or extended family member. The perpetrator pays an 'evil sorcerer' (*brujo*) to purposefully harm their rival by directing the power of his *encantos* towards the envied individual. The victim will have to visit another sorcerer who can call on the same *encantos* to heal the illness.

As this indicates, the most important difference between *mesas* to cause and cure illness is the intention of the ritual specialist (Polia 1996:

Illustration 2.2 Ritual table to cleanse sorcery illness (Kañaris). 2012. Photograph: M. Sax.

120).[11] In a *mesa* to do witchcraft, the sorcerer directs the power of the *encantos* to curse and harm a victim. He directs the power of particular spirits into a bundle containing an object closely associated with the intended victim, such as a lock of hair, piece of clothing, or photograph. The client then takes this sorcery bundle and secretly hides it in the house or business of the person they wish to harm. When the victim comes into physical contact or proximity with the witchcraft bundle, the power of the *encantos* in its sickening form enters his or her body. The victim is then cursed and contaminated, and can only be cleansed and healed by a sorcerer. As long as the *encanto*'s power remains in the victim's body, he or she will experience an illness that does not respond to any other type of medicine. Ultimately, this is because the power of the *encanto* is acting on an immaterial part of the person, their shadow-soul. If left untreated, the victim can die.

In healing *mesas*, the sorcerer must call upon the same *encanto* that caused the illness in the first place. Each *encanto* is connected to a specific power-object, which are the sorcerer's sacred rocks, staffs and swords. Each sacred object is tied to a specific *encanto*, either because the object contains the same immaterial substance that is the power of the *encanto*, or because it contains the *encanto*'s shadow-soul itself. The sorcerer uses his power-objects to 'extract' this sickening substance from the client's body, as well as 'block' or 'fight' against the *encanto* causing a client's illness.

A person can also contract an illness attributed to the power of the *encantos* through accidental contamination or direct contact, but this is rare in people's accounts. Whatever the root of the illness, if it has been caused by the power of the *encantos*, only a sorcerer can cure it, since only this type of specialist can communicate with these place-based spirits. Logically, there would be no need for healing sorcerers if there were not unscrupulous sorcerers who did witchcraft for paying clients in the first place.

Agency, Subjectivity, Responsibility

Who, or what, is responsible for causing the types of illness treated by *brujería*? This is a key question for both community members and the outside analyst. There is no simple answer. On one hand, corporally and socially manifested conditions of ill-being are connected to the power of the *encantos*. On the other hand, the involvement of sorcerers and clients is often necessary for this power to manifest as bodily experience.

Encantos are 'animated' entities and 'living things' with shadow-souls (*sombras*), by which they possess individual characters, personalities and the ability to feel and act (Polia 1996: 156). However, these entities lack the 'reason' (*razón*) that characterises people (ibid.: 163). While *encantos* display a limited degree of subjectivity, they are not demonstrably subjects in the human sense of individual consciousness, self-awareness or understanding that other subjects are also conscious to themselves (Csordas 2008: 112–13). Subjectivity matters to people in Kañaris, but not because they are interested in defining what is human in contrast to the non-human, as in the dominant Euro-American orientation. Nor do community members seek to determine what they share in common with certain animals or plants, as the theory of 'Amazonian perspectivism' implies (Viveiros de Castro 1998). Rather, community members are concerned with how they are affected by the power of spiritual entities embodied in the local landscape. The capacity for an *encanto* to act, and the ways people hold the entity accountable for what results from these actions, do matter.

The ways in which *encantos* act demonstrate two kinds of agency. In 'distributed agency', the entity acts according to its own self-generated will, and its actions produce effects in concert with the actions of other agents (the sorcerer and his client). The actions of two or more actors produce a condition of illness or healing in the body and lived context of a person (the victim or client). In witchcraft, the effect is not exclusively the results of the *encanto*'s intention, and people hold another agent accountable for the outcome of illness. In 'intentional agency', the *encanto* chooses to help or harm an individual. *Encantos* address sorcerers directly, and on rare occasions also address lay people. These are intentional actions of an *encanto*, which presupposes the entity's capacity for action of its own free will, relatively independent of larger structures.

The notion of 'distributed agency' draws on James Laidlaw's discussion of agency as the capacity for someone or something to exert power and produce a predictable effect. In Laidlaw's sense, agency is not 'an inherent quality of which individuals may have more or less' (Laidlaw 2010: 147). Rather, agency is attributed through an interpretive movement that assigns responsibility for an outcome (ibid.: 147ff.).

An analogy may illustrate how Laidlaw's discussion is relevant. If you stick your hand in a fire, you can expect the fire will burn you. This does not mean the fire had the intention to burn you, and this is why the fire produced the outcome of a burnt hand. *You* put your hand in the fire, and while you may or may not have wanted to burn your hand, the fire burned it nonetheless. Fire's nature is to burn things, but it does not possess the intention to burn your hand. The fire does not *want* anything at all, for it has no free will or consciousness by which to direct such an intention, according to both Euro-Americans and Kañarenses. Rather, fire displays agency in Laidlaw's alternative sense. Through fire's capacity to exert power and produce an effect, your hand was burned.

Similarly, *encantos* do not typically want to cause illness or healing in a person. The power of the *encanto* is mediated by the actions of a ritual specialist. The *encanto* does not intend its power to make the sorcerer's client ill or well. During a *mesa* ceremony, the *encanto* is only communicating with the sorcerer, not the client. It is the sorcerer who directs the *encanto*'s power according to his human will and intention. Thus, the *encanto*'s power is sickening in one context and healing in another. This is not a result of either the *encanto*'s intention towards the client, or an inherent quality of the *encanto* as a good or evil entity. The *encanto*'s power results in illness or healing because of the way it has been intentionally directed according to the will of the sorcerer.

Although the *encanto* is an essential participant in a chain of cause and effect that produces a predictable outcome, people do not say the *encanto* is responsible for illness or healing in a particular person. In local opinion, the intention of the sorcerer, and the client on whose behalf the specialist acts, is the socially relevant location of responsibility. In this instance, the *encanto* is displaying 'distributed agency'. Human and non-human beings share the responsibility for the outcome of the *encanto*'s power.

Yet this is not always the case. It is too simplistic to categorise *encantos* as 'subjectless' agents. Unlike fire, *encantos* are not inanimate things. They occupy a distinct ontological category in the northern Peruvian Andes. Since *encantos* have shadow-souls, they are living beings with their own knowledge and volition. *Encantos* are usually invisible to people because they inhabit the inner world that parallels this one. While lay people cannot detach their shadow-souls from their bodies to consciously enter this inner world, non-specialists occasionally encounter *encantos* who have taken human form in the everyday world. This is dangerous, and the person usually becomes ill as a result of direct contact with the spiritual entity. In this case, an *encanto* who 'grabs' the shadow-soul of a hapless traveller displays 'intentional agency', as the spirit produced an effect that arose from its own motivation.

People in Kañaris are not demonstrably interested in the agency or subjectivity of *encantos* or other non-human entities. Yet this discussion is necessary to understand what does matter to community members: determining who or what is responsible for classes of illnesses only *brujería* can cure. Ill-being brought about by malicious sorcery results in the victims altering their behaviour in relation to people they will continue to live and work beside. The sorcerer's client is the socially real perpetrator of witchcraft.

As ritual healing, *brujería* fills an important social role through determining accountability for illness and misfortune. Accountability refers to the ways people assign responsibility for a given outcome. The power of an *encanto* has made someone ill, but can the spirit be held accountable for this effect? Yes and no. The *encanto* is responsible in some way, since an individual would not have experienced this type of illness if they had not come into contact with the invisible substance of the entity's power. The power of the *encantos* is necessary to bring about well-being or suffering through *brujería*, but their intention is not. It is because of the will and desire of the sorcerer and his client that this power produces health or illness, good luck or misfortune, life or death in a particular person.

Synthesis

Sorcery (*brujería*) is a genre of both healing and witchcraft that exists alongside traditional medicine and biomedicine. It fills a distinct role in the local medical system, as it specifically treats illnesses attributed to the power of the *encantos*. These place-based spirits exist both in this world as mountains and lakes, and a parallel, inner world hidden from normal human experience and perception. The power of the *encantos* is an invisible substance that has phenomenologically real effects on people. These effects are experienced first and foremost in and through the individual body, but they are also manifested in the social and material extensions of the person. Sorcery works in the spiritual world of the *encantos*, and the sorcerer's shadow-soul enters the parallel spiritual world to learn how to extract the sickening power of the *encantos* from his client's body and restore the individual's well-being.

People in Kañaris attribute responsibility for the outcome of the *encanto*'s power through 'distributed' and 'intentional' agency. These categories are based on the implicit epistemological understandings of community members. The responsibility for witchcraft illness is shared by the *encantos*, the sorcerer and his client. James Laidlaw's discussion of agency is significant because he outlines how responsibility for an outcome can be distributed among several agents. This is clearly the case in both the cursing and healing modalities of sorcery. The *encantos* are agential entities that participate in a chain of cause and effect within a particular set of relations with the sorcerer and his client (Laidlaw 2010: 145–46). While the *encantos* are attributed with individualised names and identities, and express a self-generated will and intention towards the sorcerers with whom they have sacred relationships, *encantos* are not subjects in the human sense. They are functionally responsible for witchcraft illness, but people do not hold these spirits morally accountable for the sickening effects of their power. People only assign moral responsibility to the human actors involved.

This is where the social impact of *brujería* can be located. In small and interrelated highland communities, the local ideal is that people enjoy similar degrees of material and social well-being, and community members work together for the collective good. Yet resources and power are unequally distributed, and people can be selfish and evil, as well as generous and good. When one person envies the success and prosperity of another, the most extreme way in which they can harm their rival is through malicious sorcery (*brujería* as witchcraft). The victim goes to a sorcerer to be healed of this illness and return to their normal state of being. In the process of diagnosis and healing, however, the client may also learn which community member secretly perpetrated witchcraft against them to cause their suffering. A wise person does not attack the individual who has proven to be their enemy in turn. Rather, the conscientious person uses this knowledge to mitigate their vulnerability to future social and spiritual aggression. The person will continue to interact with their attacker within the parameters of social decency, but they will also avoid the envious individual as much as possible. Victims of witchcraft will not place their trust in someone who has demonstrated him or herself to be untrustworthy.

Conclusion

Mountain spirits and *encantos* are powerful non-human entities embodied in specific places. Andean peoples name these sacred places, and attribute them with individual identities and characteristics. In the highlands of southern Peru and Bolivia, mountain spirits play an essential role in agricultural production. In the south, human and supernatural relations are mediated by the idioms of sacrifice, payment, hunger and feeding. In this sense, ritual offerings and sacrificial payments in the southern Andes mediate the undomesticated power of the mountain spirits, and direct it towards people's desired goals.

Southern mountain spirits have an animating and vitalising power that makes plants grow and herd animals multiply. Andean peoples expect their mountain spirits to provide agricultural productivity and fertility. Community members also find themselves to be personally interpolated by these place-based spirits, who demand offerings and payments such as corn beer and coca leaves in return. If a householder neglects to make ritual offerings, the mountain spirit will make him or her ill. This is the physical manifestation of a demand the mountain spirit is making of the person. Illness attributed to mountain spirits is in part about lay people's personal relationships to tutelary divinities that animate the local landscape.

In southern Peru and Bolivia, householders can address mountain spirits directly with ritual sacrifices. These consumable offerings and payments mediate the undomesticated power of the mountain spirits, and direct it towards Andean peoples' desired goals. In the northern Peruvian Andes, place-based spirits embodied in mountains, waterfalls and high-altitude lakes are also repositories for an invisible energy that has the equal potential to help and harm people. However, lay people cannot communicate with *encantos* directly, and they are not bound to place-based spirits through a 'social contract' (Gose 2008: 280) in which people provide ritual offerings and payments in return for access to the sacred power that produces agricultural abundance and prosperity. Lay people and householders do not find themselves to be personally addressed by mountain spirits who demand ritual attention. Instead, only the ritual specialists called sorcerers (*brujos, maestros, curanderos*) can communicate with these powerful entities. Lay people must pay a sorcerer to do witchcraft, cure an illness attributed to the power of the *encantos*, or 'cleanse' and 'uplift' their luck and productive capacities.

In this sense, sorcerers mediate the relations between people and place-based spirits. While *encantos* can cause illness through accidental contamination or direct contact with a person, the spirit's power usually causes illness through ritual actions intended to damage a victim. In witchcraft, an evil sorcerer directs an *encanto*'s power towards a specific person with the intention of harming, instead of healing. Sorcerers are not motivated to do this themselves. They only do witchcraft on behalf of a paying client, who is a fellow community member who envies and wishes to harm their rival. Sorcerers therefore also mediate relations between fellow community members.

The most important difference between *mesas* to cause and cure illness is the intention of the sorcerer. The *encantos* do not care if an individual experiences ill-being or well-being. Their power has the potential to bring both health and illness, but these effects are not usually the result of the *encanto's* intention towards the person. Instead, their power is harmful or helpful according to how it has been directed by the intention of the sorcerer, and the client on whose behalf he acts. The *encantos* thus exist in a dynamic relationship that includes more than one actor.

In the northern Peruvian Andes, illness attributed to the *encantos* matters not because of people's relations to localised divinities, but because of the social and political motivations of another person that have set the condition of ill-being in motion, and the material and social consequences that result from it. For community members, what is at stake in human relations with place-based spirits is that people can use the power of non-human entities to produce destructive or generative outcomes. *Encantos* matter because the ways in which the spirit's power is used tells people something about their relations with fellow community members.

The 'mountain spirit complex' spans the Andean cultural area of highland Peru, Bolivia and Ecuador. This distinctly Andean notion of a personified and animating landscape is shared by indigenous peoples who continue to feel interpolated by place-based spirits embodied in sacred mountains and lakes. The mountain spirit complex is a common legacy of the Incan empire and Spanish colonialism. As the historical overview of mountain spirits indicates, this is not simply a matter of cultural continuity with a primordial past. In pre-Columbian times, Andean peoples venerated founding ancestors and mummified local lords as tutelary divinities who provided their people with agricultural fertility and prosperity. When the Incan cultural and political order had been definitively undermined, Andean peoples came to see mountains themselves as their protectors, sources of prosperity, and spiritual-political representatives in the emerging republican order.

The contemporary Andean mountain spirit complex thus developed out of the pre-Columbian practice of ancestor worship and divine kingship, and the constraints Andean peoples faced and the strategic responses they employed in the context of Spanish colonialism and Christian evangelisation. Today, many Andean peoples look to place-based spirits as sources of an immaterial power or energy that has the potential to bring production, health and good luck on the one hand, and loss, illness and misfortune on the other. Southern mountain spirits and northern *encantos* have the dual capacity for generation and destruction, and have dual identities as locals and foreigners. Andean peoples in both these areas attribute place-based spirits with individual identities, subjectivity, and the ability to act and produce a desired effect.

However, the relationships people have with these non-human entities and the ways in which people allocate responsibility for the effects of the spirit's power is significantly different in the southern and northern Peruvian Andes. In the south, people and place-based spirits coexist in a dyadic relationship of obligation and reciprocity, and mountain spirits distribute their spiritual power towards people as benevolence or retribution in response to the ritual offerings that householders have made towards them, or failed to provide to the spirit's satisfaction. In the north, lay people cannot communicate with place-based spirits themselves, and must seek the services of ritual specialists (sorcerers) in order to direct the power of specific *encantos* towards themselves or others according to their desired outcomes. While northern *encantos* sometimes address lay people directly and express an individualised intention to bless or curse, community members more typically distribute responsibility for the effects of an *encanto*'s power on a particular person among several agential actors, which include the place-based spirit, the sorcerer and the client.

Just why human and non-human relations are mediated through sacrificial offerings in the southern Andes and sorcery (*brujería*) in the north is a question for future research. Nevertheless, place-based spirits continue to matter to Andean peoples as overlapping nodes of relations between the human and divine, one person and another, the locality and the state, and household production and extractive industry.

Marieka Sax has a PhD in cultural anthropology from Carleton University (Canada). She is currently a postdoctoral fellow at the University of Northern British Columbia. She has two main areas of focus: sacred landscapes, peasant production and traditional medicine in the Peruvian Andes; and resource extraction, gender and Indigenous-settler relations in western Canada. Connecting these projects is an ongoing interest in socially reproduced cultural under-standings of well-being and the good life.

Notes

Research for this chapter was made possible with funding provided by the Social Sciences and Humanities Research Council of Canada through a Canada Graduate Scholarship (2007–08), Joseph-Armand Bombardier Doctoral Scholarship (2010–12), and Michael Smith Foreign Study Supplement (2012).

1. The general Quechua term for what I call here 'mountain spirits' is *tira-kuna*, which translates as 'earth-beings' (de la Cadena 2015: xxiii).
2. *Mesa* is a Spanish word that evokes both a ritual 'table' and a religious 'mass' in the Andes.
3. However, compare de la Cadena (2015) for the Cusco region.
4. Lau (2013) provides a complementary treatment of the alterity of founding ancestors in the pre-Columbian Andes as read through the archaeological record.
5. The possibility that ambiguously foreign founding ancestors may be pivotal in encounters between regimes of divine kingship and Euro-American colonisers is not limited to the Andean cultural area. A famous Polynesian example is in Sahlins (1995).
6. See also Salas Carreño, this volume.
7. Similar 'spirit-owners' of plants, animals and natural resources appear as both autochthonous to the community and racially other throughout neighbouring Amazonian regions (e.g. Kohn 2007, 2013: Chapter 5; Walker 2013: Chapter 6; and Opas this volume).
8. Here I follow the convention of the local municipality and use the spelling 'Kañaris' to identify the town and population in northern Peru. While government documents and the Peruvian media more commonly refer to this town, district and population as 'Cañaris', the spelling I employ is intended to (1) follow the orthography for the Quechua of Ferreñafe as set out in Gerald Taylor's seminal work (1982, 1996); (2) identify the town's population with the land-holding association of the peasant community of San Juan Bautista de Kañaris; and (3) differentiate this ethnically distinct community from the contemporary Ecuadorian community, colonial tributary populations, and the pre-Columbian group of the Cañar. The primary social unit of my analysis is the peasant community and ethnic group of San Juan Bautista de Kañaris, whose members form the large majority of the population of the town of K/Cañaris, and who have a legally recognised collective land-holding title to the eastern third of the district of K/Cañaris. This district is an administrative subdivision in the province of Ferreñafe, region of Lambayeque, Peru.
9. In *brujería*, the *mesa* refers to both the healing ceremony and the sorcerer's arrangement of power-objects on a blanket during the event.
10. For a similar Amazonian example of a hidden inner world, see Kohn 2007.

11. For further discussion of different types of *mesas* and other ethnographic details regarding *brujería* in northern Peru, see Sax 2014.

References

Allen, C. 2002. *The Hold Life Has: Coca and Cultural Identity in an Andean Community*, 2nd edn. Washington, DC and New York: Smithsonian Books.

Arce Sotelo, M. 2006. *La Danza de Tijeras y el Violín de Lucanas*. Lima: Instituto Francés de Estudios Andinos.

Århem, K. 1996. 'The Cosmic Food Web: Human–Nature Relatedness in the Northwest Amazon', in Ph. Descola and P. Gísli (eds), *Nature and Society: Anthropological Perspectives*. London and New York: Routledge, pp. 185–240.

Arroyo Aguilar, S. 2004. *Dioses y Oratorios Andinos de Huancabamba: Cosmología y Curanderismo en la Sierra de Piura*. Lima: UNMSM.

Bastien, J.W. 1978. *Mountain of the Condor: Metaphor and Ritual in an Andean Ayllu*. St. Paul, MN: West Publishing Co.

Brown, M. 1986. *Tsewa's Gift: Magic and Meaning in an Amazonian Society*. Washington, DC and London: Smithsonian Institution Press.

Bussmann, R., and D. Sharon. 2006. 'Traditional Medicinal Plant Use in Northern Peru: Tracking Two Thousand Years of Healing Culture', *Journal of Ethnobiology and Ethnomedicine* 2(47).

Camino, L. 1992. *Cerros, Plantas y Lagunas Poderosas: La Medicina al Norte del Perú*. Piura: CIPCA.

Crandon-Malamud, L. 1991. *From the Fat of Our Souls: Social Change, Political Process, and Medical Pluralism in Bolivia*. Berkeley and Los Angeles: University of California Press.

Csordas, T. 2008. 'Intersubjectivity and Intercorporeality', *Subjectivity* 22: 110–21.

De la Cadena, M. 2015. *Earth Beings: Ecologies of Practice across Andean Worlds*. Durham, NC and London: Duke University Press.

Fernández Juárez, G. 1997. *Entre la Repugnancia y la Seducción: Ofrendas complejas en los Andes del Sur*. Cusco: Centro de Estudios Regionales Andinos 'Bartolomé de Las Casas'.

———. 2004. *Yatiris y ch'amakanis del altiplano aymara: Sueños, testimonios y prácticas ceremoniales*. Quito: Abya-Yala.

Gelles, P.H. 2000. *Water and Power in Highland Peru: The Cultural Politics of Irrigation and Development*. New Brunswick, NJ: Rutgers University Press.

Giese, C. 1991. 'El Rol y Significado de las Lagunas Huaringas cerca de Huancabamba y el Curanderismo en el Norte del Peru', *Bulletin de l'Institut Français des Études Andines* 20(2): 565–87.

Glass-Coffin, B. 1998. *The Gift of Life: Female Spirituality and Healing in Northern Peru*. Albuquerque: University of New Mexico Press.

Gose, P. 1993. 'Segmentary State Formation and the Ritual Control of Water under the Incas', *Comparative Studies in Society and History* 35(3): 480–514.

———. 1994. *Deathly Waters and Hungry Mountains: Agrarian Ritual and Class Formation in an Andean Town*. Toronto: University of Toronto Press.

———. 2000. 'The State as a Chosen Woman: Brideservice and the Feeding of Tributaries in the Inka Empire', *American Anthropologist* 102(1): 84–97.

———. 2008. *Invaders as Ancestors: On the Intercultural Making and Unmaking of Spanish Colonialism in the Andes*. Toronto: University of Toronto Press.

Gow, P. 1994. 'River People: Shamanism and History in Western Amazonia', in N. Thomas and C. Humphrey (eds), *Shamanism, History, and the State*. Ann Arbor: University of Michigan Press, pp. 90–113.

Harner, M. 1972. *The Jívaro: People of the Sacred Waterfalls*. Garden City, NY: Anchor Books.

Isbell, B.J. 1978. *To Defend Ourselves: Ecology and Ritual in an Andean Village*. Prospect Heights, IL: Waveland Press.

Joralemon, D., and D. Sharon. 1993. *Sorcery and Shamanism: Curanderos and Clients in Northern Peru*. Salt Lake City: University of Utah Press.

Kohn, E. 2007. 'Animal Masters and the Ecological Embedding of History among the Ávila Runa of Ecuador', in C. Fausto and M. Heckenberger (eds), *Time and Memory in Indigenous Amazonia: Anthropological Perspectives*. Gainesville, FL: University Press of Florida, pp. 106–29.

———. 2013. *How Forests Think: Toward an Anthropology beyond the Human*. Berkeley and Los Angeles: University of California Press.

Laidlaw, J. 2010. 'Agency and Responsibility: Perhaps You Can Have Too Much of a Good Thing', in M. Lambek (ed.), *Ordinary Ethics: Anthropology, Language, and Action*. New York: Fordham University Press, pp. 143–64.

Lau, G.F. 2013. *Ancient Alterity in the Andes: A Recognition of Others*. London and New York: Routledge.

Murra, J.V. 2002. 'En Torno a la Estructura Política de los Inka', in J. Murra, *El Mundo Andino: Población, Medio Ambiente y Economía*. Lima: Instituto de Estudios Peruanos, pp. 43–56.

Nash, J. 1979. *We Eat the Mines and the Mines Eat Us: Dependency and Exploitation in Bolivian Tin Mines*. New York: Columbia University Press.

Platt, T. 1983. 'Conciencia andina y Conciencia Proletaria: Qhuyaruna y Ayllu en el Norte de Potosi', *HISLA: Revista latinoamericana de historia económica y social* 2: 47–73.

Polia, M. 1996. *Despierta, remedio, cuenta': advinos y médicos del Ande*. Lima: Fondo Editorial PUCP.

Rivera Andía, J.J. 2003. *La fiesta del ganado en el valle de Chancay (1962–2002). Religión y ritual en los Andes: etnografía, documentos inéditos e interpretación.* Lima: Fondo Editorial PUCP.

Rostworowski, M. 1999. *Historia del Tahuantinsuyu.* 2nd edn. Lima: Instituto de Estudios Peruanos.

Sahlins, M. 1995. *How 'Natives' Think: About Captain Cook, For Example.* Chicago, IL and London: University of Chicago Press.

Salazar-Soler, C. 2006. *Supay Muqui, Dios del Socavón: Vida y Mentalidades Mineras.* Lima: Fondo Editorial del Congreso del Perú.

Sax, M. 2011. *An Ethnography of Feeding, Perception and Place in the Peruvian Andes (Where Hungry Spirits Bring Illness and Wellbeing).* Lewiston, NY: Edwin Mellen Press.

———. 2014. 'Sorcery and Morality in the Andes: Illness, Healing, and *Brujería* in Kañaris (Lambayeque, Peru)'. PhD dissertation. Ottawa: Carleton University.

Sharon, D. 1978. *Wizard of the Four Winds: A Shaman's Story.* New York: Free Press.

Taylor, G. 1982. 'Breve Presentación de la Morfología del Quechua de Ferreñafe', *Lexis* 6(2): 243–70.

———. 1996. *El Quechua de Ferreñafe: Fonología, morfología, léxico.* Cajamarca, Peru: Acku Quinde.

Viveiros de Castro, E. 1998. 'Cosmological Deixis and Amerindian Perspectivism', *The Journal of the Royal Anthropological Institute* 4(3): 469–88.

Walker, H. 2013. *Under a Watchful Eye: Self, Power, and Intimacy in Amazonia.* Berkeley and Los Angeles: University of California Press.

3

Marking Out the Bounds of Humanity in Tsachila Ritual

Montserrat Ventura i Oller

Reflection on humanity has developed strongly in the last two decades, driven by Melanesian and Amazonian anthropology (Vilaça 2011). In the case of Amazonia, this impetus derived from a proliferation of ethnographies focusing on the construction of the person, which in turn was sparked, among other factors, by the findings of Seeger, da Matta and Viveiros de Castro (1979: 3): namely that the originality of the Brazilian indigenous societies lies in a particularly rich elaboration of the notion of person, with special reference to corporality as a local symbolic language. This emphasis has inspired studies on the concept of humanity in other parts of the Americas – in the Andean area (Platt 2001, 2009; Rivera Andía 2005; Carlos Ríos 2015), the Mesoamerican area (Galinier 1997; Gutiérrez Estévez 2010; Martínez González 2010; Pitarch 2011), and the Pacific coast area (Praet 2009a and 2009b; Ventura i Oller 2009), among others – which point to the heuristic richness of the body as a way to understand the human being and its limits. The Tsachila ethnology of western Ecuador and, in particular, the analysis of one of its curing and identifying rituals, offers up a case study that can help us to achieve such an aim.

Tsachila Humanity and Its Limits

The Tsachila people inhabit the western side of Ecuador (Santo Domingo de los Tsachila, the western lowlands, the coast of Ecuador), and could be situated at a halfway point (Ventura i Oller

2009)[1] between the highlands and the lowlands, not only geographically but also between ways of organizing subsistence and experience. They consist of around two thousand people spread over seven communes interspersed between rural estates, which are owned by non-indigenous people, and today they live by cultivating bananas, and to a lesser extent cocoa, coffee and pineapples, for domestic consumption. They maintain a relative degree of internal equality, and although the shamans have de facto power, they are formally governed by communal councils, elected annually, and a governor who unites the ethnic group, elected every four years. The ethnic statutes (indigenous regulations) promote ethnic endogamy and make it difficult for non-Tsachila to reside in the communes, as well as exerting some control over the conservative rules and practices of tradition. Although a considerable number of commune members declare themselves to be Catholic and others – fewer in number – Evangelical, the practice of these religions is scarce, serving as a complement to the spiritual life of the community and to their fairly frequent recourse to their own shamans and, to a lesser extent, those of other cultural traditions: Andean, Amazonian and Coastal indigenous, Afro-Ecuadorian and mestizos. In turn, the shamans carry on the local tradition of completing their apprenticeship with shamans from the outside: from Amazonia, the Andes, the coastal area or beyond the state borders. Most families still pass on to their offspring a position in the world that gives validity to their traditional cosmological universe. Although there is bilingual education, it is of limited success and the vast majority of the population do not reach secondary school, let alone university. Modernity is embodied in some habits of the younger generation, basically at the level of choice of clothing and the use of mobile phones and television, computers and the internet (to a much lesser extent), and the standard musical rhythms of the rural mestizo environment, as well as motorised transport. Some young Tsachila men have relations with young indigenous and non-indigenous women from other regions, but everyday life takes place with few surprises in the communities, in a society that prefers the local 'good life' to outside quests for excitement with uncertain results.

In Tsachila cosmology we find a logic of the continuum that is common in societies classified as animist in accordance with the modes of relation and identification proposed by Descola (2005), and in which humans are fated to strive permanently to identify themselves as such and not lose their condition, as noted by Praet (2013) for the Chachi indigenous society, coastal neighbours of the Tsachila.

Here, humanity is shared with other beings – animal, vegetable or spiritual – but with certain nuances. As in some other Amazonian regions, this is a relationship of degree that does not unify the universe of what is human, but rather distributes it in a scale of intensities. In order to explain it, we shall examine the system by which beings are classified, the components of the person, particularly in those attributes that constitute 'humanity' from the local point of view, and the forms taken by disease in the areas relevant to this analysis.

The ethnonym Tsachila invokes humanity, but in referential rather than absolute terms: either 'We-feminine (*chila*) of reference (*tsa*)' or the more accepted meaning of 'people (*tsachi*) + the collective (*la*)', probably a modern contraction of *tsatsachila* ('people' of reference).[2] Its referential capacity is seen in mythology and cosmology, where there are mythical beings (*tsachi kuwenta*, 'like tsachi') also known as *tsachi* without being members of the human group Tsachila. Likewise, other species designated by the indicator of reference 'tsa' (*tsakela*, the feline of reference for the jaguar; *tsapini*, the snake of reference for the *Bothrox atrox*, the most venomous one; *tsa ano*, the banana of reference for Dominican banana, *Musa paradisiaca*,[3] the most common one) become the prototype, the universal concept of the species, the sum of the attributes of the species, considered distinctive par excellence. For this reason, human beings are Tsachila even if they belong to another ethnic group, and it is the context that allows us to know which *tsachi* is being referred to.

Plants (*tape*) have a very precise category, currently well activated by shamanic healing, that does not cover all the plant kingdom. The latter is also populated by trees (*chide*), some of whose constituents are sometimes highlighted according to the purpose of their mention or use: vines (*sili*), flowers (*luli*), leaves (*japisu*). Nor is there a single term for animals as a group, with these being generically named using the designation *animalila* of Spanish origin. Although there are clear categories for birds (*pichu*) and fish (*watsa*), none of these categories are designated with the prefix *tsa*, 'of reference'. However we do find this prefix used for more restricted categories, similar to the families or the suborders of the Linnaean taxonomies, such as the felines (*kela: tsakela*) or snakes (*pini: tsapini*) mentioned above, and even in the case of fish (*tsawatsa*, but also *tsakere*, where *kere* is one of the most common fish: '*campeche*' in Spanish); but it does not appear in all the categories, as for example in the case of worms (*koro: chinikoro*, a hairy worm, with two heads; *otonkoro*, a small worm that lives in dry wood and in the intestines – a protagonist in certain myths).

Among the beings that belong to categories with which humans interact, other generic beings are also found, such as the *oko* (incorporeal beings), beings with a marked individual identity (*luban oko*, the red spirit; *son pura*), and the rest of the *ayan* (mothers, elderly women) of some animal species, such as *kela ayan* (mother of the tiger) or of the cosmos (*tsabo ayan*, mother of the stars; or *to ayan*, the mother of the Earth).

Tsachila is thus not the only referent in the world but rather the measure of many relationships. It is, in effect, a relational humanity, not a substantive one, also visible in the system of transformations of mythology, which we cannot cover in detail here (Ventura i Oller 2009 and 2012), and in other social areas, such as the field of disease (Ventura i Oller 2009 and 2011b), explored below.

The Attributes of Humanity

The Tsachila express 'thought' through the heart, as occurs among other Amerindian groups (Surrallés 2003). All humans are endowed with *tenka* in terms of heart, thorax and physical body, but also in terms of the ability to think: *tenka iton* (he has no *tenka*) = stupid, *tenka pun* = intelligent, and in terms of ability to act and to react (in the sense of soul and mobility). Lastly, *tenka* can also be conceived as a capacity to produce emotions (a certain number of expressions that refer to emotivity are formed from the root *ten*). In fact, *tenka* refers directly to the visible and tangible body organ, since all animals that possess it correspond exactly to those that are endowed with a thoracic cavity, such as mammals and birds, but also with a life pulse, such as fish and reptiles. The characters that interact with humans – of which the most frequent in mythology are the spirits, the mammals and the birds – also include snakes, especially *tsapini*, which also appear as the interlocutors of humans in the myths, and which even represent helper spirits for some shamans, able to communicate. They are, in some way, endowed with the capacity for reasoning: an ability to react to events and to intersubjective relationships in an elementary interaction (a snake that crosses paths with a human gives him or her a fixed stare and then flees). From a certain perspective, any demonstration of a being's instinct for survival is attributed to its *tenka*, and in this sense the treatment is the same for humans (men and women) and for animals. The plant world, especially big trees, also have *tenka* by virtue of having the responses needed to ensure their survival in their environment. The simple capacity of moving is enough to characterize *tenka*, as shown by the attribution of *tenka* to *to ayan* (the mother of the Earth), an entity that lives beneath the ground and whose sole known activity is to move slightly from time to time, thereby causing earth tremors or earthquakes. In some way, this shared *tenka* varies in terms of scope and attributions, depending on the being presenting it.

One of the meanings of *tenka* is superimposed on that of *silon* (life force, life itself). The *silon* of a deceased individual can return among the living in the form of an animal like the agouti (*Dasyprocta fuliginosa*), and its condition is discovered as a result of its human habits, such as coming close to the house, but also by its insipid taste when cooked and eaten. Unlike *tenka*, the *silon* is exclusive to humans and certain animals: big trees do not possess it. Those who have the strongest *silon* are the shamans, who acquire it as a result of their ability to travel to the sun.

If *tenka*, together with *silon*, brings wisdom, intelligence, awareness and the instinct for survival, *mowin* is the ability to communicate and strength, specifically the strength of attraction: *mowin* derives from *mo* (desire) and *win* (from *wino*, enter), and the best-known *mowin* is that of hunters and lovers, with their need to attract. However, once again this element is not exclusive to humans. The *mowin* of big trees was in olden times one of the beings feared in every excursion to the forest. *Mowin* is described as an incorporeal and ethereal force, yet one that can appear in the shape of a person when it makes itself visible. It is different to the *oko* (spirits), authentic beings without flesh but with a strong identity. *Mowin*, in contrast, is a force inherent to a being, whether human, animal, plant or spirit, which has the possibility of wandering in search of a new being when the one housing it dies or is no longer available, but which has no independent life. Rather than merely marking the identity of individuals, the *mowin*, as a constitutional part of the person, offers a possibility of a relationship between different individuals from the same category or from different categories, and is thus an element that allows a person to participate in social life in the broadest sense, including relationships both with the Tsachila and with individuals from other species. To this should also be added the talent for seeding, the *sen tede*, equivalent to luck (*suman*) for fishing and hunting. The latter can also be activated by means of the shaman's charms or by certain herbs that also act to counteract bad luck (*pola*) for the hunt (for the hunters, for the hunting hounds). However, the *suman* is not shared by non-humans, except for those that collaborate in the productive activities – hounds in the hunt; Biali, a mythical being, in fishing.

Lastly, the body, *puka*, is the most visible element, and a person is not considered as such until the moment at which the body is completely formed, becoming *tsachi puka*. *Puka* refers directly to completeness: the same term is used to name fruit, and the suffix *ka* is used for everything that is rounded and complete. Nonetheless, the body cannot be considered a simple container for the things that make up a person. It has a primary function, in a cosmological sense as well as an individual and social one. In Tsachila mythology, particularly in the transformational myths, animals and spirits group together into families, cooking and hunting just like humans. When they appear before humans in human form (*tsachi kuwenta*, like tsachi), they behave like humans until their identity is discovered from clues such as the way they walk or hunt, or their culinary tastes. Yet, as Descola (1986: 120) points out: 'The common referent for all the beings in nature is not man as a species, but rather humanity as a condition'. These 'characters' externalise a human social behaviour, yet they are not humans. Their difference reveals itself, not in their bodily appearance, but rather via what Viveiros de Castro (1996: 128) calls 'habitus', and Descola calls 'essence', and which can be summarised as being an affective disposition rooted in the body that determines a way of behaving. Non-humans share some human attributes, such as the ability to communicate and live in society, but the Tsachila strive to reveal their true identity and highlight the difference with body markings. The Tsachila myths teach us how they are deceived in this effort by handsome fellows or beautiful seductive women. Sometimes, as a result of these deceptions, there are sexual relations and sometimes offspring. This offspring is human, just as the appearance, the form and the relationship were human. But its humanity is diluted precisely when the transformation, experienced as a deception, is discovered (Ventura i Oller 2008). The fidelity that the Tsachila attach to facts (Ventura i Oller 2002) leads us to another snapshot of this fluid universe, in which progenitors cease to occupy the place whose nature they have usurped, and their offspring, always reluctant to stay among the humanity of reference, flees with its external parent while losing the bodily distinction of the human progenitor. The human condition is lost as a logical consequence of the discovery of the deception (the transformation, the human appearance, the seduction as a Tsachila), something that the Tsachila moral code and their standards of good conduct do not allow. And this condition is made visible on the body.

Forms of Ailments and Evils

The fluidity of the body, corroborated by the possibilities for transformation of the beings in the mythical world, is also revealed in
the local conception of illness. Thus, far from producing insensitive
people, Tsachila cosmology experiences pain and suffering as something that is fundamentally corporeal. In general, in its generic sense,
illness is caused by external agents, and is only rarely explained in
terms of a deterioration associated with the passage of time. Until the
preceding generation the Tsachila shamans would extract it from the
body in the form of a material substance such as a dart, a small stone
or a worm, as occurs in a large number of the Upper Amazonian
societies (Chaumeil 1983). The wounding object was shown after the
curing session as the physical evil that had been running through the
body during the suffering. The body was therefore conceived not
only as an external appearance that marked a prime human essence,
but also as the receptacle that contained the feelings (absent in spirits),
and which marked the difference between a living Tsachila and a dead
one, or between a complete Tsachila and a spirit. For this reason,
humans should take care of their body and protect it. Nowadays,
shamanic cures are no longer based on this visible removal, and the
illness is eliminated by means of an external cleansing of the body
with egg, in line with a curative tradition widespread throughout
Indigenous America, most likely of Hispanic origin but with different functions to those of the Iberian Peninsula (Foster 1980: 134–35).
Such cleansings are common in the medical practices of indigenous
societies that have suffered the colonial onslaught most persistently,
such as the Mesoamericans and the Andeans, but also in the so-called
'frontier of colonisation' societies in the lowlands. Apart from local
peculiarities, the basis of cleansing with egg is the rubbing of the
patient's body, carried out by the specialist, with one or two eggs,
which absorb the impurities of the patient and are then thrown into
the river or in an inconspicuous place in order to prevent the harm
from returning to humans: to the patient, to the shaman or to family
members. Today's Tsachila ritual is hence nuanced by all the incor-
porations arising from their active participation in a network of shamanic exchanges that link them to coastal, Andean and Amazonian
societies, and which spread across national borders (Ventura i Oller
2003, 2011b). Nonetheless, illness is still perceived as the result of an
external agent, as something external that needs to be expelled from
the body.

When the shamans begin a curing session, they first of all seek to diagnose the etiology of the evil with the aid of their helper spirits. By the same logic of transformations in the world of myths, bodiless beings take on physical and corporeal appearances when they appear in the shamans' visions induced during the learning process, and in the most important rituals, by means of the hallucinogen *nepi* (*Banisteriopsis caapi*). The traditional mythological narrations speak of visions of jaguars, just as the elderly recall the constant fear of the threat posed by this big feline in the everyday life of their youth. Nowadays the jungle has receded to the minimum in an environment punished by the activities of mestizo colonists – tree felling, large-scale agriculture and the pollution of rivers – and with it have disappeared most of the large mammals that featured in the myths and visions. Nonetheless, illness still takes on domestic and often ambivalent forms in the surrounding social universe.

In the etiology of ailments, *luban oko* (red spirit), an avid bloodsucker that lies in wait for hunters, the hunters' prey and everything that runs the risk of having a wound, as well as women menstruating or in childbirth, is the *seiton oko* (evil spirit) most present in the everyday life of the Tsachila, and it takes the form of a known person, sometimes already deceased, or of a specific animal. Agustín, a now elderly shaman, describes a *luban oko* thus:

> In another time in Cóngoma there were many *luban oko* ..., which took the form of parrots, of turkeys, screeching like the agouti in the night. ... *Luban oko* never leaves more than two or three footprints, then they disappear. ... *Luban oko* walked like people, like an agouti, like a horse, shouted like people, whistled, played the flute, sometimes climbed trees, like pambil leaves, like that, making noise, hacking at the trees ... never left anything alone. (Ventura i Oller 2009: 166)

Although it can appear in a variety of forms, one of the features that identifies *luban oko* is that it disappears as soon as it is in reach of humans. Apart from its frequent appearances, when it has access to blood from a body, it proceeds to suck it, causing its victims to become thinner and thinner until they die. Burning chili or colonies of termites, and chewing ginger are three of the most commonly used remedies for keeping *luban oko* away from places belonging to humans, such as the home or the bends in the river that the families have domesticated.

Seiton oko, the generic evil spirit, grabs people, hits them and kills them, and also produces the evil air, although with the decline of the jungle, it is hardly ever encountered nowadays. The elderly

Tsachila say that in the past *seiton oko* walked around in the shape of a peccary (*Pecari tajacu*), or a coati (*Nasua nasua*).

Among the beings that now only exist in myths are *Isowe*, the one which has its mouth at the back of its head, or *Sonpura*, with the appearance of a snake, living in the lakes (*wa pilu*), taking the place of the tree *pechi* when it rots, after being felled. It is considered as the *tenka* of this tree, its heart, and as a highly malevolent force (*seiton mowin*) that persecutes the Tsachila when they cut down the tree. According to some, its activity even goes so far as to provoke the growling of *to ayan*, the mother of the Earth.

The curse, the formula par excellence of the shamanic illness, is known as *yuka kika* (doing evil) or *yuka kika kiyan*. *Yuka* is a term steeped in the Christian tradition, which appears to have used it as a convenient expression for translating the notion of the devil. Augusto describes it thus:

> *Yukan* is like the *diablo* [he uses the Spanish word for devil in his discourse in Tsafiki] … it was very ugly, like black with horns, with a tail, like a dog with a tail, but like a Tsachi himself, but like black. Yukan is like that. That's what they say. There are a lot of them. (Ventura i Oller 2009: 182-183)

Leaving aside the contemporary existence of this being, which is not the subject of particular mythic narrations, the term *yuka* is usually used as an adjective to indicate something harmful, as in *yuka ofo* (lit.: 'bad flu') to describe pneumonia, or in *yuka bichi* (lit.: 'bad plague') for one of the expressions describing leishmaniasis. However, the *yuka* of the curses, certainly harmful, does not resemble the idea of an evil spirit like *luban oko* or other *seiton oko*. *Yuka kiyan* is an illness produced by an evil, sent by an enemy, and renewed in an object (admittedly, an object that the evil spirits or enemy spirits have helped to send).

Suyun kiyan, the rainbow disease, as in other regions of the lowlands and of the Andes (Kroeger and Barbira-Freedman 1992: 128, 210; Sánchez-Parga and Pineda 1985: 546), is the origin of many disorders, above all those affecting the skin. *Suyun*, as in the case of *Salun* (in some narratives named without distinction as if dealing with the same character), appears to human eyes as a handsome young man who seduces women, penetrates them and kills them during coitus (Ventura i Oller 2011a).

Among the complaints whose origin is associated with 'the whites', there are the *susto* (*wepana kika*), the evil air (*seiton wu kika*), or the evil eye (*kaka kika*), usually considered by ethnomedicine as popular diseases of Hispanic origin (Foster 1980) but rooted in indigenous traditions. They have a disembodied form, but the shamans (*ponela*) see them 'as Tsachi' during their shamanic journeys.

It is in the modern-day diseases considered *feto kiyan*, diseases of the whites, sometimes also *diochi kiyan*, diseases from God – as opposed to the local ones, which include the curse as a central cause – that we observe a variation in appearance, in many respects symptomatic of the everyday social situation. In the repertoire of Isidro, one of the young shamans with whom I worked, every disease occurs under a different human form. Thus, influenza (*ofo*) is transmitted by a mestizo trader of the *pitsa* fruit (*inga*) via the pods of the same fruit that he sells. Chicken pox is, in turn, caused by ingestion of corn on the cob served by a native merchant from Latacunga (Andes). Rubella is transmitted by an indigenous Andean vendor of *colitas* (cool drinks); dysentery by a mestizo merchant from the sierra selling bread rolls; avian flu by a small spirit with an insatiable desire for eating chicken. In contrast to the latter illnesses, *chiyaku*, tetanus, is not a disease from God but rather a disease caused by an evil spirit (*seiton oko*). This evil spirit is described as a disembodied mass that inhabits some trees of the forest, which the shamans see in the form of *du tsachi* (people of the sierra). *Chiyaku* penetrates the body in the form of a powder, so it is easier to get it when you have an injury. The (anti-tetanus) 'inyección' raises a barrier so that the disease does not penetrate. This is a logic that is repeated in other rituals which reveal the vulnerability of the body and the need to protect it, as we shall see further below.

The logic of transformation pertaining to the mythical world thus appears in the field of disease with the strength and diversity of the social imaginary. The evils are wrapped in the social bodies of the environment, both human and non-human, and mark them.

Marking Out Humanity in Ritual

Given the fragility of the body's 'casing' and the ease in passing from one bodily appearance to another in mythology and the Tsachila conception of the person, the limits of humanity are particularly vulnerable for this group. In fact, as we have shown, in Tsachila mythology the body is not an identity marker that would by itself distinguish humans from other beings, or humans from other humans; and since the body is not enough to establish a differential human identity, the Tsachila have a ritual to reaffirm the latter by strengthening it, *Patso kika* (making *patso*, 'shielding oneself').

The expression *Patso kika* (Ventura i Oller 2006) refers to a collective curing ritual, and although it is in decline like the rest of the traditional collective rituals, it is still practised in certain homes. Its objective is to cover the body with a sort of 'barrier' or 'protective shell' once cleared of any 'dirt' or foreign element caused by an 'evil' spirit. The households participating in the ritual, united by ties of kinship or neighbourhood, are joint victims of the same ailment, although the symptoms are not experienced by all of their members equally. This is in line with the indigenous concept of disease (here indeed, largely coinciding with that of so many other indigenous groups in the region), which goes beyond the physical experience of evil in a particular body to influence the collective imbalances that the cure – also collective – will attempt to amend. The 'barrier' succeeds in 'deceiving' the spirits, which otherwise, due to this ontological continuity between humans and the non-human that they are part of, have a tendency to incorporate, ignorant of the weakness of the body's casing in setting the limits of identity.

The ritual lasts two hours and usually involves at least one extensive family. And since illnesses are perceived as afflictions of the group, the remedies prescribed by the shamans, especially sex and food diets, concern the whole family, even when the illness directly affects only one of its members. Thus, besides individual cleansings, in this case with egg, the central moment of the celebration takes place when the shaman prepares a magic dye, made with *mali* (*Genipa americana*), rubber and *nepi* (*Banisteriopsis caapi*) and the men and women, separately, paint each other's bodies with black horizontal strokes. At the end of the second night, they go together to the river to take the ritual bath, rubbing themselves with a mixture of plants previously purified by the shaman. Lastly, they paint the palms of their hands with *mu* (*Bixa orellana*) and show them, in a sort of brief greeting, towards the east and west. Today, this ritual is not accompanied by words or songs, except for the litany chanted by the shaman when he invokes his helper spirits under the influence of the hallucinogenic *nepi*. More than a chant, this litany is a call to certain non-human beings to come and help to expel the evil. If the *Patso kika* ritual as a whole appears as an extreme expression of the Tsachila conception of health and disease, its practice allows us to see, in an explicit demonstration – the black strokes on the body – how the body acts as a weak material frontier: a fragile wrapping that humans themselves must occasionally fortify with this extra barrier provided by the *mali* and the *mu*. It would seem that in traditional society, the *Patso kika* allowed the Tsachila to mark out the limits of the human body in the face of those supernatural beings who did not have it: a sort of casing erected to mark and reinforce this difference between them and the other, non-corporeal, beings; a physical mark of their human identity.

The *Patso kika* ritual would thus be a demonstration of the effort that humans should make in order to remain fully human, and unsoiled by any foreign element. This is the same effort that anthropology has described vigorously since the 1980s, referring to body marking as a social marking (Turner 1995), an ontogenetic (Erikson 1996) or communicative marking (Déléage 2007; see also Taylor 2003), and an ethnic marking (Vidal 1992). *Patso kika* succeeds in distinguishing Tsachila humanity in the face of spirits and also, as the reference for humanity, from the other humans they need to stand out from, particularly the other neighbouring indigenous groups (Chachi), the Afro-Ecuadorians and the mestizo population. This distinction is achieved by emphasising their most visible external feature: the black strokes on the skin, which constitutes at the same time their 'traditional' ethnic appearance. Let us examine it.

Marking Out Frontiers in Order to Survive

The shamans have almost abandoned the celebration of *Patso kika*, at least over the last two decades. This is the period in which perhaps the most important transformations in the Tsachila's daily life have taken place. The forest and its prey have virtually disappeared, social organisation has undergone a profound transformation, the shamans have lost their political power, biomedicine has steadily been introduced – within the limitations of its precarious implementation in the region – and the Evangelist pastors and Catholic priests have continued their unremitting task of colonising Tsachila mentalities. Even so, these changes have not brought an improvement in the Tsachila's quality of life. Their economy is more dependent on the market and their diet is less diverse. They continue to suffer from diseases, with a degree of anxiety added by the fact that their shamans feel that they have lost their healing powers, while the possibility of accessing Western health care is still distant, both economically and geographically. In addition, many of the implications of this Western medicine come into contradiction with the Tsachila's notion of disease – especially when it is produced by a curse – and it thus becomes useless for solving most of their ailments, while medical interference in their bodies, such as the removal of organs or other types of direct mediation such as injections, are seen to be, if not dangerous, at least suspicious. Physical evils and social evils are too common, the shamanic cleansings are becoming too much of an everyday thing to be effective in persistent cases, and the *Patso kika* appears to solve this need for concentrating the traditional healing forces more successfully.

At the same time, from the point of view of their collective identity within the framework of Ecuadorian national society, the Tsachila find themselves at a particularly difficult moment, and are trying in some areas to reinforce some of their external ethnic marks in order to find a place in a society that demands differentiating exotic markers from them, while they attempt at the same time to adapt to the new forms of social organisation that this same society imposes on them. Whether by chance or within the same logic being described here, traditional ethnic attire also used to include body painting based on horizontal black bars – in this case drawn only with the tincture of the *mali* – on bodies smeared with red colouring, along with the cotton cloth with which men and women covered their genitals. These paintings offered the Tsachila the same external appearance as that achieved by the ritualised covering of their bodies practised during the *Patso kika*. One identifies them ethnically, the other as human beings. It is in this context that the Tsachila have, in the last couple of decades, readopted the *Patso kika* ritual. This return should thus be regarded as an effort to redefine their identity, not only in its primary sense of protecting themselves from the attacks of diseases, but also with the inexplicit but clear aim of rediscovering and rede-signing the place of their bodies in this new society: one increasingly bereft of those supernatural beings that once made up the Tsachila's cosmology and were both a complement and a mirror to their iden-tity. In a context where society is as yet unable to provide satisfactory answers to the problems it causes to its members, the ultimate goal with this effort is therefore to feel at ease with their whole persona.

We have noted that, for the Tsachila, being human is not a prop-erty of a particular species. Just like in other Amerindian animist societies, it is a 'relative position', given that any other being 'can become human when it is perceived as a congener, as a member of the species' (Taylor 2006: 71). As suggested by Praet (2013), this would appear to be a conception of humanity that forces humans to strive constantly to continue being human.

In Tsachila cosmology and mythology, in their conception of illness and in their ritual, the body is not sufficient for indicating human identity or social identity. The body is not marked out for the benefit of human Tsachila but for non-human ones (in the *Patso kika* ritual) or for non-Tsachila (in the ethnic clothing). Body marking is not purely aesthetic or a constituent part of a person in constant formation – as also pointed out by Erikson (1996), referring to the Matis of Amazonia. It is circumstantial but recurrent, and therefore ritualised. It could be an attempt to update an ancient categorisation system, or a local variant of a body-marking practice that is present in other parts of the region. In the case being studied, painting markers of humanity on the body in daily social life and in ritual helps to define and reinforce the group, and shows us that the ontological continuity between humans and non-humans is an uncomfortable initial premise that these societies have to struggle with in order to survive.

Montserrat Ventura i Oller received her PhD in social anthropology and ethnology at the École des Hautes Études en Sciences Sociales (Paris, 2000) under the supervision of Philippe Descola. Since 1991 she has carried out research with the Tsachila people from Ecuador on ethnic identity, person, human, individual and society, history, myth, nature–culture relations and shamanism. She is full professor at the Universitat Autònoma de Barcelona where, since 2002, she has led research projects on social systems of classification in the frame of the AHCISP Research Group. Her primary publications include *Identité, cosmologie et chamanisme des Tsachila de l'Équateur* (L'Harmattan, 2009), translated into Spanish as *En el Cruce de Caminos: Identidad, Cosmología y Chamanismo Tsachila.* (FLACSO / Abya-Yala / IFEA, Quito, 2012).

Notes

1. The ethnographic data come from ethnographic fieldwork conducted with the Tsachila people over several years betweeen 1991 and 2016, especially in the commune of Cóngoma and, to a lesser extent, in Naranjos and Chigüilpe. I would like to give my sincere thanks to a large number of Tsachila men and women for their collaboration at every stage of this research work. I would also like to thank the HUMANT project (HAR2013-40445-P) of the UAB's AHCISP research group for its support.
2. C.S. Dickinson: personal communication.

3. It is the most common variety nowadays, found widely in Ecuador, although it comes originally from Africa.

References

Carlos Ríos, E. 2015. 'La circulación entre mundos en la tradición oral y ritual y las categorías del pensamiento quechua en Hanansaya Ccullana Ch'isikata (Cusco, Perú)'. PhD dissertation. Barcelona: Universitat Autònoma de Barcelona.

Chaumeil, J.-P. 1983. *Voir, Savoir, Pouvoir: Le Chamanisme Chez les Yagua du Nord-Est Péruvien*. Paris: Éditions de l'École des Hautes Études en Sciences Sociales.

Déléage, P. 2007. 'Les répertoires graphiques amazoniens', *Journal de la Société des Américanistes* 93(1): 97–126.

Descola, Ph. 1986. *La Nature Domestique: Symbolisme et Praxis dans l'Ecologie des Achuar*. París: Maison des Sciences de l'Homme.

———. 2005. *Par-delà Nature et Culture*. Paris: Gallimard.

Erikson, Ph. 1996. *La griffe des aïeux: Marquage du corps et démarquages ethniques chez les Matis d'Amazonie*. Paris: Peeters/SELAF.

Foster, G.M. 1980. 'Relaciones entre la medicina popular española y latinoamericana', in M. Kenny and J.M. de Miguel (eds), *La Antropología Médica en España*. Barcelona: Anagrama, pp. 123–47.

Galinier, J. 1997. *La Moitié du Monde: Le Corps et le Cosmos dans le Rituel des Indiens Otomi*. Paris: PUF.

Gutiérrez Estévez, M. 2010. 'Dualismo y mestizaje en la identidad de los mayas del Yucatán', in M. Ventura (ed.), *Fronteras y Mestizajes: Sistemas de Clasificación Social en Europa, América y África*. Bellaterra: Universitat Autònoma de Barcelona, pp. 115–27.

Kroeger, A., and F. Barbira-Freedmann. 1992. *La lucha por la Salud en el Alto Amazonas y en los Andes*. Quito: Abya-Yala.

Martínez González, R. 2010. 'La Animalidad Compartida: el Nahualismo a la Luz del Animismo', *Revista Española de Antropología Americana* 40(2): 256–63.

Pitarch, P. 2011. 'Los Dos Cuerpos Mayas: Esbozo de una Antropología Elemental Indígena', *Estudios de Cultura Maya* 37: 149–78.

Platt, T. 2001. 'El feto agresivo: Parto, formación de la persona y mito-historia en los Andes', *Anuario de Estudios Americanos* 58(2): 633–78.

———. 2009. 'From the Island's Point of View: Warfare and Transformation in an Andean Vertical Archipelago', *Journal de la Société des Américanistes* 95(2): 33–70.

Praet, I. 2009a. 'Shamanism and Ritual in South America: An Inquiry into Amerindian Shape-Shifting', *Journal of the Royal Anthropological Institute* 15: 737–54.

———. 2009b. 'Catastrophes and Weddings: Chachi Ritual as Metamorphosis', *Journal de la Société des Américanistes* 95(2): 71–89.

———. 2013. *Animism and the Question of Life*. London: Routledge.

Rivera Andía, J.J. 2005. 'Killing What You Love: An Andean Cattle Branding Ritual and the Dilemmas of Modernity', *Journal of Anthropological Research* 61(2): 129–56.

Sánchez-Parga, J., and R. Pineda. 1985. 'Los Yachac de Illuman', *Cultura, Revista del Banco Central del Ecuador* 3(21): 511–81.

Seeger, A., R. da Matta, E.B. Viveiros de Castro. 1979. 'A construção da pessoa nas sociedades indígenas brasileiras', *Boletim do Museu Nacional* 32: 2–19.

Surrallés, A. 2003. *Au Coeur du Sens: Perception, Affectivité, Action chez les Candoshi*. Paris: CNRS.

Taylor, A.C. 2003. 'Les Masques de la Mémoire: Essai sur la Fonction des Peintures Corporelles Jivaro', *L'Homme* 165: 223–48.

———. 2006. 'Devenir Jivaro: Le Statut de l'Homicide Guerrier en Amazonie', *Cahiers d'Anthropologie Sociale* 2: 67–84.

Turner, T. 1995. 'Social Body and Embodied Subject: Bodiliness, Subjectivity, and Sociality among the Kayapo', *Cultural Anthropology* 10(2): 143–70.

Ventura i Oller, M. 2002. 'Verdades Relativas: Reflexiones en Torno a la Comprensión del Mundo. El Caso Tsachila del Ecuador', in J. Bestard Camps (ed.), *Identidades, relaciones y contextos*. Barcelona: Universitat de Barcelona, pp. 115–28.

———. 2003. 'Schamanische Austauschbeziehungen und Identität: Das Netzwerk der Colorados', in D. Schweitzer de Palacios and B. Wörrle (eds), *Heiler Zwischen den Welten: Transkulturelle Austauschprozesse im Schamanismus Ecuadors*. Marburg: Curupira, pp. 73–95.

———. 2006. 'El cuerpo, Marcador de la Condición Humana: El Caso Tsachila del Ecuador', in B. Muñoz Gonzalez and J. López García (eds), *Cuerpo y Medicina: Textos y Contextos Culturales*. Cáceres: Cicon, pp. 257–68.

———. 2008. 'Relaciones Interespecies en las Tierras Bajas de América del Sur', in V. Stolcke and A. Coello (eds), *Identidades Ambivalentes en América Latina (Siglos XVI–XXI)*. Barcelona: Bellaterra, pp. 113–29.

———. 2009. *Identité, Cosmologie et Chamanisme Tsachila: À la Croisée des Chemins*. Paris: l'Harmattan.

———. 2011a. 'Is the Past Another Time? Ancient Objects in Tsachila Cosmology', in P. Fortis and I. Praet (eds), *The Archaeological Encounter: Anthropological Perspectives*. Fife, Scotland: University of St Andrews, pp. 56–79.

———. 2011b. 'Redes Chamánicas desde el Punto de Vista Tsachila', *Nuevo Mundo Mundos Nuevos*. Retrieved 28 March 2016 from http://nuevomundo.revues.org/61200.

———. 2012. 'Entendimiento Humano para una Humanidad Compartida'. 54th International Congress of Americanists. Vienna: University of Vienna.

Vidal, L. 1992. *Grafismo Indígena: Estudos de Antropologia estética*. São Paulo: Fapesp.

Vilaça, A. 2011. 'Dividuality in Amazonia: God, the Devil, and the Constitution of Personhood in Wari' Christianity', *Journal of the Royal Anthropological Institute* 17: 243–62.

Viveiros de Castro, E. 1996. 'Os pronomes cosmológicos e o perspectivismo ameríndio', *Mana* 2(2): 115–44.

4

Losing Part of Oneself

Channels of Communication between Humans and Non-humans

Francis Ferrié

The aim of this chapter, based on my ethnographical material relative to the cure of the terror illness – a Latin American pathology known as *susto* – is to show how the Bolivian foothill region of Apolo presents an Andean conception both of the ontology (perception of the human being) and of the shamanistic practices (from aetiology to therapy). If it deals with shamanism and representation of the being, it really focuses on the relation between human beings and non-humans, as the cure involves a knowledge of the non-human entities – where they live, what they eat, how to deal with them and feed them. This chapter intends to show that there is a local conception of porosity between humans and non-humans (entities and others species such as animal, vegetal, mineral). I argue that this conception is probably Andean too, which is why I rely on Andean bibliographical references within the text to make comparisons on the following parts: anthropology of the porosity of a human anatomy riddled with holes; a landscape inhabited by fearsome entities; the shamanic negotiations between humans and non-humans; and the eating habits of non-human entities. I conclude on the porosity of the communication channels going through all species.

Illness Caused by Non-human Entities

Ana, a small 9-year-old girl arrived with her father Raúl at the house of Alina the healer, where I stayed in 2009. They had walked for several hours from a small village in the Bolivian foothills to consult Alina because Ana had been sick for a few months. She was affected by a *susto*; she had lost her *ánimu*, an immaterial part of the human body that only a healer could return to her. Ana and her father came to see Alina in Apolo, the Quechua-speaking capital of the province of Franz Tamayo.[1]

The syndrome of losing an immaterial human part falls under a pathology commonly known in Latin America by the Spanish term *susto* (terror).[2] This illness, often described as a loss of the soul, is based on the representation that an individual is composed of a material body and of one or several souls that can become detached (Rubel 1964: 270; Métraux 2013).[3]

In the Andes, the term *alma* (soul) is used, which can be distinguished from '*ánimu*', an immaterial element that leaves the individual. The two terms '*alma*' and '*ánimu*' have Latin etymologies and refer to the ontological and the eschatological, but they juxtapose the autochthonous and Christian corpuses that only become clear in the light of the vernacular concept of *camac* (Taylor 1974). The semantic field of this Quechua concept refers to the following meanings: breath, life force, heart or nucleus receiving vital energy – an immaterial human part that lights up life, perceived elsewhere as a shadow, an air flow, a double, etc.[4]

Let us note already that these two vital principles are not prisoners of the body, where they are located in healthy humans, since they can escape. The loss of the soul (*alma*) leads to biological death whereas the loss of the *ánimu* causes illness (*susto*). These two parts of the human being therefore circulate inside and outside the body. But while the soul detaches itself from the body during biological death to set out for its eschatological destination, the *ánimu* can get lost and be found during existence. The *ánimu* is the essence of the human, the *alma* that of the dead person, as summarised by Xavier Ricard Lanata (2007: 88). In short, two stages, since the body stripped of its *ánimu* for a lengthy period leads the human being to die and become a soul.

The ethnography of a therapeutic treatment of a *susto* or loss of the *ánimu* invites us to reflect on the design of the body, on the relation between humans and non-humans and on the function of the healer (*curandero*). The diagnosis of the lethargic condition of their patient enables the specialist to determine the aetiology or cause of the illness, that is to say, to identify the non-human entity responsible, to enter into communication with them, to obtain the missing immaterial part and lastly to reintroduce the *ánimu* into the patient. This ritualised relation therefore involves a patient seized by an accountable non-human entity and a practitioner healer special-ised in diagnosis and retrocession; the latter coordinates a relation of intermediation or intercession between a human and non-human to re-establish the balance.

Ethnographic material from the Bolivian Andean foothills leads to comparisons with similar Andean cases and to an anthropological reflection on both illness and healing involving non-human enti-ties. While the multitude of terms used to qualify the practitioners and their activities must be indicated, this should not discourage comparative ambition.[5] What is of interest here is rather a relation between the human and the non-human, where an entity has stolen an immaterial part of a human: a state of imbalance that is solved by the intervention of a specialist who knows how to communicate with the non-human entity to re-establish the balance and look after their patient.

Ethnography of a Therapeutic Treatment of a *Susto* (Apolo, Bolivia)

Raúl took Ana, his 9-year-old daughter, to Apolo from Santa Catalina, which is a three-hour walk through the Andean foothill valleys. They were visiting Alina, a renowned healer (*curandera*) in the region of Apolo. This town, the former capital of the Apolobamba missions, is today the administrative and commercial centre of the province of Franz Tamayo, where Leco and peasants meet, scattered between eighty villages; they all speak both Quechua and Spanish, (Ferrié 2014).

Ana was pale looking and obviously sick. Alina invited the little girl and Raúl into her cabin dedicated to consultations at the back of the house. It was there, in this small room filled with pictures and objects pertaining to 'juxtaposed' beliefs, that the nocturnal rituals were taking place, which I attended for more than a year. The spatial and temporal limits characterise the healer's ritual activities: on the one hand, the house is located on the fringe of the town, and the cabin, at walking distance from the living space, nearby a manioc field. On the other hand, night-time is favourable for ritual activities because it is believed that non-human entities are the most receptive when people sleep.

Ana and her father brought a large bag of coca, which represented an advance payment of the offering for the ritual rather than a gift for Alina. The payment or *pago* is fundamental in the ritual relation between human and non-human. Alina of course organises it and benefits from it like all the adults who are invited to take part in the ritual, but the coca is ultimately for the entities. All of us will eat it to make the payment that assures ritual efficacy in the Lévi-Strauss sense of the term (1949).

The coca cannot be overlooked: its presence is central in daily life and in rituals. The use of the plant as a social and spiritual food could be qualified as a 'total social' plant, adapting the concept of Mauss. In Apolo, coca is essential to diagnose, to socialise with patients and to call the entities. Communication takes place through it: the coca is a connecting tool. In the fields, people do not speak when working, but they interact during their break, when they share the coca to chew. In the same manner, people always eat in silence, they only talk to each other afterwards, when chewing the coca; it loosens the tongue, in a different way to alcohol, and it is during this second digestive meal that guests exchange verbally. The coca chewed in the ritual is food: it performs payment from the humans to the non-humans, and is a preliminary communication, which helps to call and mobilise them.

During that afternoon, Raúl, Alina and I began to chew the coca (*acullico*). Alina read the tarot cards[6] (*naipes*) that she had laid out one by one on the table. She had to determine what type of terror Ana was suffering from, rather than which entity was accountable. It was clear that it was terror, but how had she contracted it? Who had seized her in terror? Or who had stolen her *ánimu*? The cards and the conversation with Ana's father were decisive in determining with certitude the origin of the pathogenic disorder. But the cards and remarks by Raúl revealed even more. Ana's mother had been gone for a long time to find a job in the big city of Santa Cruz, but she was not sending money anymore and was not even calling her family. The family situation was not very bright, and there was probably also a misfortune that had been provoked by the jealousy or envy of spiteful neighbours caused by the bad curses of a witch (*brujo*), since one person's healer is another person's witch.

Alina had found the ritual solution that would take place in several phases during the night. The first practice consisted of bathing both Ana and her father who had been exposed to the infection in order to free them from the curse. Rudy, Alina's grandson, aged seventeen, who generally assisted us, was in charge of boiling water on the hearth in the forge. Alina said to him: 'We must add more spines to the *contra-mesa*, there must be more porcupine spines in my room;

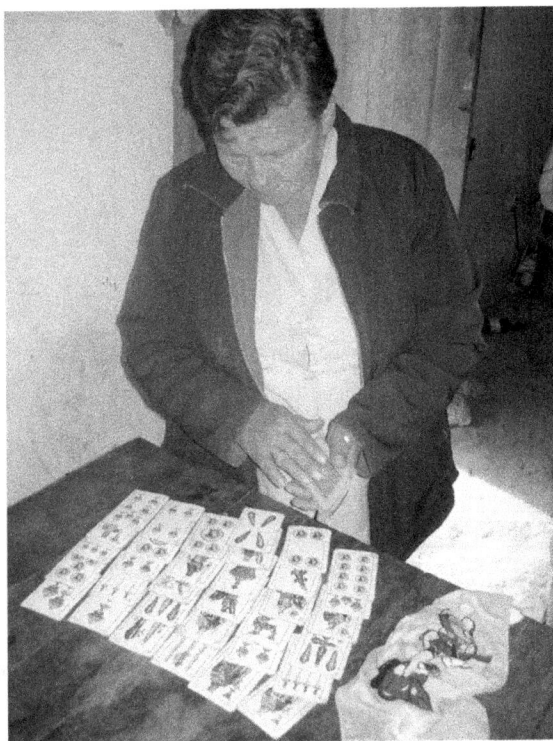

Illustration 4.1 Alina reads the cards (*naipes*). Photograph: F. Ferrié.

go and look. And we need a hen too, a black one. See if there is one and if not ask doña Blanca. Go on, hurry'.

There is an element of urgency before nightfall, as displayed above. Everything must be ready to begin to work and receive auxiliaries and messengers such as the *Ankaris*,[7] the *Pachamama*, the Divine Infant, the saints and the Virgin from whom Alina needs support to assure ritual efficacy.

Alina is part of the group of healers that do the good, not the evil, according to her. She tells us that the Divine Infant came to her in a dream and entered her little finger; she shows us that it is deformed and tells us that in fact she is not a witch, she does not touch 'the dark', implying witchery, but only practises white magic. However, the limits are never clearly defined.

Night fell, the water boiled, and Alina threw the ingredients together in the pot: the spines, dried sea stars, shells and walnuts for the *contra-mesa* – a ritual table to counter the bad spell – that had been bought mixed together at a shop in the town.

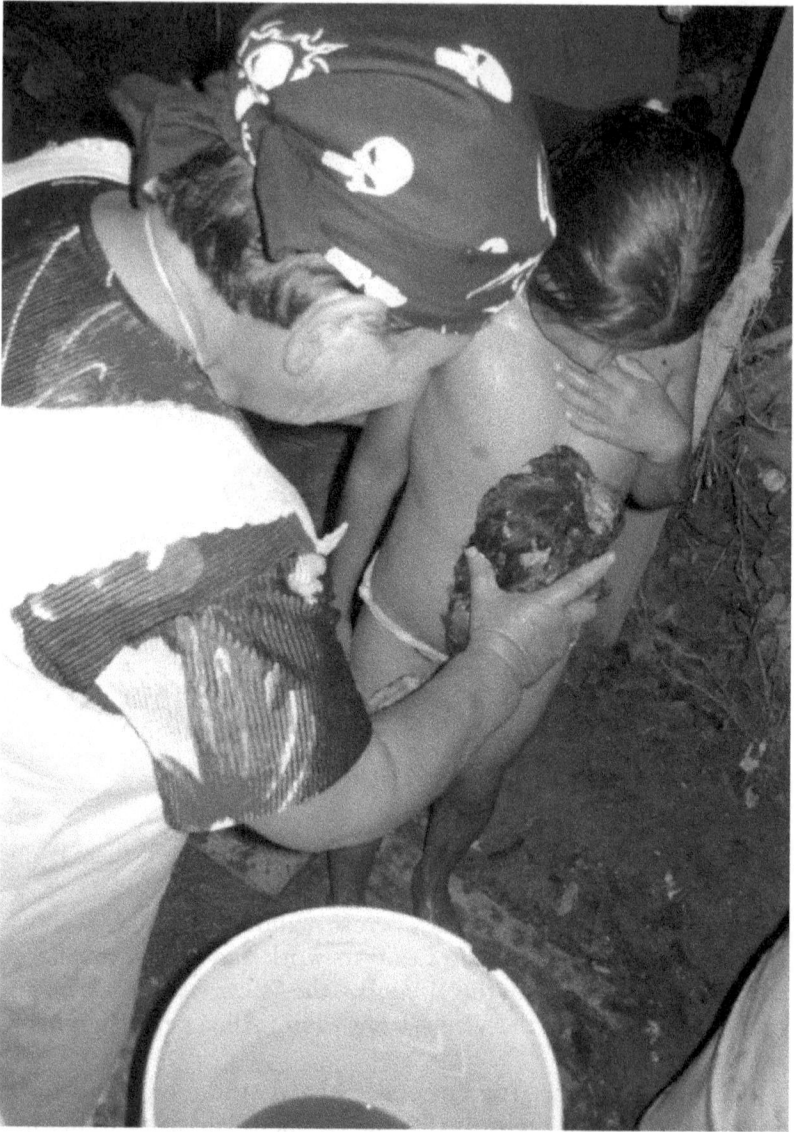

Illustration 4.2 Psycho-pump hen. Photograph: F. Ferrié.

Ana and her father both undressed in order to have the pathogen washed from them. Alina recited prayers while scrubbing them: 'In the name of the Father, the Son and the Holy Spirit, let it leave!' Then, we prepared the second propitiatory bath with a white table or *mesa blanca* composed of flower petals, honey and a sparkling wine called *champagne*. Once they had been bathed or spattered with this sticky liquid, they could not rinse it off and had to leave it on throughout the night so that the protection would penetrate and the change of fortune (*cambio de suerte*) would take place. The first bath was to remove the bad – *contra-mesa* or ritual table to counter it – and the second propitiatory bath was to send the bad spell away.[8]

Then Ana was laid on a bed. Against her tiny trembling body, Alina placed a black hen with its legs tied after being splashed with alcohol (*ch'alla*).[9] The animal probably suffocated to death; however, Ana's father and I both thought that the disease had passed from the human body to that of the animal. By transferring the pathogenic agent from Ana's body to that of the psycho-pump animal, it killed the latter.

Rudy, Alina's grandson, was in charge of taking the lifeless hen to the river to throw its corpse into the current.[10] Then he was to retrace his steps along the same path, but his grandmother told him to walk backwards, so that the disease would stay in the river and he would not bring it back with him. The hen that contained the pathogenic element removed from Ana's body was not only a psycho-pump sponge, but it was also alimentary payment to the *Wak'a* of the river like the *mesas*, which are meal offerings.

Ana was beginning to heal. The next day she would leave home with a broad smile. While Ana was asleep recovering, her father, Alina and I, were talking, chewing coca, smoking and drinking. We exchanged the local news, the secrets of some spread by others having become the subject of provincial gossip. Like everywhere, the topics of gossip encompassed politics, marriage and its deceptions, filiation, migration and its returns, the economic wealth of some, the robberies suffered by others, and so on; precious information both for the healer and the ethnologist.

Ana's diagnosis had started in her village where illnesses are treated with plants. Since this treatment failed they sought out the knowledge of an expert. They went to Alina directly, and not the municipal hospital of Apolo that had been in operation for several years, because Western medicine is not competent in the case of *susto* (terror illness). The symptoms are anaemia and aboulia: a pathological lethargy common in the Andean foothills, from the Andes to the Amazon. What causes it? What is its aetiology? The terror is due to a non-human entity that has entered the body to steal an ontological part (*ánimu*). The absence of this element leaves the body alive, but it is a shell emptied of its energy, and hence the lethargy.

If we had to put together the typical portrait of the entities responsible for terror in the province of Apolo, at the top of the list would often appear *Chisimpaye* or *Condenado*. It is a deceased person, a 'victim' of a violent death or a poor funeral treatment. But in the case of Ana, it was *Wak'a*, the master of fish, who lives in the waterfalls where no one swims. It was *Wak'a* who nearly took Ana when the child tried to cross the river. According to some, *Wak'a* takes her name locally from the cow into which the entity transforms to draw people crossing the river into the current. Others believe that *Wak'a* is an evil figure who looks like a mermaid, capable of transformation, sometimes taking the appearance of a multi-coloured toad.[11] It is said that *Wak'a* hides in the water to trap passers-by and to drown them at the bottom: especially those who have not paid the 'offering debt' (Rösing 1994) before crossing. The homophony of *Wak'a*, master of the rivers, with *Huaca* – religious entity and place associated with Andean summits – leads me to formulate the hypothesis of an appropriation of the Andean divinity inscribed in the cosmographic foothill landscape; a hypothesis maintained by the multiple Andean migratory layers that flocked to the region before even the Incas (Ferrié 2014).

We had given a meal to the renowned predatory *Wak'a*. Alina could call Ana's *ánimu* by whistling in a *wisulu* – a small hard fruit shell serving as a whistle and a bag to keep the *ánimu* once it had returned – and she called: 'Come, little *ánimu*, *hamuy*, *hamuy* (come on!)'. There was a meeting and negotiation between the shaman and the *Wak'a*. The ritual invited the *Wak'a* entity to an offering meal against the retrocession of Ana's missing *ánimu*. Alina could then restore balance in the child's body by replacing her *ánimu*.

From a regional or emic point of view, humans have holes, openings *via* which entities can enter and leave. *Wak'a* enters the human body through the vagina or anus with the aim of taking, seizing the ontological part known as the *ánimu*, in the same way that the *Kharisiri*[12] works with human fat. Newborns with a soft fontanel that is perceived as a hole are all the more exposed to the interference of a pathogenic agent. These multiple openings render them fragile. That is why their mother never places them on the ground but carries them in the *aguayo* – a back-carrying cloth – where the baby (*wawa*) is swaddled until it can walk, because a non-human entity would have quickly seized them to get her sustenance.

It is not only non-human entities that can affect a human by entering one of their orifices, but the species are contagious between themselves when in contact with each other, including from a distance. We saw that, as a precautionary measure, Alina made Ana's father have a ritual bath, in case contagion of the terror had affected him. The idea of contagion between humans extends also from humans to plant and animal species. In this regard, a menstruating woman cannot collect coca leaves without withering them. In the same way that a poison can affect a body, it is thought that certain substances produced by a human body can affect other species.

Snake bites are a major cause of death during work in the fields and forest gardens, and ritual protection is always performed against their potential danger using tobacco and coca. This danger is expressed via a taboo linked to a belief in Apolo, the Yungas and where the Chané people live, that the odour of menstrual blood attracts venomous snakes (Villar 2011: 155); and that these even suck menstrual blood from a distance in the province of Inquisivi (Spedding 1992: 311).[13] This power to cause disease from a distance is essential to understand the methods of contagion, witchery, communication and healing.[14] There are other stories of contagion that can be understood in the recommendations made to children, such as that of never pointing at a rainbow because the *kitchi*, the entity that lives there, could putrefy the organ; or that of never walking with an empty stomach along the edges of marshy areas because the morning fog enters the body and affects it. Diseases linked to the bad winds (*wayra*) refer to the pathogenic circulation of flows and fluids that threaten the human body.

In the province of Apolo, a story is told, maintained by some to be true, that a man turned into a tiger by eating a tiger flower (*tigre tik'a*). He was found dead in his human form with bullets in his body shot by a farmer when this tiger-man was hunting cattle in his animal form. Thus, that a plant had the power to metamorphose a human into an animal is not overly astonishing. These stories translate a conception of circulation of substances, which affect human and non-human groups. These disturbances emerge from the competence of the specialist who knows how to assure the rebalance.

Anthropology of the Porosity of a Human Anatomy Riddled with Holes

Let us retain from the above ethnographic data two main ideas to open the anthropological discussion. Firstly, all the bodies of different species are considered as places of passage or of the transitory circulation of substances. The porosity of the body draws a world where limits are not well compartmentalised or well defined. It is for this reason that humans adopt daily strategies to prevent risks or imbalances (intrusion of an otherness, or loss of part of oneself). Thus, eating well by filling the belly closes the body hermetically before leaving the village. This preventative technique is echoed in the debt of the offering, which warns of preying entities, based on the principle of: 'If I feed them well, they will not take nourishment from me'; in other words, by feeding them we are at less risk of becoming their prey.[15] In this case, food takes on a preventative ritual dimension.

Holes, porosities, body punctures and empty body cavities provide a way for an intruder to enter and steal. It is at this moment that the healer, a specialist at rebalancing, intervenes. They identify, call the entities, obtain the immaterial part stolen from the patient and then assure it is reintroduced into the body (endorcism). This term, proposed by Antoinette Molinié, as opposed to exorcism, fits in Apolo like in the Yucay Valley (1979: 97), since the cure of Ana consisted of a healer seeking out her *ánimu*, and reintroducing it to her anaemic body, having whistled to it and enclosed it in a walnut shell. The cure in Apolo prescribes as well that the sick person must drink water or eat soil from the place where the entity committed the robbery. Reintroducing part of the place, once the Master of the Place (*dueño del lugar*) is calmed down ritually, forms part of the recovery.

Secondly, these transfers of substances between porous bodies help one to understand the daily precautions and the ritual activity linked to the concept of the healthy body: the being is not a monad; on the contrary, body and soul are separable, and hence the gap between biological and social existence. In fact, the adult body is full of life force or good health when it is well sealed. However, a *susto* can break the balance and cause sickness on account of the lack of this life force. The life force is not fully acquired at birth, but develops, like fat (*wira*)[16] with which it is associated. Fat is healthy, an aesthetic criterion that contributes to beauty, while a thin person is perceived as sick or in poor health, emptied of their fat like a victim of the *Kharisiri*.[17] Ana, affected by the terror of *Wak'a*, was emptied of an immaterial part in a different way. But the comparison between fat and *ánimu* is relevant. The loss of one's *ánimu* provokes anaemia, which is perceived as a loss of fat. Furthermore, fat is precisely one of the substances offered to the entities in the ritual tables; fat from llama or pork efficiently feed non-human entities.

Ritual activity participates in maintaining vitality and fat in the body: the first haircut or *rutuchi* is a milestone, a rite of passage introducing the child to the social world. The second birth is when a name is given, where bonds of kinship link the child to a godfather or godmother. After an individual has passed away, they gradually dwindle: they diminish, waning like an ember that burns away until it becomes ash, and not abruptly like electricity when it is cut off.

It is in this way that the precautions taken for a child who is not yet of walking age, and who is swaddled in the *aguayo* (cloth in which babies are carried until they can walk) should be understood; the mother never puts them on the ground out of fear that the preying entities, including the *Pachamama*, might seize their tiny *ánimu*. This refers to the idea of babies or *wawas* being weaker than adults. Moreover, their fontanel, the soft part of the skull, is locally said to be an opening that exposes them to the predation of entities. It is deemed that the fontanel closes with words. The verb is at the beginning of social existence. The individual grows stronger with language acquisition.

Filling up openings or filling the body is a permanently sought strategy that exists to maintain and keep the life force, the fat. In the event of biological death, the stock gradually diminishes. During life, famished entities can always seize it from us. Education consists of turning a fragile and sickly being into a well-filled and well-closed being.

Considering that in the Andean foothills, and in the Andes, the stealing of an immaterial part by a non-human entity leaves the human body bloodless without, however, leading to its biological death, the porosity between humans and non-humans could be quite a heuristic comparative field. The intrusion of pathogenic foreign bodies and the separation of an immaterial part followed by its reincorporation represent the two nosological categories of both the Amazon (Chaumeil 1995: 64) and the Andes. The practitioner removes the pathogen or replaces the missing part. He knows how to inoculate and to heal illnesses, removing them from the sick body, even from a distance. An immaterial part has been stolen; he will seek it out or make it come. A non-human is chosen by the specialist's diagnosis; a negotiation takes place and the treatment re-establishes the balance between the accountable entity and the patient.

An anthropological study of porosity between humans and non-humans establishes a double cartography: that of the openings of the human body through which pathogenic intruders enter and leave, and that of the landscape where the harmful non-human entities are located. Both cartographies could open a field of belief and ritual practice comparisons, from negotiation to rebalance, between human and non-human entities.

A Landscape Inhabited by Fearsome Entities

This anthropological study of porosity sets forth an anatomy of the human body riddled with openings and holes: all the orifices (from the fontanel to the anus), with a geography of the pathogenic places, where humans are exposed to the risk of preying non-humans. This anthropology of porosity follows or emerges from that of 'fear' (Fernández Juárez 2008) caused by entities that populate the vivified landscape (Spedding 1992) of the Andes up to Chaco (Villar 2011). Numerous ethnographic summaries describe a landscape populated by disease-causing non-human pathogenic entities. The places of terror refer to the chthonian, to deep forests, darkness and the past. They are liminal or wild spots: caves, waterfalls and rivers; inextricable places, cemeteries and ruins on the edge of inhabited areas.

In the Yucay Valley, the *Soq'a Machu* 'evil and pathogenic force' belonging to the category of ancestral entities, appears in both liminal places and times (Molinié 1979: 85–89). *Apu*, the Andean entities from the summits of Ausangate, are sometimes auxiliaries of the shaman (Ricard Lanata 2007: 187) and sometimes pathogenic sources of the aetiology of terror (ibid: 177; Abeledo 2014: 308). Likewise, in the case of the Kallawaya from Kaata, neighbours of Apolo, the mountains were perceived as 'bodies' of the *Apus*: an anatomical map on which human geography was inscribed (Bastien 1996: 73–86).[18] In the Yungas foothills neighbouring Apolo, Alison Spedding recounts the story of a tiger associated with the *condenado* (violent death) called *anchachi*[19] (ancestor), whose sparkling eyes terrorised (*susto*) his victims at night (1992: 315). The charms of the mermaid (*mboirusu*), mistress of the waters from the Bermejo river, which Diego Villar mentions in the case of the Chané people of Chaco (Villar 2006: 139; 2011: 172), would come as no surprise to the inhabitants of the Apolo foothills who would think of *Wak'a* itself, who had instilled terror in Ana earlier.

Specialists at Negotiations between Humans and Non-humans

Indigenous aetiologies refer to the vivified landscape and time. In the Andes, illnesses that do not have a natural origin are caused by localised entities. Xavier Ricard Lanata draws up the nosological table of Ausangate (2007: 175). It matches, like in Apolo, places where the non-human entities reside and thus where diseases are contracted. The shaman practitioner has knowledge of the world of non-humans – knows their residences, their eating habits, their means of attack. Those are indices leading to the healer's diagnosis.

Andean shamans are the intermediaries who can see and identify the non-humans responsible for pathologies. They have the power to negotiate with the pathogenic entities, thanks to the help of auxiliary entities that they call upon. They know how to make them come or to seek them out, to cajole them or to fight them to recover the missing part. Knowledge of the channels of circulation and the means of communication confers to shamans the power to bring about rebalance.

In both the Andes and the foothills, the symptoms and information on the patient intersect with the shamanic knowledge of the universe where the non-humans 'live'. The landscape crossed by the patient directs the identification of the pathogenic entities: around Apolo, the crossing of a river where *Wak'a* resides, while the way back home goes through a forest at dusk or near a cemetery, will blame a bad wind (*wayra*) caused by the dead (*almas*); in the Andes, following the place crossed by the sick patient, it could be ancestors (*machu* or *Apu*), lightning (*qhaqya*) or other pathogenic entities (mermaids, *kukuchi*, *saqra*) or other diabolical entities.

Shamans therefore know how to surround themselves, to call the auxiliary entities for assistance, to call them and to welcome them. They have the power of 'injunction', to use Xavier Ricard Lanata's term (2004); that is, to enjoin the entities to help them to heal the patient. Despite the local variations, two categories can be distinguished: the first is aimed at meeting the non-human, by receiving it in the shaman's body (possession, ventriloquism), or through trips or dreams, possibly resorting to the use of psychotropic substances (tobacco, coca, ayahuasca, etc.); the second consists of ritual practices of interaction (offerings of ritual tables, songs, incantation). The tables of ritual offerings (*mesas*) involving sacrificed animals are a recurrent trait of the Andean negotiation between groups.

The Eating Habits of Non-humans

Diseases caused by non-human entities respond to therapeutic rituals that mobilise correspondences within indigenous classifying systems. The cures are based on aetiology by locally mobilising botanical, animal, mineral and sound pharmacopoeia. The therapeutic treatments involve actions such as washing, sucking, rubbing, smoking, incensing, blowing, reciting, chanting or singing, and by removing the pathogen (exorcism) or reintroducing the missing part (endorcism) through the orifices of the human body.

The Andean practice nourishes the starving entities with suitable food: it fills the voids, it fills up the holes, it decants. The Andean plan consists of satisfying the hunger of an entity, paying it in food, like in the relation of payment through sacrifice to the entity *Wak'a* of Apolo to recover Ana's *ánimu*. There is a game of taxonomic correspondence between aetiology and therapeutic cure. The Andean typology of the ritual tables (*mesas*) corresponds to the entities and pathologies: they are etiological responses. A ritual table is an offering or *despacho* sent to the entity. It is seasoned with libations on the packets of offerings, accompanied by invocations, prayers and chanted incantations. The smoke that rises from the burning of the ritual table is the nutritional channel of the entities.

The ritual counter-table (*contra-mesa*) of Apolo corresponds to the Aymaran black table (*mesa negra*) of Gerardo Fernández Juárez (1997a: 188). It is through their intermediary that the bad is washed away, by nourishing the evil and greedy entities with hard, dry, sugar-free ingredients with a dominant black colour – starfish, walnuts, plant or porcupine spines, *ñandú* feathers (*suri*), copal, pure sugar cane alcohol – but not sweet wine from grapes. The white ritual table that Alina calls locally the flowering[20] table or *florecimiento* corresponds to the *mesa blanca* (*mesa gloria* or *de salud*) of the Aymaran world (Fernández Juárez 1997a: 188), which are tables offered for those who have been seized by terror: in this case, everything is white, perfumed and sweet.

The complex of offerings of the southern Andes goes from black to white, between 'repugnance and seduction' to use the terms of Fernández Juárez (1997b). The practices of the Apolo foothills are related to this complex via the intermediary of the Kallawaya,[21] whose medical practices present affinities with ethnic groups of the southern Andes (Fernández Juárez 1997b: 174). In fact, the nosological, etiological and taxonomical categories of the pharmacopeia present equivalences. Between *apoleña* and Kallawaya pharmacopeia there are numerous botanical cases,[22] and the very similar[23] botanical taxonomical criteria are echoed in the southern Andes.

The entities are invited to an offering meal. It is a meal prepared by humans for non-humans. The 'chef' of this banquet is the practitioner who knows their eating habits. The principle is to force-feed

Illustration 4.3 Llama fat (*wira*) and *k'intu* of coca on a *mesa*. Photograph: F. Ferrié.

the entities. Eating, drinking and chewing coca is done in excess: 'force-feeding, force-drinking, force-chewing', to use the expression forged by Catherine Allen (1982), applied to the ritual context. The *Pachamama* prefers llama foetuses (*untu*); chthonian entities from the mines and the underworld love pork foetuses. Alina from Apolo knows this and explains it by the characteristics of the animal: the snout of the pig sniffs in the earth it turns over while the llama grazes the surface. This meal is in fact an 'offering debt'[24] according to the expression by Ina Rösing (1994).

The Porous Communication Channels

In the Andes and in Apolo, substances run through porous channel of communications. The libation of alcohol (*ch'alla*) is a ritual 'path' of the offering (Abercrombie 2006: 439). Thierry Saignes has shown the place of libations of alcohol in the Andes by linking alcoholic beverages to corporal[25] and cosmological representations (Saignes 1993: 69), unifying the living, the gods and the dead (ibid.: 62). Cigarette smoke 'attracts the spirits' (Bernand 1985: 158) in the same way that coca leaves chewed by humans protect the latter and attract non-human entities.[26]

The shaman is specialised in the channels of communication through which substances circulate. Therefore, the emic mode of circulation must be established as well as the correspondence between substances (blood, sperm, sugar cane alcohol or corn beer, coca, fat, tobacco, incense) that connect humans and non-humans. For instance, of a *susto* in Apolo, one might say like in the Equatorial Andes, that the weak blood 'terrorised' has turned like milk (Bernand 1985: 158). Others might say like in the southern Andes, that the urine of a healthy person can cure the *susto* caused by bad winds (Lestage 1999: 159).

Blood, fat and coca are the favourite foods of the non-human entities around Apolo (Ferrié 2015). The substances transformed with a ritual intention in diverse states (solid, liquid and gas) are first of all connectors that guarantee communication between humans and non-humans; secondly, they are foods that help to satisfy, please and calm preying non-humans. In addition, shaman healers carefully observe how the ritual tables burn, and according to the cremation, decide about the ritual performance. A full cremation is a sign that it has been well received: a table that has gone up in smoke has satiated the entity.

The consumption patterns of non-humans follow the communication channels controlled by the specialist. The shaman opens and closes access routes between the two collectives. In his therapeutic rituals, he operates an alchemical emission of transformed substances (passing from solid to liquid or gaseous). He also operates through sounds (prayers, incantations) in order to appease the pathogenic entities that inoculate the disease by penetrating into the human body or stealing an immaterial part of it (in the case of susto). The shaman performs an exorcism when the pathogen has to be extracted, and an endorcism when the missing part has to be reintroduced. In other words, the practitioner knows the substances (liquid, solid, gas, sound) that ensure communication with non-humans – their eating habits, the substances they love, drink and take nourishment from. Feeding properly, non-humans avoid their pathogenic human predation. To some extent, the shaman could be compared to a cook, or indeed to a chef, as the skilful shamanistic art mainly deals with mastering substance circulation.

Francis Ferrié is doctor in anthropology and researcher at EREA (Education and Research Center on Amerindian Ethnology), part of the Laboratory of Comparative Ethnology and Sociology (in the University of Paris Ouest Nanterre La Défense), at the Centre for Amerindian, Latin American and Caribbean Studies, Saint Andrews University, and at the Centro de Investigaciones Históricas y Antropológicas (CIHA, Santa Cruz, Bolivia).

Notes

1. The people from the Apolo province are all Quechua speakers and share as many bonds of kinship as a shared culture, but have been divided and in conflict since the resurgence in 1997 of an indigenous group, Leco (Ferrié 2014).
2. Classified by the ethno-doctor Rubel (1964) as a folk pathology or 'folk illness', the syndrome appears from Mesoamerica to South America: from Texas to Guatemala, passing by Chiapas and as far as the Paraguayan Chaco, passing by the Andes and the Amazon.
3. Alfred Métraux mentions it in the 1940s as being the 'result of the loss of the soul, which got lost or was stolen by a spirit or a goblin [a dwarf entity]' (2013: 118). It is mentioned in so many contemporary ethnographies that it would be difficult to list them all. For the lowlands bordering Apolo, see Evert Thomas et al. (2009).
4. For a summary of the variable Andean concepts, we will refer to the works of Charlier Zeinedinne (2011: 161–67), Ricard Lanata (2007: 77–90) and La Riva González (2005).
5. The healer (*curandero*) is pejoratively called *brujo* (witch). It depends on the point of view. In Apolo, there is a binary classifying distinction: some are involved in good, others in evil, despite the reputations of certain specialists. In other regions, the variety of practitioners, names and institutionalised qualifications go beyond the binary distinction (for the Andes, see for example, Virginie de Véricourt 2000: 119–26; Xavier Ricard Lanata 2007: 143ff.).
6. Like the reading of the coca leaves, that of the tarot cards is widespread in the Andes. In Bombori, Virginie de Véricourt refers to it alongside those of animal entrails and corn grains (2000: 127).
7. These are the messengers of the *apus*, entities of the summits.
8. 'The first bath is to get rid of the bad, and the second is to bring well-being': translation of '*el primer baño era para retirar el mal, y el segundo para aportar el bienestar*', explained to me by Alina in 2009.
9. Andean's ritual libation.
10. The psycho-pump hen thrown into the river is a shamanic practice of extirpation that can be related to the Kallaways; for example, the ritual of *llaki wijch'una*, which consists of removing the sadness of the mourning

by transferring it to the animal and thus throwing the sadness into the river (Rösing 2008: 411).

11. According to the anthropologist Montaño Aragón, in the 1980s, the *Wak'a* was the 'genie of Evil' of the Leco natives of the region (1989: 71).

12. This widespread and renowned Andean entity is known for attacking its victims by emptying them of their fat. It is known by different names (Kapsoli 1991; Molinié 1997; Canessa 2000; Fernández Juárez 2006; Charlier Zeinedinne 2011).

13. 'The viper is attracted by the woman with her menstruation and it sucks our blood, although from a distance' (Spedding 1992: 311).

14. This power of communication also helps to reach humans who are far away in space: the husband who has abandoned his wife can be called, during a ritual, through a piece of clothing that he has worn, so that he returns. Likewise, the young man working with the United Nations in Afghanistan who had injured his leg while fighting was healed from a distance, on his parents' request.

15. Regarding the concept of a body full like a bag, see Charlier Zeineddine (2013: 3).

16. In Quechua, *wira* and *untu* denote fat, but when we refer to human fat which the Kharisiri or Pishtaco love and extract from human bodies, we will use *wira*, while *untu* is the animal fat offered to the non-human entities in the ritual tables (Ferrié 2015). However, in 1571, *untu* denoted Indian fat sent to Spain as a medicine (Cristóbal de Molina, in Rivera Andía 2006: 36).

17. The figure of the fat-sucker is probably taken from sixteenth-century Spanish folklore, where a *sacamanteca* is mentioned (Cristóbal de Molina, in Rivera Andía 2006: 36), but its Andean use, permanence and contemporary popularity reveal an adaptation.

18. The gateway places where the offering meals are practised are devoted to circulation between the humans and the mountains, which have both a subjectivity and a family relative. In the case of the Kallawaya people and in Apolo, the worlds are permeable, contiguous, governed by a logic of circulation – an Andean concept that is suitable as a metaphor for the hydraulic system (Bastien 1985, 1996; Randall 1993).

19. See Fernández Juárez (2008) regarding the Andean entity *anchanchu* of the highlands.

20. Ingredients of the ritual table, paraphernalia or eating habits of the entities: a lichen from the altiplano (*Wira q'uwa*), which serves as a mat or base of the *mesas* is absent in the *mesa gloria* and is replaced by petals of white flowers. Above this, the following are placed: tiny lead figurines (*chiwchis*); small pieces of sculpted clay (*misterios*) representing both the wishes and the entities; silver- and gold-plated paper (*q'uri t'ant'a*); white wool; incense; llama fat (*wira*); sweet food; honey; *k'intus* of coca, which are votive pair groups of three leaves, placed with the same side facing down and in a fan shape.

21. The immediate neighbours living at a higher altitude than the people in Apolo are the Kallawaya, known for their renowned itinerant doctors of the Andes described by Girault (1984). Their herbalist knowledge was classified as an intangible cultural heritage by UNESCO in 2009.
22. There are twelve similarities of cases of botanical genres – Chillca, Wira wira, Khusmayu, Wairuru, Khari khari, Tarqu, Amakari, Paikko, Maticu, Chunta, Mokko mokko, Kuti kuti – according to a cross-checking of my ethnographic summaries gathered in a manual of medicinal plants from Apolo and the ethnobotanical summaries of Louis Girault (1984: 70–95).
23. Anthropomorphic and vegetal groups: gender, male/female (*orkkho/ china*); age, ancestor (*machu*); size: small/big (*chiñi/jatun*); anatomical attributes: nails (*uña*), phallus (*peskke*); plant: spikey (*kichka*), pepper (*uchu*), flower (*tik'a*), fruit (*ruru*), palm tree (*chunta*); landscape: plain/ forest (*pampa/sacha*); gustatory: sickly/sweet smell; colour (black/ white/red).
24. The underlying idea is an exchange between humans and non-humans. The human offerings are made in return for the propitiatory action of the non-humans. An unpaid or badly paid offering must be repaired.
25. In Apolo, sugar cane alcohol takes the place of unfermented corn beer. The eau-de-vie of Apolo presents the idea associated with *chicha* in the southern Andes: it increases virility by increasing sperm and 'adds to the sperm, menstrual blood and maternal milk triad since it can replace these and even produce them' (Lestage 1999: 163).
26. Tobacco and coca facilitate divination reading and participate in thera-peutic healing. Tobacco kills the 'bad winds' in the Andes (Bernand 1985: 158) and in Apolo, and coca is omnipresent in healings. It is impor-tant to note the exception of the Quechua area of the Andes in the north of Peru, where coca is replaced by the San Pedro cactus (Juan Javier Rivera Andía, pers. comm.).

References

Abeledo, S. 2014. 'Pastores de los Andes Meridionales: Sistemas Tradicionales de Intercambio y sus Transformaciones en Santa Rosa de los Pastos Grandes (Los Andes, Salta)'. PhD dissertation. Buenos Aires: Universidad de Buenos Aires.

Abercrombie, T. 2006. *Caminos de la Memoria y del Poder: Etnografía e Historia de una Comunidad Andina*. La Paz: IFEA.

Allen, C. 1982. 'Body and Soul in Quechua Thought', *Journal of Latin American Lore* 8(2): 179–95.

Bastien, J. 1985. 'Qollahuaya-Andean Body Concepts: A Topographical-Hydraulic Model of Physiology', *American Anthropologist* 87(3): 595–611.

———. 1996. *La montaña del Cóndor: Metáfora y Ritual en un Ayllu Andino*. La Paz: HISBOL.

Bernand, C. 1985. *La Solitude des Renaissants: Malheur et Sorcellerie dans les Andes*. Paris: Presses de la Renaissance.

Canessa, A. 2000. 'Fear and Loathing on the Kharisiri Trail', *Journal of the Royal Anthropological Institute* 6: 705–20.

Charlier Zeinedinne, L. 2011. 'L'Homme-Proie, Prédation, Agentivité et Conflictualité dans les Andes Boliviennes'. PhD dissertation. Paris: EHESS.

———. 2013. 'Manger Pour ne pas Être Mangé', *Anthropology of Food* S8. Retrieved 30 March 2016 from http://aof.revues.org/7371.

Chaumeil, J.-P. 1995. 'Du Projectile au Virus: Un Art Chamanique de l'Agression Pathogène en Amazonie', *Études Mongoles et Sibériennes* 26: 63–82.

Fernández Juárez, G. 1997a. *Testimonio Kallawaya Medicina y Ritual en los Andes de Bolivia*. Quito: Abya Yala.

———. 1997b. *Entre la Repugnancia y la Seducción, Ofrendas Complejas en los Andes del Sur*. Cuzco: Centro de Estudios Regionales Andinos Bartolomé de Las Casas.

———. 2006. 'Kharisiri de Agosto en el Altiplano Aymara', *Chungara* 38(1): 51–56.

———. 2008. 'Terrores de Agosto: la Fascinación del Anchanchu en el Altiplano Aymara de Bolivia', in *Antropologías del Miedo, Vampiros, Sacamantecas, Locos, Enterrados Vivos y Otras Pesadillas de la Razón*. Madrid: Calambur, pp. 119–44.

Ferrié, F. 2014. 'Renaissance des Leco Perdus: Ethnohistoire du Piémont Bolivien d'Apolobamba à Larecaja'. PhD dissertation. Paris: Université Paris Ouest La Défense.

———. 2015. 'A Diet of Fat Connecting Humans and Nonhumans (in the Bolivian Foothills between the Andes and Amazonia)', *Tipití: Journal of the Society for the Anthropology of Lowland South America* 13: 105–19. Retrieved from http://digitalcommons.trinity.edu/tipiti/vol13/iss2/8.

Girault, L. 1984. *Kallawaya: Guérisseurs Itinérants des Andes. Recherches sur les Pratiques Médicinales et Magiques*. Paris: ORSTOM.Kapsoli, W. 1991. 'Los Pishtacos: Degolladores Degollados', *Bulletin de l'IFEA* 20: 61–77.

La Riva González, P. 2005. 'Las reprsentaciones del animu en los Andes sur peruano', *Revista Andina* 41(2).

Lestage, F. 1999. *Naissance et Petite Enfance dans les Andes Péruviennes: Pratiques, Rites, Représentations*. Paris: L'Harmattan.

Lévi-Strauss, C. 1949. 'L'Efficacité Symbolique', *Revue de l'Histoire des Religions* 135: 5–27.

Métraux, A. 2013. *Écrits d'Amazonie, Cosmologies, Rituels, Guerres et Chamanisme*. Paris: CNRS.

Molinié, A. 1979. 'Cure Magique dans la Vallée Sacrée du Cuzco', *Journal de la Société des Américanistes* 66: 85–98.

——. 1997, 'El Pishtaco, cazador de sebo trasaltlantico', *Sieteculebras* 11: 15–23.

Montaño Aragón, M. 1989. *Guía Etnográfica Lingüística de Bolivia II*. La Paz: Don Bosco.

Randall, R. 1993. 'Los Dos Vasos: Cosmovisión y Política de la Embriaguez desde el Inkanato hasta la Colonia', in T. Saignes (ed.), *Borrachera y Memoria: Experiencia de lo Sagrado en los Andes*. La Paz: HISBOL/ IFEA, pp. 73–111.

Ricard Lanata, X. 2004. *Alfred Métraux et le Chamanisme*. Geneva: Institut Universitaire d'Etudes et de Développement.

——. 2007. *Ladrones de Sombra: El Universo Religioso de los Pastores del Ausangate*. Lima: IFEA.

Rivera Andía, J.J. 2006. 'Mitología en los Andes Contemporáneos: Un Panorama General', in A. Ortiz Rescaniere (ed.), *Mitologías amerindias*. Madrid: Trotta, pp. 129–76.

Rösing, I. 1994. 'La Deuda de Ofrenda: un concepto central de la religión andina', *Revista Andina* 23: 191–216.

——. 2008. *Defensa y Perdición: la Curación Negra: Rituales Nocturnos de Curación en los Andes Bolivianos*. Madrid: Iberoamericana.

Rubel, A. 1964. 'The Epidemiology of a Folk Illness: *Susto* in Hispanic America', *Ethnology* 3(3): 268–83.

Saignes, T. 1993. 'Borracheras Andinas: ¿Por Qué los Indios Ebrios Hablan en Español?', in T. Saignes (ed.), *Borrachera y Memoria: La Experiencia de lo Sagrado en los Andes*. La Paz: HISBOL/IFEA, pp. 43–72.

Spedding, A. 1992. 'Almas, Anchancus y Alaridos en la Noche: el Paisaje Vivificado de un Valle Yungueño', in S. Arze et al. (eds), *Etnicidad, Economía y Simbolismo en los Andes: II Congreso Internacional de Etnohistoria*. Coroico: HISBOL/IFEA/SBH/ ASUR, pp. 299–330.

Taylor, G. 1974. 'Camay, Camac et Camasa dans le Manuscrit Huarochiri', *Journal de la Société des Américanistes* 63: 231–44.

Thomas, E., et al. 2009. 'Susto Etiology and Treatment According to Bolivian Trinitario People: A "Masters of the Animal Species" Phenomenon', *Medical Anthropology Quarterly* 23(3): 298–319.

Vericourt de, V. 2000. 'Les Serviteurs de la "Gloire": une expression christianisée de l'élection chamanique dans les Andes Boliviennes', in D. Aigle, B. Brac de la Perriére and J.-P. Chaumeil (eds), *La Politique des Esprits: Chamanismes et Religions Universalistes*. Nanterre: Société d'Ethnologie.

Villar, D. 2006. 'La Religión Chané'. PhD dissertation. Buenos Aires: Université de Buenos Aires.

——. 2011. 'La Religión del Monte entre los Chané', *Revista del Centro de Estudios Antropológicos* 46(1): 151–202.

Part II

Cohabitation and Sharing

5

The Inkas Still Exist in the Ucayali Valley

What We Can Learn from Songs

Bernd Brabec de Mori

Introduction

I do not practise as a healer these days because I am still in the process of 'dieting', which I have been into for close to two years now. After concluding this diet, I should be able to meet your request. The power of this diet is supposed to make the earth tremble. There is a vast system of tunnels in the mountains wherein the Inkas dwell. You can pass through this system of tunnels and emerge in Cusco and also in other faraway places. And with this diet I will be able to enter and explore these tunnels and to meet the Inkas.

—Don Julián

Thus, or similar, in 2005, Don Julián, an indigenous Kukamiria healer about seventy-five years old, responded to my standard question during my field research; that is, if he would be willing to sing a few songs for my recordings of the musical traditions of indigenous people who live along the banks of the Ucayali River in the Peruvian lowlands. Because he was a professional healer, he did not understand 'songs' in the sense of performing tunes about drinking manioc beer at festivities or about courting women, but rather as the technique he and his peers most often use in healing, or in magically manipulating clients' conditions or circumstances. Doing a 'diet' is the common method among western Amazonian indigenous and mestizo peoples to acquire new knowledge or abilities.[1] During such a diet, the person who is 'dieting' is thought to be especially vulnerable to any forces in his or her environment. This is why a healer during his diet usually does not practise; he cannot sing magical songs. It is a great pity that during my ongoing fieldwork I lost contact with Don Julián, so I cannot relate what happened when he concluded his diet, and whether he managed to make the earth shake and to enter the Inkas' tunnel system.

Anyone who stays in the region for a while will be confronted with a multitude of similar experiences: indigenous or mestizo people tell stories that sound rather mythical and unbelievable to moderns,[2] though people insist on their literal truth. Furthermore, one may witness situations where indigenous explanations seem fairly logical while applying what one has learned during his or her socialisation in the so-called West becomes increasingly difficult. Considering this, it appears that what many local people hold as literal truth is difficult to be proven – or falsified – by the common means of scientific documentation and reproduction. This kind of truth seems to be located on an ontological level that is different from, or only in parts overlaps with, the ontology of pragmatic life that is undoubtedly shared by indigenous people and their visitors.

In a somewhat different context – in what he calls 'an anthropology of the moderns' – Bruno Latour (2013) defines fifteen different 'Modes of Existence', thereby dissecting modern life into ontological facets like 'reproduction', 'reference', 'politics', 'law', 'attachment' and 'habit'. These facets of life are ontologically different, because different entities do or do not exist; for example, 'means' from the mode 'law' do not exist in most of the other modes. Although Latour focuses on the moderns, the idea of different modes of existence can be transferred to other human (and non-human) collectives, as this author suggests himself – in the context of the Panoan Inka, especially Latour's modes of 'fiction', 'reference', 'metamorphosis' and 'technology'. Fiction resembles what most moderns who think about Panoan Inkas would resort to: stories that take one's imagination to different places. Reference is built from a network of (ideally) logically consistent indexes, usually understood as 'science', while metamorphosis is a mode that, in Latour's words, 'produces psyches'. The invisible 'beings of metamorphosis' are those who interact with human psyches or conditions commonly regarded as 'interior'. Latour (ibid.: 204) affirms that 'other cultures have practised quite systematically' the interaction with such beings. Although among the central Panoans, these invisible beings of metamorphosis certainly do not produce 'psyches', their dealings with other existents are surely perceived in a highly systematic way. The beings are named and their interactions with humans are institutionalised. In the following, the

Inkas will exemplify how fiction, science, technology and inner states can be amalgamated into one complex mode of existence.

Starting with the example of Julián's legendary Inkas, the aim of this chapter is to inquire about the ontology, or the mode of existence, of human and non-human interaction. Does this interaction take place in the 'same world' as where we sleep, eat, cook, and work in the gardens? Does it occur in dreams, in states obtained by the ingestion of psychoactive substances, during extended periods of fasting (the 'diet')? Does it depend on a professional epistemic culture (Knorr Cetina 2005) that is technically based on manipulating and sharing such altered states of perception and cognition? Or do humans and non-humans interact in a mythical space-time? If so, what distinguishes this space-time from the space-time that unfolds when I open a book and start reading a novel?

It is not within the scope of this chapter to review the many mentions of Inkas, legendary or historical, by western Amazonian peoples. This has been coherently achieved by other authors, such as Calávia Saez (2000) and McCallum (2002).[3] It is perfectly possible that there was contact between the Inka elite in and around Cuzco with people dwelling in the Antisuyo, part of the Tahuantinsuyo 'empire' located in the region east of the Andean highlands, reaching down the slopes and into the lowlands. This could prove historically probable with the Arawak-speaking groups (Asháninka, Yanesha, Matsigenka, or their predecessors) living in the higher regions of the Andean foothills (see also Hill and Santos-Granero 2002). It is less probable that there was direct contact between Quechua-speaking highland dwellers or the Inka elite with lowland groups like the Panoan-speaking Huni Kuin, Amin Waki, Shipibo-Konibo, Kakataibo and others, though the mere possibility remains. However, references to the Inkas abound, especially among the latter groups. 'The Inka' as a singular and distinguished person is regarded as a cultural hero, the instigator of today's indigenous lifeworlds, and sometimes as a direct, genetic predecessor of contemporary Panoans. By any means, the Inkas referred to by indigenous people in the lowlands are not identical to the Inkas who lived in Cuzco and governed the vast regions of Tahuantinsuyo as documented in historical sources. Nor are they identical to today's Quechua-speaking highland people, who also immigrated to the lowlands, and who constitute demographically important factions in both the urban and rural population. The Inkas in the narratives are definitely not humans of the same kind as highlanders, lowlanders, white people or others who dwell, for example, in the town of Pucallpa.

It seems that scholars dealing with the 'Panoan Inkas' can be divided into two groups: the majority who ascribe a mere 'mythical' significance to these Inkas, placing them in the remote past (Roe 1988; Frank 1994; Ritter 1997),[4] and those who believe in a literal, physical-genetic descent of the Panoans from pre-conquest Inkas/Quechuas (Lathrap, Gebhart-Sayer and Mester 1985; Tapia Arce 2013). I think that although both approaches are legitimate and possible, they do not grasp either the entire phenomenon or its significance in the indigenous cosmos. This is mainly due to the fact that both approaches leave out the Inkas' present agency among contemporary communities.

A great difficulty arises if one tries to find out from where this present agency is being executed. As indicated by Don Julián, Inkas may inhabit vast tunnel systems. From a naturalistic perspective, such unknown but inhabitable cave systems under the Andes do not exist (or the probability is minimal). In the course of this chapter, more such places will be mentioned, but they are always 'not-places' (utopia) from a naturalistic point of view. Although one may utter, for example, in Shipibo language *Inkan mai* (the Inka's land), this term is usually employed in song lyrics to denote the exact place where contemporary Shipibo live, but not any remote place hosting surviving Inkas. Similar processes occur with any topographical reference pinpointing the Inkas' whereabouts: the Inka's house (*Inkan xobo*) is 'our' house, the Inka's village (*Inkan jema*) is 'our' village. Consequently, the Inkas are at the same time 'we' and 'here', and located in faraway 'not-places' like tunnel systems.

In this chapter I will first try to outline the significance of the Inkas in Panoan cosmology by reviewing a few mentions of Inkas in narratives and song lyrics of central Pano-speaking groups (the Kakataibo and Shipibo-Konibo, where I conducted my own fieldwork). Based on ethnographic materials, I will try to find out by which means the Inkas are still able to influence the central Panoans' destiny. Thereafter, methods of finding, summoning and meeting the Inkas will be reviewed. Finally, I will try to pinpoint the region in space-time where the 'Panoan Inkas' dwell in relation to the regions where the singers of magical songs[5] usually execute their agency when dealing with non-human entities like the 'owners' of animals, plants and other entities. The chapter concludes with a topology for the contemporary Inkas in central Panoan ontology and also presents a brief and preliminary survey of 'modes of existence' (Latour 2013) among the Kakataibo and Shipibo.

Tracing the Inka

In many ethnographies, the most obvious place the Inka (as a person) repeatedly shows up is the so-called 'mythical past' of narratives (see e.g. McCallum 2002: 386), most often relating the genesis of humans, certain things, or conditions of being. The stories used by Lathrap, Gebhart-Sayer and Mester (1985: 62–65), upon which their speculative Inka history is based, are of that kind; for example, the Inka 'lived among the Conibo as their *curaca*. He was their advisor who helped them to live comfortably, to work together and be all equal. During their feasts he used to say: "Don't fight, be merry and sing". For a long time, he had been the king of the Conibo' (ibid.: 63). The same authors propose that around 25 per cent of all Shipibo-Konibo narratives would feature the Inka(s) as protagonist(s) or otherwise important characters. Without necessarily confirming the exact percentage, mentions of the Inka(s) are abundant, for example, in Shipibo, Kakataibo, Kaxinawa and Marubo mythologies.[6] In Shipibo narratives, a varied set of Inka personalities is present: *Inka bake* (Inka child, a main character in the '*diluvio*' flood narrative), *Xane Inka* (a bird-species Inka), *Kori Inka* (golden Inka, most often the 'good' character) and *Yoashiko Inka* (mean Inka, responsible for many 'bad' personality traits among today's Panoans). More names for Inkas may appear in narratives, or other names may be used for similar characters. These characters have already been mentioned and their narratives collected by other authors (for example, many Inka narratives can be found in Bertrand-Ricoveri 2010).[7] What is important here is that 'the Inka' or 'the Inkas' are not homogeneously represented in Panoan narratives but distinguished by name and attitude – and this attitude is not necessarily 'good' or morally appealing to contemporary Shipibo or Kakataibo. Moral ambiguity in combination with etiological powers among creator or trickster personalities is a common trope in indigenous narratives, not only in lowland South America, but also in the Andes, where Inkas sometimes appear as main characters too; for example, *Inkarrí* (from Spanish '*Inka rey*', the Inka king; see Ortiz Rescaniere 1986; Rivera Andía 2006).

In a journal article about magical singing among the Shipibo (Brabec de Mori 2011a), I analysed the verbal suffix *-ni*, a grammatical feature in the Shipibo language. Commonly, the suffix is understood as an indicator for 'mythical' past: 'the *-ni* suffix, which marks the tense of an action as the distant, unspecified past, that is mythic or beginning time' (Roe 1988: 113). Contrastingly, Illius (1999: 128) hints at the possibility that *-ni* may also point to some unspecified present of states of transformation. By analysing the lyrics of magical songs performed by *médicos* I could show that the same 'time' is being used to refer to the different strata of reality where the *médicos* interact with the beings they use or need for their negotiations when healing or bewitching – that is, when they are dreaming, fasting or singing. Consequently, the timescape indicated by applying the suffix *-ni* is not solely located in the past, but also in the present. This timescape can best be described as a 'remote non-future'. Similarly, narratives categorised as 'myths' (because they apply the suffix *-ni* which indicates 'mythical past') can also be understood as referring at the same time to a 'remote present', a contemporary place removed from everyday experience. Access to such 'places' is limited to people who are well prepared for this kind of venture, to the Shipibo's *yobé* and *meráya*, or among the Kakataibo to the initiated *ro oni*, 'medicine men'. If the Inkas in Panoan narratives are acting in the grammatical mode defined by the suffix *-ni* (which is true in all cases I know of), they are not only important characters of indigenous history but are still present – although in remote places – in sites that are removed from everyday experience and not at all easy to access.

To begin with the survey required to localise the Inka in the present, I will analyse a fragment of a Kakataibo song of the genre *chanin bana oti*. In a Latourian sense, we start in mode of 'fiction', taking our imagination somewhere else, into a former epoch.

Chanin bana oti songs narrate historical or mythical events and processes. According to Frank (1982: 71) and Wistrand Robinson (1976: 8–9), these songs were taught by initiated men to young candidates who had to live for a long time in the 'house of medicine' (*ro xobo*), a place outside the village in the forest, in order to be initiated.[8] Besides learning songs and other techniques, the young men had to obey a strict diet (similar to the one mentioned by Don Julián) as a prerequisite for obtaining new knowledge and abilities. During the period of initiation, older men recited the songs verse by verse and the adolescents had to repeat them word by word. Ideally, a literal transmission of the whole story could be obtained in this manner. However, following Frank (1994: 81), it seems that any Kakataibo man could provide his own 'history', or be able to recite his specific variant of these song lyrics – that is, a personalised mythology (see figure 5.1).

In any case, the present text explains in detail that the palm tree (*xebi*) that bears edible fruits was brought by 'my' Inka and planted along the river banks. The fairly humorous turn at the end explains why there are no such plants to be found in the headwaters.

1	ee / noken inka kaisa	It is told that my Inka
2	'o xebi name eo	came in order to
3	koti xebi name eo	plant (edible) palm trees.
...		
15	noken inka kaisa	My Inka, it is told,
16	beroakexai mara	brought these seeds
17	mapenara mapenatia	while going upriver
18	mapenakinbi kaisa	towards the headwaters,
19	baka ñushina isa	where a water demon (betrayed him).
20	ain xano roa	His beautiful wife
21	mebikexon kaisa	was taken away (by the demon), it is told.
22	noken inka	Therefore, my Inka
23	mapenaroama ike	did not go further upriver.

Figure 5.1 *Chanin bana oti*, performed in 2004 by Roberto Angulo (V 1722). All examples in the figures presented in this chapter stem from the corpus I collected during the fieldwork for my PhD thesis, which was funded by a grant from the Austrian Academy of Sciences (ÖAW). The recordings are archived at the ÖAW's Phonogrammarchiv and are also included in the catalogue accompanying my thesis (Brabec de Mori 2015a). With every figure, the Phonogrammarchiv's archive index is given; in this case, V 1722.

Another example may highlight the complexity of Kakataibo–Inka relations (see figure 5.2).

This is the beginning of a 'proud man's song' (*tokoriko oni*). The singer starts with a very strange parallelism: *'en papa inka / inka mane nonti / non papa inka*. It indicates that the singer himself is a son of the Inka, that the boat is connected to the Inka, while his enemy, a mestizo[9] (who killed the singer's family as if these were young tapirs) is an Inka's son, too. Regarding the boat, it is fairly common among the Kakataibo to connect the Inka (this is similar in Shipibo narratives) with the production of metallic objects, and therefore the boat which is made of 'white' metal (probably aluminium) is seen as an

1	'en papa inka	Me, (with my) father Inka
2	inka mane nonti	(in an) Inka's canoe made of metal,
3	non papa inka	the enemy, (with his) father Inka
4	inka mane nonti	(took me away in an) Inka's canoe made of metal
5	oxo mane nonti	(in a) white metal canoe,
6	'o bena penke	after turning (my people like) young tapirs,
7	penke rakekesa	turning them around and making them lie (on the floor)

Figure 5.2 *Tokoriko oni*, performed in 2004 by Gregorio Estrella (V 1719).

object originally produced by the Inka (cf. Frank 1994: 153; Calavia Sáez 2000; see also the tables at the end of this chapter). Further on, the seemingly paradoxical pedigrees of the Kakataibo singer and his enemy are based on two facets of the same narrative: first, the Inka is understood as an ancestor of the Kakataibo people (Frank et al. 1990; Tapia Arce 2013). Frank (1994: 215–16) presents narrative material indicating that, out of the Kakataibo's predecessors, the Inka emerged and engendered the contemporary Kakataibo who, thereafter, chased him away. Based on this trope, the singer is a son of the Inka. However, in addition, the Inka, after his forced departure from the Kakataibo, engendered more offspring – the white people (from the indigenous point of view, mestizos are usually called white people). Holding the technological apparatus their father Inka had given them, these white people returned to take revenge on the Kakataibo who had committed sins against their Inka father. This complex story of descent, which at the same time explains the mestizos' technological advantage and their unfriendly stance towards the Kakataibo, is masterfully condensed within nine words in the song's opening section. Here we encounter a first point of 'crossing': the mode of existence 'fiction' overlaps with 'technology'. The beings of fiction lead the listener to the emergence, or an explanation of, the beings of technology.[10]

In both examples, the relationship with the Inka is articulated. In the song about the origin of the palm trees, the singer calls him 'my Inka', which makes the Inka part of him and expresses a close, maybe emotional, relationship. Remarkably, despite being a cultural hero, 'my Inka' is tricked by a simple water demon, which portraits him as fairly 'human', and vulnerable, too. In the second example, the commonly known narrative of the parentage of both Kakataibo and whites forms the background to the war story that follows. Here again, the relationship is made closer, the Inka is mentioned as the father of both persons and as the maker (that is, father) of the boat, drawing a circle around the scene that circumscribes close family relations and makes the war appear to be a struggle among (half-) brothers. In any case, the Inka is not 'here'. He is an ancestor, and although not far removed in time or space he is not present. But he seems to be still alive.[11] He is probably just around the corner, hidden in the tunnels mentioned by Don Julián, or waiting at the headwaters of some smaller tributary to the Ucayali River.

Pascual Mahua, one of my main Shipibo research associates, insists that it was the Inka who sent all the indigenous tribes living today into the different parts of the Peruvian lowlands because they behaved badly before him; that is, they got drunk and quarrelled. Only those people who followed the Inka's advice to be abstinent were saved and became invisible. These are known nowadays as *chai-koni jonibo*, legendary and powerful 'ideal Shipibo' living in the deep woods (Illius 1987).

Pascual also told me that, in 1983, an elderly man in the native community Colonia de Caco narrated a 'true story' that he himself had witnessed a few decades ago. A great riverboat from downriver called at the village harbour. Convoking the locals, the crew gathered on the village plaza. The captain of the ship gave a great speech (in Spanish, because otherwise the Shipibo would not have understood him), explaining that the ship was cruising the Ucayali valley. It had already visited the Soaya stream on the lower Ucayali, the central Ucayali tributary Tamaya, and now the Caco River. At all these places, they set up sentinel guards who were ordered to check every person who intended to pass upriver for their moral integrity. This had to be achieved before all the mestizos and 'bad people' (the members of the Maoist organization known in Peru as Sendero Luminoso) would come here, trying to make the Shipibo become bad people too. These mestizos had stolen and appropriated the Inka Atahuallpa's palace, which they use now as their president's residence in Lima, as they had stolen all the Inkas' gold. The captain warned the Shipibo that they would suffer, but there would be salvation. The captain himself was the Inka who had taken possession of a land on the upper Ucayali, from the Pachitea River to Cumaría. There they also guarded an 'indigenous bank', a mine full of money and gold, which pertained to the different indigenous people and which they hid from the whites. After this speech, the captain and his crew boarded the ship again and entered the Caco creek, despite the ship's size: it was so big that it would not be able to pass towards the headwaters by normal means. They returned after four days, going on to other places on the Ucayali. These, the storyteller mused, were the people from Cuzco who lived in subterranean cities, developing their strike force there, waiting for the day to take back the indigenous lands from the Peruvians and whites.[12]

In addition to this narrative, Pascual produced another story which he assured he had been told by a direct witness of what had happened.[13] Without delving further into the long plot, the essence is that a group of Shipibo travellers who set out looking for the Inka found a place with abundant food. While eating there, they were surprised by the arrival of a terribly big and splendidly adorned riverboat operated by the 'returned-king people' (*rai bea jonibo*) and the returned queen (*rai bea ainbo*), who hosted the Shipibo travellers for a few days before they were sent back to their home. Here, the Inkas are considered kings, similar to the Andean *Inkarrí*, an association that will emerge again later in this chapter.

In these narratives, 'fiction' is not only crossing with 'technology' (the ships), but also with 'reference'. By reiterating that these are true stories, they provide potential points of reference for the network of indexes required to form a system of 'epistemology'. Indigenous specialists may thus use this crossing for developing methods of 'worlding' (Descola 2005). In this sense, it *is* true: the Inkas were not all murdered by the Spaniards, nor all assimilated – thereby losing all their powers – into the Quechua-speaking highland population. Some Inkas were left and took refuge in subterranean cities, in remote headwaters of rainforest streams, continued travelling on big ships, or waited in their tunnel systems that connect to the whole country for the day to strike back. Or, at least, they will take the faithful with them into lands that the whites cannot access.[14]

Contacting the Inka

This takes us to the mode of 'metamorphosis' as pronounced by Latour (2013), the construction of 'inner states'. Many people, especially moderns who have got in touch with western Amazonian 'shamanism',[15] believe that it suffices to drink big enough doses of the hallucinogenic brew *ayawaska* (Labate and Araújo 2004) in order to contact the Inka people. Contrastingly, Antonio Gómez, a renowned Shipibo *médico*, taught me that *ayawaska* was a *janson rao*, a 'lying remedy': it shows you what you want to see or what you do not want to see. It might even show you what is true, or provide access to the 'real world', but in order to obtain this distinctive faculty one has to be well trained as a *médico*, including year-long diets and much experience in dealings with all kinds of non-human entities (who may likewise betray you by appearing as what they are not, e.g. as Inkas).

The Kakataibo never fully adopted so-called 'ayawaska shamanism' for their dealings with non-humans. They nevertheless accessed a highly sophisticated system of knowledge with a broad range of applications: healing and bewitching, hunting, warfare, weather manipulation, and person-making. However, in the following pages, I will only discuss the Shipibo system because my knowledge of the (abandoned) Kakataibo system is insufficient.[16] In the past, the Shipibo system worked without the use of *ayawaska*, too (but probably used other psychoactive substances, especially tobacco). *Ayawaska* was introduced on the Ucayali River sometime around AD 1800 (Gow 1994; Brabec de Mori 2011b; Beyer 2012). Henceforth, as is well known and documented in the literature, *ayawaska* conquered the indigenous and mestizo medicinal systems of the Ucayali valley, and today the Shipibo in particular are regarded as specialists in the 'shamanic' uses of the brew. Most transcriptions of medicinal songs stem from recordings of *ayawaska* sessions (see, for example, Meyer 1974; Illius 1987; Tournon 1991; and Brabec de Mori 2002). Within these transcriptions, among many other non-human entities, the Inkas also appear here and there. As an example, I quote a short passage from a curing song by a highly esteemed, deceased *médico* (see figure 5.3).

'Having eliminated the stench' refers to the successful act of curing; it suggests that the patient was freed of an illness-causing influence, which was perceived by the singing healer as a bad odour. Therefore, the Inkas' appearance seems to take place only after the main work of curing. In the curing session Illius transcribed, however, the cleaning and curing goes on much longer, with different songs following that quoted above, but the Inkas are not present anymore after this brief dancing party. In any case, they appear here as bearers of fortune, as dancing and flying messengers of success.

In lines 13–14, the suffix *-ni* is used on the verb *joyoti*,[17] indicating that the Inkas dance in a stratum of reality, on an ontological level[18] that is different from the everyday world. The Inkas fly and dance, but only the healer perceives them visually – in his vision induced by the hallucinogenic brew – so he transmits their presence via the aural channel of song lyrics. However, it is still unsaid *where* the flying Inkas dance.

10b	nihue-n queyo-a sene(n)-man	Having eliminated the stench,
11	Inca-bo-t-ibi	all the Inkas
12	shoquit-i-ra noy-ai	are swaying from side to side while flying.
10b	nihue-n queyo-a sene(n)-man	Having eliminated the stench,
11	Inca-bo-t-ibi	all the Inkas
13	senen-ibi joyo-n-i	perfectly lined up in a row
14	shoquit-ibi joyo-n-i	are swaying from side to side in a row.

Figure 5.3 *Huehua*, performed in 1985 by Neten Vitá (from Illius 1987: 321–22). The quotation extracts Illius's transcription of the Shipibo lyrics from his interlinear translation.

A more topographically accurate mention of an Inka item occurs in a song performed by ex-*meráya* Pascual Mahua. Notably, he sang this song at a time when he had not practised as a *médico* for about fifteen years since his retirement. He performed on a small plaza in front of his house before an audience composed of my team and me and about a dozen villagers who had gathered in order to listen. He sang about his experiences on the 'other side of the sun river' (*bari paro keiba*), an unquestionably remarkable song about places and beings who dwell on ontological levels removed from laypeople's experience. The sophisticated lyrics prove fairly difficult to translate, even in the fragment that follows (see figure 5.4).

In the first lines (11–13) of this text passage, the singer defines the situation. The listeners have gathered in order to listen to him, who 'comes from there', who sings in the way he sang when he was still an active *médico*. *Médicos* sing in a transformed state, from a

11	maton oín beira je (2x)	You have come here in order to see
12	ea jain jobanon je	how I will come from there
13	neskáneskaranike	in the way it happened long ago,
14	noya rao xamanbi	when at the top of the flight medicine (tree)
15	yakani jonibo (5x)	the people sitting there (were singing).
16	kaini jonibo je (2x)	There, where these people gather
17	oxe paron toxbata je	and float downriver on the river of the moon,
18	toxbata *waporo*	on the floating steamboat [from Spanish *vapor*],
19	inkan sha *waporo*	on the Inka's whooshing [onomat.] steamboat,
20	jain naneáketa (4x)	there I embarked.
21	joé jakon *kanpana* je (2x)	The light of the good bell [Sp. *campana*]
22	nete *iromina*ya je	illuminates [Sp. *ilumina*] the world,
23	ani nete rakaya	the great world lying (at the feet of)
24	*torin* ewa nichini	the immensely standing tower [Sp. *torre*].
25	noma kewekeweya	The doves [= women] with beautiful patterns,
26	kaini jonibo	the people that dwell (there),
27	noara jain beai (7x)	we come from there.

Figure 5.4 *Onamati*, performed in 2004 by Pascual Mahua (D 5234)

'point of view' or ontological level different from that of the listeners. Pascual had accomplished the diet of the legendary *noya rao jiwi*, the 'flight medicine tree' (line 14), a diet that enabled him to take off into remote regions, to the other side of the sun river, for example. This is the region where people travel on the moon river, and notably, they travel on the Inka's steamboat, and are joined by the singer.

Whether the 'people who dwell there' (line 26) are the Inkas or not is not explicitly stated in this text, but I suppose that they are (as we shall see later). Highly interesting beside the topographical information is the technical explanation masterfully coded in lines 21–24: the strong and steady sound of the singer's voice is the bell that emits light rather than sound waves.[19] What we can perceive *here* aurally, *there* takes on a visual quality. The voice's 'light' illuminates the 'great world' – the world as seen with a *médico*'s eye, perceiving much more than what meets the untrained eye. The immense tower refers to the singer's training, his accumulated diet-power. Finally (line 27), the people who dwell in this esoteric landscape, together with the singer, come back to 'our place'.

The complicated codes in this sequence draw a 'sonic picture' and explain that this perception of the world and its beings can be 'opened' by the singing voice of a powerful *médico* who has accumulated many diets. Singing is the key to the place where the Inkas dwell. This, however, only becomes apparent within a closed, that is, esoteric epistemic knowledge that can be shared with peers by much dieting and practising (or by the teachings of somebody like Pascual). Even native Shipibo laypeople – and I tested it with various people of different ages – do not understand the meaning of the lyrics of such songs, even though they do understand the words. Understanding and consequently working with the transformative faculty of 'crossing the river of the sun' depends on a professional epistemic culture: 'fiction' here crosses with 'reference', forming a practical epistemology of producing knowledge about the world (see also Knorr Cetina 2018; Brabec de Mori and Winter 2018).

Joining the Inka

Recalling the narratives from the first section of this chapter, it seems that one can meet the Inkas if one is lucky enough to encounter them in their great steamboats that now and then cruise the Ucayali River and its tributaries. In the preceding section, on the other hand, we learned that specialist *médicos* are able to meet the Inka at their request by singing the appropriate songs. Anybody may try to sing such a song, but it only 'works' if the lyrics are perfectly set up as in the examples presented, if the tone of the voice is steady and strong (like a bell), if melody, timbre and pitch are carefully chosen, and if year-long diets provide sufficient transformative power to the singer's voice (cf. Brabec de Mori 2013). In contemporary Shipibo life, therefore, it seems unlikely that Shipibo laypeople (or even moderns) could meet the Inkas. Until around 1965, however, Shipibo people applied a technique to bring them closer, as indicated at the end of the example in Figure 5.4. This technique was called *mochai*, and but it is no longer performed among the living. During my fieldwork, I could record eleven songs (all of them exclusively demonstrated by most renowned *médicos*) that inform us how powerful *meráya* could provide the Inka experience to non-specialist participants of *mochai* events (see figure 5.5).

First of all, we can witness a common trope here: the Inka being a synonym for the (Christian) God and at the same time for a king (in line 16, literally 'the Inka's king-people'). The whole song tells of people kneeling down and singing for a brilliant world of God. Towards the end of the song, a transformation occurs and the glistening world descends, so people are singing now 'within' this world.

There are various strong indications that *mochai* events were already known and performed before the rubber boom, in a manner aimed at influencing the sun and moon in times of eclipse, turning away periods of persistent bad weather, and also fostering fertility (Brabec de Mori 2015a: 612–34). However, more recent reports of such events all point towards rituals performed in order to pray to the sun/God/Inka in a religious sense, or to summon non-human entities in order to join forces. Many *mochai* songs in my recordings stem directly from the millenarian movement around the female

16	inkan *rai* jonibo (2x)	(For) the royal [Sp. *rey*] Inka people,
17	*rios rai* jonibo	the divine [Sp. *Dios*] and royal people,
18	noara ikanai	we are singing.
...		
32	inkan bawa kenéya (2x)	The Inka's well-patterned parrot
33	yoyo imabeira	makes us imitate (its own speech),
34	noara ikanai	we are singing.
35	*rios* nete penekan	After the brilliant divine world
36	maayontaanan	has come down upon us,
37	noara mochakanai	we are (singing) *mochai*.

Figure 5.5 *Mochai*, performed in 2004 by Virgilio López (D 5291).

meráya Wasamea (Pascual Mahua's aunt) that formed in the 1950s and was based in Montebello, close to Painacu on the lower Ucayali. Wasamea then moved upriver and was reported to conduct *mochai* rituals in Junin Pablo on the shores of the Imiría Lake (Illius 1987: 124), before she was turned away by sceptical villagers who accused her of witchcraft (Roe 1988: 134). It is likely that around 1960 she had to return downriver, where her trail is lost.

The Inka connection was not as explicitly expressed in Wasamea's movement as in the millenarian narratives presented earlier in this chapter, but it was nevertheless present. Wasamea's *mochai* was reported by her nephew Benjamín Mahua[20] as being directly linked to summoning demonic beings (*yoshin*). Between religious praying and witchcraft accusations, we encounter a new synonym for the Inkas, the demonic beings *simpi jonibo*. These demons are among the most devastating forces in the Shipibo cosmos, so summoning these without being well aware of what one is doing could result in utter disaster. An elderly former *médico* from the upper Ucayali – I do not know if he was in contact with Wasamea – performed two *mochai* songs devoted to, as he said, summoning the *simpi jonibo*. These are not mentioned in the text, but kings and the Inkas are (see figure 5.6).

Mochai rituals were undertaken collectively, by non-specialist people kneeling or standing in a circle and singing, instructed by a specialist *meráya*, but without taking any type of drug. As these songs and their accompanying reports indicate, all participants probably experienced a strong alteration, perceiving arriving demons,

10	*rai* kaibobo (6x)	(Our) royal kin,
11	ja bonitoninbi (2x)	the same way that once took them away
12	inkabora beai (5x)	is now bringing the Inka back,
13	ja beaitian (2x)	and when they arrive,
14	mai nayatai (4x)	the earth is trembling,
15	shinan wekanyamawe (2x)	so do not allow your concentration to falter!
16	*rai* kaibobo (5x)	(our) royal kin,
17	noa *rai* jonibo (2x)	we are the royal persons
18	*koros* manichimea (3x)	with a cross erected in the centre (of our circle).

Figure 5.6 *Mochai*, performed in 2004 by Claudio Sánchez (D 5346). The entire song text is analysed in Brabec de Mori (2012: 93–95).

Inkas, Gods or kings. We remember that Don Julián insisted that after his diet he would 'make the earth tremble' in order to enter the Inkas' tunnels. Here we are: the *mochai* people make the earth tremble, the Inkas' arrival seems to be connected to a terrible fear that strikes the participants – they must concentrate, in order to finally *be* the royal (Inka) people. This reads rather like an account of a collective possession ritual, where participants in altered states of perception and cognition embody non-human persons. It is perfectly possible that such possessions occurred and that such invocations were targeted against the whites; or even undertaken in order to unleash diseases such as smallpox (another synonym for the *simpi jonibo*) upon their original bringers (see Brabec de Mori 2015a: 634). Whatever or whoever the *mochai* people summoned, for their adversaries (definitely all Christians) it was demons, and it is not surprising that they (or, at least, Wasamea) were accused of witchcraft.

Providing a Place for Contemporary Inkas

The Panoan Inkas appeared in this chapter as culture bringers, fathers, captains of great ships, kings, God, maybe the sun, but also as terrifying demons. In any case, they are present, and wherever they are, they are apt to repeatedly manifest in susceptible humans in order to once again take up the challenge of striking back at the invaders. The historical record of indigenous uprisings or millenarian movements presents a succession of such humans who embodied 'the Inka'. Indigenous narratives of the Kakataibo and Shipibo confirm the appearance and reappearance of Inkas, and contemporary *meráya* still seem to possess the sonic key to access the region where the Inkas dwell. The Inkas' agency, however, is rather subtle. They do not simply show up and put everything in order. Already in narratives referring to a remote past, there is not only the 'good' *kori inka*, but also his 'bad' counterpart, *yoashiko inka*, the mean one.[21] In the context of the *mochai* we witness that the Inkas are synonymous with terrifying demons. Since *mochai* rituals are no longer performed and there is no precise description of these events available, we can only speculate what the reappearance of the summoned Inka kings and their mingling with or their taking possession of the ritual participants would have looked like.

In curing rituals, Inkas are not summoned for healing. They are usually mentioned as bearers of good fortune, as was shown in Figure

5.3. Inkas do not intervene in the process of healing (or bewitching), although their artefacts and technologies are sometimes mentioned in curing songs. Their technologies are furthermore, and even more frequently, mentioned in festive songs and private poetry. See the tables at the end of this chapter for a list of Inka technologies, concepts, and their embodiment in both Shipibo and Kakataibo secular songs. By reviewing these tables, any presuppositions with which the Inkas were associated (e.g. with the unknown foreign, or with the well-known local; with specific technologies or places, or any other domain) come undone. Inkas appear in various situations, as the owners or authors of many different items or places; 'Inka' seems to be used as an adjective that adds a quality of sophistication, specialness or superiority to certain entities, objects or situations. The Inkas are therefore omnipresent, but they do not seem to be active in a specific way. Nor are they associated with a specific quality, especially not in the face of the distinction between 'us' and the 'other': the Inka is my father as he is my enemy's father (see Figure 5.1). However, they are not *here*.

In order to find out where they are, linguistic conceptualization may again give a hint. Gerhard Ritter states that in Kakataibo language, 'the difference between the states of dreaming and of vigilance is sometimes described in the same way as a difference of place. The adverb *'uxë* (on the other side, on the opposite side) is associated with the act of sleeping (*'uxcë*). Contrary to that, *nëcë* (on this side) denotes the state of vigilance' (Ritter 1997: 229, my translation).[22] This association and opposition are paralleled in Shipibo terminology (the corresponding terms read *oke*, *oxati* and *neke*, see Brabec de Mori 2015b: 32). The prefixes *o-* and *ne-* indicate that the prefixed word is associated with sleeping, dreaming, moon, detachment and distant places (*o-*), or with close places, attachment, day, light, and states of vigilance. In Figure 5.4, Pascual Mahua sang about his experience beyond the river of the sun (*bari paro keiba*), where people travel the river of the moon (*oxe paro toxbata*) on, notably, the Inkas' steamboat (*inkan sha waporo*).

It would be wrong, however, to divide the Shipibo or Kakataibo world into two parts, into the waking world, *here*, and the world of dreams, *there*. These are two sides of the same world, the world we live in, as described in detail by Fernando Santos-Granero (2003). This world is peopled by many beings, some of them close by, *here* and visible, while others are invisible and can only be perceived *there*. These invisible beings can inhabit different ontological levels, and some of them are more likely than others to be found in certain places. Under deep forest canopy, for example – that is, in the shadows (*'ota*) – the Kakataibo are scared of the commonly invisible *'otano*, the shadow-foreigners. In the headwaters of some tributary rivers (for example the Soaya, the Tamaya, the Caco, where the big ship went in Pascual's story) or in the deep woods dwell the likewise invisible *chaikoni jonibo*, those people who were once equal to the Shipibo, but who were chosen by the Inka.[23] In the same headwaters, as many narratives affirm, the Inkas' houses, mansions, lakes and animals can be found, though not simply entered or taken away. There seem to be certain 'entrances' to the world *there*, but they are well guarded by sentinel beings like the *chaikoni jonibo*.

Bruno Latour's 'Modes of Existence' (2013) provide a useful concept for identifying and localising invisible beings, because they allow for a distinction of ontological levels *within* what is called 'ontologies' by Descola (2005). An animist ontology in Descola's sense allows for a variety of ontological levels to be accessed and warranted by specialists like storytellers or singers who are often one and the same person with powerful healers and sorcerers. They form a professional epistemic culture (Knorr Cetina 2005, 2018) that is however conformed by fiction, metamorphosis, technology and reference in Latour's terms. Among moderns, these are different modes of existence, but among the central Panoans they are collapsed into one mode, warranted by those who harness the power of the transformative faculty. Here, the distinction is in ontological levels, whereas the mode of existence I would suggest to call 'transformation' is unified. Following up on these thoughts, other modes relevant and requiring different ontological facets for indigenous peoples in the western Amazon could be addressed with 'kin', 'work', 'ethnicity', 'being visited', or 'NGO', to name only a few suggestions departing from the present study towards future inquiries.

Turning back to the suggested mode 'transformation', we can see, as suggested above, that the relevant beings are consequently named and interactions are institutionalised. There are the Kakataibo's *'otano* and *kamano*, for example, and the Shipibo's *chaikoni jonibo*, all people of the deep forest whose ontological position is somewhat humanoid; further on there are invisible 'owners' (*ibo*) of visible plants and animals, of the clouds, the rivers, mountains, and so on, all of them firmly rooted in the environment. Corresponding institutions at the crossing of the habitual indigenous mode of existence (the village, *here*) and the modes peopled by these beings (the forest etc., *there*) are the Kakataibo *ro xobo* (house of medicine), which is located in the forest (outside the human, within the non-human), as well as the Shipibo diet that appears like an embodied variant of the *ro xobo*. The *meráya* and *ro oni* operate at this crossing.

The Inkas, however, are not rooted in any specific visible part of the environment. The most interesting aspect in the Inkas' own mode of existence is that they seem to share *oke*, the space *there*, with the owners of animals, plants, mountains and rivers, but do not, as these do, manifest in corresponding beings *here* (*neke*). They manifest in possessed humans, but also in people's narratives, and especially in technology.

Shipibo singers are quite explicit in that the technologies they used before the arrival of the whites – for example, bows and arrows, manioc cultivation, and ceramics – were not only taught, or 'brought', to them by the Inkas, but are still 'possessed' by them (e.g. *inkan yami wekikan*, 'the Inka's curved metal', an ironwood bow). This also applies to technologies of the moderns; for example, my tape recorder was named *inkan yami xaokan*, 'the Inka's metal bones'; and a shotgun is called *inkan yami kanakan*, 'the Inka's flashing iron'. Although the Inkas brought these technologies to 'us' as well, they are still their 'owners'. What can easily be conceptualised for technology, also applies to the people themselves. The Inkas did not only bring into existence and later on possess technologies, they did also create and later on influence humans. Many Kakataibo insist that the Inkas are their direct predecessors; some Shipibo are so beautiful that in a song they have to be called *inkan bake tsoawa*, 'the beautiful child of an Inka'; the Inka created the different western Amazonian 'tribes' (as recounted by Pascual in D 5547). Furthermore, the Inka also created white and black people (Roe 1988: 129; Pacaya Romaina 2011: 16). This is not only to be understood in a 'genetical' sense (as the first source of humanity), but as a process that has to be permanently maintained. The Inkas are still responsible for the humans' condition and their salvation. It is essential for the Kakataibo and Shipibo that their 'Inkaic' substantiality as well as mentality is maintained and continuously mentioned and made explicit, because this contributes to the making of a 'Real Person' (Santos-Granero 2012). The corresponding nurturing of a person with substances, items and rituals has to be maintained throughout their lifetime. The 'Inkaic' part of a person has to be constantly reaffirmed through song and narrative in order to stay alive.

What Latour terms the respective *beings* of fiction, technology, reference and metamorphosis, merge into one in the present case. This is specifically evident with the Inkas: the Panoan beings of metamorphosis *are* the beings of fiction. Performing fiction in rituals or songs transports these beings *into* technology and *into* persons. In effect, these beings produce 'Real Humans', as well as the references for an indigenous epistemology.

The Inkas harness, consequently, the powers of primordial production. As the 'mythical past' turns out to be at the same time a remote present, this primordial genesis of contemporary humans is at the same time the remote but current responsibility for contemporary peoples' conditions. These primordial powers are located beyond the river of the sun, in the invisible region that appears during dreams, strict diets and hallucinatory experience. This region, however, is not a parallel world but it is 'contained' in the common world, where many other invisible beings can also be encountered, if only the right entrance, a point of transformation, can be found. To meet the Inkas means to be able to travel far, *before* or *after* the difficult transformation necessary to perceive the invisible beings. Controlled transformation is achieved by singing in the correct way: it is only when lyrics, melodies, timbre and pitch are all in tune and performed by a voice that wields the power of year-long diets, that the song is correct and transformation occurs. Transformed, the singer then has to travel to the far headwaters or to the entrance point of the tunnel system. A simple diet will not be sufficient here. The singer's diet has to be especially powerful, so charged with human and non-human agency that it can make the earth tremble, in order to penetrate the disguises and convince the sentinels. In case – I do not know – Don Julián has already passed away, his peers can be quite sure that he made it and stayed *there*. There, *oke*, may therefore be right around the corner of your house.

Bernd Brabec de Mori spent five years in the Ucayali Valley (eastern Peru) mostly among people autoidentifying as Shipibo-Konibo, after studying musicology, philosophy and history of arts. Back in Austria he has been working at the Phonogrammarchiv of the Austrian Academy of Sciences and the Centre for Systematic Musicology at the University of Graz, and is currently employed as a senior scientist by the University of Music and Performing Arts Graz. His publications address the areas of western Amazonian songs, medicine, cosmologies and histories, as well as the intersections of music, religion, altered states and ontological evidentiality.

Appendix: List of Inka Items from Song Lyrics

Note: 'Reference' gives the index number used for the catalogue in Brabec de Mori 2015a. Spanish loanwords in the indigenous text column are printed in italics.

A. Shipibo-Konibo (from a corpus of 223 analysed lyrics)

Text	Theme	Meaning	Reference
inkan mai ronkeman	Shipibo tech	smoothed Inka's earth (*an earthenware drinking vessel*)	04:14:35
inkan jiwi bimi	Shipibo tech	fruit from the Inka's tree (*calabash drinking vessel*)	04:14:42
inkan tawa jashinbi	Shipibo tech	the Inka's decorated reed (*arrow for shooting animals*)	04:60:02
inkan yami wekikan	Shipibo tech	the Inka's curved metal (*an ironwood hunting bow*)	04:61:13
inkan mai matoki	Shipibo site	towards the Inka's earth (*land where Shipibo live*)	04:03:32
inkan jema senenain	Shipibo site	where the Inka's village ends (*Shipibo village's far end*)	04:12:13
inkan mai makewe	Shipibo site	the Inka's patterned earth (*floor at a dance festivity*)	04:13:41
inkan mai masenen	Shipibo site	on the surface of Inka's earth (*floor at a dance festivity*)	04:14:23
inkan mai matokan	Shipibo site	on a bump on the Inka's earth (*floor where the singing woman lies down in order to have sex*)	04:22:32
nokon tae rebon/ inkan mai wishaxon	Shipibo site	with the tip of my toes / I write on the Inka's earth (*floor at a dance festivity*)	04:22:42
eara jain joai/ inkan mai joai	Shipibo site	from there I am coming / coming to the Inka's earth (*the singer comes home for his mother's funeral*)	04:33:44
inkan maibirini	Shipibo site	on the very Inka's earth (*Shipibo village during festivity*)	04:42:21
inkan jema kaaki	Shipibo site	moving on the Inka's earth (*dancing in a village*)	04:55:03
inkan bake tsoawa	Shipibo person	the Inka's child, a *tsoawa* bird (*a beautiful woman*)	04:13:11
inkan roi chono	Shipibo person	the Inka's *roi*(?) swallow (*a beautiful woman*)	04:21:42

Text	Theme	Meaning	Reference
inkan *koros* ponyaman	Shipibo person	with the arms of an Inka's cross (*the 'strong arms' of a man when having sex with a woman*)	04:25:31
inkan joxo xawaman	Shipibo person	the Inka's white macaw bird (*here: the singer himself*)	04:85:12
inkan *tori* makero/ makeronin joyota	Shipibo concept	the Inka's tower is making / sound in a row (*the singing dancers at a festivity*)	04:01:41
inkan jiwi taponbi	Shipibo concept	the root of the Inka's tree (*manioc root*)	04:12:13
inkan mai masenen/ inkabaon banani	Shipibo concept	On the surface of the Inka's land / the Inkas have cultivated (*the calebash used as a drinking vessel*)	04:12:14
inkan tawa borebo	Shipibo concept	the tip of the Inka's reed (*used for artwork*)	04:21:45
inkan maxe toekan	Shipibo concept	broken Inka's *maxe* fruit (*maxe is used for red painting; here it refers to the blood of a wounded fighter*)	04:31:12
inkan tama xoxoni	Shipibo concept	the Inka's peanut that had grown (*clitoris in a clitoridectomy song*)	04:52:41
inkan nete seneni	Shipibo concept	the Inka's day has come (*the day of circumcision*)	04:55:03
joni benatianbi/ timpo di la inkaikobo	Shipibo concept	in the time when humanity was young / the time of the Inka's reign (*very rare Spanish reference*)	04:55:07
inkan *tori* maxketen	Shipibo concept	on top of the Inka's tower (*this describes Shipibo culture in general*)	[IPAR-08/17]
inkan yoran keyanxon	Shipibo concept	hovering above the Inka's body (*the bow that is held high before being aimed at an animal*)	04:61:13
inkan yami xaokan	foreign tech	the Inka's metal bone (*the researcher's tape recorder*)	04:03:31
inkan yami makina	foreign tech	the Inka's metal machine (*the researcher's tape recorder*)	04:03:33
inkan joxo pei	foreign tech	the Inka's white leaf (*the researcher's notebook*)	04:04:31
inkan jiwi tsekere	foreign tech	the Inka's rattling (onomat.) log (*sugarcane press*)	04:11:41

Text	Theme	Meaning	Reference
inkan yami kanaka	foreign tech	the Inka's flashing metal (*shotgun*)	04:32:41
inkan yami penekan	foreign tech	the Inka's shining metal (*scissors*)	04:52:02
rai inka bakebo	foreign person	king Inka's children (*white visitors*)	04:02:31
inkan sha *waporo*	esoteric tech	the Inka's whooshing (onomat.) steamboat (*a vessel on the 'river of the moon'; see main text*)	04:40:51
inkan bawan yakata	esoteric person	the Inka's sitting parrot (*the Inka's messenger*)	04:12:16
non inka *riosen*	esoteric person	our God Inka	04:54:06
inkan joxo xotokan	esoteric person	the Inka's white dove (*an 'angel' in a mochai song*)	04:85:12
kori inka *riosen*	esoteric person	golden God Inka	04:85:42
inkan rai jonibo	esoteric person	the Inka's royal people (*the Inkas in a mochai song*)	04:85:43
inkan bawa kenéya	esoteric person	the Inka's patterned parrot (*the Inka's messenger*)	04:85:43
ja bonitoninbi/ inkabora beai	esoteric person	what had taken them away / is bringing the Inka back (*the 'way' in a mochai summoning song*)	04:85:14
inkan mai kaaki	animal site	trespassing the Inka's land (*refers to wild animals*)	04:61:12
inkan mai tanai	animal site	exploring the Inka's land (*refers to wild animals*)	04:61:13
inkan nete xababei jo	animal concept	the Inka's day dawns (*sung by the howler monkey in his laughing song, similar to a 'human' song*)	04:70:22

B. Kakataibo (from a corpus of 24 analysed lyrics)

Text	Theme	Meaning	Reference
inka mane xeta	Kakataibo tech	the Inka's iron tooth (*arrowtip*)	05:43:02
inkan xobo tachinki	Kakataibo site	under the Inka's house (*refers to a Kakataibo house from a peccary's perspective*)	05:51:01
inkan xobo nachinki	Kakataibo site	around the Inka's house (*refers to a Kakataibo house from a peccary's perspective*)	05:51:01
inkan xobo kuechinki	Kakataibo site	digging at the Inka's house (*refers to a Kakataibo house from a peccary's perspective*)	05:51:01

Text	Theme	Meaning	Reference
inka mane nonti	foreign tech	the Inka's metal canoe	05:42:01
noken inka kaisa	esoteric person	my Inka went, it is told *(upriver, in a sung narrative)*	05:70:01
'en papa inka	ancestral person	the Inka, my father	05:42:01
non papa inka	ancestral person	the Inka, the enemy/ mestizo's father	05:42:01

Notes

I would like to thank Juan Javier Rivera Andía and Fernando Santos-Granero for their careful reading of and valuable suggestions to this chapter. I also wish to express my gratitude to Laida Mori Silvano de Brabec who, together with Artemio Pacaya Romaina, translated many hundred Shipibo songs and explained their meaning. Special thanks go to Pascual Mahua Ochavano who provided me with some insight into the knowledge of Shipibo professional healers.

1. The notion of a 'diet' that has to be undertaken in order to acquire new knowledge or abilities, or as a means to recover from illness, is well known in the western Amazonian lowlands. In regional Spanish, people use the noun *dieta* and the verb *dietar*, especially the latter in combination with an agent as idiosyncratic reference; e.g. *estoy dietando el chiricsanango*: 'I am acquiring knowledge from / fighting an illness with the plant Brunfelsia gradiflorens'. Therefore, I use the rather unusual verb 'to diet' as a direct translation to English.

2. With this term borrowed from Bruno Latour, I refer to people socialised in so-called modern environments. This generalising category defines moderns as people who argue with a commonsense ontology based on a slightly misunderstood conceptualisation of rationalism, or as Latour (2013: 94) writes, who 'propagate everywhere an accusation of irrationality about everything that needs, if we are to be able to tell what is true from what is false, a certain number of operations of transformations or displacement – operations that are, however, … a matter of reason itself'.

3. See also, for example, Frank (1994), Gebhart-Sayer (1987), Illius (1987, 1999), Roe (1988) and Tapia Arce (2013).

4. McCallum (2002), however, underlines the importance of these 'past' Inkas for the transformations occurring more recently, and the Kaxinawas' attitude towards foreigners or '*brancos*'.

5. With 'magical' songs I denote songs performed with the intention of changing conditions, influencing events or manipulating circumstances. 'Magic' will be used in this chapter to denote systems of reference that are based on logical and/or experiential/empirical networks that are not

congruent, or stand in open conflict, with Western scientific systems of reference. Hereby I regard magical systems as a means of explanation for processes performed to achieve changes that are, within the system, intersubjectively observed to 'work'. In this view, magic is not related or opposed to religion (no more than science is related or opposed to religion). For definitions of magic that allow for shared experience, research and development, see Tambiah (1990) and Brown (1997).

6. The term 'Panoan Inka' is somewhat misleading, because among many other Pano-speaking groups the Inka is not present in narratives, for example among the Yaminawa. See Calavia Sáez (2000) for an analysis of this distribution. Note that my introductory epigraph stems from a Kukamiria healer. I heard Inkas being mentioned by various Kukamiria, but could not find reliable evidence in the literature.

7. Other collections of indigenous narratives – like Estrella Odicio (1973), Frank et al. (1990), García (1993), FUCSHICO (1998) and Pacaya Romaina (2011) – relate at least two or three, sometimes many more, tales with Inka protagonists.

8. Male initiation rituals (*mekeke*) among the Kakataibo are no longer practised (officially), and have not been since around 1950. For more details on Kakataibo initiation and the 'house of medicine', see Frank (1982, 1994).

9. The Kakataibo term *no* (line 3) parallels the Panoan category *nawa*, denoting a person who is 'other-different' (as opposed to 'other-similar' brethren). In former times, *no* designated people from indigenous groups different from 'ours'. Since the Kakataibo's exposure to Peruvian society, *no* is commonly used for mestizos (or white people).

10. Among moderns, this crossing is not performed to its entirety: beings of fiction and technology only interact within fiction, forming the genre known as 'science fiction'.

11. See Calavia Sáez (2000) for a comparative view on Inkas and technology. Also in Andean mythology, beings of the past (including the Inkas) are never 'gone' completely; they go on existing in a certain way that is considered significant for contemporary people, especially because of a presumed 'mediocrity of present times' (Rivera Andía 2006: 170) in comparison with the past. For a general view on this phenomenon, see also Ortíz Rescaniere (1995).

12. Fernando Santos-Granero (personal communication, 2014) is preparing a historical study about a related millenarian movement on the Ucayali River, which will shed much light on narratives such as this one. In Andean Inka-related mythology, messianic ideas are likewise strongly present (Rivera Andía 2006).

13. These and more Inka narratives by Pascual Mahua are archived at D 5547 and D 5550.

14. Such a sacred 'Inkan' land seems to reflect on the *Tierra sin mal* from Tupí and Guaraní mythology. A *Tierra sin mal* is seldom mentioned by Panoans (but see Bertrand-Ricoveri 2010: 231–32), and in such cases it

is likely that the notion was borrowed from the neighbouring Kukama among whom this idea is present (Ochoa Abaurre 2002). In any case, there are some interesting connections – e.g. one characteristic of the *Tierra sin mal* is that the 'Lords of the authentic metal' (*señores del metal verdadero*, Villar and Combés 2013: 209) would live there, somewhere in the Andean foothills. Another detail is that a (talking/singing) parrot is often pictured as a guardian of the *Tierra sin mal*, while the same bird consistently appears in Shipibo tales and songs as the Inka's messenger (Villar and Combés 2013; cf. Brabec de Mori 2015a: 529ff.).

15. I prefer to put 'shamanism' in quotation marks, because I think that this term obscures much more than it reveals. For a concise critique of shamanism-related terminology, see Martínez González (2009).

16. The literature is not very well informed in this respect, either. Wistrand Robinson (1976: 9) mentions a few magical songs or incantations, and Frank (1982: 65) describes the *mekeke* complex that served for healing, hunting magic, war magic and male initiation. Frank (1994: 201) also explains that Kakataibo understand songs for healing as *ro*, medicine. I do not know of sources that go deeper into Kakataibo magical ontology.

17. Illius interprets the suffix -*ni* as composed of -*n*-, which turns an intransitive verb (or a noun) into a transitive one, and the modificator -*i* that is usually translated with 'in order to'.

18. With 'ontological level' I refer to a part of reality that, as conceptualised by indigenous Shipibo (among other indigenous and mestizo people in the region), requires different qualities from beings to be able to enter, see or otherwise perceive them. For example, spirits *yoshin* are generally different from Shipibo persons: they are invisible. However, they are conceived as part of reality. They require an ontological level of reality different from the level Shipibo dwell in, although these levels pertain to a shared space (e.g. the forest, the river). For a debate (in German) on the speculative ontology of Shipibo epistemology, see Sharif and Brabec de Mori (2018).

19. Treating the complex transformation of visual into sonic and sonic into visual phenomena, which is a property of powerful songs in western Amazonian magic, is beyond the scope of this chapter. For a detailed explanation, see Brabec de Mori (2015b).

20. Interview recorded in 2004 (D 5228); see Brabec de Mori (2015a: 615) for a transcription.

21. For a comprehensive correlation of these figures with the 'good' and the 'bad' mestizos and whites, see Roe (1988) and Calavia Sáez (2000).

22. Author's translation of 'La diferencia entre el estado de sueño y el estado de vigilia es, a veces, descrita como una diferencia de lugar. El adverbio '*uxë* (al otro lado, al lado enfrente) es asociado con el acto de dormir (*'uxcë*). Con *nëcë* (a este lado) se designa, oposicionalmente, el estado de vigilia'.

23. Among the Kakataibo, a loosely related concept can be found with the *kamano*. These are historically and linguistically identified as a former

(and probably extinct) subgroup of the Kakataibo (Zariquiey 2013), and they did not embrace permanent contact with Peruvian society as all the other subgroups did. They remained hidden in the woods, and although usually depicted as inferior (wild, savage, primitive) by the Kakataibo, nowadays one can observe an idealisation that brings them closer to the 'original' Kakataibo, that is, to the Inka.

References

Bertrand-Ricoveri, P. 2010. *Mitología Shipibo: Un Viaje en el Imaginario de un Pueblo Amazónico*. Paris: L'Harmattan.

Beyer, S. 2012. 'On the Origins of Ayahuasca', in *Singing to the Plants: Steve Beyer's Blog on Ayahuasca and the Amazon*. Retrieved 20 March 2016 from http://www.singingtotheplants.com/2012/04/on-origins-of-ayahuasca/.

Brabec de Mori, B. 2002. 'Ikaro: Medizinische Gesänge der Ayawaska-Zeremonie im Peruanischen Regenwald'. MA dissertation. Vienna: University of Vienna. Retrieved 20 March 2016 from http://www.emlaak.org/files/Publikationen%20Bernd/Ikaro_sw.pdf.

———. 2011a. 'The Magic of Song, the Invention of Tradition and the Structuring of Time among the Shipibo (Peruvian Amazon)', *Jahrbuch des Phonogrammarchivs der Österreichischen Akademie der Wissenschaften* 2: 169–92.

———. 2011b. 'Tracing Hallucinations: Contributing to a Critical Ethnohistory of Ayahuasca Usage in the Peruvian Amazon', in B. Labate and H. Jungaberle (eds), *The Internationalization of Ayahuasca*. Zürich: LIT, pp. 23–47.

———. 2012. 'About Magical Singing, Sonic Perspectives, Ambient Multinatures, and the Conscious Experience', *Indiana* 29: 73–101.

———. 2013. 'A Medium of Magical Power: How to Do Things with Voices in the Western Amazon', in D. Zakharine and N. Meise (eds), *Electrified Voices: Medial, Socio-Historical and Cultural Aspects of Voice Transmission*. Göttingen: V&R unipress, pp. 379–401.

———. 2015a. *Die Lieder der Richtigen Menschen: Musikalische Kulturanthropologie der indigenen Bevölkerung im Ucayali-Tal, Westamazonien*. Innsbruck: Helbling.

———. 2015b. 'Sonic Substances and Silent Sounds: An Auditory Anthropology of Ritual Songs', *Tipití: Journal of the Society for the Anthropology of Lowland South America* 13(2): 25–43.

Brabec de Mori, B., and M. Winter (eds). 2018. *Auditive Wissenskulturen: Das Wissen klanglicher Praxis*. Wiesbaden: Springer VS.

Brown, M.F. 1997. 'Thinking about Magic', in S.D. Glazier (ed.),

Anthropology of Religion: A Handbook. Westport, CT: Greenwood Press, pp. 121–36.

Calavia Sáez, O. 2000. 'Mythologies of the Vine', in L.E. Luna and S.F. White (eds), *Ayahuasca Reader: Encounters with the Amazon's Sacred Vine*. Santa Fe, NM: Synergetic Press, pp. 36–40.

Descola, Ph. 2005. *Par-delà Nature et Culture*. Paris: Editions Gallimard.

Estrella Odicio, G. 1973. *Cuentos del Hombre Cacataibo (Cashibo) y la Obra Civilizadora de Bolivar*. Lima: Ministerio de Educación.

Frank, E.H. 1982. 'MECECE: La Función Sicológica Social y Económica de un Complejo Ritual de los Uni (Cashibo) de la Amazonía Peruana,' *Amazonía Peruana* 5(9): 63–78.

———. 1994. 'Los Uni', in F. Santos-Granero and F. Barclay (eds), *Guía Etnográfica de la Alta Amazonía*, vol. 2. Lima: FLACSO, pp. 129–237.

Frank, E.H., et al. 1990. *Mitos de los Uni de Santa Marta: Enëx ca Santa Martanu Icë Unin bana Icën*. Quito: Abya-Yala.

FUCSHICO (Fundación Cultural Shipibo-Conibo). 1998. *Non Requenbaon Shinan: El origen de la Cultura Shipibo-Conibo. Leyendas-Historias-Costumbres-Cuentos*. Yarinacocha.

García, F. 1993. *Etnohistoria Shipibo (Tradición Oral de los Shipibo-Conibo)*. Lima: CAAAP.

Gebhart-Sayer, A. 1987. *Die Spitze des Bewußtseins: Untersuchungen zu Weltbild und Kunst der Shipibo-Conibo*. Hohenschäftlarn: Klaus Renner.

Gow, P. 1994. 'River People: Shamanism and History in Western Amazonia', in N. Thomas and C. Humphrey (eds), *Shamanism, History and the State*. Ann Arbor: University of Michigan Press, pp. 90–113.

Hill, J.D., and F. Santos-Granero (eds). 2002. *Comparative Arawakan Histories: Rethinking Language Family and Culture Area in Amazonia*. Urbana and Chicago: University of Illinois Press.

Illius, B. 1987. *Ani Shinan: Schamanismus bei den Shipibo-Conibo (Ost-Peru)*. Tübingen: Verlag S&F.

———. 1999. *Das Shipibo. Texte, Kontexte, Kommentare: Ein Beitrag zur diskursorientierten Untersuchung einer Montaña-Kultur*. Berlin: Dietrich Reimer.

Knorr Cetina, K. 2005. 'Culture in Global Knowledge Societies: Knowledge Cultures and Epistemic Cultures', in M.D. Jacobs and N. Weiss Hanrahan (eds), *The Blackwell Companion to the Sociology of Culture*. Malden, MA: Blackwell, pp. 65–79.

———. 2018. 'Wissenskulturen: Von der Naturwissenschaft zur Musik', in B. Brabec de Mori and M. Winter (eds), *Auditive Wissenskulturen: Das Wissen klanglicher Praxis*. Wiesbaden: Springer VS, pp. 31–52.

Labate, B.C., and W.S. Araújo (eds). 2004. *O Uso Ritual da Ayahuasca*. Campinas: Mercado de Letras.

Lathrap, D.W., A. Gebhart-Sayer and A.M. Mester. 1985. 'The Roots of the Shipibo Art Style: Three Waves in Imiríacocha or There Were

"Incas" Before the Incas', *Journal of Latin American Lore* 11(1): 31–119.

Latour, B. 2013. *An Inquiry into Modes of Existence: An Anthropology of the Moderns*. Cambridge, MA and London: Harvard University Press.

Martínez Gonzáles, R. 2009. 'El Chamanismo y la Corporalización del Chamán: Argumentos para la Deconstrucción de una Falsa Categoría Antropológica', *Cuicuilco* 16(46): 197–220.

McCallum, C. 2002. 'Incas e Nawas: Produção, transformação e transcendência na história Kaxinawá', in B. Albert and A. Ramos (eds), *Pacificando o Branco: Cosmologias do Contato no Norte-Amazônico*. São Paulo: Editora Universidade Estadual Paulista (Unesp), pp. 375–404.

Meyer, B.H. 1974. 'Beiträge zur Ethnographie der Conibo und Shipibo (Ostperu)'. PhD dissertation. Zurich: University of Zurich.

Ochoa Abaurre, J.C. 2002. 'Mito y Chamanismo: el Mito de la Tierra sin Mal en los Tupí-Cocama de la Amazonía Peruana'. PhD dissertation. Barcelona: University of Barcelona.

Ortiz Rescaniere, A. 1986. 'Imperfecciones, Demonios y Héroes Andinos', *Anthropologica* 4: 191–224.

———. 1995. 'Unas Imágenes del Tiempo', *Anthropologica* 13: 141–66.

Pacaya Romaina, A. 2011. *Shipibaon Axe (Costumbres, Arte y Cultura): Shipibo-Castellano*. Pucallpa: Centro de Capacitación y Producción de Material Impreso para Educación Bilingüe.

Ritter, G. 1997. 'Exposición de Algunos Elementos de la Cultura Cashibo-Catacaibo', *Anthropologica* 15: 217–53.

Rivera Andía, J.J. 2006. 'Mitología en los Andes', in A. Ortiz Rescaniere (ed.), *Mitologías Amerindias*. Madrid: Editorial Trotta, pp. 129–76.

Roe, P.G. 1988. 'The Josho Nahuanbo Are All Wet and Undercooked: Shipibo Views on the Whiteman and the Incas in Myth, Legend and History', in J.D. Hill (ed.), *Rethinking History and Myth: Indigenous South American Perspectives on the Past*. Chicago: University of Illinois Press, pp. 106–35.

Santos-Granero, F. 2003. 'Pedro Casanto's Nightmares: Lucid Dreaming in Amazonia and the New Age Movement', *Tipití: Journal of the Society for the Anthropology of Lowland South America* 1(2): 179–210.

———. 2012. 'Beinghood and People-Making in Native Amazonia: A Constructional Approach with a Perspectival Coda', *HAU: Journal of Ethnographic Theory* 2(1): 181–211.

Sharif, M., and B. Brabec de Mori. 2018. 'Auditives Wissen und ontologisch-epistemologischer Pluralismus: Ein Dialog für zwei Ethnomusikologen', in B. Brabec de Mori and M. Winter (eds), *Auditive Wissenskulturen: Das Wissen klanglicher Praxis*. Wiesbaden: Springer VS, pp. 93–114.

Tambiah, S.J. 1990. *Magic, Science, Religion, and the Scope of Rationality*. New York: Cambridge University Press.

Tapia Arce, A.M. 2013. 'The Kakataibo and Camano Indigenous Peoples: Perspectives on Identity of Belonging between Two Amazonian Groups'. MA dissertation. Austin: University of Texas.

Tournon, J. 1991. 'Medicina y Visiones: Canto de un Curandero Shipibo-Conibo, Texto y Contexto', *Amerindia* 16: 179–209.

Villar, D., and I. Combès. 2013. 'La Tierra Sin Mal: Leyenda de la creación y destrucción de un mito', *Tellus* 13(24): 201–25.

Wistrand Robinson, L.M. 1976. 'La Poesía de las Canciones Cashibos', *Datos Etno-Lingüísticos* 45(1): 1–27.

Zariquiey, R. 2013. 'Tessmann's "Nokamán": A Linguistic Investigation of a Mysterious Panoan Group', *Cadernos de Etnolingüística* 5(2): 1–48.

6

On Quechua Relatedness to Contemporary and Ancient Dead

Guillermo Salas Carreño

Introduction

Andean ethnography is full of references to the dead and to funerary rituals, as well as data on narratives about the dreadful 'damned
people' (*condenados*) and about the *gentiles*, *ñawpa machus* or
suqas – individuals of a previous humanity that are presented as pre-
Hispanic or early colonial mummies from non-Quechua perspectives. The analyses of these different types of dead people in the
literature, as well as the analysis of Andean kinship, largely assume
that sexual procreation, and hence ties of descent and ancestry, are
at the core of implicit Quechua notions of relatedness to what are
considered humans, whether alive or dead. In this chapter I elaborate on how this assumption is problematic and does not follow
the logic inscribed in many Quechua practices constructing human
relatedness. Other notions, beyond descent, are at the core of the
ways Quechua construct human relatedness in practice. In the first
section I will summarise previous research that shows how food provision and forms of cohabitation are crucial in the construction of the
closest kin relationships. As will become clear, the centrality of food
provision and cohabitation does not mean that sexual procreation
is ignored or overlooked, but rather that it is embedded within the
framework of food provision and cohabitation.

The second section, using previous scholarly data and analysis,
shows how these notions are also at play in the construction of

kinship beyond the nuclear family. Moreover, it elaborates on how these notions are not only present in the construction of kinship ties but in all forms of sociality.

The next three sections treat the forms of relatedness that contemporary Quechua speakers of different communities in the region of Cuzco, Peru, construct with different types of beings that, from non-Quechua perspectives, can be presented as dead humans. The third one – Death and Departure – is about how the notions of food provision and cohabitation are present in the relatedness to recently dead people. The fourth – The Damned – treats the cases of the narratives of *condenados*, dead people who cannot rest as a result of great sins, and who wander among living humans devouring them. The case of the damned is particularly interesting since the most serious sin is incest, which is of course deeply linked with sexual intercourse, and hence, with sexual procreation. The fifth – The Ancients– discusses the case of what, from a non-Quechua perspective, are seen as pre-Hispanic or early colonial cemeteries and the mummies that they contain. While many ethnographic works present these mummies as (mythical) ancestors of contemporary Quechua communities, I explain why these reiterated interpretations are misguided because they impose non-Quechua notions of descent over ethnographic evidence. From Quechua perspectives there is neither a link of descent with these beings nor a positive active relatedness that is maintained or sought with them.[1]

Food, Cohabitation and Close Kinship

In this section I summarise recent research that demonstrates the importance of food and cohabitation in the construction of Quechua relatedness.

There is a wealth of anthropological literature that describes in detail the importance of food in the construction of human sociality.[2] As Goody (1982: 2) puts it, eating is 'a way of placing oneself in relation to others'. Commensality, who eats with whom and in which contexts, constitutes a powerful mechanism to both construct social relations and to mark social boundaries (Feeley-Harnik 1994). As Carsten (1995) demonstrated for the Malay, and Taylor (2000) for the Jivaro, particular forms of commensality are at the core of culturally specific ways of constructing even the closest kin relationships between humans.

Incorporating practices of eating within the analysis of human relatedness was made possible by re-evaluating some assumptions about human kinship. Classic anthropological definitions of kinship rested on sexual procreation and ethnocentric assumptions about the universal validity of a conceptual opposition between the 'biological' and the 'social', characteristic of contemporary West European and North American societies (Carsten 1995; Holý 1996). Questioning this has allowed scholars to re-examine vernacular theories of human relatedness beyond the assumptions of the central role of sexual pro-creation in human kinship. These theories give central importance to substances beyond genes or blood (e.g. semen, milk, earth, food, sap) (Weismantel 1995; Carsten 2000, 2004; Hutchinson 2000; Parkes 2005) and typically show processual understandings of personhood associated with growth, maturation, decay and death (Fox 1971; Peluso 1996; Renne 2007). Associated with these approaches on relatedness, there is also a growing literature theorising about kinship while moving into areas previously associated with ecological and environmental studies (Hallowell 1992; Ingold 2000, 2007).

Being a person, rather than a fixed status, is a permanent process of becoming in which kinship roles are constantly being constructed in practice. '[T]he role of parents is … – by their presence, their activities and the nurture they provide – to establish the necessary conditions in the environment for their children's growth and development' (Ingold 2000: 141). Quechua social ontology is best understood in this framework. Relatively recent research in Quechua communities shows that relationships between parents, sons and daughters do not rest primarily on reproductive ties. As Van Vleet puts it in her ethnography of a Bolivian Quechua community: '[W]ho gives birth to whom is in itself insufficient for understanding Sullk'ata relatedness. Silveria claims to be Javier's mother because she *raised* him: fed him and cared for him, carried him on her back, laughed with him, and comforted his cries' (Van Vleet 2008: 58, emphasis in the original). Or, as Weismantel explains for the case of Zumbaga (Ecuador):

> The physical acts of intercourse, pregnancy, and birth can establish a strong bond between two adults and a child. But other adults, by taking a child into their family and nurturing its physical needs through the same substances as those eaten by the rest of the social group, can make of that child a son or a daughter who is physically as well as jurally their own. (Weismantel 1995: 695)

Food is the substance that constitutes and relates Quechua bodies. Levels of commensality as well as quality and quantity of food are used to construct social distances (Weismantel 1988). This is exhibited in a basic expression of the most elemental courtesy and hospitality with strangers: to offer some food to any stranger received within the house (Oxa 2005: 240).

The regular practices of sharing food define family and relatives. As Weismantel elaborates for Zumbaga, '[f]lesh is made from food … Those who eat together in the same household share the same flesh in a quite literal sense: they are made of the same stuff' (Weismantel 1995: 695). Van Vleet shows how even the process of child conception and growth before birth in Sullk'ata (Bolivia) follows similar ideas. Sexual procreation and agriculture are modelled by each other: 'A child is born nine or ten months after a man plants his seed in a woman. A child ripens during pregnancy through the *actions* of the woman who nourishes her child, just as Pacha Mama[3] nourishes the seed of corn or potatoes, allowing those seeds to ripen' (Van Vleet 2008: 59, emphasis in the original). Even before birth, the notion of feeding is important in the construction of relatedness. The new person is in the semen as a potentiality, just as plants are potentially in the seeds. The mother's body provides a caring environment for the seed and her blood is food for the foetus. Hence pregnancy is envisaged as a crucial stage that initiates the process of caring and feeding. After birth, breastfeeding is the continuation of this. If the seed is central for the existence of the new person, his or her development is impossible without the provision of food and care. This process of caring and feeding that allows a new person to exist and grow is the same that relates her to a group of other humans, her relatives.

While I emphasise caring and feeding, it should be clear that bonds of procreation are not irrelevant. This is clear in the discussion about the process of conception and intrauterine growth, as well as, for example, in the scholarship on child circulation in the Andes (when a child is raised by adults other than his progenitors). As Leinaweaver (2008: 137) puts it, '*cariño* [affection] may be forged through co-residence, sharing meals or beds, but it takes root and thrives in the fertile, if bloody, ground of genealogy'.

Continuous caring and provision of food is part of a wider process of cohabitation: living together not only means to eat the same food together every day, but also to acquire habits, etiquettes, values, tastes and accents (Leinaweaver 2008; Van Vleet 2008). The development of the new child's habitus (Mauss [1935] 1973; Bourdieu 1977) is the same process of constructing paternity and maternity, as well as becoming a sibling, an uncle, or a grandmother. Cohabitation, which implies the consumption and provision of food, is at the heart of Andean notions of the family (Weismantel 1995). 'The Ayacuchanos I knew inevitably presented having lived together, over time, as a justification for the emotional connections they experienced. Present day *cariño*, affection, is a direct result of past cohabitation' (Leinaweaver 2008: 135).

These processual ways to construct kinship resonate with the extensive Amazonian scholarship that shows similar, while not exactly the same, patterns of construction of kinship. As Rival put it for the Huaorani:

> People living in the same longhouse gradually become of the same substance, literally 'of one same flesh' … The physical reality of living together, that is, of continuously feeding each other, eating the same food and sleeping together, develops into a common physicality, which is far more real than genealogical ties. (Rival 1998: 621)

In a similar way, Vilaça (2002: 352) claims that cohabitation is crucial for the Wari' construction of kinship: '[T]he Wari' usually refer to inhabitants of the same post (a village settlement, equivalent in actuality to a subgroup) as their true kin, and on these occasions may exclude genealogical kin who live in another village'. Ethnographies carried out among the Suyá (Seeger 1981), the Piro (Gow 1991), the Araweté (Viveiros de Castro 1992), the Jivaro (Taylor 2000) and the Barasana (Hugh-Jones 2001), among others, show that these processual forms of construction of kinship that involve continuous cohabitation and commensality are widespread in lowland South America.[4]

Beyond the Nuclear Family

In this section I elaborate on how the notions of food provision and cohabitation that constitute the closest kin relations – as shown in the work of Weismantel, Van Vleet and Leinaweaver – are also present in the relations with affines and, in general, in all social relationships among kinsmen and beyond them.

In contrast to, for example, siblings who have grown up in the same household eating the same food, the affines are non-relatives who become so by constituting a new household, a new realm of cohabitation and provision of food. In general, relations with affines are based on difference, while those with siblings or parents are based on similarity (Holý 1996; Viveiros de Castro 2009: 224). Both types of relatives emerge relationally and are indispensable for the constitution of a new household.

Due to the relative preference of virilocal residence in Quechua communities within the region of Cuzco, it is usually the new wife who has to move to her husband's parents' house, and 'get accustomed'[5] there. This is not an easy process for the *qachun*[6] who stereotypically starts her new life under the critical surveillance of her husband's mother, with the latter constantly challenging her to prove her worth. The *qachun* becomes kin through a similar processual fashion by performing her mastery in food preparation and other female household tasks, as well as participating in commensality and cohabitation with her husband and his family (Van Vleet 2002). Conversely the *qatay*[7] 'intrudes himself into the intimacy of the family group, stealing their kinswoman's loyalty' (Allen 2011: 66).[8] Because affines are strangers who become relatives, being a responsible affine has to be demonstrated and publicly performed. That is why affines are in charge of labour-demanding tasks that typically involve the preparation and distribution of food and alcohol when, for example, the household is sponsoring a communal celebration or has to carry out a funeral. This role of affines in communal celebrations or in funerary rituals has been reported by several ethnographers (Isbell 1978; Harris 1982; Gose 1994). During most of these rituals the household feeds and provides alcohol to the broader community through its affines. By assuming these roles, the affine honours and strengthens the bonds with his or her partner's family; bonds created by the constitution of his or her own household.[9]

The household, the place of the strongest commensality and co-residence, is the realm of the closest kin relationships and of *generalised reciprocity* (Sahlins 1972). As shared food and companionship decreases outside the household, generalised reciprocity declines, ceding to different forms of *balanced reciprocity* (ibid.). Most of these relationships of reciprocity involve exchanges of labour that are crucial for social reproduction. Reciprocal exchanges of labour are an essential part of the wider process of circulation of food. These different arrangements of reciprocity organising agricultural production, are mediated by particular patterns of distribution of food, coca and alcohol among those who work. Provision of food is indispensable in order to organise any agricultural work. This is one of the main reasons why a man alone cannot organise exchanges of labour without a woman who cooks for the workers (see, for example, Mayer 2002).

Beyond the household, close kin is a product of cultivating ongoing relationships of close cooperation in which food is regularly given and received, as well as considerable time shared in collaborative work through a continuous exchange of labour.[10] As Isbell (1977) shows in her paper about the cleaning of canals in pre-war Chuschi

(Ayacucho), at the end of the rituals, the sponsors laid on a banquet for all those who had expressed affection by helping them out in the fulfilment of their responsibilities. The attendees were relatives by descent or affinity. The quantities and types of food offered on this occasion varied in relation to how much each relative had helped. Giving help for passing a communal work and festivity, as well as recognising those who have helped by providing food in a calculated way, are practices that are at the core of the continuous constitution of these bonds. While those who actually show affection for someone are among his or her relatives by descent or affinity, not all the people who can have bonds of descent or affinity with someone are those who actually show affection for him or her.[11] These relationships have to be cultivated by means of ongoing reciprocal exchanges of labour, work and food.

Communal rituals are, in many cases, marked by an excessive provision of food to dancers, attendees and outside visitors (Allen 1988). During carnival celebrations in Qamawara I was faced with the clear impossibility of eating all that I was offered. I soon realised, with some relief, that I was not the only one facing this problem. All attendees and particularly those who had ritual roles, such as dancers, received an especially large dish in each of the seven houses of the staff bearers in charge of the celebrations. Children played a key role in silently collecting part of the food and carrying it home to be consumed later. While this excessive communal commensality can be seen as part of the politics of prestige at play in any communal celebration, it also constitutes a powerful embodied experience of celebrating the community as a group of related people who feed and care for each other, and who collectively are able to satisfy all their members fully, and even to excess. These events of communal commensality are overstatements of what regularly, and in a more partial way, happens in everyday life via the different networks of cooperation at work within the local community. These multiple levels of commensality that constitute the social relations are only possible due to a certain level of co-residence within a set of places that are usually regarded as the landholdings of the community. As Paulson (2006) has shown for the Quechua community of Mizque (Bolivia), festive communal food consumption is crucial for the reproduction or the sense of community and belonging when community members who may live beyond the physical borders of the community reunite and reproduce their communality. As Allen (1988: 108) explained in her ethnography of Sonqo (Paucartambo), continuous co-residence with(in) a set of places – besides ties of descent – is what constitutes an *ayllu* (community). Recently, de la Cadena (2015) has re-elaborated this notion, emphasising the co-emergence of *runakuna* (humans) and earth beings in the relational constitution of an *ayllu*. Thus, an *ayllu* is not a community that is constituted only by humans but it necessarily also involves the places or earth beings.[12]

Death and Departure

As food and cohabitation are at the core of human relatedness, they are also central in marking the end of life and the departure from the community of the living. When someone dies, the deceased stops cohabitating with living humans. Moreover, he or she has to stop cohabitating with humans for the well-being of the living. When someone dies in Qamawara, it is important to ensure that both the *animu*[13] – the deceased's particular vital force now disembodied – and the *alma*[14] – the deceased's corpse – are properly separated from the community of the living. If this fails, both the *animu* and the *alma* can cause illnesses and pollute the community. The dead cannot cohabitate with the living; if this happens, human society is in danger.

In Qamawara, as has been consistently reported for many other Quechua communities (e.g. Ricard 2007 for Phinaya [Quispicanchis] and Robin 2005 for Chumbivilcas and Calca, all located in the region of Cuzco), the rituals right after death until the burial involve the separation of the corpse from the community of the living. Washing it, dressing it with clean clothes, ensuring the proper performing of *responsos* (prayers for the deceased), and the burial itself have the purpose of marking the radical separation that death entails – the termination of quotidian cohabitation. The cohabitation of living humans and a recent corpse is extremely dangerous for the former. It produces disease and misfortune. The consumption of coca, alcohol and cigarettes during the night of the wake, and in all the contexts in which the corpse is present until burial, are presented as ways of protecting living humans from the corpse's pollution. The cemetery is the place that contains the corpses and separates them from the community of the living. This is why it is important that it has walls, and that, except for burials and the day of the dead, no living human enters it. It is only in these contexts that the cemetery can becomes a social place where living humans can remain for a relatively long time. The cemetery is an unsafe and unhealthy place for living humans, who only briefly stay there, even though protected by the consumption of alcohol, coca and cigarettes. Soon after the burial is finished, the living humans leave and go to the deceased's house to continue with the mourning rituals.

The deceased's *animu*, however, remains in the community for some days after the death, until the last rituals of farewell are completed. To ensure the proper departure, all the deceased's clothes are washed so that no bodily substance remains in them. During the last rituals of departure, food has to be given to the *animu* so that it has enough strength to endure the journey to its final destiny. There is no clear agreement about where the *animu* has to travel to. Some say that it is to the country of the dead in the far-off volcanoes to the West, while others claim that it goes either to hell or to heaven, depending on the person's deeds while living. However, all the Qamawarans I talked to are very clear that the *animu* has to leave the community. Both the burial in the cemetery and the rituals of farewell are essential for preventing the cohabitation of the living and the dead.

If all goes well, the *animu* leaves and the corpse remains in the bounded realm of the cemetery. The *animus* of the dead visit the living only on the Day of the Dead. On this day, the cemetery of Qamawara is full of living humans, who clean and adorn the graves of their relatives with crosses made of qantu[15] flowers (Illustration 6.1). Nevertheless, when doing so, some coca, alcohol and cigarettes are welcome in order to ensure that no emanation from a fresh corpse endangers their well-being. In the evening, after the cleaning of the cemetery, everybody returns to their homes and each household offers a banquet for the *animu* of the dead that are coming to visit. People stay up in the house, praying and talking while they wait for the deceased to arrive and happily consume the food that is offered to them. When the day is over, the deceased's *animu* again leaves the community of the living. Several Qamawarans casually commented to me when asked about the banquet for the dead that even if the food seems to be intact there is no point in eating it. It is not nutritious or fulfilling food anymore, because the deceased's *animu* has eaten the food's *animu*. Most of these aspects of the celebrations of the day of the dead are quite consistent throughout many Quechua communities.[16]

However, this relationship with the dead vanishes with time. At some point – longer in some cases and shorter in others – people forget their dead relatives. While *musuq alma*, the recently dead, are dangerous, the old remains unattended by relatives do not do any harm. If a corpse needs to be buried, old unattended remains are removed without too much care and the space is reused. People in Qamawara did not worry about old bones on the surface of the

Illustration 6.1 Two tombs adorned with *qantu* flowers on the Day of the Dead. Notice the old unattended skulls in the niches of the wall. Qamawara, 1 November 2008. Photograph: G. Salas Carreño.

cemetery. Some fragments of old skulls were left in the niches of the cemetery wall (Illustration 6.1). Other old bones were left on the ground. People told me in an uninterested way that those were bones of very old burials and that they cannot cause any harm at all.

Similarly, the households that have recently deceased relatives have very elaborate and abundant food offerings for the day of the dead (see Illustration 6.2). The banquets in households that have old dead relatives have less elaborate and abundant banquets for the same occasions. When people no longer give food to a particular deceased person, they no longer take care of the grave and the deceased no longer appears in dreams; all relatedness with this dead person vanishes. Thus, in the long run this is a process of the deceased's individuality effacement.[17] Some people claim that they do not know what happens to them; others say that the soul is with God; and others still would say that the soul is in a faraway volcano with all other deceased people.[18] What I wish to stress here is that there is an absence of long-term relations with human ancestors. In contrast to other societies that place a strong emphasis on ancestry (Fortes 1953 for African societies; Freedman 1965 for south-east China), people in

Illustration 6.2 Banquet for a *musuq alma*, a recently deceased person. Notice the cross of *qantu* flowers. Qamawara, 1 November 2008. Photograph: G. Salas Carreño.

Qamawara usually remember two generations of ascendants. After that, all the dead come to be integrated within an undifferentiated community of *awlanchis*. This term comes from *awla* (from Spanish *abuelo* or *abuela*, grandfather or grandmother) and the suffixes *–n* (possessive) and *–chis* (inclusive second person plural). Thus, the translation would be 'our grandparents'. People also use the Spanish *abuelitos* (dear grandparents) instead of *awlanchis*. However, the translation of *abuelos* to *grandparents* is deceiving. It is important to stress that the father's father is not called *awla* or *abuelo* but *tayta* (Quechua) or *papá* (Spanish), both terms for father. The same happens with the mother's mother, who is called *mamá* (both in Quechua and Spanish), that is, mother. Hence *awlanchis* or *abuelitos* does not properly translate as 'our parents' parents' but rather refers to an undifferentiated collective of long-ago deceased and unknown kin. For example, when Qawamarans narrate about how some highland lagoons were *chukaru* (wild) but they became *manso* (tamed) after being baptised with salt; they will say that this might have occurred in the *awlanchis pacha* (the time of the *awlanchis*) or in *el tiempo de los abuelos* (the time of the grandparents). Both expressions might be better translated as 'the remote time of our old (personally unknown) deceased relatives'. Notice how this disregard of genealogy in Quechua societies is consistent with Amazonian kinship studies, which have shown how 'African' or 'Dravidian' models are of limited use for the analysis of Amazonian kinship (see Rivière 1993: 509).

When someone dies, quotidian cohabitation ceases and funerary rituals have the role of making this separation effective on all levels, including burying the corpse and ensuring the *animu* leaves. Notice how food is the substance through which social ties are still maintained with the deceased in their yearly visits on the Day of the Dead.

The Damned

Stories about *condenados* (the damned) abound in the region of Cuzco as well as throughout the Andes. Mentions of cases of *condenados* are far from being restricted to rural areas. In the mid-1990s, for example, the word spread in the city about an allegedly incestuous person who became a *condenado* and was said to be a prisoner inside Cuzco's cathedral. For two or three days a noticeable group of curious people congregated in front of the door of the cathedral trying to find out more about him, while reporters interviewed several people who claimed to have heard a *condenado*'s screams. During my field research in 2007, another notable case occurred in San Jerónimo, the old sixteenth-century *reducción* of noble Incas that currently houses the city of Cuzco's wholesale market. This case was widely covered by the local media.

A teenage girl was said to have committed suicide and to have become a *condenada*. Viviana, one of my *caseras*[19] from the San Jerónimo market, told me what she had heard:

> V: They say that this man might have taken advantage of his daughter [sexually] on several occasions … The girl met a taxi driver who was married, and had a baby with him. She had her baby. … The baby was born and she gave [the baby] to her father. He told her, 'You have to finish your studies' … She went to the *curandero* and told him, 'Sir, I want you to look in the coca leaves. My father said that he has given my baby away'. Who knows what the *curandero* said, right? In one week she hanged herself, the girl.
> G: How sad!
> V: After that, they say, she was buried, and now it is said that her grave is empty, the coffin is empty. They say that in the fields there was a girl

dressed in white with her face black and holding a black book, and several children bothered her. She told them, 'I am looking for my father; tell him I am looking for him'.[20]

Viviana mentioned that secondary school students, people going to work early and taxi drivers had met her. In these encounters the *condenada* made similar statements about her father and suddenly disappeared, leaving people unconscious and foaming at the mouth. In these two cases, as well as in the extant literature that touches on the topic for the region of Cuzco (Casaverde 1970; Payne 1984; Morote Best 1988; Lira 1990; Itier 2007; Ricard 2007; and Allen 2011 among others), while a normal human can become a *condenado* as a result of any number of serious moral transgressions, incest stands out as a very marked and recurrent offence.

Incest, as Lévi-Strauss (1969) theorised, being the negation of exogamy – the reciprocal agreement of single members to be married outside of the group – is ultimately the negation of human sociality. Incest threatens the proper reproduction of the most basic social relations on which society is built. Incestuous humans are said to become *condenados*, living-dead who wander endlessly from dusk to dawn suffering terrible pains. There are several ways to recognise *condenados*, but one of them is their inability to eat normal human food. Many stories start with a traveller arriving at night and humbly asking for shelter. Following the basic etiquette in welcoming strangers, after letting the stranger into the house, food is given to him. In some stories the *condenado* makes ridiculous excuses and refuses to eat, while in others he has a hole in the throat through which all food exits his body, and still other stories claim that the *condenado* seems to be eating, however the food on the plate does not diminish.[21] This inability to relate to humans via the consumption of food presages a horrible social disjuncture, for when the family is sleeping, the *condenado* attacks his hosts and devours them. Viviana mentioned this as well when she elaborated on other stories she had heard in order to describe what might happen to the *condenada*'s father.

V: A lady also told us about another very similar case, … the *condenado* had come and wanted to take [a man] … Where was he? [People] looked for him but he was gone, [although] his clothes were there. The damned one had eaten him.
G: What? The *condenado* eats, knows how to eat people?
V: Of course, I suppose. Several people say that this will happen. They say that [the *condenada*] will eat her father.[22]

These narratives that emerged in San Jerónimo are consistent with *condenado* narratives that have been heard not only in the city of Cuzco but also in rural communities. Consider the following summary that Michael Sallnow (1987: 128) makes regarding *condenados* according to his ethnography of Qamawara made in the late 1970s:

> If a person dies having committed a grave sin, such as incest ..., he or she becomes a *condenado* (Sp.) or *kukuchi* (Qu.), a being that ... is condemned to pass a twilight existence in *kaypacha*, the land of the living, trapping the unwary in lonely spots and feeding off their flesh. *Condenados* are greatly feared, particularly by the living relatives of a dead person suspected of being one, since they have a taste for the flesh of their own kin.

Hence *condenados* not only threaten human society by being unable to leave and prevent cohabitation, but also this cohabitation is a constant torment for the *condenado* and a serious threat for the living humans. This presence not only pollutes the community but also transforms living humans into food. By eating his or her close relatives, and particularly the living relative with whom he or she committed incest, by transforming them into food, the *condenado* demonstrates his or her capacity to destroy the same sociality that was transgressed by the incestuous acts as a living human.[23]

The Ancients

The cemeteries where contemporary people are buried are not the only type of cemetery in the landscape of Cuzco. Most if not all Quechua communities have within their lands sites that are, from a non-Quechua perspective, pre-Hispanic or early colonial cemeteries. However, most communities of contemporary Quechua people, including Qamawara, regard these cemeteries as towns of people who belong to a previous and different humanity from ours. The *ñawpa machu* (ancient [male] person) or *ñawpa paya* (ancient [female] person)[24] are survivors of an earlier and different humanity that lived under the moonlight and was destroyed by the appearance of the sun. In an attempt to escape from the sunlight, they hid in caves and small stone houses where their bodies dried out. However, they are still alive – and terribly hungry.

As with all other-than-human people with whom humans interact, the *ñawpa machu* are ambivalent beings. Humans obtain some benefits from their presence, but they are also a constant danger. For example, the people of Kuyo Grande (Pisac) told Juvenal Casaverde in the late 1960s how, in the remote past, a *ñawpa machu* of Kuyo had stolen the fertile lands of another community in a bag; since then, that community has had poor lands and Kuyo has had fertile ones (Casaverde Rojas 1970). However, the benefits that these beings bring to living humans are strongly associated with danger. Allen (1988: 56), in her ethnography of Sonqo (Paucartambo) carried out in the 1970s, states that the *machu*'s 'nocturnal labour (nocturnal for us; diurnal for them) makes the potatoes grow large in *Runakuna*'s [human's] fields, and the chullpa's wind, though it makes humans sick, is described as *wanu* [fertiliser] for the potatoes'. Similarly, Sallnow (1987: 127–28), in his ethnography of Qamawara, also carried out in the 1970s, states that

> the wind that blows from the puna at dusk might carry the soq'a machu ... which can cause sickness and even death to those who inhale it. On the other hand, the soq'a machu also promotes the fertility of the crops, while the machus themselves are sometimes spoken of affectionately, using the familiar endearment machula.

However, other scholars (Flores Ochoa 1973; Gow and Condori 1976: 27–28; Ricard 2007) consistently report that humans envisage these beings as evil and envious, capable of seriously endangering human life. During my own fieldwork in the region of Cuzco, I did not come across any instances in which the people of Qamawara or Hapu described these beings positively.

While the *ñawpa machu*'s unintended behaviour can benefit humans, these beings cannot intentionally establish positive social relationships with the latter. All their intentional interactions with human beings damage them terribly. One clear sign that they cannot establish normal social relationships with humans is that although they are hungry they cannot eat human food. Both Hapu and Qamawara people told me that these beings particularly dislike food with salt, garlic or onions. Additionally, they told me that these beings eat the product of wild potato plants and the equivalents of other upland tubers that are not considered worthy of human consumption.

Not only can these beings not establish positive social relationships with humans, they can actively attack them. The *ñawpa machu* devours humans who disrespectfully wander past their old houses without greeting them humbly and offering them coca leaves, alcohol or cigarettes.[25] The victim slowly dries out, while the *ñawpa machu* consumes his vitality and ultimately kills him. There is only one way to stop this process, one that radically reverses this relationship, and that is by burning the *ñawpa machu* (typically the bones) and then ingesting the ashes (Lira 1946; Casaverde 1970). Hence, to stop the *ñawpa machu* eating someone, this person has to eat him.

When Pedro, one of my Hapu acquaintances, and I visited the *Museo Inka* in the city we had the opportunity to see several *ñawpa machus*. They are located in an exhibit space that resembles a cave, and the visitors can see them through small windows in a wall. The *ñawpa machus* had in front of them dishes with coca leaves on them. After we left the museum I asked Pedro about the *ñawpa machus*. 'They're doing harm to people there, aren't they? Why did they allow themselves to be put there?' Pedro answered by pointing out that these *ñawpa machus* did not represent an actual threat to human beings there. They were totally out of their place, far from their old houses and their community, and faced with a constant presence of humans. This forced cohabitation in a dense human population made them uncomfortable, confused and defenceless. Furthermore, this was reinforced by the smell of garlic and onions that is present in human food and that they deeply dislike.

While humans who wander by themselves close to the *ñawpa machu* houses are exposed to the danger of being consumed by them, these *ñawpa machu* prisoners in the museum were neutralised by the overwhelming human presence in the city. The forced cohabitation with humans intimidated them. The very smell of human food, the substance of human sociality, was a constant torture for them. Social interaction between humans and *ñawpa machu* ends up damaging the former or the latter, depending on the circumstances.

This can be further illustrated in relation to these beings' sexual behaviour. Just as they are hungry, so they are sexually starved, and they have a clear inclination to deceive humans in order to have intercourse with them. This usually happens when the latter are drunk or in dreams. In order to seduce the victim, the *ñawpa machu* or *paya* take the physical appearance of the human's partner. A woman can become impregnated and give birth to a monstrous dead foetus, and die giving birth. A man who impregnates a *ñawpa paya* (the female of the *ñawpa machu*) slowly dries out over nine months until he dies when his *ñawpa machu* son is born (Casaverde 1970; Flores Ochoa 1973). Hence, while these beings can reproduce themselves by interbreeding with humans, the latter are always damaged or destroyed by this sexual activity.

Some ethnographers refer to *ñawpa machu* as 'mythical ancestors' of contemporary Quechua communities (Gow and Condori 1976; Sallnow 1987; Ricard 2007), and yet from the previous description of the relations between them it should be clear that this is not the case. The *ñawpa machu* are not ancestors or mythical ancestors of humans, since there is a clear discontinuity between them.[26] Why have contemporary Quechua communities severed their ties with what many ethnographers tend to see as their pre-Hispanic ancestors?[27] Notice that this question about the contemporary Quechua and the *ñawpa machu* is striking only when descent is assumed to be the primary way of constructing relatedness. However, the relationship between contemporary humans and *ñawpa machu* becomes clear in the framework of cohabitation and circulation of food. Since humans and *ñawpa machus* neither cohabitate nor eat the same food, it follows that they are not kin and hence one cannot be an ancestor of the other. Humans do not cohabitate with *ñawpa machus* because that destroys their sociality, but rather humans wilfully try to avoid associating with them, for to do so would entail the risk of disease or death. When the meeting is inevitable or accidental, or when people need to work in a field close to the *ñawpa machu*'s towns, coca, alcohol or cigarettes are offered to them as elemental acts of respect in order to appease their hunger and avoid becoming victims. These acts of courtesy have the purpose of preventing harm rather than establishing long-lasting and quotidian relationships as in working human kinship.

Conclusion

Currently, the majority of people of the region of Cuzco only pay close attention to their particular ascendants for two generations. Beyond this, all ascendants are referred to collectively as *awlanchis* or *abuelos*, our long-ago deceased kin. Certainly, in some contexts, the Inka are mentioned in association with one's *awlanchis* or *abuelos* in the remote past or are depicted as civilising heroes (see Flores Galindo 1986; Ortiz Rescaniere 2001). While bonds of procreation, and hence of descent and affinity, cannot be regarded as irrelevant, these are not central or essential in the construction of human sociality but rather are subsumed within logics that are constructed through notions of provision of food and patterns of cohabitation. This suggests that the strong role that ancestry plays in Andean ethnography, ethnohistory and archaeology is to a large extent the product of assuming that sexual procreation is the essential way to construct human relatedness.

The different relationships that contemporary Quechua-speaking people have with what non-Quechua perspectives recognise as dead humans could be better understood via an approach in which Quechua sociality has more to do with forms of provision of food and patterns of cohabitation than with assumptions about the universality of sexual procreation as the core of human kinship.

Through the chapter, and only in a very limited way, I have pointed to some similarities between the processual ways in which Quechua kinship is constructed and those of Amazonian societies. In this spirit, the chapter makes a counterpoint with the preceding one (Brabec de Mori) on the different ways in which the Shipibo-Konibo relate to the Inka. Part of her text deals with the Shipibo-Konibo statements about their Inka ancestry while she also shows that the Inka are contemporary beings located in a different but co-present plane of the Shipibo-Konibo world. Hence, to some extent, she shows how relationships of descent are present in an ethnographic context in which they tend to be seen as peripheral to ties built through affinity, commensality and cohabitation. In contrast, in this chapter, I am rather presenting the subsumption of descent to the contemporary and processual kinship constructed through cohabitation and commensality in an ethnographic context in which descent and ancestry have usually been treated as central.

From these two chapters emerges a regional statement regarding relations of descent and ancestry: on the one hand, they are not unimportant in Amazonian societies; and on the other, they do not overdetermine Andean sociality, allowing latitude for elective and processual kinship relations. Notice how mortuary practices favour a gradual effacement of the deceased both in Amazonian and Andean societies. In the former, they allow a certain leeway in the conceptualisation of ancestry; in the later, they are consistent with a broader system than relies more on food provision and cohabitation than on descent.

Guillermo Salas Carreño is associate professor of anthropology at the Pontificia Universidad Católica del Perú. He holds a PhD in anthropology from the University of Michigan. His research includes the semiotics of Andean world-making practices; competing narratives of modernity engrained in evangelical conversions and tourism; and the relations between mining and society. His recent publications include

'Wak'a: Entifications of the Andean Sacred' (with Bruce Mannheim, in T. Bray [ed.], *The Archaeology of Wak'as*, University of Colorado Press, 2015); 'Places are Kin: Food, Cohabitation, and Sociality in the Southern Peruvian Andes' (*Anthropological Quarterly*, 2016); and 'Mining and the Living Materiality of Mountains in Andean Societies' (*Journal of Material Culture*, 2017).

Notes

1. The primary data used in this chapter, particularly that present in the last three sections, emerged during fieldwork in the region of Cuzco between 2007 and 2008. The main site is the community of Qamawara located relatively close to the city of Cuzco, in the highlands of the San Salvador district, in the province of Calca. A one-hour bus ride connects Cuzco to the town of San Salvador, and from there it is another hour in a truck up a steep slope. Most Qamawarans, with the exception of some older women, are fluently bilingual in Quechua and in Spanish, and have a wide network of relatives living in the cities of Cuzco and Lima, and some in São Paulo (Brazil). A second site is the town of San Jerónimo. It was an old sixteenth-century *reducción* of noble Inca families. Until the 1980s it was a town surrounded by agricultural fields, but since then it has become progressively integrated into the city of Cuzco and currently houses the biggest wholesale market in the region. A third site is the community of Hapu. It is located in the Paucartambo province and is one of the Q'ero communities regarded as the hallmark of indigenous authenticity in urban Cuzco, and among New Age tourist circles in Cuzco and abroad. They practise subsistence agriculture and have high levels of Quechua monolingualism among older people. Most male youths travel seasonally to the neighbouring Amazonian lowlands to work in the hazardous informal economy of gold mining. Some older males travel periodically to intermediate towns or to the city of Cuzco as construction workers, and a few of them offer their knowledge of Q'ero practices to travel agencies and middle-class families.
2. For reviews on the anthropological literature on food and eating see Messer (1984); Mintz and Du Bois (2002); and Holtzman (2006).
3. *Pachamama* or *Pacha Mama* (Quechua): Mother earth.
4. Some of the differences between Andean and Amazonian procesual construction of kinship can be appreciated in theories of conception and intrauterine growth. As previously mentioned, in Andean societies the semen is conceptualised as seed that is cultivated and feed by the woman's body (Van Vleet 2008); among the Wari' 'procreation is a continuous act which lasts virtually up until the moment of birth or

until one or two months before' (Vilaça 2002: 353), and hence, continuous intercourses, not necessarily with the same man, are necessary for an appropriate foetus growth before birth.

5. The process of 'getting accustomed' (*acostumbrarse*) is discussed by Leinaweaver (2008).

6. *Qachun* (Quechua) Brother's or son's wife.

7. *Qatay* (Quechua) Sister's or daughter's husband.

8. These tensions around outsiders who become relatives are expressed in many *kwintus* (stories, from Spanish *cuentos*) about an animal that seduces a young woman, deceives and takes her to his house (Allen 2011: 66–67; see also Ortiz Rescaniere 2001). Those who are taking a relative or who are coming to live within the household have to demonstrate satisfactory social behaviour before they are accepted. See also Harris 1980.

9. These roles of affines are also similarly present in some Amazonian societies. The affines are those who were potentially enemies (and thus can be related to through relations of reciprocal predation) but have become kin. Affines thus are crucial for articulating the sphere of the kin with those of forces who are potentially predatory of the group. Among the Yanomami, this is inscribed in the prominent roles that the affines play in funerary rituals when the decay of the corpse's flesh is equated with its consumption by non-human predators. Similar structural roles of the affines in relation to the funerary practices are present among the Araweté and the Krahó (see Rivière 1993: 509, 512).

10. In contrast, a distant or strong hierarchical relationship is rather marked by wage labour and the provision of food by the patron to the workers. Here only very weak social bonds or a vertical patron–client relationship are present (Mayer 1977, 2002). These exchanges of labour within agricultural production provide the model by means of which other practices are carried out (Gose 1994; Mayer 2002).

11. At this point it should be made clear that *cariño* (affection) is not an abstract feeling but one that can only be expressed materially, mainly through physical work and/or the provision of food (Oxa 2005: 240).

12. Notice that the way of constructing kinship and broader relatedness among human beings through food provision and cohabitation is also present in the relationships between humans and the places where they live. Mountains, plains, hills and lands are the primary providers of food for humans, and they also provide them with somewhere to live. Places, through their materiality, give food to humans and cohabitate with them. Hence, it becomes clear how these particular places or earth beings emerge as social beings (and thus are endowed with agency and intentionality) and as parents of particular human communities. Notice that these are material beings (rather than 'spirits'). For full presentations of this argument, see Salas Carreño (2009 and 2016); and Mannheim and Salas Carreño (2015).

13. While *animu* comes from the Spanish *ánima* (soul) it is important not to confuse it with the Christian soul. Here again a comparison with an Amazonian discussion proves illuminating. The Andean *animu* is similar to the Wari' notion of *jam*: it 'only exists when the body is in some way absent (as inert): in dreams, in serious illness ... and at death. There is no soul linked to the body, and speaking about someone's soul is an indelicate act, as though their death were desired or foreseen' (Vilaça 2002: 361). Except for the last mention regarding the inference of the desire of someone's death, the rest of the citation seems to apply neatly for Andean cases. For discussions about the Andean *animu*, see La Riva González 2005 and Ricard 2007.

14. While *alma* is another Spanish word for *soul*, in Qamawara and in many other communities of the region it is used to refer to the corpse.

15. *Cantua buxifolia.*

16. For similar descriptions and attitudes in other communities in Cuzco, see: Ricard (2007, ch. 4) for Phinaya (Quispicanchis); and Robin (2005) for Chumbivilcas and other communities of Calca. Outside Cuzco, see: Gose (1994: 123–25) for Antabamba (Apurimac); Valderrama and Escalante (1980) for Awkimarka (Apurimac); and Harris (1982) for the Aymara community of Laymi in Bolivia.

17. Processes of deceased's effacement of its human form are present in many Amazonian societies, which do not follow similar patterns to those presented for Quechua societies. For example, according to Conklin (1995), the funerary practices among the Wari' that marked the end of the cohabitation with the deceased, and were also intended to help the mourners' experience of loss, involved radical processes such as dismembering, cremating and/or eating the corpse by their affines. These processes were done as compassioned practices, not only to help mourners to overcome their sadness but also the deceased to become water spirit that later would return to earth in the form of a peccary. Dismembering and consuming the body literally disentangled the kinship relations of the corpse. Thus, these funerary practices 'aimed to move mourners from experiences of loss, embodied in images of the deceased as corpse, to acceptance of the death as part of a regenerative cycle, embodied in images of the deceased rejuvenated as an animal' (Conklin 1995: 94).

18. This heterogeneity of claims regarding what happens after death is consistent with the absence of a metapragmatic discourse or exegetical discourse about practice in Southern Peruvian Quechua (see Mannheim 1991). Nevertheless, it is worth noting how Van Gennep (1960) claimed that compared with other practices, cross-culturally the funerary ones showed more heterogeneity. Additionally, he stated that compared with other theories about the world, those regarding what happens after death typically were more heterogeneous, inconsistent and contradictory within the same society. See Metcalf and Huntington (1991: 75) for a similar discussion.

19. *Casero/a* (Sp) A term with which a vendor addresses a regular client, and vice versa.

20. Conversation with Viviana, a vendor at San Jerónimo market, 2007. The Spanish transcription:

   V: Dicen que el caballero, dice, ha podido aprovecharse, en varias oportunidades dice de la hija … La chica se había conocido con un taxista que es casado, tuvo su bebe con el taxista, tuvo su bebe, … La guagüita había nacido y la había entregado a su papá, le había dicho 'tienes que terminar de estudiar', … y donde el curandero había ido a decirle 'señor … quiero que me mires en coca, mi papá ha dicho [que] lo ha entregado mi bebe' Qué le diría el curandero, ¿no? A la semana se había, ella misma, se había ahorcado, la chica.
   G: ¡Qué pena!
   V: Despuées eso, dicen, lo han enterrado. Y ahora, dice, en su tumba no hay, está cajón vacío. Han dicho que en la chacra había una chica vestida de blanco, con la cara negra y agarrando un libro negro y varios chicos la han molestando. Les había dicho 'estoy buscando a mi papá, dile que le estoy buscando'.

21. See Arguedas (1953) for similar articulation between *condenados* and their inability to eat in narratives of the Mantaro valley. See also Pino (1988) for similar narratives in Chile.

22. Conversation with Viviana, a vendor at San Jerónimo market, 2007. The Spanish transcription:

   V: Una señora así también nos ha contado pero de otra cosa, … el condenado había venido y quería llevarle … ¿Dónde está? Habían buscado y ya pues se habían ido y estaba amontonado su ropa, se lo habrá comido el condenado.
   G: ¿Qué, el condenado come, sabe comer a la gente?
   V: Claro, supongo. Así varias dicen así va a ocurrir, se lo va a comer a su papá dicen.

23. For a related discussion, see Ortiz Rescaniere's (1991) analysis of some aspects of the Huarochiri manuscript.

24. Other names for these beings are *suq'a machu*, *chullpa* or *machula* when they are male. The females are called *ñawpa paya* or *suq'a paya*. In other areas of the Andes they are called *gentiles*, Spanish for *heathens*.

25. See Rivera Andía (2000) for a narrative from Junín that frames the *gentiles* (heathens) in a similar fashion.

26. The only way in which *ñawpa machu* can be ancestors of contemporary humans is in the original sense of the Latin *antecessor*, one who precedes. The *ñawpa machu* certainly preceded the current humanity in time (while they remain also contemporaneous), but it should be clear that they and humans are not related by descent. See Ingold (2000: 141) for a notion of ancestry that does not involve descent.

27. According to Gose (2008), this relationship with the *ñawpa machu* is a consequence of the indigenous appropriation of Catholicism, particularly

in relation to burial patterns throughout the seventeenth century as well as the slow decline and erosion of the legitimacy of indigenous nobility throughout the eighteenth century. This explains why the emergence of the sun tends to be associated with already-Christian Inkas, who inaugurate the contemporary humanity; *ñawpa machu* would be non-Christian humanity previous to the Inka. That is why, in other areas of the Andes, the *ñawpa machu* are called *gentiles* (heathens).

References

Allen, C.J. 1988. *The Hold Life Has: Coca and Cultural Identity in an Andean Community*. Washington, DC: Smithsonian Institution Press.

———. 2011. *Foxboy: Intimacy and Aesthetics in Andean Stories*. Austin: University of Texas Press.

Arguedas, J.M. 1953. 'Folklore del valle del Mantaro: Provincias de Jauja y Concepción', *Folklore Americano* 1: 101–293.

Bourdieu, P. 1977. *Outline of a Theory of Practice*. Cambridge: Cambridge University Press.

Carsten, J. 1995. 'The Substance of Kinship and the Heat of the Hearth: Feeding, Personhood, and Relatedness among Malays in Pulau-Langkawi', *American Ethnologist* 22(2): 223–41.

———. 2000. *Cultures of Relatedness: New Approaches to the Study of Kinship*. Cambridge: Cambridge University Press.

———. 2004. *After Kinship: New Departures in Anthropology*. Cambridge: Cambridge University Press.

Casaverde Rojas, J. 1970. 'El mundo sobrenatural de una comunidad', *Allpanchis* 2: 121–243.

Conklin, B.A. 1995. '"Thus are our bodies, thus was our custom": Mortuary Cannibalism in an Amazonian Society', *American Ethnologist* 22: 75–101.

De la Cadena, M. 2015. *Earth Beings: Ecologies of Practice across Andean Worlds*. Durham, NC: Duke University Press.

Feeley-Harnik, G. 1994. *The Lord's Table: The Meaning of Food in Early Judaism and Christianity*. Washington, DC: Smithsonian Institution Press.

Flores Galindo, A. 1986. *Buscando un Inca: Identidad y utopía en los Andes*. La Habana: Casa de las Américas.

Flores Ochoa, J.A. 1973. 'La Viuda y el Hijo del Soq'a Machu', *Allpanchis* 5: 45–55.

Fortes, M. 1953. 'The Structure of Unilineal Descent Groups', *American Anthropologist* 55(1): 17–41.

Fox, J.J. 1971. 'Sister's Child as Plant: Metaphors in an Idiom of Consanguinity', in R. Needham (ed.), *Rethinking Kinship and Marriage*. London and New York: Tavistock Publications, pp. 219–52.

Freedman, M. 1965. *Lineage Organization in Southeastern China: Monographs on Social Anthropology, no 18*. London: University of London Humanities Press.

Goody, J. 1982. *Cooking, Cuisine, and Class: A Study in Comparative Sociology. Themes in the Social Sciences*. Cambridge and New York: Cambridge University Press.

Gose, P. 1994. *Deathly Waters and Hungry Mountains: Agrarian Ritual and Class Formation in an Andean Town*. Toronto: University of Toronto Press.

———. 2008. *Invaders as Ancestors: On the Intercultural Making and Unmaking of Spanish Colonialism in the Andes*. Toronto: University of Toronto Press.

Gow, P. 1991. *Of Mixed Blood: Kinship and History in Peruvian Amazonia*. Oxford: Clarendon Press; and New York: Oxford University Press.

Gow, R., and B. Condori. 1976. *Kay Pacha*. Cuzco: CBC.

Hallowell, A.I. 1992. *The Ojibwa of Berens River, Manitoba: Ethnography into History*. Fort Worth, TX: Harcourt Brace Jovanovich College Publishers.

Harris, O. 1980. 'The Power of Signs: Gender, Culture and the Wild in the Bolivian Andes', in C.P. MacCormack and M. Strathern (eds), *Nature, Culture, and Gender*. Cambridge: Cambridge University Press, pp. 70–94.

———. 1982. 'The Dead and the Devils among the Bolivian Laymi', in M. Bloch and J. Parry (eds), *Death and the Regeneration of Life*. Cambridge: Cambridge University Press, pp. 45–73.

Holtzman, J.D. 2006. 'Food and Memory', *Annual Review of Anthropology* 35: 361–378.

Holý, L. 1996. *Anthropological Perspectives on Kinship*. London: Pluto Press.

Hugh-Jones, S. 2001. 'The Gender of Some Amazonian Gifts: An Experiment with an Experiment', in T. Gregor and D. Tuzin (eds), *Gender in Amazonia and Melanesia: An Exploration of the Comparative Method*. Berkeley: University of California Press, pp. 245–78.

Hutchinson, S.E. 2000. 'Identity and Substance: The Broadening Base of Relatedness among the Nuer of Southern Sudan', in J. Carsten (ed.), *Cultures of Relatedness: New Approaches to the Study of Kinship*. Cambridge and New York: Cambridge University Press, pp. 55–72.

Ingold, T. 2000. 'Ancestry, Generation, Substance, Memory, Land', in T. Ingold, *The Perception of the Environment: Essays on Livelihood, Dwelling and Skill*. London: Routledge, pp. 132–52.

———. 2007. 'Earth, Sky, Wind, and Weather', *Journal of the Royal Anthropological Institute* 13: S19–S38.

Isbell, B.J. 1977. '"Those Who Love Me": An Analysis of Andean Kinship and Reciprocity within a Ritual Context', *Special publication of the American Anthropological Association* 7: 81–105.

————. 1978. *To Defend Ourselves: Ecology and Ritual in an Andean Village*. Austin: University of Texas Press.

Itier, C. 2007. *El Hijo del Oso: la Literatura Oral Quechua de la Región del Cuzco*. Lima: IFEA, UNMSM, PUCP, IEP.

La Riva González, P. 2005. 'Las Representaciones Del Animu en los Andes del Sur Peruano', *Revista Andina* 41: 63–88.

Leinaweaver, J.B. 2008. *The Circulation of Children: Kinship, Adoption, and Morality in Andean Peru*. Durham, NC: Duke University Press.

Lévi-Strauss, C. 1969. *The Elementary Structures of Kinship*. Boston, MA: Beacon Press.

Lira, J.A. 1946. *Farmacopea Tradicional Indígena y Prácticas Rituales*. Lima: Talleres gráficos El Cóndor.

————. 1990. *Cuentos del Alto Urubamba: Edición Bilingüe Quechua y Castellano*. Cuzco: CBC.

Mannheim, B. 1991. 'After Dreaming: Image and Interpretation in Southern Peruvian Quechua', *Etnofoor* 4: 43–79.

Mannheim, B., and G. Salas Carreño. 2015. 'Wak'a: Entifications of the Andean Sacred', in T. Bray (ed) *The Archaeology of W'akas: Explorations of the Sacred in the pre-Columbian Andes*. Boulder, CO: University of Colorado Press, pp. 47–72.

Mauss, M. (1935) 1973. 'Techniques of the Body', *Economy and Society* 2(1): 70–88.

Mayer, E. 1977. 'Beyond the Nuclear Family', in R. Bolton and E. Mayer (eds), *Andean Kinship and Marriage*. Washington, DC: American Anthropological Association, pp. 60–80.

————. 2002. 'The Rules of the Game in Andean Reciprocity', in E. Mayer, *The Articulated Peasant: Household Economies in the Andes*. Boulder, CO: Westview Press, pp. 105–42.

Messer, E. 1984. 'Anthropological Perspectives on Diet', *Annual Review of Anthropology* 13: 205–49.

Metcalf, P., and R. Huntington. 1991. *Celebrations of Death: The Anthropology of Mortuary Ritual*, 2nd edn. Cambridge and New York: Cambridge University Press.

Mintz, S.W., and C.M. Du Bois. 2002. 'The Anthropology of Food and Eating', *Annual Review of Anthropology* 31: 99–119.

Morote Best, E. 1988. 'La Huida Mágica', in E. Morote Best, *Aldeas Sumergidas: Cultura Popular y Sociedad en los Andes*. Cuzco: CBC, pp. 111–51.

Ortiz Rescaniere, A. 1991. 'Matrimonio y cambio cósmico: Huatyacuri', *Anthropologica* 9: 53–72.

————. 2001. *La Pareja y el Mito: Estudios sobre las Concepciones de la Persona y de la Pareja en los Andes*. 3rd edn. Lima: Pontificia Universidad Católica del Perú.

Oxa, J. 2005. 'Vigencia de la Cultura Andina en la Escuela', in C.M. Pinilla (ed.), *Arguedas y el Perú de hoy*. Lima: SUR Casa de Estudios del Socialismo, pp. 235–42.

Parkes, P. 2005. 'Milk Kinship in Islam: Substance, Structure, History', *Social Anthropology* 13(3): 307–29.

Paulson, S. 2006. 'Body, Nation, and Consubstantiation in Bolivian Ritual Meals', *American Ethnologist* 33(4): 650–64.

Payne, J. 1984. *Cuentos Cusqueños*. Cuzco: Centro de Estudios Regionales Andinos Bartolome de Las Casas.

Peluso, N.L. 1996. 'Fruit Trees and Family Trees in an Anthropogenic Forest: Ethics of Access, Property Zones, and Environmental Change in Indonesia', *Comparative Studies in Society and History* 38(3): 510–48.

Pino, Y. 1988. *Cuentos Folklóricos Chilenos: Antología*. Santiago: Universitaria.

Renne, E.P. 2007. 'Mass Producing Food Traditions for West Africans Abroad', *American Anthropologist* 109(4): 616–25.

Ricard, X. 2007. *Ladrones de Sombra: el Universo Religioso de los Pastores del Ausangate*. Lima and Cuzco: IFEA, CBC.

Rival, L. 1998. 'Androgynous Parents and Guest Children: The Huaorani Couvade', *The Journal of the Royal Anthropological Institute* 4(4): 619–42.

Rivera Andía, J.J. 2000. 'Los Gentiles de Llampa', *Anthropologica* 18: 271–80.

Rivière, P. 1993. 'The Amerindianization of Descent and Affinity', *L'Homme* 33: 507–16.

Robin, V. 2005. 'Los Caminos a la Otra Vida: Ritos Funerarios en los Andes Sur Peruanos', in A. Molinié Fioravanti (ed.), *Etnografías del Cuzco*. Cuzco: CBC, pp. 47–68.

Sahlins, M.D. 1972. *Stone Age Economics*. Chicago, IL: Aldine-Atherton.

Salas Carreño, G. 2009. 'La sustancia del parentesco entre lugares y humanos en la región del Cusco', *Crónicas Urbanas* 14: 135–50.

———. 2016. 'Places are Kin: Food, Cohabitation, and Sociality in the Southern Peruvian Andes', *Anthropological Quarterly* 89: 813–40.

Sallnow, M.J. 1987. *Pilgrims of the Andes: Regional Cults in Cusco*. Washington, DC: Smithsonian Institution Press.

Seeger, A. 1981. *Nature and Society in Central Brazil: The Suya Indians of Mato Grosso*. Cambridge, MA: Harvard University Press.

Taylor, A.C. 2000. 'Le Sexe de la Proie: Représentations Jivaro du Lien de Parenté', *L'Homme* 154–55: 309–33.

Valderrama, R., and C. Escalante. 1980. 'Apu Qorpuna: Visión del Mundo de los Muertos en la Comunidad de Awkimarka', *Debates en Antropología* 5: 233–64.

Van Gennep, A. 1960. *The Rites of Passage*. Chicago, IL: University of Chicago Press.

Van Vleet, K.E. 2002. 'The Intimacies of Power: Rethinking Violence and Affinity in the Bolivian Andes', *American Ethnologist* 29: 567–601.

———. 2008. *Performing Kinship: Narrative, Gender, and the Intimacies of Power in the Andes*. Austin: University of Texas Press.

Vilaça, A. 2002. 'Making Kin Out of Others in Amazonia', *The Journal of the Royal Anthropological Institute* 8(2): 347–65.

Viveiros de Castro, E. 1992. *From the Enemy's Point of View: Humanity and Divinity in an Amazonian Society*. Chicago, IL: University of Chicago Press,.

———. 2009. 'The Gift and the Given: Three Nano-essays on Kinship and Magic', in S. Bamford and J. Leach (eds), *Kinship and Beyond: The Genealogical Model Reconsidered*. New York: Berghahn Books, pp. 237–68.

Weismantel, M. 1988. *Food, Gender, and Poverty in the Ecuadorian Andes*. Philadelphia: University of Pennsylvania Press.

———. 1995. 'Making Kin: Kinship Theory and Zumbagua Adoptions', *American Ethnologist* 22(4): 685–704.

7

'I'm Crying for the Beautiful Skin of the Jaguar'

Laments, Non-humans and Conviviality among the Ayoreo of the Northern Chaco

Alfonso Otaegui

Introduction

This chapter examines what part non-humans play in the instauration of social conviviality in a small community of former hunter-gatherers. As part of a broader study of the relationship between speech and social life among the Ayoreo of the northern Chaco, this contribution focuses on the social values expressed in ritual wailing songs.

The notion of conviviality and the idea of continuity between humans and non-humans are essential for this research. I use the term 'conviviality' in the sense described by Joanna Overing and Alan Passes (2000). Overing and Passes study the social life of Amazonian groups, who focus on emotional comfort in everyday experience, and achieve a certain degree of social conviviality in communal life. 'Conviviality' is not used in the habitual English sense as a festive state in the company of others, but is closer to the meaning of the Spanish verb *convivir*, 'to live together'. It means a social stability that is consciously pursued and maintained in everyday interactions. This stability is based on the emphasis on social values and the condemnation of asocial ones. As Cecilia McCallum has remarked, 'sociality is not yet a theoretical concept, but rather a term used in different senses by a variety of analysts' (2001: 4). I use 'sociality' in a sense similar to McCallum (2001), Overing and Passes (2000) and Overing (2003), to indicate social relationships that are built up through performance, do not exist prior to the people involved in them, and are constantly being reinforced – or weakened – and redefined in everyday interactions. 'Sociality' involves components of affection and social ethics, defined locally. When it comes to the relationship between 'sociality' and 'conviviality', the latter entails 'an intense ethical and aesthetic valuing of sociable sociality' (Overing and Passes 2000: xiv). In my research among the Ayoreo, I have focused on everyday life – commensality, humour, gossip and songs – as the key to understanding regularities of social behaviour.

When it comes to the relationship between humans and non-humans, it has long been established that for many lowland South American groups, humans and non-humans are not separated, as they were in the old nature–culture dichotomy (Descola 2005). The myths, the notion of person, the notion of collective, and the cosmology of the Ayoreo fit in with Descola's depiction of 'animism' as a mode of identification based on the idea of similarity of interiority between humans and non-humans, and difference of physicality (ibid.). It is worth noting that, among the Ayoreo, the attribution of continuity of interiority to non-humans may in fact differ according to diverse communicative contexts (narration of tales at night, jokes and teasing interactions at mealtimes, etc.). Furthermore, the Ayoreo do not have the figure of master spirits – owners of game – from whom they would ask permission to hunt, nor do they have casual encounters with spirits in the forest, as is the case for other groups from the Chaco area (e.g. the Qom; Tola 2009). I will analyse how distinct ways of existence are attributed to non-humans in different types of interactions.

What part do non-humans play in human conviviality? In order to answer this question, I will focus on one of the Ayoreo song genres. Overing and Passes stress the importance of speech in social life, in particular the aspects related to affective life: 'emotion talk is also social talk' (2000: 3). In my previous research (Otaegui 2014) I showed how Ayoreo songs, performed and heard every night, establish an Ayoreo aesthetics of conviviality. Social values are highlighted and antisocial values disapproved of through the prism of affectivity.

To study how conviviality is depicted in speech, I will analyse Ayoreo laments. The Ayoreo perform these songs in one of the most socially tense moments, when they are confronted with the death of a loved one, or simply fear someone close to them might die. At this moment of potential social disruption and breaking of ties, these songs remind the Ayoreo of their social values in an emphasised way.

I will particularly focus on the collective-oriented aspects of lament, leaving aside the psychological cathartic ones, which would require a different and longer study. There is a rhetorical feature that will be key to this contribution: the systematic mentioning of non-humans (animals, plants, manufactured objects, etc.), which have belonged to seven different clans since the times of the First Men. An insight into the dynamics of the Ayoreo clans in everyday life will be necessary to understand these puzzling references at a moment of intense grief.

I will firstly introduce the Ayoreo and their speech, and provide a detailed description of the performance and the lyrics of the laments. I will then depict the manifestation of the clans in Ayoreo social interactions, with special focus on clan possessions. These findings will help us to understand how the Ayoreo highlight mutual interdependence – affective and economical – by means of references involving non-humans, and how this interdependence is crucial in their notion of conviviality.

The Ayoreo

The Ayoreo are former hunter-gatherers from northern Chaco. The Ayoreo number around five thousand, with half of them living in

Illustration 7.1 Ayoreo going hunting. Jesudi, Paraguay. 2008. Photograph: A. Otaegui.

Bolivia and half in Paraguay. The Ayoreo had definitive contact with white people in the 1950s, which led to the erroneous assumption that they had lived in complete isolation until then.[1] In fact, the Ayoreo had frequent interaction with other groups on the periphery of the Chaco area from at least the sixteenth century, and were reached – albeit briefly – by the Jesuits in the eighteenth century (Combès 2009). Several factors, such as oil prospecting, the settlement of Mennonite colonies in the South, and rising hostility between Ayoreo bands, pushed some small groups of Ayoreo to leave the forest and contact the outside world (Bremen 2008). The Ayoreo were sent to live in newly founded missions controlled by the Catholics (Salesian brothers) or by the New Tribes Missions. Having now been living in the missions for years, the Ayoreo have become progressively sedentary.[2]

I carried out my fieldwork in the community of Jesudi, 75 km north of Filadelfia (Paraguay) between 2008 and 2011. Jesudi is made up of around eighty people, though this number varies depending on their seasonal work on farms. The majority of them lived in the María Auxiliadora Mission in the 1970s. At the beginning of the 1980s they moved out of the mission due to the flooding of the Paraguay River. For some time, they worked on farms near Loma Plata, until they founded Jesudi in 1989. The birthplaces of each generation of the people of Jesudi tell us the story of their movements. The first generation was born in the forest, before contacting white people. The second generation was born in María Auxiliadora and near Loma Plata. The third and fourth generations (grandchildren and great grandchildren of the first generation) were born in Jesudi.

Singing is a constituent aspect of the Ayoreo's social life in Jesudi. Inspired by actual events and emotions, the Ayoreo compose a considerable variety of songs. They classify the songs into at least seven genres, according to the theme and the alleged internal state of the speaker. Any remarkable social fact in Ayoreo life can be turned into a song, from a declaration of the courage of a victorious warrior to an overt expression of sadness of an abandoned wife. They usually sing for hours at night around the fire, or just before dawn. Any Ayoreo can perform any composition he or she has heard and liked, contributing in this way to the diffusion of the story narrated in the song. These songs circulate through households and communities, and are passed on from one generation to the next. The compositions are sent as gifts in cassettes and performed during occasional visits to other communities. This transmission and perpetuation of the pieces is intended: 'Listen carefully and imitate my songs' is the usual introduction in tape-recorded messages. The repertoire of songs is the depository of Ayoreo oral memory and an example-based guideline for proper social behaviour. Among these sung stories, the *uñacai* laments are fundamental in strengthening the social ethics of the Ayoreo (Otaegui 2014).

Before focusing specifically on the sad *uñacai* songs, I would like to provide an outline of Ayoreo discourse, which can be organised into two major categories, depending on the effects the words induce on reality: *puyac* (words capable of producing changes in the world) and non-*puyac* (words without any direct outcome). *Puyac* is the base-form (Bertinetto 2009: 17) (predicative use) of *puyai*: 'forbidden; taboo; holy; consequential if misused; d.f. *puyac, puyacho*' (Higham, Morarie and Greta 2000: 279). The *puyac* words are mainly healing spells taught by the First Men in the old times.[3] The spells must be used in the right situation otherwise they produce the opposite effect. Uttering a healing spell *sarui* to cure snakebite when no one has been bitten will induce a snake to come and attack someone. The non-*puyac* words are mostly songs related to human affairs, not involving the First Men – usually about war and love stories. The *puyac* category has received much more attention in the literature than its counterpart, probably due to the exotic attraction the myths and healing spells inspired. During the course of my fieldwork I found that the 'non-powerful words' have a dominant presence in everyday speech, in contrast to their marginal place in the academic literature, and that the Ayoreo deeply value singing and talking about songs.[4]

Table 7.1 Some Ayoreo discourse genres.

puyac (forbidden, dangerous)	non-*puyac* (not forbidden or dangerous)
Spells (Mashnshnek 1991)	Songs (fieldwork data)
Sarode (healing spell)	*Enominoi* (shaman's vision)
Chubuchu (healing spell)	*Pinangoningai* (before-going-to-war song, 'I will kill you…!')
Paragapidi (protective spell; weapons purifying spell)	*Chingojnangai* (coming-back-from-war song, 'I've just killed someone')
Aguyade (garden protective spell)	*Irade* (nostalgic love song)
Erai (good luck in hunting spell)	*Uñacai* (sadness song, lament)
Uhñaune (Nighthawk spell)	*Yasitigai* ('I'm so happy…!')
	Versículo (irade-sarui on the Christian string)

The *Uñacai*, the Sadness Songs of the Ayoreo

The Ayoreo say that they sing at night because they are happy. That is true in spite of the song's lyrics, which may show the pride of a warrior after killing two people, or tell the story of a dispute between two women who wanted the same young boy as a son-in-law. The *uñacai* songs, for example, talk about someone who is mortally ill or has died, while highlighting the state of solitude and abandonment of the ones who are suffering the loss. Although the lyrics are deeply charged with sadness, the Ayoreo claim that the one singing is actually happy. In these nocturnal singing sessions, the Ayoreo do not compose the songs, they repeat the old ones they like the most. These regular performances are detached from the original circumstance and emotional state that inspired the composition of the song.

At the end of my first year in Jesudi, I witnessed a very unusual performance, one that was radically different from the habitual happy singing around the fire. One night, at midnight, I was sleeping in my tent when all of a sudden I was awoken by the voice of someone shouting and weeping rhythmically. This voice came from the house of the Dosapei family, to whom I was very attached and where I usually ate and spent the day. It was a kind of weeping in a loud voice, using phrases that were long to the point of running out of breath. Other wordless weeps could be heard from a background voice. From every corner of the village, people came to the place where the weeping and the shouts originated. I went there as well. Ome, a young woman, was standing outside the house where people were gathered. She told me: 'Jnumi is crying, go inside and see…!'

Inside the house, I could see Jnumi, a woman in her forties, sitting on her heels with her face down to the floor. She was the one crying and singing. One of her daughters-in-law was crying quietly without uttering any words. Ebedu, Jnumi's husband, was lying on the floor, totally covered by a blanket. As I could not understand the lyrics, Ome told me that Ebedu was suffering from earache. After several months of chemotherapy and corticoid treatment, Ebedu's defences were so low that he was susceptible to a range of infections. He was in pain. Jnumi feared her husband's death, announced by the doctors a couple of months earlier. I offered Jnumi an anti-inflammatory pill. All of a sudden, Jnumi stopped singing, her husband took the pill and everybody returned to their houses.

This loud and rhythmic weeping is called *uñacai* (pl. *uñacade*). Jean-Pierre Estival's exhaustive paper on Ayoreo musicology does not describe the *uñacai* category, although it mentions 'mourning songs', based on Bórmida and Califano (1978).[5] Estival believed these songs might have disappeared, as no one sang at the funeral he attended in the community of Isla Alta (2005: 459). I think this difference between Estival's data and my own findings indicates that not every song genre is performed in every community. The word *uñacai*, however, can be found in the New Tribes Mission's dictionary: *'uyacade*: wailing; grieving, with mournful crying; mourning, with loud crying' (Higham, Morarie and Greta 2000: 862); *'uñacarãi*: mourner' (ibid.: 830).

The performance of an *uñacai* is a spontaneous as well as a structured event. I have seen men and women sing in the same way, with the same combination of shouting, crying and rhythmic phrasing. Before starting, the singer does not cry at all. The mourner begins suddenly, and after a couple of minutes ends in the same way. Once the weeping and singing is finished, the individual dries their eyes, clears their nose and usually asks for water to refresh their throat. Besides this opposition between spontaneity and structure, I focus on another duality, between individual-related aspects and collective-oriented aspects of the *uñacai*.

At least three features of the *uñacai* posit this song as focusing on the individual, as an idiosyncratic expression related to a specific person. Firstly, this lament is sung individually. The performance is not collective, as is the case in other groups.[6] There is no polyphony at all: even if some people present might be moved to cry along, they do not sing. Secondly, even though some *uñacade*'s lyrics are very similar – making them look like a general expression of sadness – the Ayoreo depict every composition as the expression of the sadness of a specific individual for the loss, potential or actual, of another specific individual. In spite of its formulaic elements, every *uñacai* is unique and has a specific composer. Thirdly, the *uñacai* is the overt expression of an individual's inner state; the mourner is the origin of the emotions communicated in the song.

Other aspects of the *uñacai*, however, point to a more collective-oriented implication of the song. First, the performance summons the presence of other individuals. Sound can reach every corner of Jesudi: anyone crying-singing will be heard from anywhere in this small community. The particular combination of weeping and words can be easily identified. Although not stated explicitly, the loud weeps are a call. People immediately respond to it with their company. They come and stay next to the mourner in silence – although some might ask what is going on. They remain there, slightly knitting their eyebrows, a facial expression I attributed to sadness or worry. Secondly, since the songs can be repeated, the content can reach more people than the ones present during the first performance. As with any other song, anyone who likes an *uñacai* can later imitate it – in a song-like version without the weeping – for the sake of singing. This traumatic moment then becomes part of the repertoire of the night singing sessions. Thirdly, the *uñacai* are structured, in that they follow certain rhetoric tendencies and must be performed at the right moment. According to Greg Urban, these regularities indicate a desire for sociability. Let us examine his argument in detail.

Urban analyses the ritual wailing songs of the Bororo, the Shavante and the Shokleng in Amerindian Brazil (1988). The author finds regularities in the songs (in musical line, line length, intonation contour and voice), showing an intracultural standardisation as well as an intercultural diversity. In addition, Urban explains how wailing serves two communicative ends. On the one hand, these stylised compositions transmit sadness and feelings of loss through the icons of crying: cry break, voiced inhalation, creaky voice and falsetto vowels (ibid.: 389). On the other hand, ritual wailing indicates the individual's desire for sociability (as a manner of dealing with loss). The wailer, by using socially proper ways of crying in the appropriate context – the death of a loved one – displays social correctness: 'One wishes to signal to others that one has the correct feelings at the socially prescribed times' (ibid.: 393).

These communicative ends suggested by Urban are also present in the Ayoreo *uñacai* and correspond to what I have described as individual-oriented and collective-oriented features. The *uñacai* is a structured way of crying, which must be performed at the right moment as well. It must be sung right after a death, not several weeks or months later. As in the example shown above, the Ayoreo also sing *uñacade* when they fear the death of someone, due to illness or hunger. The *uñacai* is related to a current situation (a recent death or the possibility of one), and should not be triggered by sad memories alone.[7]

Uñacai is the proper way of crying in the socially expected moment among the Ayoreo.[8] As with the Shavante and the Shokleng (Urban 1988: 394), the Ayoreo differentiate 'just crying' from 'crying with words'. The verbs *–uñaca* and *–ungu* (to cry singing) are opposed to *–ibo* (to cry). Ayoreo say *-ibo bisideque* to stress the contrast. The word *bisideque* describes an activity as being somehow incomplete, or not fulfilling its intended purpose. For example: *ñisore* (I go hunting in the forest) vs. *ñisore bisideque* (I just wander in the forest), *yoji bisideque* (I drink *yerba mate* tea for breakfast *without eating*), *ñisiome bisideque* (I give it *for free*). According to the New Tribes Mission's dictionary, *bisidei*: adj m. free; without charge; for no reason; just for fun; of no value; of little importance. d.f. *bisidec* (Higham, Morarie and Greta 2000: 125). In a moment of grief, crying in a strict sense *–ibo* is considered meaningless, an incomplete action.

I will focus on the collective-oriented communicative end, the indication of a desire for sociability, in order to understand what sociality means for the Ayoreo. Urban says that the feeling must not be stated explicitly, in order for the indexing of sociability to be successful and the wailing convincing. This is not the case in Ayoreo, where lines such as 'I am overwhelmed by sadness' are frequent. From what I observed in Jesudi, this direct allusion to the feeling did not make it any less convincing for the people who gathered around the mourner.

An analysis of the content is necessary to understand this aspect of the *uñacai* for two reasons. Firstly, the Ayoreo themselves focus on content. They like to repeat the weeping in a song-like version in the night singing sessions around the fire. These new versions are very different to the original performance. The breathing, the rhythm and the intonation are changed and the icons of crying are absent. The words are the only remaining elements from the original composition. In addition, the Ayoreo like to comment on these words, to discuss how beautiful they are or how sad the composer of the *uñacai* had been, and why.[9] Secondly, the content of these traumatic sung moments provides an idea of how sociality is conceived by the Ayoreo. Dealing with a death or the possibility of one is a socially intense time, not only for the mourner but for the rest of the group as well. The content of the *uñacade* presents some regularity. In spite of the specificity of each composition, these laments tend to depict the mourned ones in the same fashion. In such a moment of grief, the lost loved one is presented as the ideal Ayoreo, fulfilling the essential social values of Ayoreo conviviality (Otaegui 2014).[10]

The Lyrics of the Sadness Songs

Jnumi Posijñoro composed this *uñacai* when she cried for her son Puchiejna Dosapei. He was very sick, due to the attack of an Angaite shaman. Puchiejna could not walk because 'his blood did not flow'. The doctors in Asunción (the capital of Paraguay) were clueless and had neither a diagnosis nor a cure.[11]

Uñacai for Puchiejna Dosapei
(by Jnumi Posijñoro)
*1. Oyopepaque gajine ga
ñunguamu cutemai tuqué
ñujnacari gajine.
2. Oguiyabape yu iji auatadatei
yabai uyoque gajine i quiganingo
jnacari ujadode i quigade gajine
ca chi yajiase yiquenique iji
yoquidai.
3. Oguiyabape coongopiejna
ojosogoma yabi uyoque i
quiganingo gajine pitoningai
enoñaique ujnienepise.
4. Oguiyabape yu iji cutema case
ñujnacari i quiganingo gajine
pitoningai enoñangue ujnienepise
aquesua tiachutic yape
uñengomeñu ga ca chi uñeque dei
dojoique jnacari ajnamitic*

*5. ga uñeque naiase omeñu gajine
'mama yoquicho i yocajnamite
date'
6. yichapia yu aja yoquirosori
casicaite ga yajíe putugutaroi
penojnangue ñujnacari uñeque
gajine ga ñimo duasede uñeque
i yiquenique gajine ga uñeque
doi dapaganejnai daecujat ome
nanique uyoque ca chi uñeque
dei siñeque gajine.
7. Oguiyabape aquiajna
ojosogoma yacaía gajine chagüei
urosoique ujnienepise uñaque
gajine uñeque nae 'aja bei ga agu
yigaidode cuchapibose'.
8. Oguiyabape ome uñeque
ategoningai uñeque
ategoningaique cutema case
ñujnacari uñeque.*

1. Be silent as I cry singing for my very beautiful son.
2. I am crying for my husband, the one-without-fear. We have been left behind, among the living young men, and I do not see him before me in our village.
3. I am crying for the beautiful pumpkin sprouts, my son. We have been left behind. The very ugly death has taken the very beautiful one.
4. I am crying for the one who was beautiful before. The very ugly death has taken the very beautiful one, the beautiful rainbow, my son. Perhaps he is playing soccer with the young men.
5. He said to me: 'Mummy, we have won an important match'.
6. I think of our former boss and I see my son, the very beautiful skin of the jaguar, and I see him before me; the one who used to bring us nice words, perhaps he is just somewhere else.
7. I am crying for the beautiful cow, my daughter-in-law, she is beautiful, hunger hurts her so much. That one [Puchiejna] had said 'take it and eat my food'.
8. I am crying for the one that was beautiful and generous, my son.

Half of the *uñacai* I have recorded begin with the phrase 'Be silent, I am going to cry'. This is the only line addressed to the public. It is in imperative mode and demands silence. It certainly contrasts with their everyday interactions around the fire, where several people speak at the same time. '*Oyopacho*' (Be silent!) is a call for attention; the mourner wants to be heard.

In addition to this opening line, this *uñacai* exemplifies three other regularities of the lyrics. Firstly, the mourned one is usually described as someone generous and peaceful. Generosity is illustrated with an anecdote in which the mourned one gives the mourner food, money or gifts. Peacefulness is associated with 'nice words' or, more frequently, a lack of insults (e.g. 'he did not use unkind words against me'). These two traits depict Puchiejna as *paaque* ('morally good' according to Ayoreo values) and therefore worth remembering.

Secondly, this sad moment is frequently contrasted with an image of a happy past. In this case, Jnumi remembers Puchiejna as strong and healthy, playing soccer at a neighbouring farm a couple of months earlier. The mourner is usually happy in the past as well, as he or she used to benefit from the generosity of the mourned one: '[Puchiejna said] "eat my food"'.[12]

Thirdly, the mourner names the possessions of the Ayoreo clans. As I will show, this trait links this sad moment to everyday interactions, where sociality is build up and deployed. Jnumi does not say the name 'Puchiejna'. Instead, she calls him 'the beautiful pumpkin sprouts, my son', 'the beautiful rainbow, my son' and 'my son, the very beautiful skin of the jaguar'. All these are clan possessions, *edopasade*. Puchiejna is a member of the Dosapei clan, which counts among its belongings the rainbow, the pumpkin and the jaguar's skin. Jnumi does the same with her husband and her daughter-in-law, mentioning their respective *edopasade*: 'my husband, the one-without-fear (the jaguar)' (Dosapei clan), and 'the beautiful cow, my daughter-in-law' (Posorajãi clan).

This trait is essential to the *uñacade*, as shown by its learning process. Performing an *uñacai* involves mentioning the proper clan possessions. When Jnumi was young, she did not know how to cry-sing, she only cried *bisideque*. An old woman, Puua *Chiquejñoro*, then taught her to *uñaca*. The wise Puua said to Jnumi: '*osi te...*' (do it like this...) and showed her examples for members of each of the seven clans.[13] The other aspects of the performance, such as the combination of singing and crying or the cry break, seem to be learnt by imitation. When it comes to the conscious transmission of the lament's technique, the Ayoreo focus on content, and more specifically, the mention of clan possessions (*edopasade*).

The significance of the *edopasade* in the laments needs an explanation. Why are clan possessions mentioned in such a moment of grief? One possible answer would be that they are metaphors of the individuals alluded to.[14] Nevertheless, the Ayoreo claim no similarity between the mourned ones and the clan's possessions. When asked about this rhetoric regularity, most Ayoreo refer to tradition: '*jnanibajade ore isocade, gu*' (it is the way of the First Men, that's why), while some say that hearing someone mentioning their *edopasade* (clan possessions) makes them happy.[15] This answer points to the relationships between the Ayoreo and their clan possessions. An insight into the clans' dynamics in Ayoreo everyday life is necessary to understand this rhetorical feature.

The Clans, the Weeps and the Beatiful Skin of the Jaguar

In the section I will describe how the clans are part of Ayoreo life, with a special focus on the founding of sociality in everyday interactions. Among the Ayoreo, every plant, animal and manufactured object has belonged to one of the seven clans – *cucherane* – since the times of the First Men.[16] At first, I tried to study these clans as if they were merely systems of classification. I wanted to unveil the hidden regularities of their abstract organisation. My attempt to make long lists of clans' possessions – *edopasade* – failed completely since the majority of the people did not know more than four or five of them.[17] The clans made themselves evident not through the answers they gave to my Linnean questions but in their monotonous domestic life. I found the clans in everyday life – when the Ayoreo made jokes, when they sneezed and when they cried.[18]

On Ayoreo Kinship

A few words about kinship are necessary to understand everyday social relationships. I will first present an outline of Ayoreo kinship as described in the literature, and then my observations in Jesudi.

Table 7.2 The clans of the Ayoreo

The seven *cucherane*
Chiquenoi Étacori Dosapei Posorajãi Picanerai Cutamurajãi Jnurumini

Two main structures shape Ayoreo kinship: the *iguiosode* – members of the same clan; and the *ogasuode* – members of the same residential unit. The main obligations of the members of the same clan were solidarity and hospitality: they were not supposed to harm each other (Bugos 1985: 147). Moreover, the *iguiosode* must not marry each other. Exogamy seems to be the only clearly stated fact about the clans (or *cucherane*) (ibid.: 148).[19]

The *ogasuode* are the people living in the same residential unit or *ogadi*. As the residence was uxorilocal, the archetypical *ogadi* consisted of an extended family: a married couple, their married daughters (and their families) and their single sons. According to Bórmida and Califano, the *ogasui* link is based mainly on commensality, rather than on agnatic or cognatic ties (1978: 93). Even someone not related through kinship can be considered an *ogasui* as long as he or she shares food within the residential unit *ogadi*.

I observed other peculiarities of these two kinship structures in my fieldwork in the small community of Jesudi. Clan exogamy is certainly still an important matter, even though in 2008 there were four couples of *iguiosode* – members of the same clan – in Jesudi. Jokes were made about these couples behind their backs. Moreover, on some occasions, they would even be blamed for certain diseases.[20] As Fischermann (1988: 81) said, the *iguiosode* who want to marry each other must be individuals of strong personality. People expressed a certain social disapproval, mainly through hidden laughs.

Affective closeness is one of the clearest elements of the *iguiosode* relationship. This is more evident between *iguiosode* living faraway from each other. When I visited other communities, I delivered tape-recorded messages and gifts from the people of Jesudi. They sent news, songs and gifts – clothes, tools, food – to their friends elsewhere. If there was a clan relationship, this was highlighted as such. Furthermore, it was recalled proudly and wholeheartedly. A sort of pre-existing affective bond linked the *iguiosode*. Najnua, an elderly lady from the Picanerai clan, put it very plainly: 'I am sad here in Jesudi because I have no *iguiosode*'. According to Sidi, a man of the Posorajãi clan, all the Posorajãi in Jesudi cried for the death of Caitabia, an old woman of this clan.[21] This affectivity was expressed, and built up, by exchanging stories, songs and gifts.

The word *ogasui* (member of the residential unit) is derived from the word *ogadi*, 'place'; 'residential unit' (pl. *ogadode*). An *ogadi* in Jesudi is one or two houses and the space in front of or around them. The *ogadode* are the social units of the community (there were eight in 2008). People are inside the houses mainly when they sleep. The forecourt in front of the house is the most social space, where the extended family and other individuals stay all day. This open space around the house is the place where they eat, drink *terere*,[22] talk and sing around the fire at night. This unit is also a circle of trust: people gossip here about other residential units and their members. For this reason, the *ogadode* are also political units. The *ogadi* is a space where bonds are maintained through commensality and other forms of reciprocity (cf. Salas, this volume, on the creation of kin relationships through commensality and cohabitation among Quechua).

The Funny Quarrels at Lunch

During the day, the *ogasuode* are scattered in the community, visiting other residential units, playing soccer, or looking for honey in the forest. All the members of one *ogadi* gather in their house at lunch or dinner time. On these occasions, some Ayoreo engage in a playful quarrel,[23] a sort of verbal competition between two people from different clans. Two Ayoreo tease one another about whose *edopasade* (clan possessions) are better, tastier or just necessary for life.[24]

It goes like this. A man of the Etacori clan is sitting next to the fire, eating rice and pumpkin. A member of the Dosapei clan points at the pumpkin and asks him in an ironic tone: 'Is it tasty, my *edopasai*?' The annoyed Etacori replies that without fire – Etacori's *edopasai* – the Dosapei could not cook. The Dosapei, in turn, says he does not care about fire, because he is a Dosapei and owns every plant growing in the rainy season. He may add that the Etacori are poor and have almost no *edopasade*. The Etacori reminds him of his other *edopasade* – the sun and the day – and how much the Ayoreo need those too. This discussion goes on in this way, and other members of these two clans may get involved as well. Furthermore, even members of others clans may join the conversation to praise their own *edopasade*. They will say they can live without pumpkins or fire, but certainly none would survive without water, clothes or a good four-wheel-drive vehicle.

These quarrels usually start with this provocation: 'Is it tasty, my *edopasai*?'. The underlying argument is the same: 'My *edopasade* are tasty or necessary, therefore you need them'. The Ayoreo got into the same argument when they tried to persuade me to become a member of one of their clans: 'You should be Posorajñãi, so that you will eat beef, drink milk and water, and have ice cream'; 'No, no, it's better to be Dosapei, you can eat all the fruit in the rainy season'. They were advertising their clans by highlighting the quantity of their *edopasade* or their importance in pragmatic issues. Even though they said they had many *edopasade*, they only mentioned seven or eight.

These 'quarrels' do not explain the reason why a plant or animal belongs to a specific *cucherai*. They provide no information about the logic of clan classification.[25] However, these teasing conversations do give a clue to understanding the presence of *edopasade* in everyday life. These teasing interactions remind every Ayoreo that permission is needed to eat or use another clan's possessions.

In fact, this idea of permission is stated in the answer I got when I asked the meaning of the word *edopasai*. Poro Posijno, an old lady, said: '*yedopasai yodi ga je toque jeti gosi chijna to, ñajne!*' ('Water is my *edopasai*, and nobody is going to use it, it belongs to me!'). Instead of telling a mythic story about how the water became an *edopasai* of the Posorajnãi clan, Poro preferred to emphasise the idea of property and priority of use as a definition of the concept.

This idea is also illustrated when the Ayoreo sneeze. Sneezing is attributed to someone else's anger. If a man sneezes, it means someone is angry with him. This man is supposed to say '*que ore tagu yu!*' ('They will not eat me!') or rather, to make a warning using his *edopasade*. If he is a Posorajnãi, he should say '*ijnose ti gosi que chijna jabón!*' ('It seems that someone will not use soap!').[26] It is a threat: he will not allow the hidden aggressor to use his beloved *edopasade*.[27]

The 'appropriations' of *edopasade* took place in the First Men times (Bórmida and Califano 1978; Fischermann 1988). This happened in several ways: a First Man found something new and claimed it for his clan; a Dosapei First Woman turned into an animal and it became a Dosapei's *edopasai*, and so on. The Ayoreo are born in a world of seven clans. Everything is assumed to belong to one of the seven clans, even if there are still debates about which clan owns a particular *edopasai*.

The Edopasade: *Those Shared Non-humans*

Since these verbal quarrels presuppose the mutual dependence of its participants, they are very likely to take place among *ogasuode*. In fact, the members of the household depend on each other. The *ogasuode*, the ones living in the *ogadi*, renew their communal bond every day through commensality and general reciprocity. The *ogasui* relationship is not restricted to cognatic relatives. Furthermore, kinship links may even be absent in some cases: a widower without children, for example, can be a member of an *ogadi*, as long as he

Illustration 7.2 Ayoreo women gathering *caraguatá* fibre plants (*Bromelia hieronymi*). Jesudi, Paraguay 2009. Photograph: A. Otaegui.

shares food and lives in the household. Giving and receiving food are the basic collective-oriented activities, which communicate sociality. Offering food creates and reinforces social linking, while not accepting it indicates social rejection, as illustrated by Jnumi and her elder son Tamocoi. After a lifelong marriage, Tamocoi had left his wife and children and taken a new wife. Jnumi, facing the possibility of not seeing her grandchildren anymore – as Tamocoi's ex-wife had decided to leave Jesudi – greatly disapproved of Tamocoi's decision. In order to express her rejection, Jnumi did not accept his son's food. She also refused to allow her new daughter-in-law to work for her in the *ogadi*. Food is an indicator of social relationships. In disputes between *ogasuode*, threats like this can be heard: 'Go elsewhere and find out if other people will feed you as we do!'. *Ogasui*, then, is better described as a performatively established relationship, reinforced by sharing food on a regular basis.

This mutual dependence is not unexpected in an area where the availability of food is very irregular. There are times of relative abundance but several of scarcity, depending on the season, the demand for farm workers in the area and the government's assistance policy. Food consists mainly of rice and noodles bought with money obtained from working and selling craftwork. During the rainy season, from December to April, the diet is enriched with some vegetables and occasionally some prey. Hunting is not very frequent, though, because the forest around Jesudi has become limited in resources. From time to time the Ayoreo travel on a bulldozer to neighbouring areas to find game, honey and *caraguatá* fibre for making bags. On occasions the Paraguayan government declares a state of emergency in the area and sends trucks loaded with food, which lasts for some weeks. This interdependence, however, means not only subsistence, but also the founding of social life.

The teasing interactions at lunch are a *mise-en-scène* of the actual interdependence among *ogasuode*. It is a dramatic representation of how everyone is actually using other's people *edopasade*. Even though it is carried out in a humorous fashion, it helps to establish the idea of reciprocity as a basic fact. This 'staged' interdependence is not a strict parallel to the actual interdependence inside the residential unit. The result of the humorous quarrels is the general notion that everyone is using another clan's possessions, but there is no 'equal exchange of *edopasade*'. The need for permission to use *edopasade* is symbolic, as Fischermann reminds us (1988: 156). No one will stop using fire or eating beef just because the Etacori and the Posorajãi did not give their permission. As a matter of fact, this permission is never asked for. The teasing conversations stem from the interdependence being recognised as a given fact. This resulting idea of 'everyone needing everyone else' is actually not coherent with the uneven distribution of *edopasade* among clans. There are rich clans and poor clans, according to the number of their *edopasade* (Bórmida and Califano 1978; Fischermann 1988). However, as the Ayoreo of Jesudi usually know only a small number of their possessions, this fact does not play an important role in their discussions. These teasing interactions stress the fact of interdependence, while at the same time they offer an image of what would happen if everyone decided to keep their clan possessions for themselves. The *edopasade* (which are mostly animals and plants) as a metaphoric language of interdependence, depict the relationships between humans not as performative, but as extremely necessary. The *edopasade* – those shared non-humans – inscribe relatedness (Carsten 1995) in everyday experience.

Conclusion

The path I have followed in my research may be considered quite peculiar, since it originated from a crying song in the night and then led to teasing conversations at mealtimes. The performance of an *uñacai* makes this solo lament a collective event: people come to the mourner's place and get involved in the act as the audience. The sad *uñacai* songs present some rhetorical regularities in their content. Firstly, there are declarations of the virtues of the deceased – specifically, generosity and peacefulness. Secondly, the songs present the opposed images of a happy past and a sad present. Lastly, they allude to people by mentioning their clan possessions, the *edopasade*. In order to understand the meaning of these references to the *edopasade* (mostly animals and plants) in the sad songs, it was necessary to take a closer look at everyday life in Jesudi. Everyday events, such as people teasing each other, gossiping, and jokes after sneezing, provided the clue to understanding the clans in Ayoreo life.

The clans establish two types of relationships, one between two people (two *iguiosode*) and another between a person (a human) and an item or a living being treated as such (an *edopasai*). The relationships between *iguiosode* – humans of the same clan – involve two equal individuals who exchange messages, songs and gifts. This is a mutual relationship, marked by affection and reciprocity. They are expected to defend each other and provide hospitality when needed. Since many animals and plants were humans in the First Men times, and as all entities belong to one of the seven clans, I wondered if a human being could have an *iguiosode* relationship with a non-human. Among other groups in the Chaco area, it is not unusual for humans and non-humans to interact as regular people. For example, Qom hunters from Argentinean Chaco dialogue with master-spirits to request permission to hunt (Tola 2009). Nevertheless, as we said at the beginning, this is not the case among the Ayoreo: there are no master-spirits. Non-humans seem to act as people with an interiority similar to humans only in the stories of the First Men times. The *iguiosode* is a relationship between two human beings.

The relationship between a human and a non-human of the same clan – *edopasai* – implies the idea of use and property. The old woman's definition of the term *edopasai* ('that thing nobody can use because it's mine') made that clear. A clan possession is something used – for example, fire – or consumed – for example, pumpkins. It is not a 'non-human person'. The *edopasade* are not treated as people, at least in the specific relationship with the human owners. There is no interaction or communication between humans and their clan possessions. In the myths, to the contrary, non-humans are actually people, with human will and speech, indicating continuity of interiority with human beings (Descola 2005). This observation does not contradict the depiction of Ayoreo's mode of identification as 'animism' made in the introduction, but it points out that distinct ways of existence appear in diverse and concrete contexts (cf. Willerslev 2007 on bringing animism 'down to earth', to the concreteness of everyday experience). A peccary is a prey, food to be shared, in the relationship between a human and his or her *edopasai*. In the First Men stories, however, the peccary is a young man with long teeth and thick hair on his back (Fischermann 1988).

The non-human *edopasade* also play a part in relationships between humans from different clans. These relationships between humans point in turn to the notion of conviviality, which is implicated in the sad *uñacade* songs, which are normally performed at moments of profound grief. At these socially intense occasions, the *uñacade* laments highlight three concepts essential to Ayoreo conviviality: interdependence, generosity and peacefulness. The social interdependence – enacted inside the *ogadi* – is symbolically referred to by the *edopasade*. Generosity is depicted by means of anecdotes, in which the griever receives food or gifts from the mourned one. Peacefulness is usually stated as the negation of aggressive behaviour: 'He did not use unkind words against us'. The mourner produces an essential reframing: what is individual becomes a social matter. The *uñacai* is not – or not only – the expression of grief of an individual for another individual. This sad song presents death – or the possibility of one – as a wound in the social fabric of Jesudi. The mourner has not (only) lost a loved one, but a link in a network of reciprocity.

What is the relationship between conviviality and non-humans? Conviviality is symbolically established in the *uñacai* songs through the circulation of non-humans. The network of reciprocity is actually conviviality in motion. The previous section showed that the non-humans belonging to different clans – the *edopasade* – are terms mediating between humans. As everything in the world belongs to one of the seven clans, then everything is borrowed from people of other clans or lent to them. The reference to *edopasade* is a reminder of interdependence assumed as basic fact. In the case of the Ayoreo of Jesudi, these non-humans are not people with whom it is possible to establish relations of sociality. Instead, non-humans – in the relation of *edopasade* – are in fact what constitute relationships between humans. The clans are a metaphoric language of relatedness. Two *iguiosode* – members of the same clan – share a common origin, and a common relation to several animals, plants and manufactured objects – their *edopasade* – which have their roots in the First Men times. Two people of different clans need each other's clan's possessions, as reminded everyday by funny jokes and sad songs. This interdependence by means of non-humans is also expressed in the most concise way in oral memory. According to a tale of the First Men times, the First Men of each clan tried at one point to live using only their own *edopasade*. As life was not possible like this, they decided to share their possessions again.

The Ayoreo case is a good reminder of the importance of everyday life in the construction of sociality. It illustrates the importance of humour, affective relations and reciprocity in achieving and maintaining a state of social conviviality. Humour is not independent of the social and cultural background of the people who produce it. The aforementioned jokes at lunch clearly illustrate the basic components of Ayoreo social life: their expectations of reciprocity and their need for others are depicted as central in the idea of conviviality. It is worth noting that I have only cited the jokes related to the clans, while there are certainly many others – usually about couples' fights or infidelities – that also expose, criticise or reinforce accepted and non-accepted behaviour and concepts. Humour is definitely an important source of information for gaining a better understanding of sociality in these virtue-centred groups (Overing 2000). These teasing interactions constitute a theatrical display of a possible different way of life, one in which the basic obligations of commensality and reciprocity are not respected. Humour implies a slide of meanings, a reversion of expectations (as in the well-known tricked jaguar stories), a way of imagining a parallel state of things with a little twist. This little, yet fundamental, change is the pretended refusal to the exercise of reciprocity ('What would you do without my *edopasai*...?'). The teasing interactions seem to be closer to Villar's idea on Chacobo humour as a way of collective thinking (2013: 492). The expected reciprocity leads to another of the main points of this chapter: commensality as a basic social bond. Commensality entails not only material exchanges, such as food sharing, but also affective relations between two or more people. Affectivity is an undeniable aspect of the teasing interactions about *edopasade*, in the relations between *iguiosode*, and is always expressed by exchanging specific items, such as gifts, money and even dedicated songs in tape-recorded cassettes. The *uñacai* laments explicitly present this indissolubility of sociality, affectivity and materiality – which is not, I believe, exclusive to the Ayoreo – in one phrase that is repeated in all of them. According to the Ayoreo, this phrase expresses sadness in the strongest possible way: '*chaguei urosoique*', 'Hunger hurts me'. Hunger, of course, is not only a physiological state, but also a sign of abandonment. '*Chaguei urosoique*' means no one is there to give food to the mourner, to create and maintain the basic social bond. The mourner is hungry and sad: he or she is completely alone.

Alfonso Otaegui obtained his PhD in anthropology from the EHESS (Paris). He then spent a year as a postdoctoral researcher at the University of California, Berkeley (Fyssen Foundation fellow) and two years at the Philipps-Universität Marburg, Germany (Alexander von Humboldt Foundation fellow). He is based at the Center for Intercultural and Indigenous Research (CIIR), Pontifical Catholic University of Chile, and is currently doing research among migrants working in Santiago (Chile), focusing on communicative practices related to ageing and healthcare in new digital environments. He is a member of the research team of 'Anthropology of Smartphones and Smart Ageing', a global comparative project coordinated at University College London.

Notes

I would like to thank William Hanks, Charles Briggs and Laura Graham for their valuable comments on this subject. I am also very grateful to Juan Javier Rivera Andía and the anonymous reviewers, who provided me with insightful comments and useful critics on a previous version of this chapter. All remaining errors or shortcomings are my own responsibility.

1. A couple of families still live in the forest without contact with whites, even if these families' territory is getting smaller due to the establishment of farms by Mennonite and Brazilian landowners. Several NGOs are fighting for the autonomy of these groups and the restitution of their lands: Survival International, Iniciativa Amocotodie, UNAP (Unión Nativos Ayoreo del Paraguay), GAT (Gente Ambiente Territorio), OPIT (Organización Payipie Ichadie Totobiegosode) and APCOB (Apoyo para Campesino-Indígena del Oriente Boliviano).
2. Despite over fifty years of contact, the Ayoreo are fluent speakers of their language (Zamuco language family) and some of them speak Spanish too, with very different levels of fluency. Although young adults understand the words related to traditional culture less and less (Bertinetto 2009), the prognosis for the survival of the Ayoreo language is good.
3. The First Men (*Jnanibajade*) and the First Women (*Chequebajedie*) are people from mythic time, when animals and humans were not yet different. Most of these myths tell the story of a First Man who decides

to transform himself into an animal, right after teaching the humans a healing spell and the specific instructions for its use.

4. Jean-Pierre Estival (2005, 2006) and Jürgen Riester and Graciela Zolezzi (1999) are the only ones who have transcribed and published non-*puyac* songs. Daisy Amarilla's (Amarilla-Stanley 2001, Amarilla and Posoraja 2011) and José Zanardini's (1981, 2003; Zanardini and Amarilla 2007) contributions present a large repertoire of stories, most of them non-*puyac*.

5. Bórmida and Califano mention mourning songs in their very brief depiction of funerary rites. These authors do not describe the laments at all (1978: 160).

6. For collective ritual wailing, see, for example, the Warao from Venezuela (Briggs 1992, 2008, 2014) or the Kaluli from New Guinea (Feld 1990).

7. Jnumi gave me the example of a woman who had cried an *uñacai* for her son a year after the young boy's death. The Ayoreo considered this '*poitac*' (ugly). Jnumi realised, however, that the memory had not triggered the *uñacai*, but a current situation. This woman had another sick son and she feared his death. Even if the *uñacai* was 'old', the fact that it was linked to an ongoing situation made it one that was 'performed at the right moment'.

8. I was able to witness ten performances of *uñacai*, none of which was related to a death. In all cases but one the singer feared the death of someone, caused by disease or starvation. In addition, I recorded seventeen song-like versions of *uñacade*; ten of these were related to the deaths, while the rest were concerned with severe diseases.

9. This emphasis on meaningful words presents a stark contrast with other groups in Lowland South America: the Shavante wailing songs, for example, consist of repeated vowel sounds with no semantic content at all (Graham 1987).

10. Other authors analyse the relationship between laments and social structure in a different way. Feld (1990), for example, finds in the ecopolyphony of the voices in Kaluli laments a parallel with the egalitarian social structure. As the *uñacai* is an individually performed lament, I cannot make this comparison between musical and social structure among the Ayoreo. Briggs (1992) explains how the Warao women use the *sana* songs to subvert the social subjugation they suffer from men in everyday life. I have not seen specific political implication in the *uñacade*, but an idealised depiction of expected social interactions. In addition, the Ayoreo make no accusations in the *uñacade*, not even when a shaman has caused the disease or the death. The Ayoreo focus rather on how nice the mourned individual was. The lyrics of the *uñacade* are mainly examples of Ayoreo sociality and conviviality.

11. A few weeks later, a Nivakle shaman healed Puchiejna. The healer also revealed the identity of the attacker: an evil shaman from a neighbouring Angaite community.

12. This contrast (happy past vs. sad present) can be found in several groups' laments (e.g. Briggs 2014 on Warao laments).
13. This teaching was then passed on. In 2011, Jnumi tried in the same way to teach Meri, a young girl, how to cry-sing. Meri was sad about her cousin who was in hospital, but 'didn't know how to cry'.
14. In a war song *pinangoningai* for example, the singing warrior may say that he is as brave as his *edopasai*, the wild pig.
15. This explanation is related to an old expression of gratitude, which consisted in praising the clan possessions of the benefactor. For example, the expression '*Daju poro penojaaaaae!*' (The white *caraguatá* is beautiful!) was employed to thank a member of the Etacori clan for a gift.
16. The *cucherane* do not fit in with the classic definition of clan (Murdock 1960). Even though 'clan' is not an accurate translation of *cucherane*, I will use it for the sake of simplicity. Moreover, it is the Spanish translation used by the Ayoreo. I try to follow Bartolomé's idea. He suggested that instead of forcing the concept of *cucherane* to fit into old categories such as 'sibs' or 'clans', it would be better to unveil its particular meaning (Bartolomé 2000: 256).
17. I erroneously believed, inspired by the long lists of *edopasade* found in literature (Bernand-Muñoz 1977; Fischermann 1988), that every Ayoreo knew many clan's possessions. Some elders in Jesudi do know several *edopasade*. My aim, however, is to understand the most common and shared knowledge about the clans.
18. For an analysis of the Ayoreo clans as classification systems, see Bernand-Muñoz (1977), Fischermann (1988), Bartolomé (2000), Bórmida and Califano (1978) and Dasso (2006). For a study of the social implications of clans – exogamy and residence – see Bugos (1985). These so-called 'clans' (see note 16) among the Ayoreo may lead one to think that we are in the presence of what Descola (2005) has called 'totemism'. However, in spite of certain superficial similarities (e.g. the fact of humans, non-humans and objects gathered together in several groups), the Ayoreo actually fit better into the 'animism' category (ibid.) due to a series of features in the mode of identification, the instituted collectives derived out of these, and the mode of relation between human and non-human.

The Ayoreo myths are the classical examples of this mode of identification, animism, so widely present in lowland South America: they tell the stories of existents with human and non-human physical traits who transform for good in a particular non-human entity. The non-humans end up being characterised as persons with the same traits of interiority as humans (e.g. the ability to speak) but with different physicalities.

When it comes to the institution of collectives, the tale of the man who was turned into a peccary (see one version in Casalegno 1985: 188) is very instructive. It is the story of a human hunter who is kidnapped by the peccaries and then socialised by them. He then puts long teeth on and thick hair all over his body, and by this bodily transformation he becomes a member of this non-human group. He ends up teaching his new fellows how to avoid human hunters. This myth shows us that 'every species has their own collective' (Descola 2005: 342), and that we are not dealing with hybrid collectives, as it is the outcome of a totemist mode of identification. Besides, the mode of relation with non-humans is predominantly predation, which is usually the case in animist ontologies.

The *cucherane* (clans) do not fit with the idea of totem presented in Descola's work (2005: 203). There is no foundational myth of the clans, nor a tale that would explain the origin of everything that is related to a specific *cucherai*. The stories of why a non-human or an item belongs to a specific clan are as the Ayoreo First Times tales in general: 'a multiplicity of *individual decisions*' (Sebag 1965: 117, italics in the original, our translation). In some cases it is someone from a clan who finds something, and therefore it belongs to this clan (e.g. a man from the *Etacori* clan keeps walking until he finds the day, and that is why the day is an *edopasai* of the *Etacorone*). On other occasions, the non-human is presented as having belonged to a clan since the very beginning of times.

There are not common features (material or essential) shared by humans and non-humans of the same *cucherai*. Even though some general traits may be attributed to humans belonging to the same *cucherai* (e.g. 'the *Dosapei* have a clearer skin'), these are vague and limited to humans. Besides, there is no species or object that would be the best exponent of a *cucherai* identity, as is the case in totemism – as analysed by Descola (2005: 231). Finally, it is not forbidden to eat one's own clan possessions, the *edopasade*. There are food prohibitions among the Ayoreo, but these are the classical examples of not eating jaguar (an eater of raw meat) or scavenger birds (eaters of rotten meat), who were powerful shamans in the First Men times tales.

19. Bugos's detailed study on Ayoreo kinship in Bolivia provides concrete data about *iguiosode* solidarity and exogamy. Only 6 of 52 violent deaths involved members of the same clan, and only 13 of 750 unions broke the exogamy rule (Bugos 1985: 147–48).

20. This, of course, was not taken as absolutely certain. The attribution of the cause of a disease is always open to discussion (Otaegui 2011).

21. Actually, I have seen people from different clans crying for the same person. Nevertheless, Sidi's statement shows how *iguiosode* are expected to care about each other.

22. Infusion of *yerba mate* prepared with cold water.

23. The domain of Ayoreo humour – if such a domain is definable – is of course larger than the teasing interactions described in this contribution. There are myths that make Ayoreo laugh. In one of them the jaguar is tricked into eating his own cub (cf. one version of this myth in Amarilla-Stanley 2001: 45), which reminds us of Clastres's idea that Amerindians laugh from what they fear (Clastres 1974). There is also a set of jokes on people who break the clan exogamy rule, which could allow us to think of humour as a way of social control or a reinforcement of certain habitus. Examples can also be found among the Ayoreo of what

Villar (2013: 482) has described among the Chacobo as 'sadic humour', which consists in laughing from suffering animals (in the case of Ayoreo, they may find amusing the situation of a tattoo trying unsuccessfully to escape from the fire where it is being cooked alive). Moreover, there are many other teasing interactions leading to moments of joy and laughter, usually related to sex, infidelity and some individuals' particular traits of personality. I will focus on these funny quarrels at lunch, as this theatrical display of what life could be, if certain habitus changed, turns out to be fundamental in the reinforcement of certain values of Ayoreo conviviality.

24. Humour is not of course an independent dimension of life among the Ayoreo. It is related to affective relations, myths, verbal art and many other constituents of everyday life. Humour has been analysed in several ways since the classical contribution by Clastres (1974) based on the study of three Nivacle myths. Other researchers have also related humour to myths (Lagrou 2006; Overing 2000, 2017). Lagrou analyses the presence of humour in Kashinawa myths as guiding their particular understanding of the world and their relation to it. In a discourse-centred approach, Sherzer presented a Kuna trickster story as a reflection or commentary on everyday life (Sherzer 1990). Surrallés has addressed the relation between humour and affect expressed in poems sung by women among the Candoshi (Surrallés 2003). Overing's (2000) analysis on the importance of humour in everyday life and in the instauration of a certain sociality, and Villar's paper on Chacobo humour (2013) as way of collective thinking, constitute the main references for this work.

25. Some *edopasade* are clearly linked by contiguity: the cow, the milk and the ice cream belong to the Posorajnãi; the sun, the day, the fire and the fuel (*yote piroi*, 'water of fire') belong to the Etacori. Nevertheless, contiguity can be seen linking only few *edopasade* (Fischermann 1988: 150–60 counts 115 *edopasade* belonging to the Etacori).

26. For most of the new items, the Ayoreo just refer to contiguity: 'Trucks are made of metal [metal or iron are Chiquenoi], so they belong to the Chiquenoi clan'. In same cases, a myth explains how a new item has become a possession of a clan. The myth of the origin the iron – discovered by the Ayoreo during the Chaco war (1932–1935) – tells how animals of the Chiquenoi clan became owners of this metal by extracting it from the body of the white stork (Fischermann 1988: 114).

27. There is also an affective dimension in the idea of *edopasade*. Since early childhood the Ayoreo learn to be proud of their clan possessions. A child is taught by his or her grandmother: 'As you are *chiquenoi*, honey is your *edopasai*'. The child smiles happy and surprised, as when he or she gets a toy or a chocolate. '*Unejna yedopasai!*' ('my *edopasai* is tasty!') is an expression of satiety, and pride as well, after drinking water or eating fruit.

References

Amarilla-Stanley, D. 2001. *Oé chojninga: Relatos bilingües ayoreo-castellano*. Biblioteca Paraguaya de Antropología, 40. Asunción, Mexico: CEADUC.

Amarilla, D., and J.I. Posoraja. 2011. *Captura del ayoreo José Iquebi*. Biblioteca Paraguaya de Antropología 80. Asunción: CEADUC.

Bartolomé, M. 2000. *El Encuentro de la Gente y los Insensatos: La Sedentarización de los Cazadores Ayoreo en el Paraguay*. Asunción, Mexico: Instituto Indigenista Interamericano.

Bernand-Muñoz, C. 1977. *Les Ayoré du Chaco Septentrional: Etude Critique à partir des Notes de Lucien Sebag*. La Haya: Mouton.

Bertinetto, P. 2009. 'Ayoreo (Zamuco): A Grammatical Sketch', *Quaderni del Laboratorio di Linguistica della Scuola Normale Superiore* 8: ns.

Bórmida, M., and M. Califano. 1978. *Los Indios Ayoreo del Chaco Boreal: Información Básica Acerca de su Cultura*. Buenos Aires: FECYC.

Bremen, V. Von. 2008. 'Impactos de la Guerra del Chaco en la Territorialidad Ayorea', in N. Richard (ed.), *Mala Guerra: Los Indígenas en la Guerra del Chaco (1932–35)*. Asunción and París: ServiLibro, Museo del Barro, CoLibris, pp. 333–54.

Briggs. Ch. 1992. '"Since I Am a Woman, I Will Chastise My Relatives": Gender, Reported Speech, and the (Re)production of Social Relations in Warao Ritual Wailing', *American Ethnologist* 19: 337–61.

———. 2008. *Poéticas de Vida en Espacios de Muerte: Género, Poder y Estado en la Cotidianeidad Warao*. Quito: Abya-Yala.

———. 2014. 'Dear Dr. Freud', *Cultural Anthropology* 29(2): 312–43.

Bugos, P. 1985. 'An Evolutionary Ecological Analysis of the Social Organization of the Ayoreo of the Northern Gran Chaco'. PhD dissertation. Evanston, IL: Northwestern University.

Carsten, J. 1995. 'The Substance of Kinship and the Heat of the Hearth: Feeding, Personhood, and Relatedness among Malays in Pulau Langkawi', *American Ethnologist* 22(2): 223–41.

Casalegno, H. 1985. 'Les Ayoré du Gran Chaco par leurs mythes: essai de lecture et de classement des mythes Ayoré I-II-III'. PhD dissertation. Paris: Paris Diderot University.

Clastres, P. 1974. *La Société contre l'État: Recherches d'anthropologie politique*. Paris: Les Éditions de Minuit.

Combès, I. 2009. *Zamucos*. Cochabamba: Nómades, Instituto de Misionología.

Dasso, M. 2006. 'Notas acerca de los clanes ayoreo del Chaco boreal', *Acta Americana. Journal of the Swedish Americanist Society* 14(1): 39–68.

Descola, Ph. 2005. *Par-delà nature et culture*. Paris: Gallimard.

Estival, J.-P. 2005. 'Introducción a los Mundos Sonoros Ayoreo: Referencias, Etnografía, Texto de Cantos', *Suplemento Antropológico* 40(1): 451–502.

————. 2006. 'Memória, emoção, cognição nos cantos irade dos Ayoré do Chaco Boreal', *Mana* 12(2): 315–332.

Feld, S. 1990. 'Wept Thoughts: The Voicing of Kaluli Memories', *Oral Tradition* 5: 241–66.

Fischermann, B. 1988. *Zur Weltsicht der Ayoréode Ostboliviens*. Bonn: Rheinische Friedrich-Wilhelm-Universität.

Graham, L. 1987. 'Three Modes of Shavante Vocal Expression: Wailing, Collective Singing and Political Oratory', in J. Sherzer and G. Urban (eds), *Native South American Discourse*. Berlin: Mouton de Gruyter, pp. 83–118.

Higham, A., M. Morarie and P. Greta. 2000. *Ayoré-English Dictionary*. Sanford, FL: New Tribes Mission.

Lagrou, E. 2006. 'Rir do poder e o poder do riso nas narrativas e performances kaxinawa', *Revista de Antropologia* 49(1): 55–90.

Mashnshnek, C. 1991. 'Las Categorías del Discurso Narrativo y su Significación en la Cultura de los Ayoreo del Chaco Boreal', *Anthropologica* 9: 19–38.

McCallum, C. 2001. *Gender and Sociality in Amazonia: How Real People are Made*. Oxford: Berg Publishers.

Murdock, G. 1960. 'Cognatics Forms of Social Organisation', *Viking Fund Publications in Anthropology* 29: 1–14.

Otaegui, A. 2011. 'Los Ayoreos Aterrorizados: Una Revisión del Concepto de Puyák en Bórmida y una Relectura de Sebag', *Runa – Archivo para las Ciencias del Hombre* 32(1): 9–26.

————. 2014. 'Les Chants de Nostalgie et de Tristesse des Ayoreo du Chaco Boréal Paraguayen' (Une Ethnographie des Liens Coupés). PhD dissertation. Paris: EHESS.

Overing, J. 2000. 'The Efficacy of Laughter: The Ludic Side of Magic within Amazonian Sociality', in J. Overing and A. Passes (eds), *The Anthropology of Love and Anger: The Aesthetics of Conviviality in Native Amazonia*. London: Routledge, pp. 64–81.

————. 2003. 'In Praise of the Everyday: Trust and the Art of Social Living in an Amazonian Community', *Ethnos* 68(3): 293–316.

————. 2017. 'An Amazonian Question of Ironies and the Grotesque: The Arrogance of Cosmic Deceit, and the Humility of Everyday Life', in J. Shaffner and H. Wardle (eds), *Cosmopolitics: The Collected Papers of the Open Anthropology Cooperative, Volume I*. St Andrews: Open Anthropology Cooperative Press, pp. 209–26.

Overing, J., and A. Passes (eds). 2000. *The Anthropology of Love and Anger: The Aesthetics of Conviviality in Native Amazonia*. London: Routledge.

Riester, J., and G. Zolezzi (eds.). 1999. *Cantaré a mi gente: canto y poesía ayoreode*. Santa Cruz de la Sierra: APCOB.

Sebag, L. 1965. 'Le chamanisme Ayoreo (II)', *L'Homme* 5(2): 92–122.

Sherzer, J. 1990. 'On Play, Joking, Humor and Tricking among the Kuna. The Agouti Story', *Journal of Folklore Research* 27(1–2): 85–114.

Surrallés, A. 2003. 'Por qué el humor hace reír? Humor, amor y modestia ritual en la lírica amazónica', *Amazonia Peruana* 28–29: 87–102.

Tola, F. 2009. *Conceptions du Corps et de la Personne dans un Contexte Amerindien: les Toba du Gran Chaco*. Paris: L'Harmattan.

Urban, G. 1988. 'Ritual Wailing in Amerindian Brazil', *American Anthropologist* 90(2): 385–400.

Villar, D. 2013. 'De qué ríen los chacobos', *Anthropos* 108: 481–94.

Willerslev, R. 2007. *Soul Hunters: Hunting, Animism, and Personhood among the Siberian Yukaghirs*. Oakland: University of California Press.

Zanardini, J. 1981. 'Vida y misterio de los indios Moro Ayoreo', *Suplemento Antropológico* 16(2): 167–185.

——— (ed.). 2003. *Cultura del pueblo ayoreo: Manual para los docentes*. Biblioteca Paraguaya de Antropología 44. Asunción: Centro Social Indígena, CEADUC.

Zanardini, J., and D. Amarilla. 2007. *Sabiduría de la selva: Cuchade uje jnoi chigo uyoque*. Biblioteca Paraguaya de Antropología 60. Asunción: CEADUC.

8

Substantiated Wealth

Morality, Local Economy and the Body in Indigenous Amazonia

Minna Opas

'Money is mad, like madness. It makes one go mad.'

—A Yine woman

Introduction

People's responses to changes taking place in their social, economic and medical environments – especially those brought about by different processes of modernisation – are prone to become negotiated in the socio-cosmological field. In indigenous contexts, encounters with the Other (e.g. white people representing religious or nongovernmental organisations), novel medical treatments (e.g. vaccinations and operations), inclusion in national social systems (identity cards and birth certificates), and institutionalised education are examples of transformations that generate ambivalence among local people. An exemplary topic in this respect is the introduction or advancement of a monetary economy and capitalistic principles of commerce, which seem to pose a challenge to the underlying social principles – for instance reciprocity – of the local economy. Various studies from different parts of the world demonstrate how the introduction of a monetary economy or the increased availability of commodities creates a situation of moral ambivalence, although examples of the contrary abound as well (Taussig 1980; Parry and Bloch 1989; Guyer 1995; Gregory 1997; Akin and Robbins 1999; Maurer 2006; Keane 2007). Economic change and the possibilities it presents are welcomed, although the apparent costs of the novelties for the society, family and the individual are considered threatening (Mitchell 2001). An important site for the negotiation of such ambivalent situations are people's relationships with different non-human or semi-human beings. Often, in relation to subsistence activities, the negotiation tends to take the form of pacts between humans and beings glossed as 'devils' owing to Christian influence.

In the Latin American context there are plenty of examples of how changes in the socio-economic and medical environment have boosted the occurrence of narratives concerning different kinds of evil personages and demons. Extremely common figures both in the South American highlands and lowlands have been different 'extractors' – the face-takers, and fat and blood-stealers – known, for instance, by the names *sacacaras* and *pelacaras* in the Spanish-speaking lowlands, *kharisiris* and *lik'ichiris* in the Aymara-speaking areas, and *ñak'aq* and *pishtakuq* in the Quechua-speaking highlands (Siskind 1973; Weiss 1975; Stoll 1982; Rivière 1991; Salazar-Soler 1991; Bastien 1992: 183–86; Gow 2001: 256–66; Fernández Juárez 2008). These beings are thought to extract human bodily substances – fat, blood and skin – to be used in the production of 'white' technology, for instance medicine and cosmetics. Narrations of these figures were already common in the early colonial period and they are also known in the Iberian Peninsula (Fernández Juárez 2008).[1] However, in contrast to these malevolent beings, which have mostly been interpreted as responses to technological advances and medical treatments, and which cannot be reciprocally interacted with, the beings that work as sites for the negotiation of changes in the economic field are often understood as being more interactive. Typically, these beings are masters or owners of natural resources – guardians of game animals, of the forest and the river (see also Brabec de Mori and Sax this volume). Although in the normal daily life, interaction with these beings may be characterised by control on the one hand, but care on the other (Fausto 2012), within the framework of economic changes they frequently become demonised or associated with demonic forces, and the results of interacting with these beings are often disastrous (see e.g. Nash 1979; Taussig 1980; Ingham 1986; Parry and Bloch 1989; Harris 1989; Sallnow 1989; Smith 1996; Jamieson 2009). With regard to the changes in the economic environment, perhaps the best-known example in literature dealing with the masters of resources is Michael Taussig's (1980) discussion on the Bolivian tin miners and the Colombian sugar plantation peasants. In his analysis, devil beliefs were a way for these people both to resist and to 'come to terms' with the implications of the new economic situation.

Two issues that Taussig and various other authors have identified as being common to such cases have to do firstly with excess and individualisation, and secondly with the body. Firstly, the ambivalent moral situation caused by the changed economic scene tends to culminate in the demonisation of excess (Mitchell 2001), which becomes epitomised in the interaction with different beings. The inequality between the indigenous or peasant and the capitalist modes of production – whereas the first rarely generates surplus, the latter offers a promise of excess – is prone to affect social relations and thus destabilise social order. The demonisation of excess is therefore one way of dealing with and trying to resist the changes in social relations. For instance, in the cases discussed by Taussig (1980), peasants in Colombia and Bolivia enter into secret contracts with devilish figures in order to increase production and their profits (i.e. to generate excess). For Taussig, such entering into the capitalist system, especially the shift from a reciprocal exchange-based economy to a market-based one, causes 'alienation' of the individuals in a society. It changes the emphasis from human relationships to fetishised commodities. The contracts made with devilish figures epitomise the dangers of such overt individualism, since they are considered non-productive and, in the end, fatal for the person who is accused of having sold his soul to the devil.

The observation that different processes of modernisation cause a movement away from emphasising sociality towards valuing individualism and independence has been common in ethnographies of the 1980s and 1990s (Taussig 1980; Parry and Bloch 1989). More recent studies have also pointed in this direction, perhaps perceiving the issue with greater complexity. In his study of the relationship between modernity and Protestant Christianity among the Indonesian Sumbanese people, Webb Keane notes how changes in human subjectivity derive from one of the central characteristics of modernity: the distinction made between subjects and objects (Latour 1993; Keane 2002). 'Protestant modernity characteristically involves a certain dematerialisation of the human world, a denial of some of the ways human subjects are enmeshed with material objects' (Keane 2007: 271). Thus, the transformation from exchange practices to monetary interactions does contribute to promoting a change in the human subject. The human subject becomes a free, autonomous individual, separate from the world of objects. In such a context, money may also become a detached commodity freed from its social connections. It does not get its value from being part of human social relations in a particular way, but becomes desired first and foremost for its cash value (Keane 2002; 2007: 270–84.)

The second issue in common in interaction narratives concerning demonised guardian/master/owner figures is the centrality of the body. The body is the central locus for negotiating transformations and the ambivalence caused by economic changes, and the effects these have on social life. The uncertainty about the contemporary socio-economic transformations becomes visible as anxieties about the possession of the body (Mitchell 2001). In situations involving the introduction and advancement of a market economy, it is often the body that faces the consequences of the demonised excess. The body becomes ill, violated, and in many cases even dead.

In this chapter, I shall look at the connections between monetary/market economy, capitalism, individualism and the body in the context of interaction with owner-master figures. My discussion will focus on the indigenous Amazonian Yine people, among whom the two themes delineated above – excessive wealth and individualism, and the body – figured prominently in their interactions with the guardian of the forest, *Kaxpomyolutu* or the Hand-whistler, often demonised owing to the influence of Evangelical Christianity. The Hand-whistler's name derives from its ability to mimic animal and bird sounds by whistling through its hands. Whereas many previous works on the processes of modernisation related to economy and non-human others have largely concentrated on the society or community-level processes taking place as a result of economic changes, in which the human body is understood primarily as a symbol, and have examined the relationship between the local group and the foreign capitalist actors (the outside world), I shall try to shed light on the process of demonisation of the guardians of nature by shifting the analytical focus to the individual and the individual body.[2] As in many other cases, among the Yine the human body was also the locus of negotiations of excessive wealth. Nevertheless, it was not a passive receptor of the consequences but rather a site for active negotiation of the socio-economic changes and their significance, both for the individuals themselves and for the community, or more generally the society.

I aim to show firstly how the interactions with and the narrations of the Hand-whistler, or hand-whistlers since different forest areas were considered to have their own guardians, worked as a framework for the Yine within which the tension between individualism and sociality – in particular as it concerns the local economy and wealth accumulation – could be played out at the level of the body; and secondly, how this took place through the processes of substantiation. Occupying a key place in these processes was the ability to remain in control of oneself, which in the end came down to a person's corporeal moral condition. In particular, I shall show how the Yine attempts to find a balance between individualism – which is to be understood as a passivity in rehearsing one's sociality rather than an active self-interest – and sociality took place and were reworked at the level of the body through the socio-moral value of sharing, as expressed by its counterpart, the negative value of excess. The relationships the Yine had with the hand-whistlers highlight the destructiveness of excess in terms of physical strength and money, and exemplify the undesired effects of the social and moral imbalance in situations where personal profits are stressed over and above communal welfare. Furthermore, the challenges to people's ability to control the social and economic changes taking place in the environment in which the Yine live were negotiated not only in the personal interaction with the Hand-whistler, but were also seen to affect the composition of the Yine social cosmos more generally – in other words, the actions and incidence of different non-human beings.

The chapter also aims to contribute to the discussion on the question of human to non-human kinship relations in Amerindia – and in Amazonia, in particular. In these discussions, predation and commensality have been observed to be 'distinct yet dynamically articulated forms of producing people and sociality' (Fausto 2007: 500) in interspecies relationships (including spirits and owners of resources). The exclusivity of perspectives has been understood to be at the heart of such processes. For instance, a case of soul capture by a non-human may appear as seduction and commensality from the perspective of the person's soul, but suffering and withering away from that of their bodily experiences (see ibid.: 502). The chapter pays attention to two points, in particular, in such interactions. First, the interspecies or human–non-human interactions have often been analysed as relations between masters and adoptees, or as non-human attempts to build kinship relations. The case of the Yine relationships with the Hand-whistler, however, directs the examination of this dynamism towards a mode of relatedness best described with the notion of formalised personal friendship (see Santos-Granero 2007; Killick 2010). It invites the analysis of formation of bodies through infliction of pain as generative of relatedness rather than otherness, but still not directed towards the formation of enduring kin relations. Rather than radical transformation or metamorphosis, the result of these processes is a condition of 'in-between'. Second, the chapter contributes to the examination of human–non-human relations separately from the framework of predation (Fausto 2005; Vilaça 2009). Even though the dimension of predation does feature in many Yine human–non-human interactions, it is rarely the central organising principle in them (Opas 2014; see also Hill this volume). Instead, different beings appear to relate to others through pacific processes of consubstantialisation aimed at achieving 'good life'.

The Yine Local Economy

The Yine (also known as the Piro) are an Arawak-speaking people, numbering between five and seven thousand, and living mainly in the central and south-eastern Peruvian Amazonia. My work concentrates on the Yine people of the south-eastern lowlands, of the Madre de Dios region, where their economic situation is quite different from that of the Yine from the central parts of the country. Despite their long history as merchants, the basic subsistence activities of the Madre de Dios Yine people have been, and still are, hunting, fishing and agriculture. The products of these activities have been given and exchanged according to family relations and the godparent system known in Spanish as *compadrazgo*, in which the godparents of a child become the co-parents of the child's parents. Nevertheless, especially during the past half a century, the need for money to buy commodities has constantly increased, which has also disturbed the exchange relations. Money does not enter the exchange system like other products, but tends to stay with the person or within the nuclear family. Although the possibilities for generating income have not kept up with the need for money, there are nowadays many possible sources of income for the Yine, such as working as boatmen and selling handicrafts to tourists. Nevertheless, few of them provide income on a regular basis and in most cases the profits are low. This is why over the past ten years or so logging has become an extremely important business among the Yine. It is considered to produce unparalleled income in a relatively short time compared to other sources. For instance, at the end of the first decade of the twenty-first century, every member in one of the Yine communities was allowed to sell seven thousand board feet of timber a year, amounting to a sum of approximately 4,000–18,000 Peruvian Nuevos Soles (1,300–6,000 USD) depending on the species. This was much more than the other means available for generating income were capable of providing.

However, logging was also prone to causing severe disputes and uncertainty. The most active loggers were accused of selling more timber than the quantity assigned to them by the community. People, both indigenous and non-indigenous, were also said to cut down trees in spite of the official ban against felling valuable trees in certain areas. The Yine also resented the fact that they were paid only a fraction of the income gained by the intermediary loggers selling the timber on. In addition, foreign exploiters extracting wood without permission from the legally recognised Yine territory were a constant source of trouble. The problem of illegal logging often took the form of witchcraft accusations. During my stays among the Yine, several cases of illness were thought to have been caused by foreign loggers. One central way for negotiating this changing economic environment and the controversies it generated was the relationships the Yine had with the guardian of the forest of their social cosmos, *Kaxpomyolutu*.

Crafting Morally Legitimate Bodies by Fighting

The Yine guardian of the forest, *Kaxpomyolutu* or the Hand-whistler, is related to the guardian figure common in Amazonian indigenous and mestizo social cosmoses and generally known as either *Shapishico*[3] or *Chullachaqui*, which comes from the Quechua words *ch'ulla*, meaning 'uneven', and *chaki*, 'foot'. Nevertheless, and unlike many other cases, the *Kaxpomyolutu* was not pictured as having one foot pointing backwards.[4] Among the Yine the guardian was described as being as short as a six- or seven-year-old boy but extremely strong. It wears a small *cushma*, the painted cotton gown worn by Yine men in the past, and therefore resembles a very short Yine person. The Hand-whistler is the owner of game animals and the forest at large. Most Yine adults had at least heard its calls in the woods, and they all also personally knew someone who was said to have encountered one. When encountered in the forest, the Hand-whistler was said to ask for a man's hunting intentions and could either approve or condemn them, in the latter case with fatal results for the hunter. In the first case, however, the Hand-whistler could show the hunter where game is to be found. Nevertheless, it was said to make sure that no one hunts in excess and that everyone has an equal possibility of finding animals and thus participating in the exchange of food among the family and co-parents.

One woman in her fifties told me how her father had encountered a Hand-whistler in his youth and had subsequently established a lifelong relationship with it. The man had been alone in the woods searching for game when a midget-like being, which he recognised as hand-whistler, had appeared before him. The Hand-whistler asked what the man was looking for in the woods and he replied that he was searching for food for his family and wanted to kill a partridge (*Traylor's tinamou*; Yine, *yoko*). The Hand-whistler told him that all the animals, including the *tinamou*, were his, as he had brought them up and that the man was not to kill them. Instead, the Hand-whistler wanted to fight the man but the latter resisted saying that he had no reason to, nor did he wish to start fighting. However, the Hand-whistler insisted and assaulted the man, throwing him against a tree trunk with tremendous force. Then he urged the man to strike him in turn. In this manner, the Hand-whistler and the man continued throwing each other around until they were both exhausted. When the battle was over, the Hand-whistler declared that from now on the two of them would be friends.[5] He blew on the top of the man's head so that he would become as strong as he himself was, after which the man was finally able to return home. Reaching home, he felt totally deprived of his strength and remained in bed for several days. After a while he felt that he had regained his strength and, to his surprise, he had in fact become unusually strong. From then on, he always encountered hand-whistlers in the forest and these showed him where he could find game animals to feed his family.

This was a fairly common storyline among the Yine. Nevertheless, whereas the Hand-whistler usually acted as the owner of game animals, in recent years it had assumed new tasks, such as the guardian of valuable trees. Some Yine people said that instead of game animals, it could show loggers the whereabouts of mahogany and other trees with commercial value. In this way, it could help them to earn money. Given the changes in the economic environment briefly outlined above, it does not seem surprising that the Hand-whistler had gained more significance as the guardian of valuable trees than of game animals.

However, what at first appeared curious to me in these narrations – when the Hand-whistler was depicted as the guardian of both the animals and trees with commercial value – was the insistence of the Hand-whistler on fighting the men it encounters. It seemed logical enough that if one denies their similarity and kinship, the Hand-whistler kills the self-declared stranger or 'enemy'. One woman explained the encounters with the Hand-whistler, saying that 'it appears to you like a person, it tells you, it asks you: "Are you my brother?"; you have to reply "Yes, I am", because if you don't it kills you right away'. It was thought that if a person in this situation opposes the Hand-whistler, the result is lethal: the Hand-whistler fights the man until he is killed. But the fact that the Hand-whistler was always said to fight even those men who accept it as their kin or friend seemed peculiar. Why would the Hand-whistler wish to hurt his newly gained friends or kin?

Considering this in connection with Amerindian relational construction of personhoods/bodies gives us an insight. As already noted early on by Anthony Seeger, Roberto da Matta and Eduardo Viveiros de Castro (1987), Amazonian social groups can be characterised as communities of substance (see also Turner 1980; Conklin and Morgan 1996; McCallum 1996; 1997; Vilaça 2002; Londoño Sulkin 2012). It is through sharing substances – food and sexual fluids – and through physical proximity that people become consubstantial and thus kin, or at least more kin-like. Recently it has been shown how different objects and manufactured items also work in a similar way (Santos-Granero 2009). Harry Walker (2012), for instance, demonstrates how, among the Peruvian Urarina people, baby hammocks act as active agents contributing to forming the body of a child and thus producing legitimate personhood through physical contact. Among the Yine, people are made kin by producing and consuming 'real food' – especially game meat – together (Gow 1991). Similar processes appeared to take place in relation to the fights the Yine have with the Hand-whistler and his enormous powers. In them, the making of kin took place through physical hardship.

Among the Yine the process of making the body strong was initiated early on in a child's life. Beginning from birth, several different practices were customarily undertaken in order to manipulate the body. Different herbal and other treatments were widely used in order to strengthen the body, especially the limbs, and to generate beautiful and fitting Yine bodies. Different herbal drinks were prepared and herbal baths were taken. Children were also advised to bathe in the river very early every morning so that their bodies would not become lazy but strong. As adolescents and adults, when fat and other impurities had accumulated in the body, people drank bitter herbal infusions, causing vomiting, which was thought to purify the body, let the laziness out and make the body willing to work. Girls in particular also whipped their legs and arms with nettles or other pain-inflicting plants in order to make their limbs grow fat and enduring. Treating bodies in this manner was considered vital, for sociality could only be achieved through the labour of bodies capable and willing to work: to construct houses, to clear fields and to produce food by cultivating, hunting and fishing.[6] Although many of these measures were still in active use during the childhood of the present-day grandparent generation, they have gradually become less common. Nonetheless, some of the measures mentioned above were still actively practised during the first half of the 2010s.

It was especially the practice of whipping one's arms and legs with nettles that caught my attention, perhaps because it seemed to deviate most from the meanings I had personally attached to physical pain. Whereas for me physical pain carried primarily negative connotations, slight physical pain seemed to be viewed positively among the Yine, who still considered it one of the central ways of making bodies strong. In addition to girls whipping their limbs with plants, even small babies' bodies were treated in a similar manner. It initially took me by surprise when I observed the Yine women cooing at their babies and simultaneously gently slapping them on the cheeks with the palm of their hand. This kind of practice was very different from the way I had been used to seeing babies being nurtured, and it became understandable to me only after examining it in relation to practices such as that of the adolescents' limb whipping. I soon realised that I had never actually seen Yine children older than perhaps two or three years, let alone adults (except drunken men), crying. Some children, when joining in nurturing small babies, also gently slapped them, and were amused if the baby started crying owing to the treatment; often commenting on the situation with excitement and surprise in their voice: 'Look, she is crying!' Crying, then, at least in public, seemed to be considered not only unaesthetic but also a sign of weakness and therefore a reaction strongly repressed by the Yine. Thus, the process of making people capable of bearing physical discomfort is begun early on with measures suited to the child's age. In the case of small babies, I think they get used to such mild discomfort relatively soon and no longer start crying because of it. These treatments commonly applied in childhood were largely aimed at manipulating children's bodies so that they would grow up to be tough and adept at acting in ways that would enhance the production of everyday sociable life.

These practices seem to be akin to the forms of ritual pain infliction, which aim not at punishment but at making the body enduring and resistant and able to produce sociality, such as the Mariwin spirit whipping among the Matis (Erikson 1999).[7] Viewed from this perspective, the fight between a Hand-whistler and a man, when they have agreed to be friends or kin to each other, does not appear destructive and violent but rather constitutive of bodies and relationships. Firstly, by fighting, the man's body would become strong and capable of bearing physical hardships in the future. Secondly, the process is also a form of making bodies, and more generally person-hoods, similar to others. In this sense the Hand-whistler could be seen to conform to the general endeavour of most beings in the Yine social cosmos of expanding their network of social relationships by making others similar through corporeal activities. Whereas other beings begin making others similar through sharing substances such as food and semen, the Hand-whistler does it through another form of physical interaction, namely fighting.

Not all fights, however, were considered constitutive in such a positive way. It was only fighting that is somehow regulated – agreed beforehand or supervised by adults – and not induced by anger, which was productive. The cases of violent fights prompted, for instance, by drunkenness that I witnessed among the Yine were condemned by everybody. They were considered inappropriate, even mad, behaviour and destructive of relatedness. Like other unwanted characteristics (such as homosexuality, which is viewed negatively especially by Protestant Christian Yine) (Opas 2008), it was feared that such angry ways of acting could also influence other people's ways of being. As shown also by people's experiences in interacting with hand-whistlers, mad behaviour expressed as violent action was thought to be caused largely by an inability to keep one's physical powers under control.

Even though fighting between the Hand-whistler and Yine men aims, from the Hand-whistler's point of view, to make the two bodies similar, the process of consubstantialisation is *not* similar to processes of 'making kin out of others' (Vilaça 2002) in regard to its aims and end result. Rather, it could better be characterized as one of 'making friends out of others'. The aim and result of the consub-stantialising fighting appears not to be the drawing of the human person away from the human sphere and their human condition but rather the formation of a certain kind of alliance – a kind of friend-ship between the Hand-whistler and the human person. In fact, in a number of narrations I was told, the Hand-whistler specifically asks whether the person wishes to be his friend (rather than kin). Owing to its limited scope – the relationship actualises only when a person goes out to hunt or to find suitable trees for logging – I would not, however, go as far as to equate the Yine friendship relations with the Hand-whistler with their human-to-human friendship relations. One rather obvious possibility would be to talk about these relations as those between owner-masters and their adoptive children or pets, common throughout Amazonia. As is emblematic to such relations, the relations between hand-whistlers and Yine are characterised by both the aspect of control and that of care (Fausto 2012). However, such relationships do not easily extend beyond the two members of the dyad. The focus remains in the interaction between the master and the child. As will be examined below, in the Yine relationships with hand-whistlers the focus was equally on the effects of the relationship on the human community and on the person vis-à-vis his human kin. Therefore, rather than exploring the relationship here as one between master and adoptee, I wish to study it within the framework of friendship. In general, friendship relations in Amazonia can be understood as less defined and more voluntary and flexible than master–adoptee or kin relations (cf. Killick 2010: 4). Nevertheless, owing to the great variation in the modes of friendship in Amazonia, no single definition of friendship can be given (Santos-Granero 2007: 9). Perhaps most accurately, then, the Yine–Hand-whistler relations can be talked about as 'formalised personal friendships', which are not 'totally altruistic but fulfil important pragmatic objectives: acquisition of exotic goods, allies, prized knowledge, and, above all, security', and extend beyond the two members of the relationship (ibid.).

Among the Yine, such formalised personal friendship relations formed between hand-whistlers and Yine men resulted in the men gaining magnified qualities as hunters, and so in a sense becoming more-than-human and more like hand-whistlers; but it did not signify their drifting away from the human bodily condition, as consubstantialising interaction (aimed at generation of kinship) with many other non-humans would. Rather, the new condition was somewhat reminiscent of the 'in-between' condition of shamans, who are capable of interacting with beings with different perspectives but can still return to their human point of view without undesired consequences (cf. Hill this volume). That is, however, only if the Yine men's bodies were morally able and trustworthy enough (see Santos-Granero 2007)[8] to deal with the magnification, as will be discussed below.

Substantiation of Power and Wealth

While physical strength and endurance were highly valued among the Yine, powers that are too great were considered menacing. In narrations concerning the Hand-whistler, the enormous powers men could receive from hand-whistlers were thought to lead easily to trouble. It was said that men who have become strong also become mad: they do not know how to control their powers. As one Yine man observed about such a person: 'He was no longer as he used to be. His body was now mad'.

The theme of the danger of possessing a certain quality in excess – knowledge, 'wild substance' and power, for instance (Arguedas 1961; Overing 1985; Pollock 1992; Wright 1992; Conklin 2001) – is common among Amerindian peoples and, at least in Amazonia, is related to the fabrication of personhoods examined above. Taming and gaining control over one's newly acquired powers or other constituents, especially those concerned with the success of the everyday production of sociality and relatedness, cannot normally be achieved all at once in Amazonia but requires a gradual domestication process in which these qualities are woven into one's body, into one's personhood (Londoño-Sulkin 2012; Walker 2012). This domestication achieved through substantiation necessarily requires a social context: a person cannot construct their body or personhood alone but only in social interaction with others, whereby the qualities' social and moral aspects become both constitutive of a person and harnessed for the good of the collective. This explains why too great a quantity of a given quality received at one time makes a person mad: since the quality has not been gradually entwined into a person in social interaction with others, it has not become substantiated, and so it cannot be mastered. In the Yine case, physical strength was thus not only a bodily achievement but was part of defining the person's socio-corporeal and moral condition.

Whereas in the case of the Hand-whistler as the guardian of the forest and game animals it was excess power that needs controlling, in the case of the Hand-whistler as the guardian of valuable trees the substance to be controlled was money.[9] Unlike the first case, in relation to the economic profits gained from logging the Hand-whistler also became demonised – its devilish nature became activated in some people's explanations and descriptions. As discussed above, the Yine people felt exploited by outsiders in that they had to sell timber at a bargain price whereas mestizos made a profit. Nevertheless, I argue that among the Yine the actualisation of the devilish nature of the Hand-whistler was not, at least in the first place, a way of criticising the market economy or capitalism, as many previous works on devil-belief traditions have argued. It derived neither from the mestizo loggers taking advantage of indigenous people nor from the difference between 'peasant' and 'capitalist' modes of production (Parry and Bloch 1989; Harris 1989; Sallnow 1989). Firstly, the Hand-whistler was thought to be encountered just as frequently by mestizos as by indigenous people, and to help them in finding valuable trees. Secondly and more importantly, in Yine narrations the emphasis was not solely on how money was earned, on its modes of production, but equally, or even more so, on how it was used, on the reasons for its circulation. The Yine explained that the Hand-whistler watches people, and if they 'go mad' because of the money, if they use the money gained from logging for diversion, such as drinking, instead of buying necessities, it will not show them the location of valuable trees anymore. The 'contract' made with the devil, the Hand-whistler, will be beneficial for the person if he sticks to it and does not use the money for alcohol or other unnecessary commodities, but for the benefit of the family. Money is therefore not to be detached from the mechanisms of social reproduction (Keane 2002; 2007: 270–84).

The demonisation of the Hand-whistler then derived from people's inability to put the money into generative use – that is, from the lack of a properly moral body willing and able to act sociably. As in the case of physical power, the morality that people associated with the production and circulation of money could be seen as becoming substantiated in them, as becoming generative of them as people. The socially destructive morals related to (excess) money as an object detached from the cycles of complementary labour or as a tool for sensuous enjoyment and luxury, for instance, could (when the money was used) not only become constitutive of a person but also disrupt the social process. The person using his or her money to drink alcohol, for instance, could be considered selfish, since the money thus used could not contribute to the continuation of productive reciprocal social relations. Money can therefore be understood as becoming productive for Yine sociality only when it can be properly controlled. Money needs to be domesticated, to be associated with work and social relations, as it usually is when gained little by little. But in the case of logging, the problem was the same as with suddenly obtaining excess physical power: it overwhelms a person, usually not allowing the process of substantiation to take place, and thus making the person 'mad'. Therefore, gaining control over the money acquired from logging comes down to a person's general moral condition. If a person wishes to produce and share food with others, desires to live close to their family and highly valued tranquil domestic life, it is more likely that such a person would not be overwhelmed by great amounts of money but could put it to generative use. Logging and narrations concerning the interaction with the Hand-whistler were therefore instances that make visible and tangible the concerns the

Yine had in their economic life, and in relation to which a person's moral condition could be evaluated.

Nevertheless, what needs to be stressed here is that the individual's well-being made possible by economic assets should not be juxtaposed with the asocial individualism often considered to prevail in the so-called Western thinking. As has been noted for many Amazonian peoples, among the Yine personal autonomy and the ability to be social were equally valued and the one could not exist without the other (Overing and Passes 2000: 21). Able hunters, well-off families and skilled artisans were not only envied but also admired, especially when their abilities worked to benefit the whole family. Yet even in the opposite case when a person acts individualistically, I suggest it is not merely a matter of active self-interest. It is rather generated through passivity or disinterest in rehearsing the body in order to make it social. The end result, however, begins to bear a strong resemblance to the so-called Western type of individualism characterised by asociality, in that the wealth accumulated as a result of logging tends to remain, to a large extent, in individual hands.

Being in Control of the Lived Environment

As has been seen, being able to control one's body, to keep it sociable, in spite of sudden profits or income, was a task the Yine people were struggling with in the current logging-driven local economy. A sociable body was, for the Yine, not only a proof of a person's legitimate moral condition but also a guarantee of, and a precondition for, the continuation of the ongoing production of the current form of Yine social life. The threats to this continuation were discussed in particular through the Yine relations with the Hand-whistler.

This was not, however, the only manner in which the human–non-human relations in the Yine social cosmos worked in coming to terms with current socio-economic changes. Despite their general disinterest at least in the distant future – a characteristic common to many Amazonian groups – the Yine people had started thinking about the socio-economic changes awaiting them in the foreseeable future. Their major concern was the dirt road, which would eventually reach the Yine communities in the south-eastern Peruvian Amazonia – perhaps in five, ten or fifteen years' time. People believed quite strongly that, even though the road would make their access to the city easier and more affordable, and would act as a route for commercialising their agricultural products, it would significantly alter their forms of subsistence and thus their social life. There would be a significant increase in the number of mestizo and city-dwelling people coming to live in the region, which would have the effect of diminishing the number of game animals in the area available for hunting. Furthermore, people anticipated, all the remaining valuable trees would be cut down by the newcomers – if they had not been finished before then – so that logging would no longer generate income. In general, in the Yine view, the forest would no longer provide subsistence for the people. Instead they would have to become farmers, clearing the forest for plantations, and selling their fruits and other products to people in the cities.

These future prospects were also reflected in Yine views of the non-human world. I by no means aim to reduce Yine interaction with the Hand-whistler or other non-humans to the position of a mere instrument of reacting to change. Rather, owing to their centrality in Yine daily life and economics, it would be surprising if they did not feature in one way or another in Yine practices of dealing with change. The Yine suspected that in the future the hand-whistlers would recede deeper into the forest and they would hardly ever be seen again. The uncertainty in the face of the overwhelming situation of the outside world penetrating into the forest in an uncontrollable way was reflected in the idea that the hand-whistlers will no longer be around, but that cases of witchcraft, for instance, will increase. When the local economy was considered to still be, to some extent, in the Yine people's own control despite the continuous changes and problems with illegal logging, the guardian of the forest as an interactive being worked as one site for negotiating the changes. It was anticipated, however, that when the hand-whistlers are forced to retreat, interaction with non-humans will diminish and will be replaced by more anonymous and one-way relationships of witchcraft and of assaults by semi-humans: face-takers and fat-stealers. Interaction and control will be replaced by a situation in which people could no longer influence the relationships in their social cosmos, no matter whether these were with different non-human beings or with other humans. There seemed to exist an underlying fear that people's bodies – no matter how morally reinforced their bodily condition was – will be unable to cope with the excesses that the market economy entering their lived world would bring. The result of all this could be that people will become 'mad' by the current standards. As was already observed about the Yine people moving into cities: 'They are mad – leaving their families behind like that'. In general, then, the Yine views towards the socio-economic transformations appeared to conform to Mitchell's (2001: 3) observation that '[t]he fear [was] of excessive change, rather than [of] change per se'.

Conclusion

In this chapter I have discussed the ways in which the transformations in the socio-economic field become negotiated in Yine people's relations with the guardian of the forest, the Hand-whistler. As the guardian of both the most important foodstuff and the basis of the exchange system, game meat, and of the most important source of income, namely logging, the figure of the Hand-whistler worked for the Yine as a meaningful way to negotiate the relationship between individuality and sociality, and the influences of market economy and capitalism on these relationships and on the social and moral life at large. The chapter has shown how these articulations were being rethought and reorganised at the level of the body, as bodily moral processes of substantiation.

Approaching the question of devil belief tradition in this manner from the perspective of the individual actor has had the advantage of diversifying the picture of the local peoples' ways of adapting to the changes in the economic environment and of domesticating new influences and structures. Local people appear as active agents in dealing with the changes in the local economy. This derives to a large extent from the tendency to view the 'representatives of capitalism' not as evil, or as something to be kept at a distance and rejected, but as something needed for the generation of sociable life among one's kin and social sphere at large. The Yine understandings of capitalism and monetary economy highlighted in the Hand-whistler narrations could thus be seen not just as reactions to the changing economic scene, but also in a way as proactions aimed at simultaneously guarding the integrity of the community and its members, and embracing the change in a controlled manner. In this regard, the interaction with the Hand-whistler was in stark contrast to the prospects the Yine envisioned for their future possibilities of coping with socio-economic changes. Fat-stealers and face-takers are not needed for the ongoing production of social life. Rather, they destroy it, and thus exemplify the damaging power of excessive wealth and of the type of individualism that is not intertwined with sociality.

Minna Opas is researcher in comparative religion at the University of Turku, Finland. She has been doing fieldwork among the Yine of south-eastern Peruvian Amazonia since 2000. Her research interests include anthropology of Christianity, indigenous peoples and religions, materiality, and religious imagination. She has been editorial secretary of *Temenos: Nordic Journal of Comparative Religion*, secretary of the Finnish Society for the Study of Religion, visiting scholar at the Université de Paris X – Nanterre, Centre Enseignement et Recherche en Ethnologie Amérindienne (EREA), and academic visitor at the University of Edinburgh, UK, Department of Social Anthropology.

Notes

I am grateful to the Academy of Finland for funding this research (no. 252542) and to the two anonymous reviewers and Juan Javier Rivera Andía for their insightful comments on the earlier versions of this chapter.

1. Other authors have also discussed similar figures, e.g. in the African context (White 1993; Weiss 1998). In the Yine myth corpus, such a figure is the Mother of Smallpox (Yine, *Moro* from Quechua *muru*; Sp., *viruela*). According to the most common storyline, the Mother of Smallpox – depicted as a male figure – travelled from village to village killing people and extracting fat from them, which was needed for his nutrition.
2. On master-owner figures and processes of modernisation and colonisation in Amazonia and Latin America, see e.g. Nash 1979; Taussig 1980; Ingham 1986; Perrin 1988; Renard-Casevitz 1988; Albert 1988; Hugh-Jones 1988; Harris 1989; Descola 1996; Gow 2001; Albert and Ramos 2002; Kohn 2007; Gose 2008; Jamieson 2009.
3. It is probable that that word *shapishiku* (just like the words *shapi* and *shapingu*) are variants of the word *supay* meaning owner, shadow, spirit, and malevolent being (Taylor 1980: 60).
4. Among the Yine this is a quality assigned to another being, the red brocket deer (*Mazama Americana*), which is considered to be able to adopt human form.
5. A similar theme is found in the Andean folklore in the story of John the Bear, who is half human half bear, and has great, but uncontrollable and thus destructive physical powers (Arguedas 1961).
6. On the practices of generating beautiful Yine bodies, see Gow 1999; 2001: 158–64.
7. On ritual violence and fighting in Amazonia, see e.g. Clastres (1974) 1989; Whitehead 2002; Santos-Granero 2005; Beckerman and Valentine 2008.

8. According to Santos-Granero 2007 (see also Rosengren 2004: 44), trustworthiness is a key aspect of friendship relations in Amazonia. Trust is also of focal importance in Yine relationships with the Hand-whistler: the act of a person telling other people of their relationship with the Hand-whistler, and so betraying the latter's trust, is said to lead to serious consequences. Space does not allow me to develop this point further here.

9. On indigenous Amazonian engagements with monetary economy, see e.g. Hugh-Jones 1992; Albert and Ramos 2002; Fisher 2000; Santos-Granero 2009.

References

Akin, D., and J. Robbins (eds). 1999. *Money and Modernity: State and Local Currencies in Melanesia*. Pittsburgh, PA: University of Pittsburgh Press.

Albert, B. 1988. 'La fumée du métal: Histoire et représentations du contact chez les Yanomami (Brésil)', *L'Homme* 106–7(2–3): 87–119.

Albert, B., and A.R. Ramos (eds). 2002. *Pacificando o branco: cosmologias do contato no Norte-Amazônico*. São Paulo: Unesp.

Arguedas, J.M. 1961. 'Cuentos Religioso-Mágicos Quechuas de Lucanamarca', *Folklore Americano* 8–9: 142–216.

Bastien, J.W. 1992. *Drum and Stethoscope: Integrating Ethnomedicine and Biomedicine in Bolivia*. Salt Lake City: University of Utah Press.

Beckerman, S., and P. Valentine (eds). 2008. *Revenge in the Cultures of Lowland South America*. Gainesville: University Press of Florida.

Clastres, P. [1974] 1989. *Society against the State: Essays in Political Anthropology*. New York: Zone Books.

Conklin, B. 2001. 'Women's Blood, Warriors' Blood, and the Conquest of Vitality in Amazonia', in T. Gregor and D. Tuzin (eds), *Gender in Amazonia and Melanesia*. Berkeley: University of California Press, pp. 141–74.

Conklin, B., and L. Morgan. 1996. 'Babies, Bodies, and the Production of Personhood in North America and a Native Amazonian Society', *Ethos* 24(4): 657–94.

Descola, P. 1996. *The Spears of Twilight: Life and Death in the Amazon Jungle*. New York: The New Press.

Erikson, P. 1999. *El sello de los antepasados: Marcado del cuerpo y demarcación étnica entre los Matis de la Amazonía*. Quito: IFEA/Abya-Yala.

Fausto, C. 2005. 'Se Deus fosse jaguar: Canibalismo e cristianismo entre os Guarani (séculos XVI–XX)', *Mana* 11(2): 385–418.

———. 2007. 'Feasting on People: Eating Animals and Humans in Amazonia', *Current Anthropology* 48(4): 497–530.

———. 2012. 'Too Many Owners: Mastery and Ownership in Amazonia', in M. Brightman and O. Ulturgasheva (eds), *Animism in Rainforest and Tundra: Personhood, Aniumals, Plants and Things in Contemporary Amazonia and Siberia*. New York and Oxford: Berghahn Books, pp. 29–47.

Fernández Juárez, G. 2008. *Kharisiris en Acción: Cuerpo, Persona y Modelos Médicos en el Altiplano de Bolivia*. Quito: Abya Yala.

Fisher, W.H. 2000. *Rain Forest Exchanges: Industry and Community on an Amazonian Frontier*. Washington DC: Smithsonian Institution Press.

Gose P. 2008. *Invaders as Ancestors: On the Intercultural Making and Unmaking of Spanish Colonialism in the Andes*. Toronto: University of Toronto Press.

Gow, P. 1991. *Of Mixed Blood: Kinship and History in Peruvian Amazonia*. Oxford: Clarendon Press.

———. 1999. 'Piro Designs: Painting as Meaningful Action in an Amazonian Lived World', *Journal of the Royal Anthropological Institute* 5(2): 229–46.

———. 2001. *An Amazonian Myth and Its History*. Oxford: Oxford University Press.

Gregory, C.A. 1997. *Savage Money: The Anthropology and Politics of Commodity Exchange*. Amsterdam: Harwood Academic.

Guyer, J.I. (ed.). 1995. *Money Matters: Instability, Values and Social Payments in the Modern History of West African Communities*. Portsmouth, NH: Heinemann.

Harris, O. 1989. 'The Earth and the State: The Sources and Meanings of Money in Northern Potosí, Bolivia', in J. Parry and M. Bloch (eds), *Money and the Morality of Exchange*. Cambridge: Cambridge University Press, pp. 232–68.

Hugh-Jones, S. 1988. 'The Gun and the Bow: Myths of White Men and Indians', *L'Homme* 106–7, 138–56.

———. 1992. 'Yesterday's Luxuries, Tomorrow's Necessities: Business and Barter in Northwest Amazonia', in C. Humphrey and S. Hugh-Jones (eds), *Barter, Exchange and Value: An Anthropological Approach*. Cambridge: Cambridge University Press, pp. 42–74.

Ingham, J.M. 1986. *Mary, Michael and Lucifer: Folk Catholicism in Central Mexico*. Austin: University of Texas Press.

Jamieson, M. 2009. 'Contracts with Satan: Relations with Spirit Owners and Apprehensions of the Economy among Coastal Miskitu of Nicaragua', *Durham Anthropology Journal* 16(2): 44–53.

Keane, W. 2002. 'Sincerity, "Modernity", and the Protestants', *Cultural Anthropology* 17(1): 65–92.

———. 2007. *Christian Moderns: Freedom and Fetish in the Mission Encounter*. Berkeley: University of California Press.

Killick, E. 2010. 'Ayompari, Compadre, Amigo: Forms of Fellowship in Peruvian Amazonia', in A. Desai and E. Killick (eds), *The Ways of*

Friendship: Anthropological Perspectives. Oxford: Berghahn Books, pp. 46–68.

Kohn, E. 2007. 'Animal Masters and the Ecological Embedding of History among the Ávila Runa of Ecaudor', in C. Fausto and M. Heckenberger (eds), *Time and Memory in Indigenous Amazonia: Anthropological Perspectives.* Gainesville: University Press of Florida, pp. 106–29.

Latour, B. 1993. *We Have Never Been Modern.* Cambridge, MA: Harvard University Press.

Londoño Sulkin, C.D. 2012. *People of Substance: An Ethnography of Morality in the Colombian Amazon.* Toronto: University of Toronto Press.

Maurer, B. 2006. 'The Anthropology of Money', *Annual Review of Anthropology* 35: 15–36.

McCallum, C. 1996. 'The Body That Knows: From Cashinahua Epistemology to a Medical Anthropology of Lowland South America', *Medical Anthropology Quarterly* 10(3): 347–72.

———. 1997. 'Comendo com Txai, Comendo como Txai: A Sexualização de Relações Ètnicas na Amazônia Comtemporânea', *Revista de Antropologia* 40(1): 104–47.

Mitchell, J.P. 2001. 'Introduction', in P. Clough and J.P. Mitchell (eds), *Powers of Good and Evil: Social Transformation and Popular Belief.* New York: Berghahn Books, pp. 1–16.

Nash, J. 1979. *We Eat the Mines and the Mines Eat Us: Dependency and Exploitation in Bolivian Tin Mines.* New York: Columbia University Press.

Opas, M. 2008. 'Different but the Same: Negotiation of Personhoods and Christianities in Western Amazonia'. PhD dissertation. Turku, Finland: University of Turku.

———. 2014. 'Ambigüedad epistemológica y moral en el cosmos social de los yine', *Anthropologica* 32(32): 167–90.

Overing, J. 1985. 'There Is No End of Evil: The Guilty Innocents and Their Fallible God', in D. Parkin (ed.), *The Anthropology of Evil.* Oxford: Basil Blackwell, pp. 244–78.

Overing, J., and A. Passes (eds). 2000. *The Anthropology of Love and Anger: The Aesthetics of Conviviality in Native Amazonia.* London and New York: Routledge.

Parry, J., and M. Bloch. 1989. 'Introduction', in J. Parry and M. Bloch (eds), *Money and the Morality of Exchange.* Cambridge: Cambridge University Press, pp. 1–32.

Perrin, M. 1988. 'Du mythe au quotidian, penser la nouveauté', *L'Homme* 106–7(2–3): 120–37.

Pollock, D. 1992. 'Culina Shamanism: Gender, Power, and Knowledge', in E. Matteson and G. Baer (eds), *Portals of Power: Shamanism in South America.* Alberquerque: University of New Mexico Press, pp. 25–40.

Renard-Casevitz, F.-M. 1988. 'L'histoire ailleurs', *L'Homme* 106–107(2–3): 213–25.

Rivière, G. 1991. 'Lik'ichiri y Kharisiri… A Propósito de las Representaciones del "Otro" en la Sociedad Aymara', *Bulletin de l'Institut Français d'Études Andines* 20(1): 23–40.

Rosengren, D. 2004. 'Los Matsigenka', in F. Santos and F. Barclay (eds), *Guía etnográfica de la alta amazonía, vol. IV: Matsigenka, Yánesha*. Lima: Smithsonian Tropical Research Institute/IFEA, pp. 1–157.

Salazar-Soler, C. 1991. 'El *Pishtaku* entre los Campesinos y los Mineros de Huancavelica', *Bulletin de l'Institut Français d'Études Andines* 20(1): 7–22.

Sallnow, M.J. 1989. 'Precious Metals in the Andean Moral Economy', in J. Parry and M. Bloch (eds), *Money and the Morality of Exchange*. Cambridge: Cambridge University Press, pp. 209–31.

Santos-Granero, F. 2005. 'Amerindian Torture Revisited: Rituals of Enslavement and Markers of Servitude in Tropical America', *Tipití: Journal of the Society for the Anthropology of Lowland South America* 3(2). Available at: http://digitalcommons.trinity.edu/tipiti/vol3/iss2/4 [accessed 31 January 2017].

———. 2007. 'Of Fear and Friendship: Amazonian Sociality beyond Kinship and Affinity', *Journal of the Royal Anthropological Institute* 13: 1–18.

——— (ed.). 2009. *The Occult Life of Things: Native Amazonian Theories of Materiality and Personhood*. Tucson: University of Arizona Press.

Seeger, A., R. da Matta and E. Viveiros de Castro. 1987. 'A Construção da Pessoa nas Sociedades Indígenas Brasileiras', in J. Pacheco de Oliveira Filho (ed.), *Sociedades Indígenas and Indigenismo no Brasil*. Rio de Janeiro: UFRJ/Marco Zero, pp. 11–29.

Siskind, J. 1973. *To Hunt in the Morning*. Oxford: Oxford University Press.

Smith, N.J.H. 1996. *The Enchanted Amazon Rain Forest: Stories from a Vanishing World*. Gainesville: University Press of Florida.

Stoll, D. 1982. *Fishers of Men or Founders of Empire? The Wycliffe Bible Translators in Latin America*. London: Zed Press.

Taussig, M. 1980. *The Devil and Commodity Fetishism in South America*. Chapel Hill: The University of North Carolina Press.

Taylor, G. 1980. 'Supay', *Amerindia* 5: 47–63.

Turner, T. 1980. 'The Social Skin', in J. Cherfas and R. Lewin (eds), *Not Work Alone: A Cross-cultural View of Activities Superfluous to Survival*. London: Temple Smith, pp. 112–40.

Vilaça, A. 2002. 'Making Kin Out of Others in Amazonia', *Journal of the Royal Anthropological Institute* 8: 347–65.

———. 2009. 'Conversion, Predation, Perspective', in A. Vilaça and R. Wright (eds), *Native Christians: Modes and Effects of Christianity among Indigenous Peoples of the Americas*. Farnham: Ashgate, pp. 147–66.

Walker, H. 2012. *Under a Watchful Eye: Self, Power, and Intimacy in Amazonia*. Berkeley: University of California Press.

Weiss, B. 1998. 'Electric Vampires: Haya Rumors of the Commodified Body', in M. Lambek and A. Strathern (eds), *Bodies and Persons: Comparative Perspectives from Africa and Melanesia*. Cambridge: Cambridge University Press, pp. 172–94.

Weiss, G. 1975. *Campa Cosmology: The World of a Forest Tribe in South America*. New York: American Museum of Natural History.

White, L. 1993. 'Cars Out Of Place: Vampires, Technology, and Labor in East and Central Africa', *Representations* 43: 27–50.

Whitehead, N. 2002. *Dark Shamans: Kanaimà and the Poetics of Violent Death*. Durham, NC: Duke University Press.

Wright, P.G. 1992. 'Dream, Shamanism, and Power among the Toba of Formosa Province', in E.J. Matteson Langdon and G. Baer (eds), *Portals of Power: Shamanism in South America*. Albuquerque: University of New Mexico Press, pp. 149–72.

Part III

Transformations and Slow Turbulences

9

Signifying Others

The Musical Management of Social Differences in Amazonia

Jonathan D. Hill

Prelude

In March 1985, a group of indigenous people from the Arawak-speaking Wakuénai-Curripaco of the Guainía River in southernmost Venezuela celebrated a male initiation ritual, called *wakapéetaka iénpitipé* ('we show our children'). The name of the ritual refers to the central importance of sacred wind instruments – flutes and trumpets – that are shown to young men as they are being initiated into adulthood. This particular male initiation ritual was held for several young men between the ages of ten and fifteen, who were members of the Dzáwinai and Muriwéni phratries. Audio recordings of the entire ritual, including performances of instrumental music, ritual speeches, women's drinking songs, and the ritually powerful singing and chanting (*malikái*) for the boys' sacred food, are available at Indiana University's Archives of Traditional Music (Accession No. 85-526-F) and at the Archives of Indigenous Languages of Latin America (www.ailla.utexas.org, KPC002 collection).[1]

These recordings had their genesis in a field trip I had made to the Venezuelan Amazon Territory in June through August 1984. During most of those three months, I was travelling up and down rivers in the western portion of the territory and combing the neighbourhoods of Puerto Ayacucho and San Fernando de Atabapo for information on the social and ecological processes through which the Wakuénai and other Arawak-speaking peoples were adapting to more permanent interethnic relations with non-indigenous individuals and institutions. In the course of my travels, I arranged to spend several days at the principal site of my doctoral research, a village along the lower Guainía River, where I hoped to refine my interpretation of *malikái*, a genre of ritually powerful singing and chanting that employs a sacred language that differs from the dialects of everyday speech. After so many days and nights on the river, it was a relief to settle back into the rhythms of village life among friends. Within a few days, I had answered many new questions and was ready to continue on my journey up the Guainía and Atabapo rivers. Before my departure, however, the headman and senior ritual specialist in the village asked me if I would be willing to leave my stereo recording equipment until the following year so that his son could learn the various performances of singing, chanting and praying that make up the genre called *malikái*. The first stage in learning *malikái* requires the apprentice to memorise long lists of spirit-names, and having access to tape recording equipment would clearly provide a very useful way of assisting the traditional learning process. So I decided to leave my recording equipment with enough blank tapes and batteries to allow the headman's son, Felix Lopez de Oliveira, to practise learning *malikái* singing and chanting. In return, I asked Felix to make recordings of any rituals or ceremonies, or any other occasions at which people were performing instrumental and/or vocal music.

I returned to the village in July and August 1985 and was pleased to learn that our experiment in native ethnomusicology had fully succeeded in both of its objectives. Felix had recorded several hours of *malikái* singing and chanting, and was making considerable progress in memorising the long lists of powerful spirit-names for initiation rituals and other rites of passage. He had also made recordings of female and male initiation rituals, both of which had taken place in March of that year. Over the next several weeks, I spent many hours listening to these tape recordings with Felix and his father, Horacio, who was a powerful chant-owner with tremendous knowledge of the mythic and other hidden meanings of the spirit-names that form the central feature of *malikái* singing and chanting. At one point, Felix and I sat and listened to the final musical performance that marked the end of the male initiation ritual, the moment when the primordial human being of myth (*Kuwái*) departs from the village to return to the sky-world of mythic ancestors. For more than two full minutes, the sweet, repetitive sounds of three *waliáduwa* flutes gradually faded until they became completely inaudible. From time to time, a blast or two of high-pitched sounds from the *molítu* flute punctuated the continuously flowing melody of the three *waliáduwa* flutes. Felix described how the group of men playing the flutes had danced in single file down to the port at the river's edge, where they had entered a large dugout canoe and were paddled off into the distance without missing a single beat. He then asked me what I thought about this recording; did I like the way he had decided to leave the tape recorder running for several minutes as the men's flute playing gradually faded into the distance at the end of the ritual? I told him that I thought his recording was exceptionally beautiful and that he had great talent, not only for the technique of sound recording but also for understanding how placement and movement are such vital parts of the ritual's meaning. At the time, I considered the slow fading of musical sounds in Felix's recording to be an interesting and pleasant ethnoaesthetic effect (Whitten and Whitten 1988: 12). Over the years since 1985, I have spent much time and effort studying the instrumental and vocal music of Wakuénai rituals and associated narrative practices (Hill 1993, 2009), and in the course of making these interpretive studies I have come to understand that the long, slow fading out of musical sounds in Felix's recording is more than merely an interesting ethnoaesthetic effect.

In the mythic narratives about the life of the primordial human being, *Kuwái*, the sacred flutes and trumpets are taken away from the centre of mythic space to various downstream and upstream locations. In myth, the playing of musical sounds on sacred flutes and trumpets in different places is said to open up the world. Felix's recording of the flutes and trumpets at the end of the male initiation ritual in March 1985 brilliantly captured this mythic process as a movement of musical sounds across the landscape of forests and rivers – a collective process of musically opening up the social and historical space of humanity.

Musicalising the Other

Musicalisation, or the production of musical sounds and words as a way of socialising relations with affines, non-human beings, and various categories of 'others', is perhaps best understood as a process of creating a naturalised social space in which human interactions are densely interwoven with the sounds and behaviours of fish and other non-human animal species. I have introduced the term musicalisation in a number of previous publications (Hill 1993, 1994, 2002, 2011, 2013, 2015) as part of a sustained effort to accurately describe and translate a complex set of indigenous cultural practices that I experienced in the course of fieldwork with the Arawak-speaking Wakuénai of Venezuela in the 1980s and 1990s.[2] Through collaborative work with ethnomusicologists and linguistic anthropologists who have done field research on indigenous musical and verbal artistry in various locations across lowland South America, I have found the concept of musicalisation, or 'musicalising the other', to provide a valid basis for developing new comparative approaches to understanding indigenous cultural creativities (Hill and Chaumeil 2011; Hill 2013, 2015).

Given the central importance of speech and sound, listening and hearing, in Amazonian communities (Menezes Bastos 1978, 1995, 1999; Seeger 1979, 1987, 1991; Basso 1985; Beaudet 1993, 1997; Hill 1993; Santos-Granero 2006; Hill and Chaumeil 2011), it is appropriate to develop theoretical models of sociality that are grounded in specifically Amazonian semiotic ideologies that privilege sound over vision and other senses for managing the transformative relations between humans and various kinds of 'others' (non-human species and objects, affines, spirit-beings, etc.). Musicalisation refers to processes of using non- or semi-verbal patterns of sound to enact various kinds of social transformation: life cycle transitions, shamanic journeys, affinal exchanges, revitalisation movements, political-economic resistance, and so forth. By paying close attention to the details of musical sounds and their organisation in ritual and ceremonial performances,[3] we can better understand how indigenous Amazonian peoples enact these transformations between self and other, human and non-human, living and dead, kin and affine. My approach to musicalisation builds on Ellen Basso's approach to ritual communication as a process of acknowledging the otherness of the other (2009, 2011) by demonstrating how musicalising the other is a nuanced process of making history through engaging others, sharing the space-time of others, and always returning to one's own identity.

In this chapter, I will broaden the scope of my previous efforts to use the concept of musicalisation as a method for comparison of cultural practices in linguistically diverse and geographically widespread indigenous communities (Hill and Chaumeil 2011; Hill 2013, 2015). Musicalisation does not operate in isolation but in tandem with a variety of other verbal and non-verbal activities, such as: verbal interpretations of natural and/or humanly fashioned sounds; giving animal names to musical instruments, melodies, or associated dances; naming animal spirits in ritual chants and songs; and narratives about mythic space-times in which human and animal beings are not yet differentiated. In the following sections, I will draw upon ethno-graphic materials from my fieldwork with the Arawak-speaking Wakuénai of Venezuela to illustrate how musicalisation works within broader contexts of verbal art, animal spirit-naming, and native interpretations of natural sounds and species. I will also provide a comparative perspective on these musical and verbal processes through a brief exploration of a genre of ritual singing called 'shout songs' (*akia*), performed among the Gê-speaking Suyá of Central Brazil. My goal is to suggest how the concept of musicalisation can be used to arrive at more general, cross-cultural understandings of how non-human animal species come to be regarded as 'signifying others' through the use of their sounds, names and other attributes as basic elements in the construction of humanly fashioned social spaces in Amazonia.

Natural Sounds in Social Contexts

These processes of musicalisation, or constructing social identities through poetic transformations of natural objects and species, are central features of traditional modes of subsistence and the spe-cific landscapes of the Upper Rio Negro. Among the Wakuénai of Venezuela, the interrelations between musicalisation and practical economic activities are particularly clear in the tradition of *pudáli* ceremonial exchanges. *Pudáli* ceremonies were closely connected to the annual cycle of fishing and gardening, and expressed the comple-mentarity between male and female subsistence activities. The ideal time for initiating the two-part cycle of *pudáli* ceremonies was in the month of *Wariperihnume* (the 'mouth of the Pleiades', or late April to early May), when the heavy rains of the long wet season are beginning and the rivers rise above their banks to create vast areas of flooded forest. Shortly after this, large schools of *Leporinus* fish migrate into the newly flooded forests to spawn, and Wakuénai fishermen capture vast quantities of these fish in weirs as they return to the main channel of the river. This brief period of superabundance of fish is the ideal moment to begin the cycle of *pudáli* ceremonies by sponsoring an opening, male-owned ceremony in which a large pile of smoked fish is taken and offered to a host group of affines, or potential affines. The recipients of this food gift are then obligated to sponsor a closing, female-owned *pudali* ceremony several weeks later in which they bring a large quantity of processed manioc pulp to their hosts' village (see Figure 9.1).

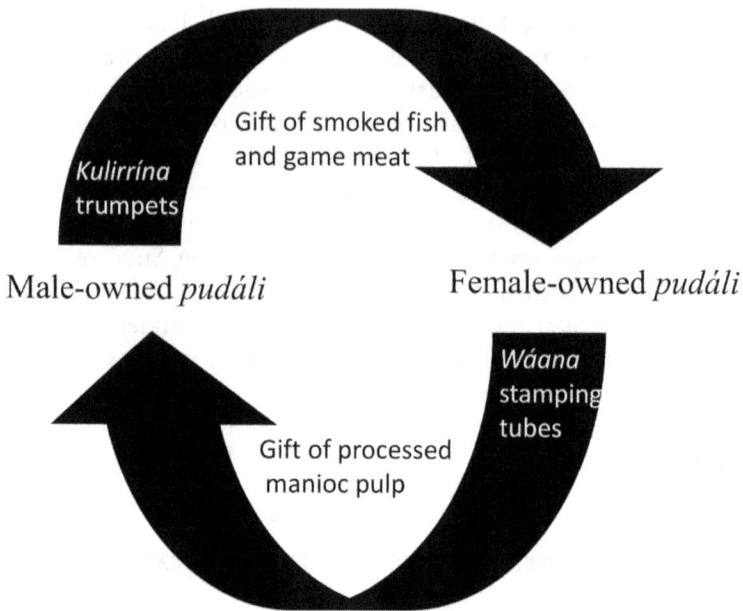

Figure 9.1 *Pudáli*: gender complementarity and the musicalisation of intercommunal exchange. Figure created by the author.

In the opening, male-owned *pudáli* ceremonies, groups of men played *kulirrína* trumpets that replicate the sound of rivers and streams filled with spawning, migrating *Leporinus* fish at the beginning of the long wet season (Hill 1987, 2011). In these collective performances, groups of male trumpet-players and their female dancing partners circled around a pile of smoked fish and game meat that would later be presented to the ceremony's hosts. These collective dances were named after three species of *Leporinus* fish, and the human activity of dancing and playing music were referred to by the same verb (*-irrápaka*) used to describe the spawning behaviours of *Leporinus* fish.

Kulirrína trumpets are named after a species of large catfish (*kulírri*; *surubí*, Yeral; *raiao*, Spanish) that has a thick black stripe running along each of its sides. In 1927, Kurt Nimuendajú travelled through the north-west Amazon and concluded that these 'catfish' (*surubí*) trumpets were the most distinctive material artefacts produced by Arawak-speaking 'Baniwa' of the Isana River (Nimuendajú 1950). By the time of my first fieldwork with the Wakuénai in 1980, these unique instruments were no longer in use in villages along the Guainía River. However, in the course of studying the music of ceremonial *máwi* flutes and related kinds of vocal and instrumental music, my indigenous hosts decided to construct several of the *kulirrína* trumpets as a way of teaching me about them and as a demonstration for people in the village. News of the catfish trumpets spread across the region, and soon there were not only Wakuénai visitors but Yeral-speakers from the Casiquiare, Guarequena from Guzman Blanco, and Baniwa[4] from Maroa, who were all interested in seeing and hearing the catfish trumpets.[5]

In technical terms, the *kulirrína* are complex trumpets, or ones in which a separate mouthpiece or embouchure is attached to a tubular resonator (Izikowitz [1934] 1970: 232). The use of basketry covered with resins, waxes and paints to make bell-shaped resonators is found only in the Upper Rio Negro region among the Wakuénai and Curripaco of Venezuela and Colombia, and the Baniwa of Brazil. Making catfish trumpets begins with weaving tubular resonators (the body of the fish) out of *pwáapwa* strips around a balsawood mould. The lower ends of the woven resonators are later sewn and flared out to make the fishtails. After several identically sized and shaped resonators have been woven and sewn, short tubes of hollowed-out *máwi* palm are fastened to wheels made from *dzamakuáapi* vines just large enough to fit snugly into the 'heads', or upper ends of the woven resonators. The mouthpieces are then inserted into the resonators and cemented into place with several layers of palm leaves covered with hot, melted resin from a tree species called *peramá*. As this combination of resins and palm leaves cools, it hardens and holds the mouthpieces in place. The long ends of *pwáapwa* strips are then tied securely around the *máwi* mouthpieces, and excess lengths of *pwáapwa* are cut off with a knife. The instruments are not considered to be dangerous or sacred except at the moment when men close up the resonators by tying them to the mouthpieces. It is said that women of childbearing age must not see or be present at this moment because their future unborn children could become stuck inside their wombs, causing death to both the mothers and their unborn children.

Once the instruments have been closed up, the entire exterior of the resonators, from the 'heads' where they are joined to the mouthpieces down to the 'tails', must be covered in thick layers of *peramá* resin so that they will be airtight and capable of functioning as resonating sound cavities. Heated knives are used to smooth the coating of resin until the trumpets have a smooth, shiny, jet-black appearance. Long strips of palm leaves are tied to the outsides of the

Illustration 9.1 Masking and painting trumpets to make black stripes. Photograph: J. Hill.

resonators to serve as masking, while the other surfaces are painted white and decorated with designs representing the mythic ancestors of the trumpets' makers (Illustration 9.1). After drying the trumpets on the same racks used for sun-drying manioc breads, the palm leaf masking is removed, revealing the long black stripes that complete the instruments' resemblance to *kulírri* catfish (see Figure 9.2). The upper ends, or 'heads', and lower ends, or 'tails', of the trumpets may also be decorated with white heron feathers mounted on thin sticks.

The use of woven basketry, palmwood mouthpieces, vines and resins to make complex trumpets is unique to the Wakuénai, Curripaco, and 'Baniwa' of the Upper Rio Negro region and is not found anywhere else in South America or the rest of the world. My research with the Wakuénai of Venezuela thus confirms Nimuendajú's assertion (1950) that these catfish trumpets are the most distinctive cultural artefacts produced by the 'Baniwa' of Brazil. The making of such unique and highly visible, sound-producing artefacts is a statement of collective identity, a way in which the Wakuénai, Curripaco and Baniwa express who they are and distinguish themselves from all the other Arawak-, Tukano-, Maku-, Yeral-speaking and non-indigenous peoples living in the region. Yet if these quintessential indigenous artefacts, or the local cultural 'logo', are unique and culturally specific, the materials out of which

Illustration 9.2 Drying newly painted trumpets. Photograph: J. Hill.

the catfish trumpets are made – *máwi*, *pwáapwa* and *dzamakuáapi* – are signifiers of socio-economic and religious themes that are found throughout indigenous Amazonia: the reciprocal giving and taking of foods and other gifts, the processing and transporting of vegetable foods, and the power of secret or restricted knowledge. *Kulirrína* trumpets unite all three themes into single objects, a fashioning of plants that connects the annual spawning runs of fish to the episodic regeneration of human social relations; men's hunting and fishing to women's gardening and manioc processing; kin to affine; and invisible secret to the experiential world of sounds, shapes, colours, objects and species.

All the music, singing and dancing of *pudáli* ceremonial exchanges is said to have originated in mythical times as a way in which *Kaali*, the mythic owner of manioc and other cultivated plants, taught his sons how to ask their hosts for gifts of food and drink. The use of singing and instrumental music as a way of respectfully 'asking' for food and drink marked a crucial turning point in Wakuénai mythic history, since these were the first signs of socialised interactions between kin and affines (or hosts and guests) based on reciprocal giving and taking of cooked foods rather than violence. Musicalisation is thus strongly associated with the origins of social exchange between kin and affine; through placing both social categories within the broader symbolic framework of naturalised social beings, musicalisation creates a space

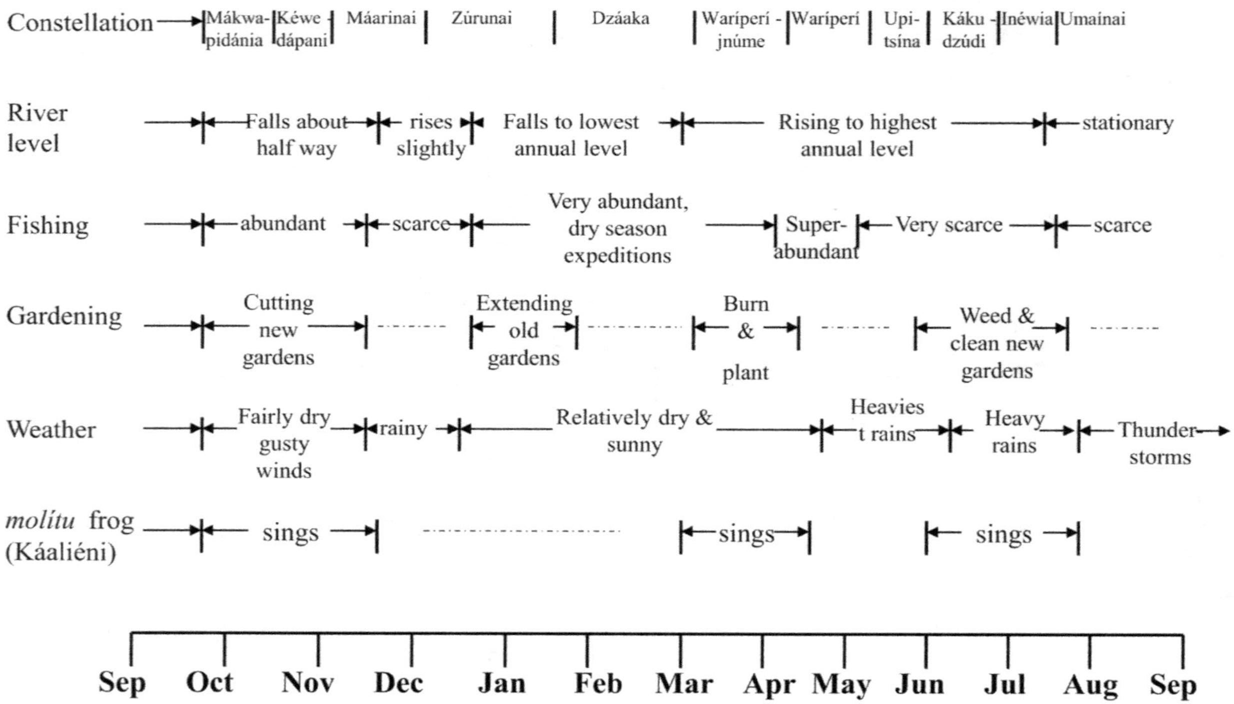

Constellation — |Mákwa-|Kéwe | Maarinai | Zurunai | Dzáaka | Wáriperi -|Wáriperi |Upi- | Káku -|Inéwia|U'mainai
pidánia| dápani| jnúme| tsina | dzúdi

River level — Falls about— rises — Falls to lowest — Rising to highest — stationary
half way slightly annual level annual level

Fishing — abundant —scarce Very abundant, Super-— Very scarce — scarce
dry season abundant
expeditions

Gardening — Cutting Extending Burn Weed &
new old & clean new
gardens gardens plant gardens

Weather — Fairly dry—rainy Relatively dry & Heavies Heavy — Thunder-
gusty sunny t rains rains storms
winds

molítu frog — sings sings sings sings
(Káaliéni)

Sep Oct Nov Dec Jan Feb Mar Apr May Jun Jul Aug Sep

Figure 9.2 Annual cycle of fishing and horticultural activities, showing the periods when the *molítu* frog sings. Figure created by the author.

that allows for experiencing and acknowledging (rather than negating, subjugating or violently consuming) the other's otherness.

Another illustration of how natural species can become signifying others within the human social world is the species of small frog known as *molítu*. As an animal species, the *molítu* is regarded as one of *Káali*'s children (*Káaliéni*) and forms part of the process of musicalisation in *pudáli* ceremonies. The singing of the *molítu* frog is said to 'tell' men and women when it is time to select and clear forest lands for new manioc gardens, when to burn the felled vegetation, and when to plant new gardens. The *molítu* frog sings in September and October, telling men to cut new gardens. It stops singing in November and does not start up again until late March or April, when it is believed to tell people to burn and plant their new gardens before the heavy rains of the long wet season begin in late April and May. The *molítu* frog stops singing in late April until the slightly drier months of June and July, when its singing is said to tell people to weed and clean their gardens. In August, the frog stops singing until the beginning of the short dry season in mid-to-late September, when it is time for men to fell trees for a new manioc garden (see Figure 9.2). The general belief is that when people work in synchrony with the voice of the *molítu* frog, or *Kaalieni*, their gardening activities proceed more smoothly and quickly; but if they ignore the mythic calendar of the *molítu* frog's singing their labour is slow and difficult.

In male and female initiation rituals and in sacred ceremonial exchanges called *kwépani*, men play a kind of flute named after the *molítu* frog and carry on semi-lexical musical dialogues with women, who perform drinking songs (*pakamarántakan*) from inside a special house where they have been secluded. As a musical instrument, the mythic meaning of *molítu* frogs is that of an army of male warriors who accompanied the trickster-creator, Made-from-Bone (*Iñápirríkuli*), in his pursuit of the first woman (*Ámaru*) and her female companions after they had stolen the sacred flutes and trumpets of the primordial human being (*Kuwái*). As mythic symbols of men's ability to regain control of the sacred flutes and trumpets from women, *molítu* frogs are embodiments of masculinity and male-controlled ritual power. Thus the same frog species whose name signifies masculinity in sacred rituals and ceremonies is also a natural acoustical sign for regulating the timing of seasonal horticultural activities through its singing. The multivocality of *molítu* frogs thus demonstrates how musicalisation can simultaneously work at different levels – as a natural species signifying calendrical information

		Specific Spirit- Name D			
Specific Spirit- Name A	Specific Spirit- Name B	Specific Spirit- Name C	Specific Spirit- Name E	Specific Spirit- Name F	Specific Spirit- Name X
Generic Spirit- ➡ Name I	Generic Spirit- ➡ Name II	Generic Spirit-➡ Name III	Generic Spirit-➡ Name IV	Generic Spirit-➡ Name V	Generic Spirit- Name IX

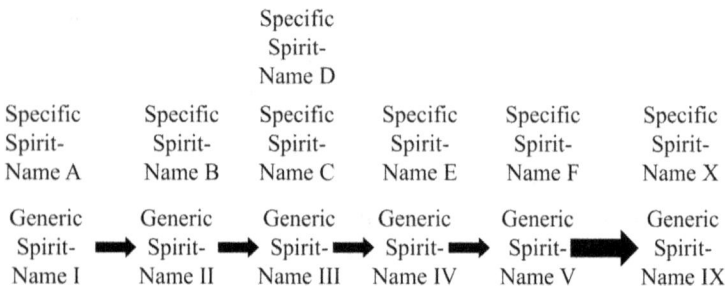

Figure 9.3 The more dynamic process of 'going in search of the spirit-names'. Figure created by the author.

to human horticulturalists, or as a musical instrument embodying the mythic competition between men and women and its playful re-enactment in ceremonies and rituals.

Chanting the Animal Spirit-Names, Making Men and Women

For the Wakuénai, the most powerful forms of musicalisation are practised in sacred singing and chanting (*malikái* and *malirríkairi*) performed only by ritual specialists. In *malikái* songs and chants for childbirth and puberty initiation rituals, processes of spirit-naming provide the basis for musicalisation. Chant-owners (*malikái limínali*) understand their ritual performances as a verbal art form in which the spirit-naming of edible animal species is the primary source of ritual power. When teaching an apprentice to perform *malikái* singing and chanting, the emphasis is placed on exact memorisation of complete taxonomies of animal spirit-names. There are two distinct processes of spirit-naming: (1) a more dynamic, or 'hyperanimate' process called 'going in search of the names'; and (2) a more stabilising process called 'heaping up the names in a single place'. 'Going in search of the spirit-names' requires the chant-owner to invoke a number of different categories of animal spirits in rapid succession, while attaching only one or two specific animal names to each category (see Figure 9.3). 'Heaping up the names in a single place' is a more gradual process in which the chant-owner invokes a single category of animal spirits and then fills it up with a long list of specific animal names (see Figure 9.4). The contrast between these two processes of spirit-naming is one of relative salience rather than an absolute or binary opposition. The more dynamic process of

Specific Spirit-Name X	Specific Spirit-Name Y	Specific Spirit-Name Z
↑	↑	↑
Specific Spirit-Name B	Specific Spirit-Name D	Specific Spirit-Name F
Specific Spirit-Name A	Specific Spirit-Name C	Specific Spirit-Name E
Generic Spirit-Name I	Generic Spirit-Name II	Generic Spirit-Name III

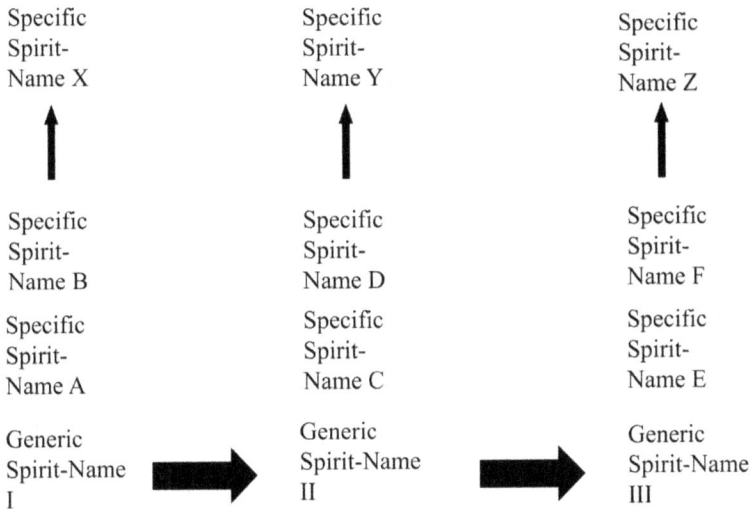

Figure 9.4 The more stabilising process of 'heaping up the spirit-names in a single place'. Figure created by the author.

'going in search of the names' places greater emphasis on the movements *between* categories of animal spirits, but it still allows for some instances of naming more than one specific animal spirit within each category. The more stabilising process of 'heaping up the names in a single place' is a far more orderly process of putting large numbers of specific animal names into a relatively small number of categories. However, there are examples of seemingly anomalous spirit-names that appear to violate the more general orderliness of 'heaping up the names in a single place'. Spirit-names that appear to be 'out of place' (e.g. a bird spirit named within the category of water animal spirits) are usually more powerful than other spirit-names because they are intertextually linked to mythic episodes of transformation (e.g. a bird that transformed itself into a water animal).

This hierarchy of spirit-naming principles forms the basis of an indigenous theory of musical sound, or the musicality of ritually powerful speech, as an instrument of power that allows ritual specialists – chant-owners and shamans – to effect life-cycle transitions and to control semiotic transformations between unborn and born, living and dead, ancestor and descendant, animal and human, affine and kin, white and indigenous people. Musicalisation (or 'going in search of the names') in these ritual performances refers to the use of musical dynamics – such as microtonal rising, loud/soft contrast, crescendo/decrescendo, acceleration/deceleration – to transform and energise the relatively stable categories of mythic being into an expanding historical world of peoples, natural species, rivers, and terrestrial places. The complementary process of lexicalisation (or 'heaping up the names in a single place') is a more stabilising activity of using verbal categories of spirit-naming to constrain or minimise (but not negate or deny) the transformative power and creativity of musical dynamics.

Female and male initiation rituals are complex social events at which chant-owners must sing and 'chant-into-being' the names of all the places, foods and peoples making up the world. They tap out the rhythms and tempos of this mythic-historical 'opening up' of the world with ritual whips by striking an overturned basket that covers a pot of hot-peppered, boiled meat (*káridzamái*) that will form the initiates' first food as adult women or men.

The central activities of both male and female initiation rituals are fasting and seclusion. During the period of seclusion, the initiants must survive on drinks made from wild palm fruits, water, and manioc flour. The culmination of male and female initiation rituals is a long series of *malikái* songs and chants in which all species of edible animals, fish, birds and plants must be named in all the places where *Ámaru* and the women played the sacred flutes and trumpets of *Kuwái* during the second creation of the world. For both male and female initiation, the opening *malikái* song is a movement between distinct pitches at the mythic centre of the world, *Hípana*, the place of ancestral emergence. After invoking the places of sacred power in the sky-world, the chant-owner names the celestial umbilical cord (*hliépule kwá éenu*) that connects the sky-world to the terrestrial world of human beings at the 'navel of the world' (*Hípana*) and that nourishes the latter with the power of mythic ancestors. From that point of departure, the chant-owner and an accompanying chanter 'go in search of the names' of the mythic ancestors of the initiants' patrisibs. The chanting continues for at least six hours and makes use of microtonal rising, different starting pitches, acceleration, crescendo and other musical dynamics. Between each chant, the chant-owner kneels on the ground, lifts the overturned basket covering the pot of hot-peppered, boiled meat, and blows tobacco smoke over the food. Finally, after chanting the last places along the Isana and Aiarí rivers leading back to *Hípana*, the chant-owner sings a closing song using exactly the same four pitches as the opening song, and invoking one last time the celestial umbilical cord connecting the sky-world and the human world.

Despite the similarities between *malikái* singing and chanting for male and female initiation rituals, there are also important differences.

For female initiation, the first song is performed at noon, and the chanting continues throughout the afternoon. The closing song is performed shortly before sunset. The naming of places moves across an area that roughly approximates the ancestral territories of the Wakuénai phratries living in the Isana and Guainía river basins at the headwaters of the Rio Negro (see Map 9.1). For male initiation, the first song is performed at night, with chanting throughout the night and the closing song coming just before dawn. In these chants, a much larger area covering the entire Rio Negro, lower Amazon, and middle and lower Orinoco basins must be named (see Map 9.2). This vast set of rivers, forests and savannahs corresponds approximately to the areas that were inhabited by Northern, or Maipuran,

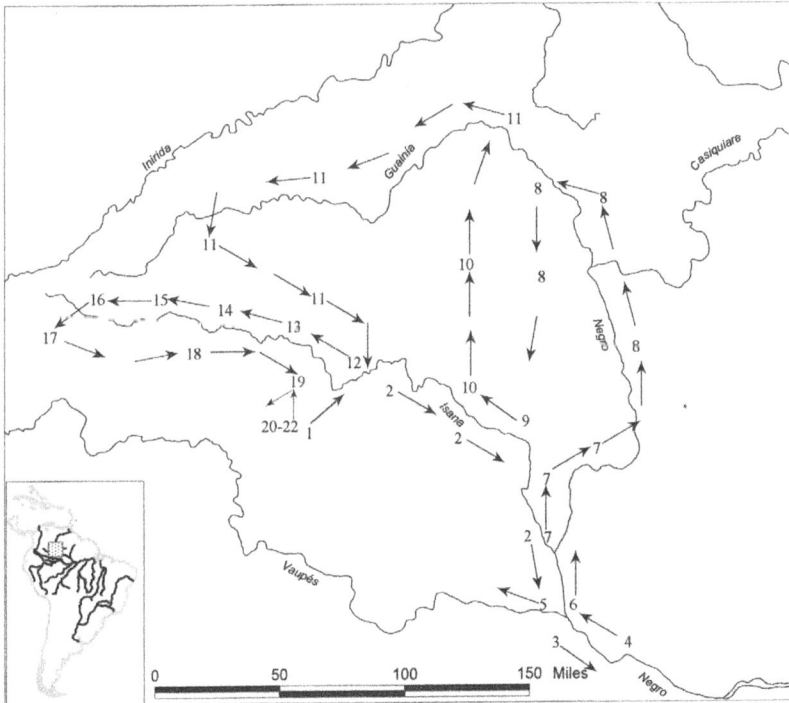

Map 9.1 Place-naming in ritual chanting for female initiation (*wakáitake iénpiti*). The numbers 1–22 refer to sacred chants in the order of their performance during female initiation rituals. Map created by the author, previously published in Jonathan D. Hill and Fernando Santos-Granero, *Comparative Arawakan Histories: Rethinking Language Family and Culture Area in Amazonia*, Champaign: University of Illinois Press, 2002. Reprinted with permission.

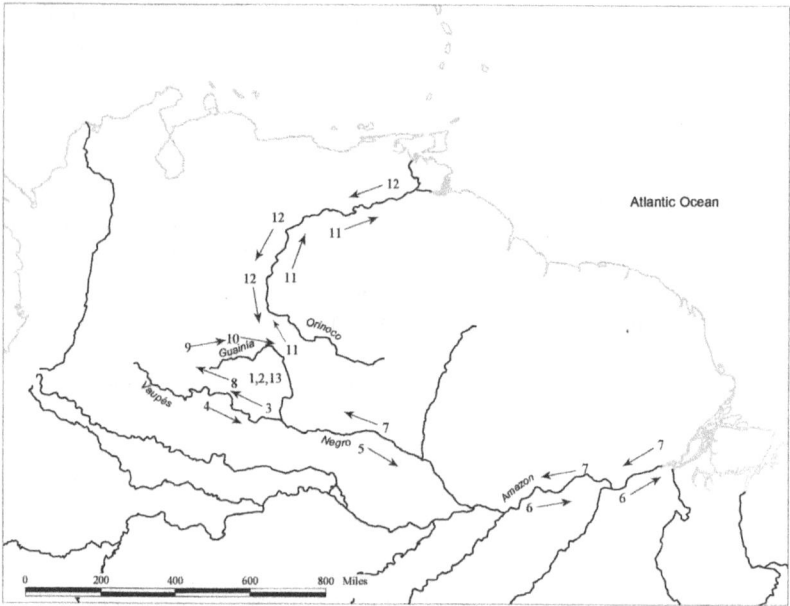

Map 9.2 Place-naming in ritual chanting for male initiation (*wakapéetaka iépitipé*). The numbers 1–13 refer to sacred chants in the order of their performance during male initiation rituals. Map created by the author, previously published in Jonathan D. Hill and Fernando Santos-Granero, *Comparative Arawakan Histories: Rethinking Language Family and Culture Area in Amazonia*, Champaign: University of Illinois Press, 2002. Reprinted with permission.

Arawak-speaking peoples at the time of the arrival of European colonisers in the sixteenth century (Key 1979).

For a girl, initiation is an individual ritual that takes place shortly after she reaches her first menses, and the emphasis is on attaching moral and historical meanings to her sexuality and fertility. Female initiation rituals are called *wakáitaka iénpiti* ('we speak to our child'), referring to the ritual advice that the girl receives from the chant-owner, her grandparents and other elders. There is less emphasis on teaching practical skills to the girl-initiant, since she has already demonstrated mastery of these activities prior to reaching puberty. Male initiation, however, involves prolonged training in adult male activities, such as weaving baskets, making tools and weapons, and felling trees for new gardens. The boys are initiated in groups, and they are expected to learn sacred narratives about the mythic creations of the world during the life cycle of *Kuwái*, the primordial human being. Most importantly, boys are shown how to make and play the sacred flutes and trumpets of *Kuwái*, which is why male initiation rituals are called *wakapéetaka iénpitipé* ('we show our children').

The contrast between place-naming in female and male initiation rituals can be understood as two complementary forces of political history. In female initiation rituals, place-naming outlines a relatively closed, hierarchical pattern of movements that reasserts and commemorates connections between specific social groups, or localised sets of patrisibs organised into ranked phratries, and sacred places *within* the Upper Rio Negro region. Place-naming in male initiation rituals depicts a more open, expansive pattern of interconnections *between* Wakuénai phratries of the Upper Rio Negro region and other, downstream regions in the Orinoco and Amazon basins that were inhabited by other large Arawak-speaking polities prior to the nineteenth century. The pattern of place-naming is more centripetal for female initiation and more centrifugal for male initiation. The former is mainly concerned with defining relations between Wakuénai phratries and a shared site of origins at the mythic centre of the world, whereas the latter aims at defining a number of widely dispersed regional centres in relation to a single mythic centre in the Upper Rio Negro region. In both cases, the mythic centre at *Hípana* is verbally depicted in opening and closing songs as the 'navel' where a 'celestial umbilical cord' (*hliépule-kwa dzákare*) connects the sky-world of mythic ancestors to the terrestrial world of human descendants. And in both male and female initiation rituals, the mythic centre is also defined through the use of four stable pitches that are sung in opening and closing songs before and after the chanting of place-names, which 'opens up' a sacred landscape.

Suyá Shout Songs and Ceremonial Singing

The process of musicalisation, or the production of musical sounds and words as a way of socialising relations with affines, non-human beings, and various categories of 'others', is equally important among the Suyá, a northern Gê-speaking group of Central Brazil. Like the other Gê-speaking communities of Brazil, the Suya do not make or play the kinds of flutes, trumpets and other wind instruments that are so central to the ritual and ceremonial activities of the Wakuénai as well as many other Arawak-, Carib- and Tupi-speaking peoples of lowland South America (Hill and Chaumeil 2011). Nevertheless, musicalisation as a process of creating a naturalised social space through singing the names of animal, fish and other non-human species is strikingly illustrated in the two genres of singing that make up the central activities of Suyá ceremonial and ritual life. *Akia*, or 'shout songs', are performed by individual males aged eight and up, and are self-affirmations of an individual singer's physical strength and emotional state. A man who sings for many hours is express-ing happiness with the way things are. 'People who do not sing are implicitly saying that they are not "happy". They may be in mourn-ing for a dead relative, be angry about something, or have a particu-lar grudge' (Seeger 1979: 375). *Akia* singing is unique to the Suya, who use it to distinguish themselves from neighbouring indigenous groups (ibid.: 379). In contrast with the individually performed *akia* songs, *ngere* are ceremonial songs that are collectively owned and performed by age- and sex-based groups of men and women.

Both *akia* and *ngere* genres of singing must be understood in the context of Suyá social organisation, which is based on an uxorilocal process of removing young boys from their natal family households so that they can become fully integrated into their wives' family households after reaching full adulthood. A long (fifteen or more years) period of initiation takes place in the bachelors' hut at the centre of the village plaza (Seeger 1981: 156ff.). Once a man has con-summated his marriage by becoming a father and moving from the bachelors' hut into his wife's family household, he is forbidden from returning to his natal family household to visit his mother and sisters except under special ceremonial circumstances. He must never sleep or eat at his sister's household, and he can never go near it when his sister's husband is present. The avoidance between male affines (ZH and WB) means that an adult man's relations with his natal family household are spatially distant. The primary audience for men's *akia* shout singing are their mothers and sisters, who listen closely for their son/brother's voice, the strength of which is considered to be a measure of his physical, social and emotional well-being.

> Specifically men say they want to be heard by their mother and sisters. They say that if a man sings well, his mother and sisters (a single refer-ential kinship term exists that includes them both) will be happy. But if a man sings an old *akia*, or sings badly, they will be sad. When a lot of men sing *akia* together they all want to be heard. They must sing loudly and have distinctive songs to sing. (Seeger 1979: 380)

Suyá men sing *akia* songs while standing in the village plaza or *outside* the periphery of the village, so their voices must be loud enough to travel across considerable spatial distances in order to reach their intended audience. Moreover, several men sing *akia* simultaneously, and each tries to be heard above the sounds of other men's shout singing.

In contrast, *ngere* ceremonial songs are performed *inside* the men's house (or bachelors' hut) at the centre of the village or *inside* the residential houses on the edge of the village plaza. When singing *ngere* in residential houses, groups of men repeat the same song in each of the households, and each man blends his voice into the group of singers so that it will be indistinguishable. 'In this case a man does enter his sisters' and mother's house as well as other houses he may never enter on normal occasions. But he enters as an equal member of a sex-and age-defined group, not as a brother, lover or individual' (Seeger 1979: 387). In other words, *ngere* ceremonial singing inverts the pattern of spatial and social relations established in performances of *akia* shout songs. In the former, the individual's voice is subordinated to that of a group of singers who perform inside residential households, regardless of the kinship ties between singers and the members of the households. In *akia* singing, the individual makes every effort to have his voice heard over and above that of other men who are singing at the same time, and the individual singers are positioned at a considerable distance from the residential households of their mothers and sisters, who are the primary intended audience. In both genres of singing, however, musical sounds and words are used to create socialised spaces that require the acknowledgment of the otherness of the other at the same time as they include both kin and affines.

And in both *akia* shout songs and *ngere* ceremonial singing, musicalisation acts as a process of creating a 'naturalised' social space through singing the names of animal, fish and other non-human species. 'Men learn their *akia* from specialists who have the ability to hear and understand the songs of certain animals, fish, bees and trees' (Seeger 1979: 385), and the most important part of each song arises in a central passage which is known as 'telling the name'.

> In the 'telling the name' (2) the animal is important, and songs are often identified by the animal named in them (there is apparently no vocabulary for musical features such as syncopation or melodic figures, although these are obviously important in remembering the song itself). (ibid.: 388)

Animal names thus form a central part of Suyá ways of speaking about *akia* songs. *Ngere* songs are remembered for longer than *akia*, since they are associated with whole seasons of ceremonial activities during which entire groups of men are initiated into the men's house rather than individual men who sing at particular moments in time. 'Like *akia*, many *ngere* are learned from mammals, fish, birds, bees and plants, and taught to the men of the village by living men. Other *ngere* are "old" and were taught in the mythical past by some animal or enemy Indian' (Seeger 1979: 387). Both *akia* and *ngere* singing are ways of creating a naturalised social space in which musical sounds and words both acknowledge and encompass the other's otherness.

Closing Thoughts

In this chapter, I have shown how instrumental and verbal musical sounds, collective dancing, natural sounds and musical naming of animal spirits serve as ways of giving cultural recognition to non-human beings as signifying others, or voices that play a central role in processes of specifically human socialisation and social reproduction. The concept of musicalisation, or the production of musical sounds and words as a way of socialising relations with affines, non-human beings, and various categories of 'others', allows for the development of new ways of understanding indigenous Amazonian cultural practices across vast geographic, historical, linguistic and other differences.

The ethnographic cases discussed in this chapter show that analogous processes and patterns of musicalisation are discernible even in such widely divergent regions of Amazonia as the north-west Amazon and Central Brazil. The ranked patrilineal and patrilocal phratries of the Upper Rio Negro, with their collective ensembles of flutes and other wind instruments, and their highly restricted forms of ritually powerful singing and chanting, could hardly be more different from the uxorilocal villages, age grades, and moieties of Central Brazil with their radically egalitarian genres of ritual singing. And yet, in spite of such vast cultural and historical differences, the underlying process of musicalisation works in both regions to acknowledge the social otherness of affines as well as to encompass it within ritually and ceremonially constructed spaces of historical engagement, allowing individuals and groups to share in others' social lives. Whether it be in the sounds of a frog's singing, the low rumbling bass tones of migratory schools of fish during their annual spawning runs, or the naming of animal spirits in songs and chants, indigenous Amazonian peoples use the sounds, behaviours, and verbal namesakes of these signifying others to create naturalised social spaces for managing biological, social and cosmic diversity.

Jonathan D. Hill is professor and former chair of the Department of Anthropology at Southern Illinois University, and has done extensive fieldwork with the Wakuénai (also known as Curripaco) of Venezuela in the 1980s and 1990s. He is the author of *Keepers of the Sacred Chants: The Poetics of Ritual Power in an Amazonian Society* (University of Arizona Press, 1993); *Made-from-Bone: Trickster Myths, Music, and History from the Amazon* (University of Illinois Press, 2009), and numerous articles and chapters on music, myth and history in lowland South America. In addition, he is editor of various compilations.

Notes

1. I deposited the original copies of audio recordings from my fieldwork with the Wakuénai at the Interamerican Institute for Ethnomusicology and Folklore (INIDEF) in Caracas, Venezuela, in December 1981 and August 1985 (VEN 866-874-M).
2. Elsewhere (Hill 1994, 2002) I have demonstrated how musicalisation serves as a way of collectively engaging with historical changes introduced by non-indigenous actors and institutions. The invention of a novel genre of evangelical singing among the Suruí of Brazil provides another clear example of how an indigenous Amazonian people have musicalised 'others' – in this case, American and German missioniaries – in ways that creatively reproduce pragmatic dimensions of their traditional verbal artistry, even as they embrace drastically new cosmological representations (see Yvinec, this volume).
3. The distinction between ritual and ceremonial performances is one of degree rather than kind. Ritual performances are invariably characterised as sacred activities, whereas ceremonial performances may be either sacred or secular. Also, all ceremonial performances are collective actions that require entire groups of men and women, whereas rituals may be either small, relatively private gatherings or larger public events.
4. The Baniwa of Maroa share many of the mythological and ritual traditions with the Wakuénai, Curripaco and 'Baniwa' of Brazil. However, the Baniwa language spoken in Maroa is radically different from that of the 'Baniwa' of Brazil.
5. See 'Ethnomusicological Interlude: The Catfish-Trumpet Festival of 1981, or How to Ask for a Drink in Curripaco' (Hill 2009) for a detailed description of this event.

References

Basso, E.B. 1985. *A Musical View of the Universe: Kalapalo Myth and Ritual Performances*. Philadelphia: University of Pennsylvania Press.

———. 2009. 'Ordeals of Language', in M. Carrithers (ed.), *Culture, Rhetoric, and the Vicissitudes of Life*. New York: Berghahn Books, pp. 121–37.

———. 2011. 'Amazonian Ritual Communication in Relation to Multilingual Social Networks', in A. Hornborg and J.D. Hill (eds), *Ethnicity in Ancient Amazonia: Reconstructing Past Identities from Archaeology, Linguistics, and Ethnohistory*. Boulder: University Press of Colorado, pp. 155–71.

Beaudet, J.-M. 1993. 'L'Ethnomusicologies de l'Amazonie', *L'Homme* 126–28: 527–33.

———. 1997. *Souffles d'Amazonie: les Orchestres 'tule' des Wayãpi*. Nanterre: Société d'Ethnologie.

Hill, J.D. 1987. 'Wakuénai Ceremonial Exchange in the Northwest Amazon Region', *Journal of Latin American Lore* 13(2): 183–224.

———. 1993. *Keepers of the Sacred Chants: The Poetics of Ritual Power in an Amazonian Society*. Tucson: University of Arizona Press.

———. 1994. 'Musicalizing the Other: Shamanistic Approaches to Ethnic–Class Competition in the Upper Rio Negro Region', in Alicia Barabas (ed.), *Religiosidad y Resistencia Indígenas hacia el Fin del Milenio*. Quito: Abya-Yala, pp. 105–28.

———. 2002. '"Músicalisando" o Outro: Ironia Ritual e Resistencia Etnica entre os Wakuénai (Venezuela)', in B. Albert and A. Ramos (eds), *Imagens do Branco na Historia Indigena*. Saõ Paulo: Unesp, pp. 347–74.

———. 2009. *Made-from-Bone: Trickster Myths, Music, and History from the Amazon*. Urbana: University of Illinois Press.

———. 2011. 'Soundscaping the World: The Cultural Poetics of Power and Meaning in Wakuénai Flute Music', in J. Hill and J.-P. Chaumeil (eds), *Burst of Breath: Indigenous Ritual Wind Instruments in Lowland South America*. Lincoln: University of Nebraska Press, pp. 93–122.

———. 2013. 'Instruments of Power: Musicalising the Other in Lowland South America', *Ethnomusicology Forum* 22(3): 323–42.

———. 2015. 'Musicalizando o Outro: Etnomusicologia na Epoca da Globalização', in D.L. Montardo and M.E. Domínguez (eds), *Arte e Sociabilidades em Perspectiva Antropológica*. Florianopolois: UFSC, pp. 13–46.

Hill, J.D., and J.-P. Chaumeil (eds). 2011. *Burst of Breath: Indigenous Ritual Wind Instruments in Lowland South America*. Lincoln: University of Nebraska Press.

Izikowitz, K.G. (1934) 1970. *Musical and Other Sound Instruments of the South American Indians: A Comparative Ethnographical Study*. East Ardsley, UK: S.R. Publishers.

Key, M.R. 1979. *The Grouping of South American Languages*. Tübingen: Günter Narr.

Menezes Bastos, R.J. 1978. *A Musicológica Kamayurá: para uma Antropologia da Communicação no Alto Xingu*. Brasilia: FUNAI.

———. 1995. 'Esboço de uma Teoria da Música: para além de uma Antropologia sem Música e de uma Musicologia sem Homem', *Annuário Antropológico* 93: 9–73.

———. 1999. 'Apùap World Hearing: A Note on the Kamayura Phono-auditory System and on the Anthropological Concept of Culture', *The World of Music* 41(1): 85–96.

Nimuendajú, C. 1950. 'Reconhecimento dos Rios Icana, Ayarí, e Uaupés: Relatorio Apresentado ao Servico de Protecão ãos Indios do Amazonas e Acre, 1927', *Journal de la Societe des Americanistes* 39(1): 125–82.

Santos-Granero, F. 2006. 'Sensual Vitalities: Noncorporeal Modes of Sensing and Knowing in Native Amazonia', *Tipití: Journal of the Society for the Anthropology of Lowland South America* 4(1): 57–80.

Seeger, A. 1979. 'What Can We Learn When They Sing? Vocal Genres of the Suyá Indians of Central Brazil', *Ethnomusicology* 23: 373–94.

———. 1981. *Nature and Society in Central Brazil: The Suya Indians of Mato Grosso*. Cambridge, MA: Harvard University Press.

———. 1987. *Why the Suyá Sing: A Musical Anthropology of an Amazonian People*. Cambridge: Cambridge University Press.

———. 1991. 'When Music Makes History', in S. Blum, P. Bohlman and D. Neuman (eds), *Ethnomusicology and Modern Music History*. Urbana: University of Illinois Press, pp. 23–35.

Whitten, D.S., and N.E. Whitten. 1988. *From Myth to Creation*. Urbana: University of Illinois Press.

10

Inventing a New Verbal Art from Traditional Issues

The Evangelical Songs of the Suruí of Rondônia

Cédric Yvinec

Several ethnographical studies have described the conversion of indigenous Amazonian people to Christianity, which is a widespread phenomenon. However, these studies have often focused on the insertion of Christian discourses and practices within their cosmologies (e.g. Capiberibe 2007; Bonilla 2009; Grotti 2009; Vilaça 2009) and they tend to explain why the indigenous cosmology was somehow prepared to incorporate some elements of Christianity, while reformulating or neglecting others (Vilaça 1997). Thus, conversion is mainly described on the semantic level of representations – and, of course, on the level of sociological relationships that these inform (relations with kinsmen or with neighbouring groups). However, the semantic content of religious representations is often poor, confused, or not really taken into account by many individuals who claim to 'believe' in a religious doctrine. Indeed, for other phenomena of transmission of religious representation, such as prophetic movements, it has been shown that the semantic content was less important than the pragmatics of transmission (Severi 2004). As a matter of fact, before turning into beliefs and representations, Christianity first appears as a set of discursive and ritual practices, which are defined by some generic forms and legitimate contexts, such as prayer, preaching and praising. These pragmatic issues are closely connected with sociological issues. In indigenous Amazonia, these new discursive practices have to be implemented into a cultural context in which verbal arts play a prominent role, particularly in the sociological differentiation of knowledge – it is unlikely that, in Amazonia, someone can secure himself a position of chief, ritual leader or shaman without mastering some kind of verbal art. Consequently, in that context, conversion can be described as the interaction between two systems of verbal practices – the indigenous one and the Christian one. More specifically, due to the importance of musical (instrumental or verbal) speech in most relationships with Amazonia's many figures of otherness – affines, strangers, non-human beings, spirits – conversion can appear as a case study for the concept of 'musicalising the other' (Hill, this volume).

Here, I thus argue that the success of Protestantism among a population of the Brazilian Amazon, the Suruí of Rondônia, can be analysed as the invention of a new system of verbal arts. First, I give some ethnographical information on the historical process of conversion among the Suruí, in order to show that a specific verbal art, evangelical song, played a key role in the success of Christianity in that population. Then I turn to a comparison between the 'traditional' system of verbal art and the new one promoted by Protestant missionaries, in order to show that the pragmatic issues that underpinned the former remain at stake in the latter.[1]

Traditional Social Morphology and Recent History of the Suruí

The Suruí of Rondônia (also known as *Paiter*, their auto-denomination) are a Tupi-Mondé-speaking population of Brazilian Amazonia that numbers about twelve hundred today. They were first contacted in 1969, when their territory, which lay in the interfluve of the Rio Machado and the Rio Roosevelt, was opened up to agricultural development for settlers from southern Brazil. Before this contact, in classical Amazonian fashion, they relied on hunting and slash-and-burn horticulture, and maintained a warlike relationship with their neighbours. They lived in one or two big villages of several longhouses, which they moved every two or three years. Their population probably numbered around five hundred. Hierarchy and social differentiation were strongly marked among men, with a high proportion of polygynous families. Men, constrained by an avuncular rule of marriage, married at a relatively late age (over twenty), but some of them could have three or four wives, or more; this led to a high percentage of single men. The tensions that arose from these inequalities were partially reduced by two practices that provided young men with the opportunity to become political leaders, or at least to marry earlier: war and agonistic beer festivals, which both required the composition of a specific kind of ritual song. However, elders remained very dominant over the young.

This traditional order collapsed in the decades following the contact with 'Whites' (*yaraey*, who are defined as owners of metallic tools and firearms). First, the Suruí met a FUNAI contact team, and soon afterwards, pioneer farmers.[2] Most of the Suruí lands were invaded by settlers and deforested, while boom towns grew in the vicinity of the Indian reservation Sete de Setembro, which was delimited for them in 1977, in the states of Rondônia and Mato Grosso. The generation of men in their twenties at the time of contact were the first to be able to handle trade and working relationships with Whites. They first earned money as employees of the FUNAI. In 1980, as the Suruí succeeded in expelling the farmers that had settled on their lands, these young men became 'owners' of the fields of coffee trees that the farmers had grown, while the others had to work for them. In the late 1980s, they turned to selling timber and controlled most of the monetary income of the Suruí until the mid-2000s. While that generation gained an economic prominence over the older one, they also had an opportunity to get round the avuncular obstruction. Indeed, the contemporaneous pacification of most indigenous groups of the region entailed access to foreign Indian women. Many Suruí men took women from Cinta-Larga, a neighbouring Tupi-Mondé population and former enemies, while the reverse never occurred. However, at the height of timber selling, in the early 1990s, the abundance of monetary resources was quickly spent on consumption goods, especially on manufactured alcoholic beverages, while maize-beer drinking waned, as people gradually gave up growing maize. Although industrial beer and liquors are consumed in a festive and somehow prestigious way, this kind of drunkenness had never been completely channelled in a ceremonial way and it frequently caused quarrels. Logging companies rapidly took advantage of the competition between Suruí men to gain access to their lands, so that almost every man eventually got to have 'his' logger and needed to control a piece of land and a trail to smuggle his timber out. Consequently, the villages, which had already split along the coffee plantations, became more scattered. Matrimonial instability grew, because wealth attracted many White women of easy virtue, whereas Suruí wives were suspected of having affairs with White men in the villages while their husbands were out in the forest with their logger. Such a condition is described as 'scattered' (*pamitota*, 'all following each one's face'), 'dissipated' (*wawala*) and 'lawless' (*paweitxaesame õm*, 'without law of living together').

Conversion to Protestantism

Conversion to evangelical Protestantism took place in this context. The Suruí had been in contact with missionaries from the Summer Institute of Linguistics (SIL) since 1974. However, for two decades the missionaries barely preached and mainly dedicated themselves to translating the Bible into Suruí, which gave them a good command of the Suruí language. In the late 1980s, a few Suruí men encountered a couple of the Deutsch Indianer Pionier Mission (DIPM). These missionaries started to preach actively and to convert the Suruí even though they could not speak the native language at all (they had to rely on linguistic assistance by the previous ones). The first believers were recruited from among second-rate leaders; later, a number of people who did not succeed in the timber economy became believers, as well as the elderly. However, within a decade, almost all Suruí, male and female, had become *crente* ('believers' in Portuguese, a category that refers to all Protestants in that region, except Lutherans) or 'masters of God' (*palobiwayey*). Some of these converts have remained *crente* since then; others gave up going to church after a few months or years. In the ideology of the DIPM – or at least, in the interpretation of that ideology by the Suruí – being *crente* means 'giving oneself to God' (*palobǧa aweyõ*).

Long before they had converted any Suruí, the SIL missionaries had translated the notion of 'God' by the already existing locution *palob*, 'our father (inclusive of addressee)'. In the traditional cosmology this locution refers to a mythological male character who provoked the differentiation of animal species and their separation from humanity, and to an unremarkable shamanic spirit, whose song claims it 'made' sundry beings ('daylight', 'stones', 'shamans', 'benches'). The mythological character is related to the Amazonian figure of the Twins, since he usually appears with his 'Skin-Flake' (*palobleregud*), which was subsequently associated with the Christian 'devil' (in spite of the fact that Our-Father does not behave in a kinder way than his Skin-Flake). The missionaries managed to convince the Suruí that God/Our-Father had the power to cure diseases, solve tensions with kin and spouses, and protect believers from any aggressions, physical or magical. All these misfortunes define 'sin' (*ñan*, 'bad') as 'entanglement with difficulties' (*meresotepãy*). 'Giving oneself to

God' is not a matter of faith, since no one ever questioned his existence. Believers explain their conversion, not because they realised that God exists, but because they interacted with him personally, meeting him in dreams. However, meeting God is not a significant occurrence: people may experience this quite frequently. Conversion is not a very dramatic process: the new *crente* simply states his will to live in a Christian way and starts going to church; sometimes, baptism by immersion is practised. Thus, no Suruí is a non-believer: there are only sinful believers.[3] After a few years of observance, many individuals go through a time of sin, then mend their ways, and so on.

First and foremost, being a 'believer' depends on one's behaviour. This requires abstaining from several activities that had been intensely practised at the time the Suruí met the DIPM. Believers must not drink alcohol, smoke tobacco or dance; this meant that both the consumption of manufactured alcohol and traditional beer festivals were prohibited; shamanism became impossible too. They could not indulge in adulterous relationships – however, polygynous marriages were not prohibited and the missionaries never interfered in the Suruí matrimonial rules. Believers could not fight with other Suruí or with foreigners; in their sermons, the DIPM missionaries advised their audience to yield to political authorities, both to the Brazilian state representatives and to the indigenous leaders (even if Suruí leaders often refused to observe Protestant rules). Finally, believers could not 'interact with idols' (*soeyalapa*), that is, practise shamanism, since the notion of 'idol' refers to any invisible power other than God; the missionaries failed to persuade the Suruí that the 'idols', that is the shamanic spirits (*soey*), do not exist. Believers state that these spirits are lower gods, whose power is just weaker than God's.

These prohibitions obviously met some expectations of the elder Suruí men and of all those who did not succeed very well in the timber economy. Indeed, the elderly could hope to dissuade the young from stealing the wives they had and did not lose much in the prohibition of violence and beer festivals. The poor, who had no money to spend on alcohol or other luxury goods, would not lose much in the dancing and drinking prohibition either. However, Protestantism spread far beyond these social groups, at least as a temporary state. This was probably made possible because evangelical Protestantism did not only act in a prohibitive way: it also offered new tools and means. Protestantism successfully promoted various verbal arts, most noticeably songs that were able to supersede those it banned: shamanic songs, which were important therapeutic devices,

and beer festival songs, which were major symbolic goods, especially for those – the young – who were traditionally deprived of real
goods (women). As a matter of fact, some of these new verbal arts
enjoyed some of the performative properties and symbolic values
of the traditional ones: some started to be used as therapeutic or
magical devices; others became prestigious performances that new
believers particularly valued, just like performing beer festival songs
was appreciated by the young. In the Protestant tradition – at least in
that to which the SIL and DIPM missionaries are heirs – no verbal art
really enjoys such properties and values. So the success of these new
verbal arts lies in the interaction between Suruí issues and these new
verbal forms, and it is this question that I address here. First, I set
out the traditional verbal art system. Then I describe the evangelical
verbal art system and I detail rhetoric of evangelical songs. Finally, I
explain the issue of authorship and the performative expectancies of
these songs.

Overview of Suruí Traditional Verbal Arts

In the Suruí tradition, there are two marked forms of speech, which
may be labelled as 'verbal arts' in so far as they are considered as different from ordinary talking and as requiring specific abilities. These
are 'singing' and 'performing spirits', which hereafter I will refer to,
respectively, as 'profane songs' and 'shamanic songs'.

'Singing', *merewá*, literally 'saying repeatedly', refers to any kind
of sung speech. It is only considered as an intensive form of speech,
defined by its repetitive structure. Repetition and redundancy are
the basis of the high expressivity of profane songs: this is what the
particle *pere* – which means 'repetitively, completely, throughout' –
denotes. 'Singing' is the most perfect way of telling something:
when, in a narrative, the narrator announces: *eebo dena iwewá e*
('then [he] said that'), he or she implies that the character sung about
the event in question – and usually a quotation of the song follows.
However, the Suruí do not credit profane songs with any symbolic
efficacy: 'singing' has no material consequences whatsoever. The
topics suitable for singing are numerous, ranging from exceptional
events (homicide) to humdrum occurrences (fishing, hunting). Each
of these define a subgenre of profane song: *paloakabewá*, 'recounting a homicide', *ayõrewá*, 'recounting an adultery', *ihtxakabewá*,
'recounting a fishing party', and so on, each distinguished by
a tune and a lexical style. Most of the topics of songs include a

confrontational feature. Only the individual who initiated the event in question is entitled to sing about it – consequently, singers are almost always male. But anyone who has initiated such an event is allowed to sing about it, no matter how old or young he is. As a general rule, 'singing' claims both that the singer initiated a noteworthy sequence of actions and that this sequence is now completed. Indeed, some meaningful sequences – war, beer festivals – cannot be completed as full events or acts until their initiator sings. To this extent, 'singing' can be labelled as an illocutionary act, in Austin's (1962) terms. For every new occurrence, a new song must be composed: it should comply with the stylistic rules of the subgenre in question, but a minimum poetic novelty is expected. This will prove both the authorship and the genuine responsibility of the singer and actor of the event. 'Singing' is the hallmark of agency: to prove that you have done a deed of some kind, you must be able to compose a song of *that* kind – the generic conformity of the song proves the act belonged to that class of acts (killing, drinking, etc.) and the singer is a man of that kind (killer, drinker, etc.) – and you must be able to compose a *new* song, as the novelty of the song proves that an act of that kind was achieved on *that* occasion. Thus, every profane song denotes the 'eventhood' of a particular sequence of actions and the authorship of its speaker.

'Performing spirits', *sopereiga* – literally 'repeatedly picking a spirit'; that is, shamanic singing – is a special kind of 'singing' (*merewá*), defined by its authorship: indeed, spirits are said to 'sing' their own songs (only shamans can hear them), whereas the shaman is only said to 'perform' the spirits' songs – this 'performance of spirits' is what the ordinary human can hear when a shaman is singing. Due to their foreign authors, the lyrics of shamanic songs resort to a language that is quite different from everyday Suruí and hard to understand for many listeners. Their tune is radically different from profane songs too. Although the performer – the shaman – is not the author, this speech is credited with perlocutionary effects, in Austin's terms, since it is not only able to cure the sick, but also to kill its speaker. 'Performing spirits' is a very dangerous act, because when practised illegitimately, it leads the speaker to death; only shamans – that is, always adult men chosen by spirits – can perform their songs without making them angry and being consequently punished by them. Each song is expected by the spirits (and the patients) to be performed in a similar manner each time by every shaman. 'Performing spirits' is limited to a corpus of songs. In theory, each spirit owns one song and all shamans know all the spirits, which means that they all perform

Table 10.1 Characteristics of profane songs and shamanic songs.

	Profane songs (*merewá*, 'singing')	Shamanic songs (*sopereiga*, 'performing spirits')
Understandability	Full	Low
Authorship	Human	Non-human
Performativity	Illocutionary	Perlocutionary
Variability	Mandatory	Negated
Event	Denoted and constituted	Prevented or negated

the same corpus of songs in the same way. In practice, the shamans do perform the most important songs in a roughly similar way; but their ways of performing minor songs probably vary a lot more. What is more, minimal variations on some specific part of the song prove that the shaman is attuning his singing to the invisible presence of the spirit, not trotting out words he learned by rote. Shamanic songs are performed, always in a ritualised way, whenever the help of the spirits is needed, either to heal an individual or to drive away diseases from the village. In every shamanic session, the shamans enumerate songs in an organised way until the expected outcome (recovery) is reached or until the corpus of songs they know is exhausted. Thus, 'performing spirits' is aimed at preventing or remedying events such as breaks in the usual, healthy state of affairs, by displaying a whole, well-ordered speech. To a certain extent, since many spirits bear names of natural species (although their ritual connection to their natural eponym is rather weak), Suruí shamanic singing can illustrate the concept of 'musicalisation as a process of creating a naturalised social space through singing the names of animal, fish and other non-human species' (Hill, this volume).

The stylistic and pragmatic properties of these two verbal arts can be contrasted and summarised in Table 10.1.

Evangelical Verbal Arts

When they converted the Suruí to Protestantism, the missionaries introduced three new verbal arts:

- Preaching, *palomakobáh palobğa*, literally 'teaching God to everybody';
- Prayer, *palobmayã*, literally 'talking to God';
- Evangelical song, *palobewá*, literally 'saying/singing God'.

The most valued of these verbal arts, in the missionaries' practice, are preaching and prayer, far more than evangelical songs. Of course, this is never explicitly stated, but the missionaries imply that preaching and praying can return some material benefits, whereas singing hardly does.

Preaching is specialist work, initially performed by missionaries; it is now carried out by trained Suruí, during church services. The content is very technical, expounded in quite scholarly ways through reading and commenting on the Bible, partly in Portuguese, standing behind a desk, on a platform in front of a blackboard. The congregation usually pay little attention to what is said and find it boring and tiresome – they consider themselves as engaged in the specific activity of pupils, *sodigĩkin*, 'studying', 'looking at written things', even though they are not actually reading. On the contrary, the various actual or potential speakers vie with each other in their erudition, carefully prepare their lecture and call themselves various bureaucratic titles ('pastor', 'assistant', 'missionary', 'usher').[4] In stark contrast to local Brazilian preachers, who affect impassionate enthusiasm, the Suruí pastors opt for tedious earnestness, probably in the wake of the DIPM missionaries. The preachers' legitimacy relies on their personal training in evangelical institutes in distant cities (Porto Velho, Cuiabá), which only rather young individuals can attend, because this requires a fair command of Portuguese. The individuals, including a few women, who are selected by the missionaries to do a training course in preaching are motivated by the search for new horizons through experiences reserved for a few specialists. They particularly value the annual meeting with other Christianised tribes and the various trips they go on with missionaries. Such pragmatic settings and sociological issues of 'teaching God' are akin to the position of shamans in respect to helping ordinary people whenever the latter have no need of it: shamans are rather eager to talk about their experiences, and vie with each other, but ordinary (healthy) people are not really interested in listening to them. The efficacy of preaching is not really assessed according to its effects on the congregation (either by their attention, or by the improvement of their behaviour). However, some benefits seem to be expected by the preachers and the congregation: performing and attending 'teaching God' should favour God's blessing for both in a very general way. The exact kind of benefits (health, wealth, afterlife, etc.) and the nature of the connection (reward for care, enhancement of skill, etc.) between 'teaching God' and its salutary consequences are never stated though.

In contrast to preaching, prayer can be performed by everybody, in everyday Suruí language, and its communicative function is prominent. It is always spoken publicly and aloud, by only one individual, while others keep mute. Everybody is expected to close their eyes. It starts with a vocative (*palob!*, 'God!')and is usually made of two parts: first, it lists some attributes of God ('you made forest, you made rivers' and so on); then, it requests God's practical help, in a very specific way for some people ('cure them', 'give them enough money to pay their bus ticket'), and carefully lists them, without giving any justification; finally it concludes with only one foreign word, *amen*, repeated by the audience. In theory, the first part is stable and relies on the speaker's remembrance of the Genesis and his or her inspiration by the Suruí natural environment and mythological tradition ('you made the Brazil nut tree'). This is probably supposed to set his or her authority to pray. However, almost all adult men and women dare to pray. Believers claim that 'talking to God' has perlocutionary effects – and sinners tacitly agree. Of course, this belief is explicitly supported by the missionaries since the supposed efficacy of prayer is one of their main arguments in favour of Christianity. The varying efficiency of prayer does not elicit any discussion; when questioned about its failure to achieve its goal, Christian Suruí will answer that prayer should either be repeated and carried on, or performed by another speaker, or both. The Suruí have an idea that all speakers are not equally good at praying, but there is no explicit ranking of them and women can pray while men stay mute. Although prayer is verbally addressed to God, there are always one or several real human addressees in the audience: the expected beneficiaries of God's help – if God is requested to cure a sick person, the speaker will lay his or her hand on the former's head. Thus, 'talking to God' is tantamount to a public expression of the commitment of the speaker to the addressee's interest. This interactional issue is very similar to shamanic singing, since shamans are supposed to carry on performing one spirit after another, until their patient gets better; and their effort is assessed by the time they spend listing spirits' songs.[5]

As a matter of fact, evangelical songs are not as valued as preaching and prayers by the missionaries. Of course, they do not discourage praising God by singing and there is no explicit ranking of the various evangelical verbal practices. But the missionaries do not reward evangelical singing with a prestigious social status such as the position of preacher, and they do not grant it clear perlocutionary effectiveness. That which the Suruí call 'saying/singing God' is supposed to play the ritual function, in the missionaries' views, of praising God, since it translates the Portuguese locution *louvar a Deus*. Admittedly, celebrating, praising may be an aspect of 'singing' in profane songs. However, it is important to note that by denoting evangelical songs by a locution made of the verb -*ewá* ('say/sing') and of God as its direct object, the Suruí classify this verbal art as a subgenre of 'singing' – that is, as a genre of profane song (in contrast to shamanic song). Consequently, 'God' or 'God's deeds' appear as a topic suitable for singing, which is, in some respect, similar to a human activity such as killing, hunting, seducing, being intoxicated, and so on. The little interest missionaries take in Suruí traditional culture probably prevented them from noticing this odd equation from a Christian point of view. In spite of its lesser significance in the missionaries' views, compared to preaching and praying, evangelical singing is undoubtedly the verbal art that the Suruí appreciate most, both as speakers and as an audience. Such an unexpected preference is therefore worth analysing.

Genres and Uses of Evangelical Songs

Evangelical singing is the most complex of the verbal arts that appeared with conversion to Protestantism. Indeed, one can distinguish three forms of evangelical songs. The first distinction is obvious: there are, on the one hand, evangelical hymns in Portuguese, and, on the other, songs in Suruí. But among the latter there are songs whose lyrics have been written down in a hymnal, and others whose lyrics have not. These distinctions are not purely linguistic or formal.

Evangelical hymns in Portuguese, available in the hymnal or orally taught by the missionaries, are learned by rote and sung collectively during church services, either by the whole congregation or by a choir of teenagers. Out of church, they are only sung by the young, especially teenage girls. Their performance without the help of a choir remains difficult for the elderly, who can neither write nor speak Portuguese. The aim of the performance is apparently to pass time, and especially to entertain the children who are often left in these young girls' care.

The hymnals that the SIL have supplied to the Suruí since 1992 contain 148 songs in Suruí. Some are obviously mere translations of classical hymns. Their tunes display a strong evangelical influence and their lyrics often refer to classical biblical themes. Most of these songs were composed by the first generation of converted Suruí, both male and female, probably with the help of SIL missionaries. However, some written songs were undoubtedly composed by Suruí by themselves. These display typical features of Suruí traditional songs that the non-written evangelical songs also display. The names of their composers, often illiterate individuals, also prove that many of these songs were first composed in a purely oral way. Although the name of the composer is mentioned above each lyric in this booklet, many singers do not pay any attention to it; consequently, they may sing works by their close kin or political rivals indiscriminately. Indeed, these are usually sung collectively, during church services only.

Finally, adult men and a few elderly women regularly compose new songs and sing them immediately, without writing them down. These songs do not explicitly refer to any specific event – or, more exactly, the audience cannot guess what the song refers to without an explanation from the composer. They usually allude to various biblical themes – especially salvation – and emphasise the relationship between the singer and God or Jesus. The motivation for composing a song – according to statements of both composers and listeners – is usually an interaction of the singer with God at night, in dreams.[6] The author of such a song will often sing it again, during a church service and out of church as well. Some of these songs are well known, at least to the kin of their author; some quickly fall into oblivion. Respectable composers seem to own (i.e. to be recognised as the author of) no more than five or six songs, which is far less than the average number of profane songs owned by composers; pastors apparently compose more songs. Whenever asked, the author will proudly sing his or her song again. But for some time, no one will dare to sing a new song in its author's place. The authorship is thus quite emphasised in these songs. Consequently, songs of this kind are never sung collectively – moreover, collective singing is mostly performed by the young, while the authors of these songs are mostly rather old. I collected a dozen of them, from a pastor about sixty years old, a fifty-year-old man and a seventy-year-old woman.

These subcategories of 'saying/singing God' are not explicit, and their boundaries are porous. While some of the written Suruí songs were probably first composed as oral songs, before the missionaries selected them to be written down, some composers perhaps hope to have their compositions included in future editions of the SIL booklet, since they do not conceal their pride in being recognised as 'God singers'. Conversely, the corpus of songs included in the booklet is obviously used as a source of inspiration by composers of new songs, either by directly reading the lyrics or by listening to the performance of this corpus during church services. The latter way is undoubtedly more productive.

Stylistics and Pragmatics of Evangelical Songs

Most songs, especially non-written ones, are composed by middle-aged or old Suruí, who used to compose profane songs. Unsurprisingly, they have inherited numerous formal characteristics of profane songs. From a melodic point of view, they display an overall pattern that can be found, on a different scale, in many profane song subgenres: the first segments of a sentence, which often are the same syntagms repeated two or three times, are sung rather loudly, with a slightly rising pitch, and then the last one is sung by a lower voice, with a descending pitch. On the lexical and syntactic levels too, non-written evangelical songs inherited the mannered style of profane songs: they have conspicuously complicated locutions, including rare or foreign words inserted in strings of genitive or objective constructions:

meresotepãyepabepekotigta
'carrying the width of arms [= cross] of entanglement with difficulties [= sin]'
or:
*oma*paraiso*iway*
'the master of the paradise of mine'

However, the most interesting patterns that evangelical songs share with traditional ones are rhetorical: these are the parallelistic structure, the quoting pattern and the evidential modality specific to those genres. Evangelical songs have clearly the same parallelistic structure as profane songs – this pattern is conspicuously absent from the written Suruí evangelical songs that are obvious translations of hymns of the Protestant tradition. This parallelism relies on a leitmotif and development pattern: a similar syntactic structure is expanded and enriched throughout the song by inserting and varying some syntagmatic elements, usually direct objects or subjects. For instance, consider the following fragment of a song composed by an old woman:

1. *Ate meyxa omerepi i, Palobağa pağay*
   Ate meyxa omerepi, ate meyxa omerepi, omerepi i, Palobağa ena
   Ate meyxa Noeperemi meyidağa ma, ibapna ma, olade meykay
   ewepi oğay i, Jesusağa ena

> *Ate meyxa omerepi, ate meyxa omerepi ğaraesiyõpabilī ibapağa ma*
> *Noeperemi maloypoyha makoy ma, olade meykay ewepi oğay i,*
> *Jesusağa ena*
> *Ate meyxa omerepi, ate meyxa omerepi, omerepi i, Jesus ağa pağay*
> 'Don't you listen to me?' God is saying to all of us
> 'Don't you listen to me, don't you listen to me, listen to me?' God is
> saying so
> 'Don't you hear what I'm saying to you, "Just like Noah, make your
> own, your canoe!"' Jesus is saying so
> 'Don't you listen to me, don't you listen to me, don't you hear what I'm
> saying to you, "In the middle of the swamped forest make a canoe,
> just like Noah shunned the downpour!"' Jesus is saying so
> 'Don't you listen to me, don't you listen to me, listen to me?' Jesus is
> saying to all of us.

Its parallelistic structure relies on the following semantic and syntactic pattern:

> *Ate meyxa o-*[developmental slot No. 1]*-epi i* [developmental slot No.
> 2]*-eğa* [developmental slot No. 3]
> 'Don't you hear me saying [No. 1]' [No. 2] is saying to [No. 3]

Developmental slots No. 2 and No. 3 are syntactically loose – they are made up of a free subject with an indirect object or an expletive locution – and they are semantically simple, as they only refer to Christian deities and indefinite addressees. Developmental slot No. 1 is the direct object of the transitive verb *epi*, 'to hear', and can grow to become a complex clause set that contains most of the lexical variations and semantic information of the song. It is worth noting that what is developed initially appears as a simple personal pronoun, *o-*, 'me'; thus a deictic pronoun is later replaced by a whole discourse ('make a canoe like Noah's', and so on). Such development of deictics is particularly productive, as Suruí sentences include numerous exophoric and endophoric pronouns whose reference often remains uncertain. This uncertainty is especially pronounced in evangelical songs, since the relevant context is noticeably vague, as the song refers to events that the audience has not witnessed (e.g. interactions in dreams) and/or cannot identify accurately (e.g. Biblical comparisons).

This whole pattern – Leitmotiv part No. 1 / Developmental slot / Leitmotiv part No. 2 including minor developmental slots – is a classical structure of profane songs.[7] It is worth noting that in profane songs this structure is usually both more complex and more rigid. On the one hand, the leitmotif nature can be more syntactical or abstract, allowing more developmental slots to appear. On the other hand, the classification of subgenres requires developments to include some sets of metaphors specific to each subgenre – to some extent, such a lexical or semantic classification of evangelical songs is only assumed by the references to Christian deities. Thus, this developmental pattern is probably easier to handle in the evangelical context than it has ever been traditionally.

As the previous example shows, evangelical songs are scarcely a direct discourse: they often include quotations, and these sometimes contain other quotations. Even if a song does not claim to quote God's speech but only refers to the singer's speech, this will usually be reported as a quotation, as in the following fragment of a song composed by a middle-aged man:

2. *'"Yena te bo oih ter", olade ihkarsonimaibikoy moribmoyhpiabpa-beka, eetiga Palob ya ihkarsonimaibikoy moribmoyhpiabpabepi oiga po', oğa ena pağay*
'"So I'm really dying", as I was thinking so, at the bottom of the vast lake inside the belly of the big fish, then God picked me out of the belly of the big fish at the bottom of the vast lake, they say', I'm saying this now to us all.

This embedding of quotation is perfectly in the style of profane songs. It seems closely connected to the very act of 'singing': in many written songs, although they probably rely on translations of some Christian themes, the Suruí composers apparently added such quotation-framing phrases to embed the whole song. This quotation device is articulated with the parallelistic structure described above. As a general rule, quoted sentences appear in an anaphoric way, at the head of a whole sentence, while quotation-framing sentences appear as an epiphora. Thus a quoted sentence usually provides the first part of the leitmotif, while the quotation-framing sentence provides its second part and some minor developmental slots. The main develop-mental slot is filled in by some parts of the quoted material. If there is only one level of quotation, a syntactical part of the quoted sentence will be developed; if there are two levels of embedded quotations, one of those will be developed. As a result, quoted elements are fore-grounded, while quotation-framing elements appear last, somehow backgrounded rhetorically and musically – since the last part of the musical phrase is sung in a lower voice.

Finally, the evangelical songs also display a pervasive rhetorical feature of traditional songs, both profane and shamanic – a complex authorship pattern, due to the avoidance of the witnessed evidential mode. In Suruí, two evidential modes contrast with each other: witnessed and non-witnessed evidentiality. The former is marked by the verbal particle *de* and by the sentence-final marker *e*; the latter is marked by the verbal particle *ya* and/or by the sentence-final markers *a* (assertive) and *i* (non-assertive). This evidential opposition is clear-cut in affirmative sentences dealing with past events: then *de* claims that the speaker witnessed the event that he or she is talking about, whereas *ya* states that it was not, but that it was known through hearsay. In other types of utterances, *ya* only states that the speaker did not or could not witness the events, without positively referring to hearsay – perhaps just because the events may not have occurred yet, like in an interrogative sentence. In some sentences, aspectual particles may take the place of verbal evidential particles; then, only the sentence-final markers allow the evidential status of the utterance to be inferred. However, if no evidential markers can be identified, this usually means that the witnessed mode is avoided – for instance, the present marker *eğa* is seemingly incompatible with the witnessed sentence-final marker.

Although non-witnessed evidentiality (*ya... a* or *ya... i*) does not positively appear in all songs, any kind of sung speech – shamanic, profane or evangelical – is explicitly incompatible with witnessed evidentiality (*de... e*). In shamanic songs, witnessed evidential particles just do not occur, and speakers have no reason to worry about it, since these songs are supposedly fixed. As regards profane songs, informants state this as a rule: 'When you sing (*merewá*), you do not say "*de*". You say "*de*" when you tell something (*iwema*)'. This rule was elicited as I had tried to sing a basic profane song of my own composition, but I was corrected by an old woman and her adult son. I was not given any more justification of this rule, except that 'This is our way'. Similarly, in the evangelical songs, witnessed evidentiality does not occur (except in a few embedded clauses) and these songs pervasively use the particles *ya* and *eğa*, contrasting or incompatible with it. These non-witnessed evidential particles especially occur in the main, quotation-framing clauses:

3. *Waba meypah meyxa, ye ya Palobla pağay a, pağay ma, oğa ena pağay*
   Let's teach us all this: 'God told us all, they say, "You are going to disappear"', I'm saying so to all of us
4. *Anode, anode ena e, iwepide oğay eweiway ya Jesus ya iweariwa ena*
   'This one standing there thinks about me "That's true"', the one in charge of that, Jesus, delights of that, they say
5. *Jesus ya awewá oğay*
   Jesus talked to me, they say

'So you are going to come here, as owner of my paradise, aren't you?' thus he talked to me, he talked to me

Thus the song as a whole is always affected by a doubt surrounding the identity of the ultimate source of its utterance.

Of course, these characteristics of evangelical songs are, in a sense, 'inherited' from the traditional songs: the composers of evangelical songs have gone on developing leitmotifs, embedding quotations and denying witness because they had learned to sing that way in their traditional verbal art system. This is particularly true from the point of view of the rhetorical technique: composers have had to resort to the skills they already managed, and the developmental structure has provided them with a routine technique for composing songs. However, they were not compelled to embed quotations or to keep a non-witnessed evidentiality – the missionaries are probably not very keen on the sceptical innuendos that the latter feature may arise. Eventually, whatever the historical reasons of these patterns, the inferences they allow the audience to make, the relationship they set between the speaker, its utterance and the audience, the ideological consequences they have on the understanding of Christianity by the Suruí and the epistemological and sociological issues that they deal with are still to be analysed.

The combination of these three patterns – developmental structure, quotation embedding and non-witnessed evidentiality – creates a complex assertive system and an elusive authorship in these songs. Indeed, until the singing ends, the audience cannot be certain that some developmental potentialities do not remain unnoticed, hidden in some pronouns; and until the end, they cannot be sure that some utterance will not end up embedded in a discrete, delayed quotation frame; and even then, the paramount evidential authority will remain unidentified, due to the framing non-witnessed particle.

Authorship in Traditional and Evangelical Songs

Actually, such delusiveness can be found in traditional songs, profane or shamanic, and to an even higher degree, since they display the same feature in a very systematic way. Elsewhere (Yvinec 2011, 2012), I have suggested that the avoidance of witnessed evidentiality in traditional songs always introduces at least two kinds of co-speakers or co-authors of the sung utterance, along with the singer.[8] In short, in shamanic songs, these co-authors are the spirits – who

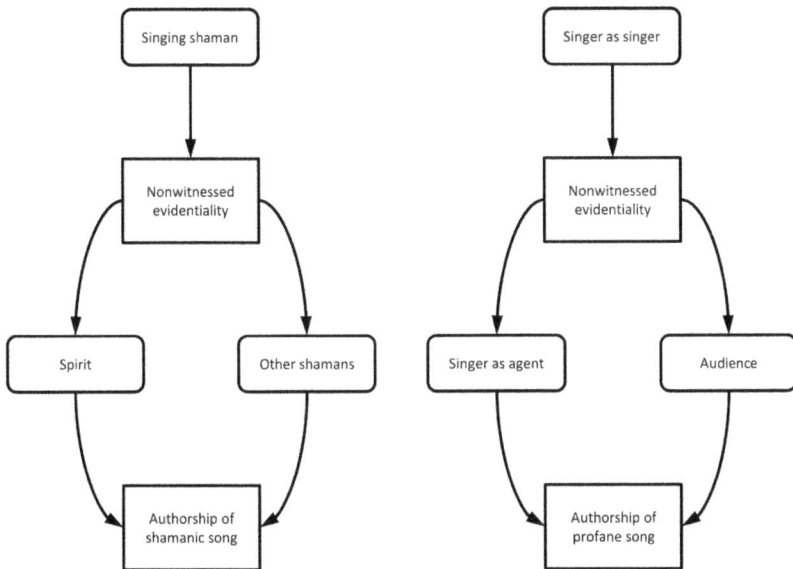

Figure 10.1 Authorship pattern in shamanic songs (left) and profane songs (right). Figure created by the author.

are the official authors of the songs that the shamans perform – and the other shamans, who all claim to sing exactly the same songs, and who obviously assess the correctness of the singer's performance. In profane songs, such co-authors are less obvious. However, since one cannot sing without having previously achieved some act that deserves being celebrated, the co-authors can be identified as, on the one hand, himself (not as the singer he is now but as the agent he was before – at the time he performed the event that justifies his present singing); and, on the other hand, the audience, who tacitly recognise his action as worthy of song. Thus, in each case, there are two kinds of co-author: one that is singular and absent – invisible (spirit) or past (individual as agent); and one that is plural and present – the audience, either a specialist or a general one (see Figure 10.1). Since such a homology can be found between the authorship patterns of two radically contrasted genres of songs, it is worth trying to search for a homologous tri-partition of authorship in evangelical songs.

The first candidate for co-authoring these songs is obvious: God himself, who could play the part of the shamanic spirits. Indeed, many songs claim to report what God did or said. Evangelical singers admit that they consciously composed their songs – they thought about them before singing them aloud, they hummed them first, and so on. Nonetheless, they ascribe the decision of composing to some personal interaction with God. Ascribing one of the positions of co-author to a supernatural agent (i.e. an entity that is invisible, powerful and impossible to interact with under ordinary circumstances) thus sets us in the shamanic songs' authoring pattern, since the profane model does not call on any such agency. So, if we follow this shamanic model, then the third pole of authorship should be attributed to a human audience that masters a specialised knowledge. Within the evangelical world, such an audience could be identified as the missionaries (and, secondarily, as the previous evangelical song composers). Such a cast for the present, plural, audience-like co-author part does suit one kind of evangelical song: those that have been written down. As a matter of fact, by being selected by the missionaries to appear in the hymnal, these songs have been approved and co-authored by them. Of course, the Suruí individuals who are already recognised as good evangelical composers, especially those who are employed by the SIL as Bible translators, might influence the missionaries' choice and share their position of co-authors. These songs, by being recognised, collected, materialised and distributed in a standard booklet, become a common heritage that all the believers are entitled to sing, regardless of the identity of the individual human author. Once it has been written down, a song is less identified by its human composer than by its subject or inspirer, since it is the latter that motivated it being written down. As the human author is forgotten, the agency that supposedly inspired all the songs of the corpus, God, can appear as their main author.

Such a homology of authorship pattern between the written evangelical songs and shamanic songs is relevant because it can account for various similarities in their uses. Just like shamanic songs are more or less fixed, and various shamans (who do not claim to have authored them but still allow themselves to assess every performer of these songs) perform these with minimal variations, so also the singers of written evangelical song are multiple. They do not claim to have composed them, and they try to perform them in a stable way, which is always likely to be assessed and corrected by other potential performers, particularly by the supposedly skilled ones, such as evangelical leaders and missionaries. Although evangelical songs do not have a perlocutionary effectiveness by themselves, they are collectively sung in a ritual setting that is monitored by specialists – the church service led by pastors and/or missionaries – and from which some benefits are expected; this echoes the performance of shamanic songs in collective rituals, in which the whole population sings along to the shamans' performance in order to protect the village from disease and disorder. Just like shamanic singing is not by itself efficient in curing the sick but sets into action the powerful agency of the song's spiritual author, evangelical singing during a church service gains God's favour and opens up the way for the efficacy of prayer. Indeed, the corpus of written songs and its tangible materialisation, the SIL hymnal, are considered as 'God's holy things' (*palobasoeymaǧuy*), endowed with some protective powers. People sleep with the Bible and hymnal at their side, just like they used to sleep with shamanic paraphernalia by their hammock. Of course, there are important differences between shamanic songs and written evangelical songs in terms of linguistic understandability, modality of learning and allowed performers. However, a similar kind of authorship, denied for him- or herself by the speaker, and indeterminately attributable to supernatural agencies and human specialists, is correlated both in shamanic songs and written evangelical songs with an analogous way of performance and expectancies about its perlocutionary effects.

The shamanic pattern of authorship can account for the use of non-witnessed evidentiality in written evangelical songs, but it would be inadequate for non-written ones – and this is rather troublesome, since many written songs were probably initially composed as non-written ones. Indeed the divine authorship of songs is problematic. God, as an invisible agency and authority, may undoubtedly be convoked by the singers to legitimise their singing. However, tempting as it may be to assign him the part of the shamanic spirits after he turned them silent, I do not think the Christian God is mighty enough to author songs exactly in the same way as shamanic spirits. No shaman would dare to claim a shamanic song as his; by contrast, evangelical singers do claim authorship of their compositions, at least until these are selected to be written down. Evangelical singers do not describe themselves as modest 'performers', always in fear of the author of their utterance. They do not sing God's words, but sing *about* God words and deeds.

In their description of the song-composing process, singers do not say that God taught them a song's content, but that they interacted with God and afterwards composed a song. Admittedly, interactions with God, which usually take place while the individual is sleeping, often amount to verbal messages from God to the human person, whether they result in a song or not. Nevertheless, if the song inspired by such a message may reproduce God's words in direct speech, this will always appear as quoted speech, with an explicit quotation-framing clause – moreover, God's quotations in songs are not always verbatim reports, according to informants. This is consistent with the classification of such a discourse as a 'saying/singing' (*ewá*), rather than as a 'performing' (*pereiga*). Consequently, that which authors the song, in the sense of that which legitimises the singing, is not an entity, but an event, and this event includes the singer as a participant, just like in the profane authorship pattern.

If we follow the latter authorship pattern, the other co-author of the non-written evangelical song should be identified as the audience in the wider sense – that is, as an unrestricted, unspecialised audience. As a matter of fact, these songs are initially sung in front of such an audience. Composers recount that they listened (*epi*) to God 'while they were asleep' (*akereibita*) – an epistemic situation that is not mere dream, because it has the same ontological value as waking – then they woke up and immediately sang their new song for the first time. This means that the first audience of the song is made up of people who live in the same house – that is, close kin and spouse(s). Then the song may be sung during the day among kin and neighbours, and afterwards, during a church service. If it is sung directly at church, this will only occur during a routine church service, not on a special occasion, such as a meeting of parishioners from different villages or a service in which missionaries or visitors coming from afar participate. Thus, the first audience of non-written evangelical songs can be defined as not very impressive, rather familiar, informal and usually well disposed towards the singer. From an epistemic point of view, it is an audience of peers, since they do not master any specialised knowledge that would allow them to judge the singer's composition or performance. This does not mean that all the new compositions will be equally welcomed, but praise and criticism will not be able to rely on some specific, recognised competency, so that everybody will know that they are influenced by the everyday relationship between kin. Once again, the similarity of the authorship pattern between profane songs and non-written songs correlates with analogies in their way of performance and the expectancies about their perlocutionary effects. Both are sung by one singer alone, in front of people who are potential singers of songs that ought to be both similar and different, and who are thus entitled to judge that song. No perlocutionary effect is expected from such songs, since they are neither sung in a particularly ritual context nor are they a prelude to any efficacious verbal practices, such as prayer. As speech acts, they only testify that the singer somehow interacted with God, just like a profane song only testifies that its singer claims to have previously achieved a deed of some kind, that of the song's genre.

Therefore, an interesting correlation between, on the one hand, the kind of audience and, on the other hand, the performative properties and the supposed powerful co-author of the utterance, can be detected in both traditional and evangelical sung verbal arts. In both cases, a non-specialist audience correlates with the denial of perlocutionary effectiveness, whereas a specialist audience allows the singer to claim perlocutionary effectiveness for his or her song. Performative properties depend upon the relative competence of the audience, probably because a specialist audience is able to introduce some supernatural agencies as co-authors of the utterance, whereas when singing in front of peers only, the singer has to assume authorship of his or her utterance. Thus the presumption in the symbolic efficacy relies on a split within the whole audience, between ordinary members and a few members whose special competence is acknowledged by the others. Furthermore, there needs to be a kind of incommunicability between these two parts of the audience. Indeed, Suruí shamans cannot fully explain to their non-shaman kin how they learned their songs. Admittedly, missionaries do not look for any exclusive mystical relation with their deity, but the historical, political and linguistic settings do separate them from their Suruí flock.

As regards traditional verbal arts, this split in the audience relies on obvious linguistic devices, such as lexical opacity and syntactic irregularity, which impair the parsing and understanding of shamanic songs. These characteristics are absent in evangelical songs, or they are ineffective, since Portuguese songs are used in the same way as some Suruí songs. One could argue that writing plays that part: indeed, the use of a song will change once it has been written down. However, this would bypass an important element: it is not writing by itself – many Suruí can write and read nowadays – but writing down by a third party that appears as a determining factor in the perlocutionary expectancies about some evangelical songs. So, first and foremost, it is a pragmatic, interactional setting that is at work, not a technical, cognitive device. It is for this reason that, although they are formally similar to profane songs, some evangelical songs have the performative properties of the traditionally opposite genre – that is, shamanic songs.

Conclusion: Pragmatics of Innovation

The success of Christianity among the Suruí undoubtedly relied on various factors, and verbal arts were probably not the most decisive.

However, the success of evangelical singing among the Suruí was probably favoured by the ambivalence of its authoring pattern, since this allowed the advantages of both traditional genres to be combined: individual recognition and perlocutionary effectiveness. These can be combined by one song, but only successively, not simultaneously: individual recognition of its singer before it is written down, and perlocutionary effectiveness afterwards. By combining these, each suffers some diminution: the singer is recognised only for some time, and the most acknowledged ones will be forgotten by having their songs written down; the perlocutionary effectiveness is only relative, subordinate to that of prayer.

The impossibility of simultaneously holding these advantages shows that this pragmatic issue – combining personal authorship and belief in symbolic efficacy – is a long-lasting, stable element of the Suruí tradition of verbal arts. Indeed, this pragmatic issue remains the same while verbal practices and cosmological representations drastically change. Furthermore, this pragmatic issue has an obvious dynamic part in the composition of new songs and, consequently, in the renewal of verbal arts. Thus, the core of a tradition of verbal arts appears to lie not in some stylistic devices or in beliefs about the performative properties of some discourses, but in these kinds of pragmatic issues that structure a system of verbal arts by organising relationships between the authors', performers' and audiences' expectancies about the performative properties of various genres, which can support various cosmological lexicons.

The importance of singing for the integration of Christian deities in the Suruí discourse appears as an ethnographical case that could exemplify the concept of 'musicalising the other' that Hill (this volume) defines as a pan-Amazonian 'way of socialising relations with affines, non-human beings, and various categories of "others"', so that their otherness is 'both acknowledge[d] and encompass[ed]'. Indeed, the musical genre 'singing God' has rearranged the socialised interactions with the non-human being 'Our-Father/God', by defining its specific position within the set of Suruí musical genres, which often refer to various kinds of others – enemies, affines, others' spouses, shamanic spirits, and so on. Evangelical singing has also created a space for newly arrived human others – the missionaries – among the various voices than can co-author sung discourses. However, in contrast with the ethnographical cases studied by Hill, from the north-western Amazon and Central Brazil, the natural dimension – animal or vegetal names – plays a lesser part in this process of musicalising the otherness of Christian beings, while its dynamic, historical, event-oriented aspect is more salient. Of course, this is linked both to the well-known cultural style of Tupi-speaking groups, in contrast to the Arawakan- and Gê-speaking populations, and to the novelty of the 'others' at stake. Nevertheless, this shows that the concept of musicalising the other should be extended to the question of dynamic otherness – that is, historical changes. Thus, musicalising the other is not only creating new sounds, melodies and metaphors but inserting the new others into the set of contrastive features that define a musical tradition.

Cédric Yvinec conducted ethnographical fieldwork among the Suruí of Rondônia (Brazilian Amazon) for twenty months between 2005 and 2015. He is now a researcher at the CNRS (Mondes Américains, Paris), after being a postdoctoral researcher at the Max Planck Institute for Psycholinguistics (Nijmegen) and at the Laboratoire d'Anthropologie Sociale (Paris), thanks to grants from the Fondation Fyssen (2012–13) and the Fondation Thiers (2013–16). He received his PhD in social anthropology from the EHESS (Paris) in 2011. His research deals with linguistic anthropology, ritual, cosmology and history.

Notes

1. I refer to the verbal arts of the Suruí that existed before they converted to Protestantism as 'traditional' for the sake of convenience of reference, because they form a system that had stabilised and had been passed down from generation to generation, when the Suruí lived in voluntary isolation. I do not mean that these verbal arts display any intrinsic feature that would distinguish them from any so-called 'modern' ones. In my view, the Protestant verbal arts are not in any way more 'modern' or less part of a 'tradition' than the Suruí ones; they were just introduced into the Suruí system of verbal arts more recently.
2. The Fundação Nacional do Índio (FUNAI) is the Brazilian federal government agency responsible for protecting indigenous populations.
3. There are heretics among the Suruí, since a few villages, because of political rivalry, left the 'Suruí Church' to follow other Protestant churches (Adventist, Assembly of God, and various local Pentecostal churches). However, those that I observed – Adventist – still used the SIL material (translated Bible, hymnal) that they had received before they dissented, and their verbal practices were still similar.

4. Some Suruí preachers acquire a good knowledge of biblical narratives and can argue sophisticatedly about theological matters.
5. The opening of perlocutionary effectiveness – here, therapeutic efficacy – to anybody by prayer causes a problem: indeed, experience will soon contradict such a claim. Perhaps the characteristics of preaching somehow meet the disequilibrium caused by the 'democratization' of alleged verbal efficacy in Protestant prayer. In fact, preachers claim a kind of perlocutionary power too, but restrict it to a difficult technique that requires specialised training.
6. Among the profane subgenres, there is *akersonmabewá*, 'song of dream'. Songs of this subgenre allude to auspicious dreams in a very opaque way. They are mainly composed by young singers.
7. The survival of this traditional structure in non-written evangelical songs can be compared to the structure of written evangelical songs obviously based on translation. Indeed, such a parallelistic structure tends to disappear in many of the latter: either the song is purely repetitive, or it is purely narrative with no lexical or semantic recurring features. The repetitive songs are sung at church only, in a very ritualised way, to open or close the service. The narrative ones are never sung.
8. Complex authorship is frequent in Amazonian verbal arts, especially in shamanic songs, which led Cesarino (2011) to prefer the concept of translator, instead of author, to describe the relationship between Marubo shamans and their songs.

References

Austin, J. 1962. *How to Do Things with Words*. Oxford: Oxford University Press.
Bonilla, O. 2009. 'The Skin of History: Paumari Perspectives on Conversion and Transformation', in A. Vilaça and R. Wright (eds), *Native Christians: Modes and Effects of Christianity among Indigenous Peoples of the Americas*. Farnham: Ashgate, pp. 127–45.
Capiberibe, A. 2007. *Batismo de Fogo: os Palikur e o Cristianismo*. São Paulo: Annablume.
Cesarino, P. 2011. *Oniska: Poética do Xamanismo na Amazônia*. São Paulo: Perspectiva / FAPESP.
Grotti, V. 2009. 'Protestant Evangelism and the Transformability of Amerindian Bodies in Northeastern Amazonia', in A. Vilaça and R. Wright (eds), *Native Christians: Modes and Effects of Christianity among Indigenous Peoples of the Americas*. Farnham: Ashgate, pp. 109–25.
Severi, C. 2004. 'Capturing Imagination: A Cognitive Approach to Cultural Complexity', *Journal of the Royal Anthropological Institute* 10(4): 815–38.

Vilaça, A. 1997. 'Christians Without Faith: Some Aspects of the Conversion of the Wari' (Pakaa Nova)', *Ethnos* 62(1–2): 91–115.

———. 2009. 'Conversion, Predation and Perspective', in A. Vilaça and R. Wright (eds), *Native Christians: Modes and Effects of Christianity among Indigenous Peoples of the Americas*. Farnham: Ashgate, pp. 147–66.

Yvinec, C. 2011. 'Les monuments lyriques des Suruí du Rondônia: chants, événements et savoirs'. PhD dissertation. Paris: EHESS.

———. 2012. 'Arousing and Mastering Feelings of Alien Inspiration in One's Own Speech: Pragmatics of the Shamanic Songs of the Suruí of Rondônia', *Anthropological Linguistics* 54(4): 371–401.

11

Prosperity and the Flow of Vital Substances

Relating to Earth Beings in Processes of Mobility in the Southern Peruvian Andes

Cecilie Vindal Ødegaard

The ways in which people in the rural Andes communicate with the earth beings through ritual and reciprocal means have been widely documented. Less attention has been paid, however, to the significance of these practices in processes of mobility. In this chapter, I explore how Quechua- and Aymara-speaking people moving to the city relate to the powerful entities of the landscape, and how these relations are reproduced or changed. Examining mobility beyond the usual tropes of de/reterritorialisation, I illustrate the significance of people's relations with earth beings when they resettle in new surroundings, more specifically in the city of Arequipa, Peru. In particular, I focus on ritual offerings related to the creation and maintenance of well-being and prosperity, and how the powerful surroundings are drawn upon also in an urban context to attract money and business. In doing so, I explore the ontological underpinnings of human relations with entities of the landscape[1] in order to analyse the significance of these relations across rural–urban differences, and discuss why movement may in itself require offerings. In my exploration of these issues, I embark upon some comparative discussions by drawing upon Amazonian ethnographies too.

Earth Beings and the Question of Animism

In Andean communities, human relationships with entities of the landscape – like the powerful surroundings of earth and mountains – involve ritual activities concerned with maintaining the health and fertility of humans and earth beings alike. This way of relating to the animated landscape in rural areas is connected to agricultural and pastoral activities and cycles, and realised through offerings to *pachamama* (earth spirits)[2] and the *apus* (mountain spirits).[3] In order to secure their goodwill and thus the fertility of the fields and flocks, these powerful beings are paid through the offering of food, alcohol, coca, llama fosters, herbs, and so on. Such offerings demonstrate the understanding of earth beings as persons, in the sense that they, like humans, have needs and feelings, and may become hungry, angry or revengeful. If their needs and desires are not responded to – that is, if people do not share with them – they will withdraw their goodwill and possibly do harm. These ways of mediating the relations to earth beings contrast with the Amazonian relations with spirits, which are not mediated through offerings. Further, Andean relations with earth beings cannot be considered egalitarian, as are relations to non-human beings among hunters and gatherers in Amazonia, Siberia and other places. Rather, the relations with earth beings in the Andes are more of a hierarchical kind, as are the relations *between* different *apus*, as they are positioned in hierarchical relations to each other, depending on their size and powers (Urton 1981: 48–53; Sallnow 1987: 129). The power of *apus* is also specific to a certain place and region, in the sense that the powers of an *apu* may be limited to a certain area, although the more powerful ones can have a wide geographical reach (Lund Skar 1994). People generally make offerings to the most powerful *apu* in their local surroundings. In contrast, *pachamama* encompasses a generalised idea of the powerful earth or ground, implying that its powers are not necessarily space-specific but may be at work anywhere. By securing the well-being of these entities of the landscape, humans not only prevent the illness and misfortune that these beings may cause, but likewise maintain their own health and prosperity by contributing to maintaining and nurturing the earth beings as important sources of fertility and prosperity.

According to Allen, the ritual practices and offerings in Andean communities involve an idea that all beings are intrinsically interconnected, and that 'all beings share a matrix of animated substance' (Allen 1998: 21). According to this perspective, it is impossible to separate spiritual beings from their physical manifestations or places, as in the Euro-American dichotomisation between body and soul, nature and culture. In the Andes, all matter is in a sense alive, and all life has a material base (Allen 1998). As the anthropological critique of the Cartesian dualism has intensified during the last two decades, the interest in animism has been revitalised. Problematising the long-standing impact of Tylor's (1871) work on animism, developed within a modernist spiritualist/materialist dichotomy and implying a notion that 'animists' understand the world childishly and erroneously, Bird-David (1999) has suggested replacing the term with 'relational epistemology'. Relational epistemology is about 'knowing the world by focusing primarily on relatedness, from a related point of view, within the shifting horizons of the related viewer. The knowing grows from and *is* the knower's skills of maintaining relatedness with the known' (ibid.: 69). Viveiros de Castro (1992, 1999) criticises this concern with animism in terms of epistemology, arguing that such practices should not primarily be understood in terms of knowledge. He thus problematises the ways in which anthropologists often try to explain non-Western ontologies by deriving them from (or reducing them to) epistemology. According to him, 'this massive conversion of ontological questions to epistemological ones is the hallmark of modernist philosophy' (1999: 79). Instead, he defines animism as an ontology 'concerned with being and not with how we come to know it'. In this perspective, animism postulates the social character of relations between humans and non-humans, where both are immersed in the same socio-cosmic medium (Viveiros de Castro 1998: 473). By suggesting this approach, Viveiros de Castro stresses the importance of 'taking the Indians seriously' (2004: 129), and seeks to avoid an understanding of animism simply as a projection of differences and qualities of the human world onto the non-human world (1998: 474). This involves an emphasis that non-human beings may not just have feelings, expectations and intentions, like humans do, but they may also have impact in the world in ways that may cause harm to humans. Similarly, in the Andean context, it is important to understand human relations with mountains and other earth beings as more than simply a 'cultural interpretation' of 'nature' (de la Cadena 2010: 365). People relate to these entities of the landscape as persons, and consider them to have a real-life impact on their life situations.

With the notion of 'perspectivism', Viveiros de Castro has proposed a way to understand the Amerindian ontologies of the Amazonian region, ontologies that involve a conception that the world is inhabited by different sorts of subjects or persons, human and non-human, who apprehend reality from distinct points of view (1992, 1998). Perspectivism involves an understanding of animistic practices that recognises how surroundings and animals may be considered as active agents with their own will and intention – and not simply being acted *upon* as in Euro-American thinking. This conception supposes 'a spiritual unity and a corporeal diversity', implying that animals are people, or see themselves as persons (Viveiros de Castro 1998: 470). By underlining this, Viveiros de Castro seeks to revert the dichotomy in Euro-American discourse between nature (as given) and culture (as variable) by suggesting the term 'multinaturalism'. The manifest form of each species is a mere envelope (a 'clothing') that conceals a shared internal human form, which is only visible to certain beings and shamans. This internal form is the 'soul' or 'spirit' of the animal: an intentionality or subjectivity identical to human consciousness (ibid.: 471). In this perspective, there is a spiritual commonality to all animate beings, both humans and animals, with a variable bodily appearance. Bodily appearances are thus not fixed attributes, but 'changeable and removable clothing' (ibid.). In this 'highly transformational world' (Rivière 1994: 256), spirits may shift clothing and take animal form, and humans may turn into animals. Viveiros de Castro suggests that the notion of the body as a 'clothing' is probably Pan-American (1998: 471).

While perspectivism has travelled far and wide in scholarly research, there may be several problems related to the use of this perspective both within and beyond the Amazonian region, as has been discussed by Ramos (2012), among others. She problematises the ethnographic homogeneity involved in a perspectivist approach, and how it is sometimes applied regardless of linguistic affiliation, and leaving out a large sociocultural residue (ibid.: 483). She notes that perspectivism involves an attribution of so much uniformity to native thinking that it flattens down (if not denies) people's inventiveness and aesthetic sophistication. In this manner, she argues that indigenous diversity is being reduced and oversimplified. 'The voice we hear is not indigenous, but an alien verbalisation ... a sort of hyperreal Indian ... that is much easier to absorb than the real native' (Ramos 2012: 490). While Viveiros de Castro points to important flaws in the term 'multiculturalism', Ramos notes that, by reverting to the dichotomy between nature and culture, he at the same time appears to reproduce the nature–culture dualism by proposing a view where nature is considered variable, and culture as given (ibid.: 486). Along similar lines, and as discussed in the introduction of this volume, Turner has noted that non-human entities' possession of subjectivity does not necessarily mean that an animal or plant identifies itself as human (Turner 2009: 17).

In Andean contexts it may not be accurate to say that there is one spiritual interiority taking on different clothing, as in the spiritual universality implied in Amazonian perspectivism. Rather, there are different spirits and beings, which all have different personalities and characteristic traits, such as *pachamama* and the *apus*. There are also the spirits of the *antepasados* (ancestors), *mal sitios* (bad places) and other spirits and beings that are, like humans, entangled through animate substance and the same vital force (Allen 1998: 21), and having the same desires and feelings as humans. They thus share certain commonalities with humans, and rely on the same vital substances. What I would like to suggest in this chapter is that the notion of an animate force or substance, vital to humans and earth beings alike, is in different ways made relevant in processes of mobility. In doing so, I argue that a focus on mobility may contribute to enhancing our understanding of human relations to earth beings, by exploring how these relations are actualised in and through movement. A focus on mobility may enable us to understand the historical and cultural continuities of people's relations and practices related to entities of the landscape, and their significance for questions of prosperity in different forms. My intention is therefore twofold. First, I discuss how a focus on the different forms of transformation and conversion related to earth beings may help us to account for the continued importance of earth beings in an urban context. Considering how all beings in the Andes can be seen to share a matrix of animated substance, I posit that earth beings are connected to powers and prosperity also in their urban forms. Second, I show how a focus on mobility and migration can provide insight into the ways in which interactions with earth beings are subject to variation and negotiation in everyday life. In this regard, I explore human relations with earth beings as part of ontological dynamics (Remme 2016), where boundaries and flows of powerful substances are mediated through offerings, but in ways that are subject to change and negotiation too. It might illustrate Willerslev's (2013) point that although we should take animism seriously, it might be wise not to take it too seriously, as illustrated by the Siberian Yukaghirs' ridiculing of the spirits, which is integral to the game of hunting.

In her study of mobility in the Andes, Lund Skar (1994) has noted that while wealth in rural areas is characterised by the connectedness to the surroundings and land, wealth in urban contexts is no longer synonymous with the total state of interpersonal human–landscape relations that create prosperity in agriculture. According to her, this is because migrants in the city engage in new forms of work that generate wealth on different terms. Divorced from the land and the context of the ancestors, Lund Skar argues that wealth becomes associated with a notion of luck, more in keeping with Euro-American ideas of fate. One of my concerns in this chapter is to demonstrate that there are significant continuities in human relations with earth beings when people move to the cities, and that ritual and relational understandings of wealth and prosperity continue to carry importance. Ritual relations and offerings to earth beings are considered an important source of prosperity in the urban context also, and are seen to influence people's prosperity in its urban forms. In this regard, Harris (2000) has made an important point concerning notions of prosperity in the Andes, by stressing that agricultural fertility and money are not necessarily opposed, since money comes from the same sources that ensure the harvest and reproduction of flocks. This is an issue to which I shall return.

While studies of mobility in Andean contexts abound, few of them have explored the significance of people's relations with earth beings in processes of mobility (see Ødegaard 2011 for an exception). In the Amazonian context, studies have paid relatively little attention to the question of mobility due to the widespread assumption that its indigenous peoples are spatially static. One exception is an edited volume by Alexiades (2009), demonstrating how mobility and dislocations in Amazonia have been more common than is generally assumed. Rather than entailing simply knowledge loss or acculturation, authors in this volume show how mobility may instead entail processes of appropriation, experimentation and innovation when it comes to environmental knowledge, practices, ideologies and identities. The volume does not primarily deal with questions of animism or cosmology, except for one chapter (Feather 2013) showing how travel among the Nahua is closely associated with establishing or severing relationships to the land – and to living and dead people. The study shows how a focus on mobility may provide new understanding of indigenous identities and of different ways of inhabiting and relating to space in processes of mobility.

My chapter is based upon several periods of fieldwork in a migrant neighbourhood called Jerusalén in Southern Peru, in the city of Arequipa in 1997, 2001, 2003, 2007, 2011 and 2016. A group of migrants occupied this previously desolate location on the slopes of the Misti volcano in the 1960s. The inhabitants in Jerusalén have migrated from different parts of the departments of Cuzco and Puno, but as well from Apurímac, Ayacucho and rural parts of the Arequipa department. Most speak Quechua as their mother tongue, while a few speak Aymara. Several inhabitants in Jerusalén were barely in their teens when they left their villages, often to look for a

Illustration 11.1 Powerful landscapes in an urban context. Arequipa, 2016. Photograph: C. Ødegaard.

job or because they had relatives already living in the city. Kinship is therefore significant for the process of moving to and settling in the city. In addition to kin, settlement composition tends to be defined also by the different departments, districts or villages of origin of the inhabitants (see Altamirano 1988; Lund Skar 1994). In the following section, I explore how migrants to Arequipa relate to earth beings in processes of mobility, and connect this to questions of prosperity in different forms.

The City and the Powerful Surroundings

When I spoke with my interlocutors in Jerusalén about the reasons why they had moved to Arequipa, many said it was in order to *progresar*, or to *buscar modernidad* (look for modernity), and to acquire paid labour, money, goods, or the standard of living and knowledge they associated with the 'urban'. The quest for an urban or modern way of life was thus central for many, while this quest came to expression also in the continued significance of ritual relationships and offerings in an urban context. In Jerusalén, many of my contacts have continued to communicate with and bring offerings to the animated landscape – that is, to the *apus* of Arequipa and particularly to the Misti volcano, as well as to *pachamama* – so that the powerful surroundings will be benign and not harmful. During the construction of new houses, for instance, it is common to make offerings as a way to ask for the goodwill of the powerful surroundings, and to bring prosperity and luck to the house and the people living there. The *ch'alla* (offering) in these cases consists of alcohol that is thrown on the ground or sprinkled towards the mountains. The pattern that the liquid makes on the ground gives an indication of whether the offer has been accepted. If the liquid creates a long-stretched and symmetrical pattern, it is said that the offer has been well received and that the earth beings will provide money and prosperity in return. House construction work in these cases commonly takes place through reciprocal labour, by the organisation of work parties involving neighbours and kin. For the arrangement of the *techamiento* (roofing), the house owners also appoint *padrinos* (godparents) for their new house. Workers are invited to eat and drink, and everyone participates in making offerings. Offerings are made on a daily basis too, by the use of coca leaves. Although the use of coca is often frowned upon in urban contexts (Allen 1988; Ødegaard 2010), it is not uncommon for people to bring coca to their workplace, where the coca chewing is initiated by an offering. For instance, at the market places of Arequipa, traders often invite each other to chew coca during breaks. First they make an offering by finding three nice and complete leaves that are gathered in the hand and blown upon. They may then say a few words of appraisal to *pachamama* and the *apus*, mentioning who or what they want them to protect or benefit, and rolling some earth or ash inside the leaves. After breaking the leaves into little pieces, the offering is thrown in three different directions. Similarly, on festive occasions, when making or greeting *compadres* (ritual co-parents), welcoming someone, or saying farewell before a journey, payments are performed through the offerings of coca leaves or drinks. More grand-scale offerings, for instance of an animal, are generally performed once or twice a year, often by hiring a *curandero* (healer). Through these offerings, people seek the goodwill of the powerful surroundings and their positive influence in securing the health and well-being of household members, their ability to work and possibilities to prosper.

While most of the cities that receive migrants from the highlands are located along the coast (such as Lima, Ica, Tacna, Chimbote and Chiclayo), Arequipa lies at about 2,500 meters above sea level and is surrounded by mountains and volcanoes. It is worth noting that the change of environment may therefore not be experienced as abrupt for those who move to Arequipa compared to other cities. My interlocutors in Arequipa sometimes spoke about the Misti as more powerful than the mountains of their places of origin, and due to its physical proximity it became clear that they considered themselves primarily under the influence of Misti. Many continued to appeal similarly to the powers of the mountains at their birth village, especially when making visits there. For instance, when Angelina[4] and I went to visit her mother in Arapa, close to the highland town of Asangoro, one of the first things she did on arrival was to take out the bread that she had brought from Arequipa and present it to the *apus* while saying the names of the mountains surrounding us, in addition to Misti. On such journeys it is indeed considered important to bring something from the city to share upon arrival, as it is also important to bring a product from your birth place when returning back to the city. While making the offering, Angelina asked the *apus* for everything to go well on our journey and for her business to prosper. Then she gave the remaining bread to her mother, nieces and nephews, and myself. In the city, and when at work in the market, Angelina similarly pays the *apus* in Arequipa in order to secure success in her business and to prevent theft. These offerings are thus not intended to increase the fertility of agricultural land as such, but rather to stimulate other forms of prosperity, well-being and luck, or what could be conceptualised as prosperity on wider terms (Harris 2000). In Jerusalén, offerings are made in order to appeal for goodwill, for example in work, trade, educational matters, or in life as such. While payments to the *apus* are performed with appeals for economic success or progress in the urban context, payments to *pachamama* are made to seek well-being more generally, such as to prevent illness and secure the family and household.

As already mentioned, Harris (2000) has argued that the performance of ritual payments in the rural Andes is informed by general notions of fertility associated not only with production and reproduction, but is seen as created and maintained through a logic of reciprocity, circulation and exchange as well. In this manner, *pachamama* and the mountains are considered guardians not only of the fertility of fields and stock – as well as the mines – but also, as in my study, of the fertility of business and money (see Harvey 2001). My argument in this regard is that while the forms and intentions of the payments may vary, they are based on the same ontological underpinnings of exchange as necessary to maintain fertility – that is, the fertility of agriculture and domestic animals as well as prosperity in its urban forms, including money. Different forms of prosperity are thus seen to depend upon the fertilising mechanisms involved in exchange and circulation; but, as I return to later, the powers of earth beings can as well be harmful. *Pachamama* may get hungry if people fail to make offerings, and such failure may result in her attacking people (*quiere agarrar*), for example by making them fall. In order to avoid illness in cases when experiencing a fall, some people therefore make an offering or simply urinate on the spot, thus providing *pachamama* with vital substances. In similar ways, the *apus* require offerings to prevent them from causing accidents, illness and even death.

Compared to Amazonian ethnographies, the issue of transformation and metamorphosis has received less attention in ethnographies from the Andes, although similar transformations and conversions can be important here too. The powerful mountain spirits may for instance manifest themselves in different bodies, such as large birds, or humans. When an *apu* appears in human form, it is often as a blond man, although they may appear as women or children with either black or white skin (Gose 1994: 212; Stensrud 2011). The mountain spirits are additionally associated with and manifested in devil figures – as illustrated in the offerings made to figures shaped after images of the devil – and they may similarly be manifested in the figures of Catholic saints (Nash 1979; Harris 2000). Earth beings may thus manifest in different shapes, and their inherent powers can be realised in different kinds of prosperity, including money and modern goods. As I have explored elsewhere (Ødegaard 2016), the widely debated *kharisiris* in the Andes, who steal blood or fat from unsuspecting humans, are known to change forms too. While most often appearing as a blond, blue-eyed man, *kharisiris* may also take the form of a dog or a snake. In addition, *kharisiris* have the capacity to convert – through illicit exchange – human blood or fat into prosperity and money (see e.g. Canessa 2000; Weismantel 2001). Several of my contacts in Arequipa have become seriously ill after experiencing *kharisiri* attacks; among them my friend Juan. One night he opened the door to his house upon hearing a knock, and there was a dog outside; two weeks later he fell ill, and was left unable to work. This dog was apparently a *kharisiri* who had converted himself. The capacity for such transformations not only enables the *kharisiris* to attack people without them noticing, but is likewise considered to help them to escape law and justice. This point is illustrated by my contact Norma's account of a *kharisisi* attack in her home village Zepita close to the border with Bolivia, where a young man was killed by a *kharisiri* a few years back. In the aftermath of the killing, inhabitants in Zepita organised a demonstration to demand justice, so that the *kharisiri* would not go unpunished. The local police finally managed to arrest a man they suspected was responsible for the killing, but when a police officer came to his cell the following day, the man had turned into a wolf. The next day, when a police officer again came to check on the prisoner, the man had turned into a snake. When a police officer came in on the third day, the man stood there as a person, but with his body covered in dollars. Instead of taking the man to justice, the police officer – and apparently the tax agents too – removed all the dollars from the man's body and let him go. The *kharisiris'* theft and disruption of the flow of vital substances may depend on this ability to convert – for example, into an animal in order to escape justice, or into a person who can bribe the authorities.

The prosperous powers of the surroundings may also take animal form, and be manifested in different entities and beings. A few people in Jerusalén reported having seen mules carrying cargo at night, accompanied by the sound of bells. Such mules are said to be loaded with riches which can be obtained if you make an offering. On one such occasion, after seeing a mule from afar, on the very outskirts of Arequipa, my *compadre* Pedro regretted not immediately making an offering, on the spot. It might have made him rich, he said, but he was too frightened to react. In such encounters with prosperous entities or beings, wealth may sometimes 'chance' upon people. As I return to below, the outcome of such encounters depends on whether you make an offering there and then; you must react quickly and with a certain determination, without being distracted by fear or doubt, or the riches will be lost on you and you may fall ill. To have certain knowledge about how these powers work, and how you should respond to them, is therefore important, especially when you resettle or work in new places, as is illustrated below. However, people sometimes said that while most people previously knew how to handle these powerful entities, many now fall ill since the knowledge is gradually disappearing.

Upon returning one day from his job on a construction project, Angelina's husband Juan was feeling very ill. From that day, for several months, he was unable to work due to bad headaches and dizziness. Although I was living in their house at the time, they did not explain to me what had happened until a couple of weeks had gone by. Juan had chanced upon a prosperous, but also potentially dangerous, entity while he was digging the ground that day. He had suddenly touched upon a ceramic object hidden underground, considered as originating from 'el tiempo de los Incas' (the time of the Incas) or *los antepasados*, and thus of ancient origin and containing ancestral powers. As Juan in this case fell ill almost immediately, he was not able to take a second look at the ceramics, but had had to leave it for the other workers to explore. In retrospect, Angelina emphasised that Juan became ill because he had come too close to a bad place, a badness that was related to the ceramic object. They confirmed this suspicion shortly afterwards when they consulted the coca leaves. Angelina was certain that Juan had actually hit an ancient grave with his stick and that the ceramic object had contained gold meant for him. However, as Juan had not been saying his prayers, been chewing coca or making an offering as she always reminded him he should, the wealth and power had made him ill instead and was lost to him. If only Juan had protected himself when at work in such an unfamiliar place, he would probably have gained possession of the gold instead of falling ill. The ceramics in this case were considered to have a direction or intention of their own (e.g. ancient wealth meant for Juan), something that Juan had failed to respond to. It was not simply that Juan could have taken possession of the wealth if he had made an offering, but that the wealth was *meant* for him. This understanding of the intentionality and agency of the ceramics indicates how non-human entities or beings are not regarded simply as the object of human manipulation, but as having the power – and even the intention – to bring prosperity or, alternatively, to do harm. Through the payment of gifts or food, people may influence this capacity to bring prosperity – and thus avoid harm. It indicates how prosperity – as well as harm – is understood in relational terms, and resonates with Bird-David's (1999) emphasis on relatedness. The outcome of these relations and encounters is defined by whether you manage to mediate through offerings or not.

Prosperity, Desire, Danger

The classical anthropological concern with the *culture* of social relations of production (Polanyi 1957; Sahlins 1972) includes a concern with the existence of different cultural understandings of how wealth and well-being is constituted and maintained (see Harris 2000, and more recently Mintchev and Moore 2016). In light of the Andean emphasis on prosperity, it is interesting to note Gow and Margiotti's (2012) argument that there seems to be a lack of interest among Amazonian people in notions of prosperity or fortune. Among the Kuna people in Panama, for instance, as among the Piro of Bajo Urubamba, it is not common to seek good luck through rituals that aim to control or summon fate and destiny. They further argue that Amazonian languages rarely possess fortune terms, and that metaphors concerning the division, apportion and allotment of luck receive no particular cosmological elaborations. Nor are there any superior principles or divinities specifically involved in endowing humans with luck or fortune (ibid.: 43). In contrast, their Andean neighbours attach notions of prosperity not only to the powerful surroundings as discussed above, but also to domestic animals, as illustrated in Rivera Andía's study (2003, 2005) of livestock branding rituals in villages near Lima. Among the Kuna and Piro, Gow and Margiotti relate the absence of fortune terms to how their subsistence strategies are based primarily on vegetable staples from beyond the cultivated domestic zone. Other studies (Santos-Granero 2015) have aimed at showing the existence of indigenous views of wealth in the Amazonia too. In Santos-Granero's volume, it is argued that notions of wealth in Amazonian societies are closely linked to the maintenance of good health, convivial relations, and the creation of strong, productive and moral individuals and collectivities. This differs significantly from capitalist societies, which are more inclined towards the individualist accumulation and consumption of material goods. While it is beyond the scope of this chapter to go further into such regional similarities and differences regarding notions of wealth and prosperity, it is important to note that we must not reduce these variations to a question of ecological determinism (Descola 2011). This point brings us back to the issue of studying human relations with entities of the landscape within a framework of mobility.

Despite their similarities, the *apus* in the city and those in the highlands may differ and require different payments. The *curandero* Manuel came to Juan's house one day to perform a cure, of which an expansive offering represented a central part. While Manuel was preparing the guinea pig that he would use in the cure, he explained that the *apus* in the highlands are generally paid in a much simpler and less expensive manner than the *apus* in the city. In the highlands, the liquid offered to the *apus* generally consists of some anise spirits, chicha⁵ or the like. *Apus* in the city, however – like Misti, Pichupichu or Chachani – prefer expensive drinks such as whisky or beer; that is, goods that are mainly consumed by people in the city, or people with money. Manuel explained that the *apus* in the city thus have different desires compared to those in the highlands, and he drew a parallel with how the desires of people can also differ or change, for instance when migrating. These ways in which earth beings share the desires and preferences of humans differ from Viveiros de Castro's description of how animals and spirits *see* their food as human food, in the sense that jaguars see blood as their manioc beer (1998: 470). The Andean *apus* rather seem to have the same food preferences as humans (beer, coca, meat) – that is, as long as humans treat them with respect, and share with them through offerings. If not, the *apus* may see humans as their food (prey), and there are various accounts of how people get ill, have accidents or die if they fail to make an offering. In this manner, the character and outcome of these encounters depend on whether you make an offering or not, as the earth being may either be benign or cause you harm. With perspectivism we could say that the *apus* respond with aggression if they are not recognised for their commonalities with humans through sharing (although these commonalities relate to their common reliance on the same vital substances, and not necessarily on a common spiritual interiority, as in Amazonian perspectivism). The *apus* can be seen as dividual persons (Strathern 1988), being constituted in and of social relationships that are mediated through vital substances in the form of offerings. Human relations with these entities of the landscape are based upon a notion of sharing, and the failure to do so may transform the relationship from one of sharing to one of predator and prey. Humans are therefore potential prey to a spectrum of powerful beings, due to their common reliance on vital substances.

The notion of sharing creates the backdrop for the ways in which the objects used in ritual payments may be subject to change when people move to the city, as illustrated above. These changes can be related to the way in which the highlands and the city are locations for different sorts of prosperity,[6] where the city is associated with the access to money and modern goods, differing from the forms of prosperity associated with the highlands (e.g. the fields and flocks, and their produce). Prosperity in its different forms is considered as a rather unstable entity though. As one of my interlocutors formulated it, prosperity may benefit you one day and leave you for someone else the next day. And, while prosperity may be promoted by the performance of ritual offerings, the flows of vital substances, on which prosperity depends, can also be interrupted by the powers of *curanderos* and *brujos* (healers who speak with the devil). They know how to influence or redirect these flows. If someone has bad luck in business, it is said that 'la plata no para en sus manos' (money won't stop in their hands), a condition that may be caused by the harmful acts of *brujos*. The flow of powerful substances may be disrupted by the actions of *kharisiris* too (see Canessa 2000), who are known to steal body substance (both human and animal) to exchange it with money from the devil, or from the *apus*.[7] In the following section, I illustrate how movement may in itself require offerings, and then I go on to discuss how such payments are also subject to negotiation in everyday life.

Movement

Since the powerful surroundings are seen as located and manifested in different local and regional landscapes, movement from one place to another may disturb the communication between people and surroundings and put the person who moves in danger. People who move across distances therefore need to protect themselves, for instance by making offerings or bringing stones, earth or food from the place left behind (Allen 1988; Lund Skar 1994; Harvey 2001). According to a woman called Olinda, movement can be dangerous because the earth of a new place does not yet 'know you' (*conocerte*), a situation that can threaten one's health and general well-being. In order to make the earth beings at a new place 'know you', one can bring a piece of earth or a stone in a bag or pocket, or otherwise make some kind of offering. By bringing such objects from the place left behind to a new place, the powers from the place left behind are seen to work protectively against the dangers found in new surroundings. This is not just an attempt to relate to and communicate with the earth beings at a new place, but also to anticipate or influence how they will perceive you and your arrival. It indicates how the question of 'knowing' here is a question of relating, through the interchange or flow of substances, and illustrates the material basis of 'knowing' in these encounters. It is a widespread opinion that the success of an offering or a gift will depend on the extent to which you have knowledge of the recipient's preferences. These examples indicate how people see themselves as related to and affected by the powerful surroundings, and how, when they move, they seek to mediate between the powers of a place of origin and the powers at a new place of arrival. These ways of maintaining or creating a relationship with the surroundings is therefore significant for a person who moves. Before one of my own journeys, I was even advised to put my clothes on backwards in order to avoid disorientation, dizziness and travel sickness. One way to understand such advice is that the person travelling with the clothes the other way around can confuse the powers that are activated during a journey and prevent them from reacting to the traveller's intrusiveness by, for example, causing sickness. In this and other ways, humans may try to anticipate – and manipulate – how they will be perceived by the earth beings when travelling to a new place.

Central to the exchanges of vital substance with entities of the landscape is the notion that all persons are considered to have an *ánimo*, a term that shares connotations with soul, agency, will and intention (Gose 1994). The experience of shock or fear (*susto*) may cause the *ánimo* to leave the body and stay behind at another place. My interlocutor Olinda for a time thought that she might have lost her *ánimo*, since she was feeling unwell and kept dreaming of her village of origin. In order to be cured, she was advised to go back to her birth village, and once there, she should encourage her *ánimo* to return by calling her own name and waving with her hat (or clothes). Place-specific powers may thus affect the state of the *ánimo*, and illness or well-being may be affected by movement in space. To go back to a place where the *ánimo* was lost is seen as an act of curing, by reuniting an animated dimension that has been separated from its source (Lund Skar 1994: 231). The use of clothing is furthermore interesting in the sense that it might help the *ánimo* to recognise its source, or where it should return to.

These ways of dealing with movement, and the relationship between people and place, was also a central theme in the myths of the Incas, who saw their ancestral origin as connected to Lake Titicaca, on the border between Peru and Bolivia (Dover, Seibold and McDowell 1992: 9). In one of these myths, it is said that the first Incas, Manco Capac and his brothers and sisters, were created at Lake Titicaca, from where they travelled through subterranean channels to Cuzco (de Molina 1943: 11–12). Since this primordial time, the Titicaca origins of the Incas have been symbolically remembered by bringing water from Lake Titicaca to Cuzco for the ritual anointment of each new king. Such an anointment with Titicaca water might have served to legitimise the displacement of the Inca centre from its site of emergence to Cuzco (Sherbondy 1992). Additionally, when common people moved around, the re-foundation of an *ayllu* (descent group) at a new site was ritually accomplished by carrying water from the *ayllu*'s previous water source into a new territory, where it was poured into the springs of the new land (ibid.: 57). There are clear similarities between these precolonial practices and the current significance of bringing stones, earth or food when moving to a new place. These similarities indicate not only the long-standing continuities of these practices in the Andes, but also their significance specifically for mobility.

Variation, Negotiation, Labour

On the hillsides rising towards the Misti, several inhabitants in Jerusalén have made a living by collecting stones in informally established mines. As the land here is the property of the municipality but not officially in use, these mines represent an opportunity for anyone to come and work in them. People come to dig out stones that are used in the production of stone-washed jeans and collected in trucks that come once a week. Those who work like this have to protect themselves from the evil *duendes* – that is, small, bearded, human-like creatures that are said to live in these mines and sometimes cause the miners to have accidents or become ill. For the purposes of protection, people have to consume coca, cigarettes or spirits, as well as make offerings to the *duendes* and pray to God. Similarly, when making use of new land, people are advised to protect themselves against dangerous powers and entities of different kinds. The hillsides of Misti are considered especially dangerous, being the location of different kinds of bad places (*mal sitios*) influenced by the powerful volcano, as well as the ancestral Incas, which may all cause the sickness *mal viento* (bad wind). These are places associated with evil spirits, and sites where accidents have already happened and have thus intensified the sense of danger. It is said that people who have to pass through or accidentally come across such places ought to protect themselves by making offerings – and prayers to God.

While these accounts are common in the neighbourhood where I did fieldwork, there is at the same time a significant variety in the extent to which people continue to make offerings in the city. Some people say that the *apus*, *pachamama* and other powerful beings lose their powers in the urban context, and hence they choose to perform such payments only occasionally. According to the *curandero* Pablo, this is because people think there are too many buildings and people in the city for these powers to work. So while the influence of earth beings and spirits in the urban context can be significant, it is considered to be more so on the outskirts of inhabited areas, such as those close to mountains and volcanoes (the Misti, for instance).

Eduardo is another *curandero* who regularly makes offerings to the powerful earth beings and the Misti, and who knows how to cure people's illnesses. Together with some of his kin, he is involved in conducting a surveillance of the volcanic activities of Misti, in an attempt to assess the possibilities of future eruptions. In this manner, people who make offerings to earth beings, like the Misti, may treat Misti simply as a mountain, or make the mountain subject to scientific or economic ventures. Other people prefer not to involve themselves in ritual offerings at all, or they agree to take part only when socially obliged to. There are also people who deny the importance of the *apus* and *pachamama* by rationalising about a lack of proof and effect, or complaining about the high expenses involved in ritual payments. If the situation requires it, such as in the case of illness or social obligation, many would nonetheless seek a traditional healer or occasionally make an offering, but would not do this on an everyday basis. In the case described above when Juan got ill upon finding some ceramic objects, for instance, he had failed to make an offering when at work in a new place, either because he forgot to or he just did not care about it. For this reason, his wife was annoyed, arguing that it was his own fault that he fell ill instead of obtaining a possible fortune. In this and other situations, I found that people were often reluctant to talk about their involvement in ritual payments. Not only do these offerings require knowledge that is considered secret, but many migrants also actively seek to under-communicate this and other dimensions of their background from the highlands, due to the experience of being stigmatised or discriminated against. This stigma provides some of the background against which the significance of earth beings is continually negotiated in everyday life. Among those of my interlocutors who had taken a serious decision about converting to Evangelism, it was common for them to refuse involvement with ritual payments altogether. Interestingly, some converts explicitly explained their conversion with reference to the high expenses involved in offerings to the earth beings.

People's involvement in these ritual payments may vary with the kind of work they are engaged in, indicating an interconnectedness between ritual activity and labour as has been discussed by several Andeanist scholars (Gose 1994; Harris 2000; Harvey 2001). In Arequipa traders, in particular, tend to be concerned with making ritual payments and thus maintain relations with the sources of prosperity to secure their business (Ødegaard 2010, 2011). Pointing out the significance of a connection between ritual activity and labour is not the same as reducing ritual activity to pragmatics, but to underline the ways in which different kinds of work may involve different ways of relating both to humans and earth beings.

While movement may expose people to danger, movement and circulation are also important cultural values, being considered as necessary conditions for the generation of prosperity, as I have already indicated (see Harris 2000). This is precisely the traders' concern: to earn money and promote prosperity by bringing, circulating and selling goods. Success in a trader's business depends on relationships of trust and cooperation, and there is an intense cultivation of social relations among traders, through sharing and giving, and the establishment of godparenthood relationships. Many traders perform ritual payments as a way to maintain good relations with the sources of health and prosperity; they depend on mutual relationships and exchange with humans as well as earth beings for their businesses to prosper. Their payments to the entities of the landscape are meant to reproduce the sources of prosperity and improve success in business, and grand-scale traders have a particular responsibility for serving as sponsors for festivals or parties. Due to the very nature of their work, traders make sure that things circulate and that money changes hands, and are thus thought to perform a valuable social service by making money 'give birth' (Harris 2000: 61). As illustrated by Harris, there is even an understanding that money itself can grow and give birth, in the sense that money is made fertile through circulation and exchange. In Jerusalén, money is involved in offerings as well as in rituals of transition, like in the hair-cutting ritual (corte-del-pelo) where a child's hair is exchanged for money (Ødegaard 2010). Some traders also make offerings to money in order to make the money grow and be fertile; similar to the practices described by Taussig (1980) of how money is brought to the priest to be baptised. These offerings take place as some money is placed within a white cloth, so that it is completely covered, and wine or beer is poured onto each corner of the cloth. In order for this money to be fertile, it must not be spent until fourteen days have passed. In Jerusalén, I myself never witnessed how this offering to money is performed, but I was told that it is a *secreto* (secret) that not everyone knows. My *compadre* Victor learned it from one of the traders at the market. When he was younger and feeling sorry that his mother did not have her own proper house as she had always wanted, he started to perform payments to money in order to make the money grow. He did so hoping that he could help his mother with money to construct a house made of cement, and then painted.

According to Harris, money is associated with agricultural fertility as well as the nation state, and prosperity can be seen as having different sources – one ancient, underground, and the other less ancient, that is, today's money (Harris 2000: 73). Among people who move to the cities, the notion of different, coexisting sources of power and prosperity can be illustrated by the meanings people attribute to progress. On the one hand, inhabitants in Jerusalén associate notions of prosperity and progress with the modern goods and ways of living found in cities, and on the other hand they see prosperity as dependent on and influenced by the powers of the past and earth beings. Different forms and sources of power and prosperity are thus seen to coexist in the urban landscape, and in people's quest for progress they appeal to earth beings as important sources of prosperity. Money, in this manner, can be seen to *be* different things. It can be what you earn as a wage, or it can be the riches that circulate from the source of *apus*. This understanding of money and prosperity indicates the importance of understanding processes of change, not only or primarily in terms of a response to external influences and power structures, but, as emphasised in the Introduction of this volume, how changes in Amerindian cultures must be explained also in terms of indigenous patterns.

Conclusions

This chapter has explored how human relations with the powerful earth beings are reproduced as people move to the city. My intention has been twofold. First, and having in mind how all beings in the Andes are seen to share a matrix of animated substance (Allen 1998: 21), my focus on migration has served to illustrate how the significance of earth beings is not simply a projection of social attributes to 'nature'. Rather, human relations with earth beings in processes of mobility can be seen as a question of relating. Humans and earth beings share the same matrix of animated substance, and depend on the same vital substances, where relations must be mediated through gifts and offerings. I have argued that a focus on these forms of mediation, and different forms of transformation and conversion, may help us to account for the continued importance of earth beings in an urban context. *Apus* can be manifested in different forms, and their powers may be realised in the form of different kinds of prosperity, including money, and the chapter has illustrated how humans try to anticipate the reactions of earth beings, for example in processes of movement. Second, I have explored human relations with earth beings as ontological dynamics, where boundaries and flows of powerful substances are mediated through offerings, but in ways that are subject to significant variation and negotiation in everyday life. People's offerings to the earth beings do not exclude the fact that they may also view these practices at a critical distance, and estimate their cost and expense in relation to other priorities and concerns. It indicates how animistic practices do not necessarily enjoy an authoritative status as *the* way to deal with and relate to non-human beings, as similarly noted by Bird-David (1999), since these practices are as well subject to negotiation and change. It is nonetheless striking to see how these practices are being reproduced over time and across space.

Differing from the dominant, capitalist notion of prosperity as individualist accumulation and consumption of material goods, there is a widespread notion in rural Andean communities that well-being and prosperity depend on gifts and offerings, and the flow of substances between humans and earth beings. This notion continues to hold significance among those who migrate, as they see prosperity in the urban context as still being dependent on social and ritual relationships. Ritual gifts, relationships and offerings are understood to influence people's well-being in the city too, and so urban prosperity depends on maintaining these relations. Among traders, for instance, it is considered important to provide gifts and offerings to maintain the fertilising mechanisms of exchange and circulation, and thus secure a successful business.

By focusing on the mediation of human relations with earth beings through offerings, I have illustrated how earth beings share the food preferences of humans, and that, like humans, the *apus* in the city may have different desires to those in the highlands. This sharing of food preferences does seem to depend, though, on the extent to which humans share with earth beings through offerings. If not, the *apus* may see humans as their food (prey). Central to my argument is therefore that offerings to the landscape entail a notion that earth beings share certain commonalities with humans; related to their common reliance on vital substances, although not necessarily sharing a common spiritual interiority, as in Amazonian perspectivism. In this manner, the character and outcome of encounters with earth beings will depend on whether you make an offering or not. An important point to draw from this is that a failure to share transforms the relationship from one of sharing to one of predator and prey. This potentiality reveals the transformative capacities of relations of reciprocity and sharing, in that a failure to give involves not just an absence or lack, but an active denial that may turn the commonalities and interdependence between humans and earth beings into a relationship of predation.

Acknowledgements

My thanks to the people in Peru who agreed to participate in this research and generously shared with me their everyday lives, experiences and points of view. I would also like to thank Juan Javier Rivera Andía for his efforts to realise this book project, and for his constructive comments and suggestions on this chapter. In addition, I am grateful for the inspiring suggestions and constructive criticisms of the reviewers.

Cecilie Vindal Ødegaard is associate professor in the Department of Social Anthropology University of Bergen. She has a doctoral degree in social anthropology, and is author of the monograph *Mobility, Markets and Indigenous Socialities: Contemporary Migration in the Peruvian Andes* (Ashgate, 2010). Based on several periods of fieldwork in Peru since 1997, her work has been published in *Journal of the Royal Anthropological Institute*, *Ethnos*, *Journal of Development Studies*, *Journal of Ethnobiology and Ethnomedicine*, and *Journal of Borderlands Studies* among other journals. Her research interests include questions of indigeneity, gender, animism; mobility and urbanization; territoriality, state, extractivism, work and informality.

Notes

1. While earth beings in the Andes (like animals in the Amazonian region) are often categorised in the literature as 'non-human' beings, I will mainly refer to them as 'entities of the landscape', or earth beings. This is related to one of the points that I would like to make in this chapter, namely that the offerings to entities of the landscape entail a notion that earth beings share certain commonalities with humans, and rely on the same vital substances.
2. *Pachamama* is the feminine principle of fertility, life and growth, able to give or withhold the rains and the harvests (Lund Skar 1994: 173–74).
3. *Apus* are often seen as the incarnations of ancestors, and regarded as a masculine principle.
4. The names (and birth places) of my interlocutors have been altered for purposes of anonymity.
5. Chicha is beer made of corn, and is the most common form of alcohol consumed in many highland areas.
6. The fact that the Andean countryside is increasingly entangled with the domestic and global economy does not undermine this point.
7. *Kharisiris* are thus not only closely identified with *apus*, but are seen to make exchanges with the *apus*.

References

Alexiades, M.N. (ed.). 2009. *Mobility and Migration in Indigenous Amazonia: Contemporary Ethnoecological Perspectives*. New York and Oxford: Berghahn Books.

Allen, C. 1988. *The Hold Life Has: Coca and Cultural Identity in an Andean Community*. Washington, DC: Smithsonian Institution Press.

———. 1998. 'When Utensils Revolt: Mind, Matter, and Modes of Beings in the Pre-Colombian Andes', *RES: Anthropology and Aesthetics* 33: 18–27.

Altamirano, T. 1988. *Cultura Andina y Pobreza Urbana Aymaras en Lima Metropolitana*. Lima: Pontificia Universidad Católica del Perú.

Bird-David, N. 1999. '"Animism" Revisited: Personhood, Environment, and Relational Epistemology', *Current Anthropology* 40: 67–91.

Cadena, M. de la. 2010. 'Indigenous Cosmopolitics in the Andes: Conceptual Reflections beyond "Politics"', *Cultural Anthropology* 25(2): 334–70.

Canessa, A. 2000. 'Fear and Loathing on the *Kharisiri* Trail: Alterity and Identity in the Andes', *Journal of the Royal Anthropological Institute* 6: 705–20.

Descola, P. 2011. *L'Ècologie des Autres: L'Anthropologie et la Question de la Nature*. Versailles: Quae.

Dover, R., K. Seibold and J. McDowell. 1992. *Andean Cosmologies through Time: Persistence and Emergence*. Bloomington and Indianapolis: Indiana University Press.

Feather, C. 2013. 'The Restless Life of the Nahua: Shaping People and Places in the Peruvian Amazon', in M.N. Alexiades (ed.), *Mobility and Migration in Indigenous Amazonia: Contemporary Ethnoecological Perspectives*. New York and Oxford: Berghahn Books, pp. 69–85.

Gose, P. 1994. *Deathly Waters and Hungry Mountains: Agrarian Ritual and Class Formation in an Andean Town*. Toronto: University of Toronto Press.

Gow, P., and M. Margiotti. 2012. 'Is There Fortune in Greater Amazonia?', *Social Analysis* 56: 43–56.

Harris, O. 2000. *To Make the Earth Bear Fruit: Ethnographic Essays on Fertility, Work and Gender in Highland Bolivia*. London: Institute of Latin American Studies.

Harvey, P. 2001. 'Landscape and Commerce: Creating Contexts for the Exercise of Power', in B. Bender and M. Winer (eds), *Contested Landscapes: Movement, Exile and Place*. Oxford: Berg, pp. 197–210.

Lund Skar, S. 1994. *Worlds Together, Lives Apart: Quechua Colonization in Jungle and City*. Oslo: Scandinavian University Press.

Mintchev, N., and H.L. Moore. 2016. 'Super-diversity and the Prosperous Society', *European Journal of Social Theory* 21: 1–18.

Molina, C. de. 1943. *Fábulas y ritos de los Incas*. Lima: Miranda.

Nash, J. (ed.). 1979. *We Eat the Mines and the Mines Eat Us: Dependency and Exploitation in Bolivian Tin Mines*. New York: Columbia University Press.

Ødegaard, C.V. 2010. *Mobility, Markets and Indigenous Socialities: Contemporary Migration in the Peruvian Andes*. Farnham, UK: Ashgate.

———. 2011. 'Sources of Danger and Prosperity: Mobility and Powerful Surroundings in the Andes', *Journal of the Royal Anthropological Institute* (Incorporating *Man*) 17: 339–55.

———. 2016. 'Alterity, Predation and Questions of Representation: The Problem of the *Kharisiri* in the Andes', in B. Bertelsen and S. Bendixsen (eds), *Critical Anthropological Engagements in Human Alterity and Difference*. New York: Palgrave Macmillan, pp. 65–87.

Polanyi, K. 1957. 'The Economy as Instituted Process', in K. Polanyi and C.M. Arensberg (eds), *Trade and Markets in the Early Empires*. Glencoe, IL: Free Press, pp. 243–70.

Ramos, A.R. 2012. 'The Politics of Perspectivism', *The Annual Review of Anthropology* 41: 481–94.

Remme, J.H.Z. 2016. 'Chronically Unstable Ontology: Ontological Dynamics, Radical Alterity, and the "Otherwise Within"', in B. Bertelsen and S. Bendixsen (eds), *Critical Anthropological Engagements in Human Alterity and Difference*. New York: Palgrave Macmillan, pp. 114–32.

Rivera Andía, J.J. 2003. *La fiesta del Ganado en el Valle de Chancay (1962–2002). Religión y ritual en los Andes: etnografía, documentos inéditos e intepretación*. Lima: PUCP.

———. 2005. 'Killing What You Love: An Andean Cattle-Branding Ritual and the Dilemmas of Modernity', *Journal of Anthropological Research* 61: 129–56.

Rivière, P. 1994. 'Wysinwyg in Amazonia', *Journal of the Anthropological Society of Oxford* 25: 255–62.

Sahlins, M. 1972. *Stone Age Economics*. New York: Aldine de Gruyter.

Sallnow, M. 1987. *Pilgrims of the Andes: Regional Cults in Cuzco*. Washington, DC: Smithsonian Institution.

Santos-Granero, F. (ed.). 2015. *Images of Public Wealth or the Anatomy of Well-Being in Indigenous Amazonia*. Tucson: University of Arizona Press.

Sherbondy, J. 1992. 'Water Ideology in Inca Ethnogenesis', in R. Dover, K. Seibold and J. McDowell (eds), *Andean Cosmologies through Time: Persistence and Emergence*. Bloomington and Indianapolis: Indiana University Press, pp. 46–66.

Stensrud, A.B. 2011. '"Todo en la Vida se Paga": Negotiating Life in Cusco, Peru'. PhD dissertation. Oslo: University of Oslo.

Strathern, M. 1988. *The Gender of the Gift*. Berkeley and Los Angeles: University of California Press.

Taussig, M. 1980. *The Devil and Commodity Fetishism in South America*. Chapel Hill: The University of North Carolina Press.

Turner, T. 2009. 'The Crisis of Late Structuralism, Perspectivism and Animism: Rethinking Culture, Nature, Spirit, and Bodiliness', *Tipití. Journal of the Society for the Anthropology of Lowland South America* 7(1): 3–42.

Tylor, E.B. 1871. *Religion in Primitive Culture*. New York: Harper and Row.

Urton, G. 1981. *At the Crossroads of the Earth and the Sky: An Andean Cosmology*. Austin: University of Texas Press.

Viveiros de Castro, E. 1992. *From the Enemy's Point of View: Humanity and Divinity in an Amazonian Society*. Chicago, IL: University of Chicago Press.

———. 1998. 'Cosmological Deixis and Amerindian Perspectivism', *The Journal of the Royal Anthropological Institute* 4: 469–88.

———. 1999. 'Comments to "Animism Revisited: Personhood, Environment, and Relational Epistemology"', *Current Anthropology* 40: 79–80.

———. 2004. 'Perspectival Anthropology and the Method of Controlled Equivocation', in *Tipití. Journal of the Society for the Anthropology of Lowland South America* 2(1): 3–22.

Weismantel, M. 2001. *Cholas and Pishtacos: Stories of Race and Sex in the Andes*. Chicago, IL: University of Chicago Press.

Willerslev, R. 2013. 'Taking Animism Seriously, but Perhaps Not Too Seriously?', *Religion and Society: Advances in Research* 4(1): 41–57.

Epilogue

The Wild Boar Is Out Again and Knows Better than the Jaguar

Mark Münzel

Two invisible guests have been present at the Round Table on Non-humans in South America: the jaguar and the wild boar.

I am using these two species here as an animal metaphor (which is nothing alien to Amerindian ways of expression) following an observation of Claude Lévi-Strauss (1964: 102) on their roles in South American mythologies. He found (as always) a pair of oppositions in the case of two mythical transformations of man: one, of a man into a jaguar, and the other into a wild boar. In the first case the man is elevated to a higher rank, above culture; thus the shaman approaches the celestial beings. In the second case, the man who becomes a wild boar is degraded below culture.[1] Today, decades later, most of us think that the contrast between nature and culture underlying his assumptions was exaggerated, including his distinction between the jaguar who reaches above culture and the wild boar who remains below it. In a more general way, the structuralist transformation of fieldwork data into abstract theory has provoked a reaction of a return to solid field data. But we can still use his metaphors.

I take the jaguar metaphorically as the elevation to a higher level, to more than culture; this means, for science, where shamanism is substituted by higher teaching, to theoretical abstraction sterilised of impure field data. The wild boar, on the other hand, is field research not yet ennobled to the level of pure theory. Of course, the humanities always have to find a path between abstraction and empiricism, between the jaguar and the wild boar, but in the specific moment that the study of South American Indian ritual and mythological life has reached today, the question is more acute than ever. I should like to call this book a manifesto of post-perspectivism, as the jaguar (perspectival over-abstraction and over-generalisation) has to give room to the wild boar (fieldwork) again; and we discover that even without high-level abstract theorising the wild boar is able to speak, to think – and, by searching on the ground, we discover new paths that may serve as a solid base for generalisation.

The Jaguar

'Perspectivism' has rocked South Americanist anthropology since Viveiros de Castro's fundamental 1996 article, which developed further and generalised ideas he proposed in his 1986 PhD (Viveiros de Castro 1986). This dissertation connected the long-term Brazilian discussion on anthropophagy to a tradition of joking among the Indians, taking an anthropophagic indigenous statement of the sixteenth century as 'a burst of humour: black or Zen … a declaration of a revealing non-sense'.[2] But in 1992, the title of the English translation suppressed the reference to anthropophagy, so typical of a certain Brazilian anthropological tradition, by substituting '*The Cannibal Gods*' of the Brazilian Portuguese title with the more abstract '*Humanity and Divinity*', and introduced the 'Enemy's Point of View' (evoking the 'Other' that is so important to French philosophy from Levinas to Latour). In the same vein, the translation substituted the key quotation of the original text – in which the South American author Jorge Luis Borges claimed that even if reality is not always fascinating, the hypothesis of it must be – with a quote from a French writer, Michel Leiris, who speaks about the interface between spirits: ours and the *others*. The changes of title and epigraph are significant: from the Brazilian concern for indigenous humour and fantasy, to the French philosophy of the Other.

A Note on Masking Fun

Viveiros de Castro's keen sense of indigenous humour is in line with a Brazilian tradition of understanding based upon field experience with Amerindians. An old Brazilian anthropologist[3] once explained it to the young and inexperienced newcomer to field research I was at that time by one of his many fieldwork anecdotes. Once he had met a fierce Indian chief at the entrance to a village of warriors. Gesturing like a jaguar, the chief warned him: 'I am very wild! I shall eat you!'

The Brazilian anthropologist replied in an even more theatrical way with an even wilder gesture including the hills around them: 'I am wilder than you! I eat up anything, even the hills and the trees!' The fierce warrior understood the irony, broke into a grin, put his arm around the anthropologist's shoulder and said: 'Let's go to my village and have a good meal!' In another case, a Brazilian lady visited an indigenous village where I was on fieldwork. She happened to arrive during a ritual dance when masked male dancers threatened the women with clubs. Some trees from the spirits' forest had been cut in order to create space for a new garden, and now the spirits, being the owners of the woods, asked for an indemnity: the women had to serve food to them. It was a wild scene with the masked men brandishing their clubs and the women crying in an apparent fear that did not always hide their giggles. The serious background was, on one hand, the idea that the forest and its ferocious inhabitants had to be compensated for the loss of their trees, and on the other, that the men who had cut the trees and were now hiding under the masks had to be paid for their labour. The white lady was afraid to tears of the whole awful racket. But at this moment, a masked man who had been brandishing his club at her lifted his mask briefly, and told me with a grin, 'Tell the lady everything is fine', and then went on again uttering horrible, threatening cries.

It is this kind of play between gravity and jokes that characterises much of the indigenous ritual life that Viveiros de Castro seems to understand so well. But it is precisely this sense of humour that has been submerged in his later works by a philosophy that fulfils desires of an international public in want of deepness. '"Isn't the cannibal always the other?" asked Clastres and Lizot' (Viveiros de Castro 1992: 271). This tendency was always there in Viveiros de Castro's work, but now it took over control.

A Note on Masking Field Research

This was already the second transformation that Viveiros de Castro's publications on the Araweté had undergone. They were originally based upon solid fieldwork from 1981 to 1983, but were not published as a classical monograph before 2000, and (from a career point of view: 'only') in Portuguese, not in a prestigious English or French edition – the same goes for his earlier, thorough and inspired fieldwork on the Yawalapíti. Reading this truly captivating report on a non-European culture, one wonders how the author managed to forget it all in order to write – obviously later on, although with an earlier publication date compared with the field report – a highly theoretical PhD dissertation in which it is often difficult to find behind the European philosophy the original indigenous sentences that had been included in the earlier field report. In fact, the way the author manages this transformation is by mixing up the ethnographic facts of his field research with colonial sources of the Tupinambá of the sixteenth century and with general sources of anthropology. It was this alienation from the field that guaranteed the international success of Viveiros de Castro's work. The jaguar went up to heaven and left behind the wild boar.

A Note on Masking Indigenous Sufferings and Multiple Cultures

Is it a pure contingency or an unconscious hint at a specific tradition that with perspectivism the term 'ontology' has spread again in anthropology? In fact, in the history of anthropology, there was an important precedent case set in 1945: the Bantu 'ontology' of Father Placide Tempels ([1945] 1949).[4] This fascinating piece of European (in this case, Thomistic) philosophy found among Congolese mission disciples was offered to the European public as the proof that there was an indigenous ontology that European missionaries could admire, and it had an important function in the late colonial period by showing that Africans were able to think (an astounding miracle for many a European at that time). After fifteen years of living among Congolese Bantu, Father Tempels had achieved a deep insight into their ways of thinking and had translated them into the terms of European religious philosophy he had learnt during his theological formation. Even today, his work continues to be an important contribution to our understanding of African thought. Yet, two objections quickly arose.

First, African revolutionary leaders and writers of the decolonisation period accused him of turning the general public's attention away from the actual social and economic problems Africans were suffering. As the Antillean poet and political activist Aimé Césaire commented with bitter irony:

> Let them plunder and torture in the Congo, let the Belgian colonizer seize all the natural resources, let him stamp out all freedom, let him crush all pride, let him go in peace, the Reverend Father Tempels consents to all that. But take care! You are going to the Congo? Respect I do not say native property (the great Belgian companies might take that as a dig at them), I do not say the freedom of the natives (the Belgian colonists

might think that was subversive talk), I do not say the Congolese nation (the Belgian government might take it much amiss). I say: You are going to the Congo? Respect the Bantu philosophy! ... Since Bantu thought is ontological, the Bantu only ask for satisfaction of an ontological nature. (Césaire [1950] 1972: 57–58)

Eduardo Viveiros de Castro cannot be accused of this way of neglecting the indigenous sufferings by restraining himself to philosophy. His fieldwork report does not spare the authorities severe criticism for the actual policy of destruction of the environment, of the indigenous culture, and of indigenous lives. These chapters are written with obvious engagement, even with wrath. But those were his field notes, not the books he gained international prestige with and which are cleaned of untheoretical descriptions of indigenous sufferings. Now it is ontology. As Aimé Césaire might have put it:

Let them plunder in the Amazon, let them go in peace, the anthropologist consents to all that. But take care! You are going to the Amazon? Respect I do not say native property (the great companies might take that as a dig at them). I say: You are going to the Amazon? Respect the Amazon Indian ontology!

Second, Father Tempels' analysis of Bantu thought, as much as it was based upon years of conversations with Bantu thinkers, could easily be traced back to a European interpretation: the learned theologian had translated African thought into European (in his case Christian) ontology. Moreover, he had underestimated the richness of varieties of African cultures, lumping them all together into one 'Bantu philosophy'.

The analogy with the actual perspectival ontology is obvious. Sentences pronounced by South American indigenous thinkers are adapted to and lumped together into one ethnophilosophy. As Alcida Rita Ramos puts it in an article cited in this book by Rivera Andía and Ødegaard:

The enormous indigenous diversity is currently in danger of being compressed into formulas and principles of an alien philosophy. [Perspectivism] runs the risk of spawning a new ethnographic species: a generic Amerindian forever trading substances and viewpoints with animals in a cosmological orgy of predation and cannibalism. [This] theoretical proposition hinges on its philosophical rhetoric, which is more appropriate to generalizations than to the understanding of specific worlds of meaning. (Ramos 2012: 483)

Ramos also criticises the depoliticisation implied in the perspectival focus on indigenous thought: 'Perspectivism in a Political Neverland' (ibid.). Similarly, Terence Turner (amply mentioned by Rivera Andía in this book) argues

> that closer attention to the detailed structure of indigenous conceptions, both of natural beings and human embodied persons, is essential to avoid the distortions inherent in attempts to treat all Amazonian (or even all Amerindian) cultures as a single, homogeneous philosophical system. (Turner 2009: 39)

But this does not mean that perspectivism could just be dismissed. On the contrary, it is widely recognised to have opened new horizons and furnished deeper insights into indigenous thought. Oscar Calavia Sáez (2012 – another article of this author is cited in this book by Rivera Andía) pleads for demystification: let us just take perspectivism as one way of understanding among others and see what insights it may furnish us with. Ramos's and Turner's criticisms of the abstraction from fieldwork in some perspectival writings are true for the later works of Viveiros de Castro. Yet as Calavia finds, while many scholars of perspectivism have done thorough fieldwork, their verbal adherence to perspectivism hides their efforts to just do a serious work based upon the data they collected in the field. This may parallel what happened with structuralism: it continued to be used as a theoretical frame, if not to say facade, behind which serious fieldwork on indigenous belief systems had been carried out. One might also think of ethnological works written in the last period of East German socialism: many a preface published at that time stressed the importance of Marxism (often together with the latest Party Congress) for each respective work, while the subsequent text bore no relation whatsoever to either the Party or to Marxism. In the conclusion of such works, of course, the author would summarise how the preceding chapters had confirmed the findings of Marx and Engels.

A Note on Masking Indigenous Ontodiversity

During my first field trips I tried to find out how an indigenous community[5] categorised certain spirits within the world's order. I established a list of ghosts and asked if they were living in the woods or in the lakes, if they had competence over forest game or over trees or over fish. My indigenous counterparts quickly understood what I was aiming at: the discovery of a system of extra-human beings, the arrangement of each one in a case. This amused them, and they mocked me. When I asked where a certain spirit of the waters that gave or refused fish to the fishermen lived, they answered 'in the forest, of course'. And when I asked where a jaguar ghost lived, they answered 'deep in the river'. The spirit of a bird was placed below the roots, not up in the tree tops. This was just a game, a joyful invention of an inverted world in response to the simplicity of my questions. But it was also a reaction to my efforts to systematise their world's order. Beyond the momentary joke, they made me understand that there is movement and disorder in the world. In fact, as they then explained to me, the fish spirit is not always a fish, but may undergo a transformation into a jaguar, and the jaguar sometimes is able to change into a certain bird. Thus, they introduced me to their world of permanent change. Things are not what they seem to be – or if they are, they will soon become something else.

This is, if not the contrary, at least not exactly what is usually understood as 'ontology', a term of European philosophy derived from the Greek το ὄντος (the being), the doctrine of what is and, in most cases, will always be. If we look beyond the realm of anthropology, we find a wide range of philosophical discussions, from Heidegger's irrationality to the rationalist antipodes, who would prefer analysis to the mystics of Being they consider an 'illness', which has spread like a pestilence since the nineteenth century but has now passed its peak (Stegmüller 1969: 5). This is not the place to enter deeper into that discussion, but to recommend an awareness: 'ontology' is not an innocent word that anthropologists may use as 'just another word for culture' (as they are criticised for in Venkatesan et al. 2010), but a term heavily charged with traditions we should be aware of before using it. Resuming and simplifying, I should range it among either the Heideggerian mystics or (more frequently, as in phenomenology) among the descriptive systems of the timeless order of things. It is usually meant to be universal (except with Heidegger, but he is certainly not of much influence on South Americanist anthropology): 'Ontology, as philosophers understand it, grasps at truths that transcend the experience or history of particular human groups, while anthropology is concerned with human differences and the uniqueness of perspective' (Paleček and Risjord 2013: 3).[6]

Underlying the use of 'ontology' (again, except with Heidegger) is the conviction that beliefs are based upon a timeless order. This means that when we speak of an indigenous 'ontology' we presuppose (consciously or not) a worldview that takes the world to be based upon immutable, eternal, timeless truths. This is certainly true for some basic ideas – for instance, for ethical principles – but it does not fully describe the richness of indigenous imagination. In many an indigenous system of understanding of the world, disorder and change are immanent. Many an indigenous thinker does not like permanent systems; and many an indigenous mythology is a story of reversals of order. Indeed, perhaps one of the reasons for the spread in European science of the 'pestilence' (Stegmüller) of finding an Ontology of Being everywhere was the fear of change and disorder.

Now, it is interesting to note that most of the authors of the present, post-perspectivist or post-ontological volume do not use the term except when referring explicitly to the theoretical context of perspectivism or animism where, naturally, this main keyword must be noticed and discussed. Ødegaard is among those in this book who explicitly cautions against 'reducing cultural variation, creativity and everyday negotiation to rigid ontological schemas', or even 'understanding of these ontologies as closed, monolithic and totalitarian'. She only seems to admit the term without any hesitation when speaking not of beings or things but of a principle such as the necessity of exchange. Dransart uses the word only with respect to strong, 'ontological' power; Sax speaks of ontological classes and relationships between power objects, not of an ontology of spirits.

As Rivera quotes in this book, Descola has raised concerns about how the 'ontological turn' neglects ontodiversity, meaning the richness of differences between indigenous thoughts. Halbmayer (cited by Rivera in this book as another recent critic of the ontological turn), although using the term ontology, gives it a sense contrary to the usual one: not monolithic, but against unified systems. He introduces 'mereology' (a formal theory of parthood relations within philosophical or theological ontology) to describe 'an ontology based on partial encompassment resulting in a multiverse and multiple beings' (Halbmayer 2012: 120). One is tempted to think of Husserl's problem of establishing the material relations of wholes to parts to find an equilibrium between the formal and the material a priori (the system and its mereologies).[7] Halbmayer is careful not to go beyond the empirical data from indigenous groups he studied, and it is with much caution that he arrives at the question of whether the importance of mereologies he found there is 'a specific feature of Carib-speaking groups' or is 'widely dispersed among lowland South American groups' (ibid.). Yet the term 'mereologies' usually still presupposes that there is always a system (meaning a whole or a formal a priori, as Husserl would have said) of which mereologies are the parts. I should go a bit further and ask if it could not be the other way round. Why should indigenous worlds of multiplicity and dissidence always form parts of a whole? Could not indigenous thinkers be strong enough to endure a multiversity of systems, and live without systematising a whole?

The Wild Boar

As several authors of this book note, the problem with perspectivism is that it tempts alienation from the realities of the field. It is in this context that Turner (2009) traces it back to structuralism. I have tried above to describe this problem in a nutshell through the evolution of Eduardo Viveiro de Castro from an excellent field researcher to an excellent theoretician who lost his solid empirical ground.

In fact, there *is* solid empirical data on indigenous perspectivism and, of course, Viveiros de Castro and other perspectivists refer to them. It is only that these data do not encompass a general world-view, but refer to specific cases, especially to wild boars – and here, I am not speaking of the species as a metaphor, but of real wild boars running through the forests of the Amazon. According to what some Amerindians are reported to say, the perspectives of wild boars are contrary to ours: they think that it is them who hunt men, whereas we think hunters are hunting wild boars. This is the empirical evidence from the Juruna society brought upon by Tânia Stolze Lima (1996): it is wild boars.

Lima is frequently quoted by Viveiros de Castro, who emphasises that one of his main chapters on perspectivism and multinaturalism 'has its origins in a dialogue with Tânia Stolze Lima', while his key article on perspectivism from 1996 'was written and published at the same time as the article of Lima about the Juruna perspectivism which I recommend to the reader' (Viveiros de Castro 2002: 347–48, note 1). Another main source Viveiros de Castro quotes is the field research of Gerhard Baer, and there again it is wild boars (and tapirs) (Baer 1984: 198).[8] In another context, not quoted by Viveiros, the wild boars appear again, this time seen from the other side, and mistaken: 'The dead of the Secoya speak about the living in an erroneous way and think fish are wild boars' (Cipolletti 1992: 167). Cipolletti sees this as one part of a more general view of the Secoya, namely that those who abandon their society are no more able to understand it, but see it through a 'deforming mirror' – an idea expressed in mythology through the narrative strategy of 'the paradox, the inversion, and the reduction to absurdity' (ibid.: 171).

The fact is surprising: in a great part (though not in all) of the cases of Amerindian explanations cited as the empirical basis for perspectivism, the indigenous people were talking about wild boars. Could it be that what has served a whole perspectival ethnophilosophy was just an observation of how a horde of wild boars, persecuted by human hunters or on the run for other reasons, seems to scurry without reason, trampling down whatever they find on their way?[9] Or how some old wild boars separate from their band to live a solitary life outside their society? Or to put it in a more general way, has the old structuralist and more recent perspectivist bias to generalisation led anthropologists astray from the empirical observations of certain species that Amerindians had transformed into mythical cases of *specific* behaviour, and not meant to be generalised at an overarching non-human level? Mythology often describes not rules but rather *un*-usual behaviour – who would suppose that the sexual adventures of Zeus might provide rules of social conduct for humans? Of course, perspectivism has found many cases of relations between humans and non-humans other than wild boars, but it is precisely when field research permits a closer look at so many cases that we find that there is more to Amerindian cultures 'than the animist and perspectival ontologies have so far revealed', as they 'ultimately discard or ignore the rich base of biological knowledge that underlies the natural and cosmogonic classifications of native Amazonians' (Rival 2012: 132, 127), and, may we add, of other indigenous South American peoples as well.

A return to the details of fieldwork results is precisely what is happening in the chapters assembled in this volume. As the editor puts it, this volume 'offers bottom-up approaches ... Following the evidence of their own fieldwork findings, the authors have compiled here work from ethnographic phenomena to theoretical frames, and their texts stand in contrast to projects mostly concerned with locating examples of already posited typologies'.

May the jaguar climb up to the heaven of abstract ideas. Meanwhile, let us listen to the wise observations of indigenous thinkers and experts of nature and non-humans, even when the jaguar thinks those are just wild boars running around on this too-material world and failing to reach ontological schemas invented in heaven. This rehabilitation of the wild boar is the message of the book. And let us not forget that among the animals of South America, the boar (and not the jaguar) is the one most similar to man inside his or her body (heart, liver, etc.), as any hunter may observe. As a metaphor, the boar is human, and field research is to observe human life and thinking, not the theories of those jaguars who lost ground in the heaven of their theories.

Mark Münzel is Professor Emeritus at the Philipps-University of Marburg in the Department of Social and Cultural Anthropology. Born in Potsdam in 1943, he studied in Frankfurt, Coimbra and Recife. He obtained a Ph.D. at Goethe University in Frankfurt 1970 with a thesis on Amazon Indian shamanism and has conducted research among indigenous peoples in Brazil, Paraguay, Ecuador and Peru. He was curator of the Ethnographic Museum of Frankfurt 1973–89 and chair of Anthropology at the University of Marburg 1989–2008. He has also been actively engaged in solidarity movements of indigenous peoples and was member of the Board and Chairman of the International Workgroup for Indigenous Affairs from 1979 to 1982. His main themes of interest are South American indigenous religions, mythologies and arts.

Notes

1. The South American wild boar is akin to, but not of the same family as, the Old World boar. The New World Tayassu family includes two species that Lévi-Strauss distinguishes carefully, but I skip these details here. Strict differentiations are also observed in at least those South American indigenous languages I have come across. Besides the words for the two zoological species, the Aché idiom (of Tupí-Guaraní stock) specifically designates a pecari that is living solitarily outside the band with a word for 'wild, solitary'. The degradation below culture that Lévi-Strauss attributes to the mythical wild boar seems to me to fit to this term for an animal that is living outside the animal society. On the other hand, although jaguars, in distinction to wild boars, do not live in bands, there is also a word for an especially solitary, unsocial jaguar. Lévi-Strauss would have been pleased to learn that the unsocial wild boar and the unsocial jaguar might be seen as one kind of a linguistic pair.
2. English translation (Viveiros de Castro 1992: 271).
3. Protásio Frikel, of German origin, but acculturated in Brazil.
4. For a recent discussion, see Obanda 2002.
5. The Kamayurá in northern Mato Grosso.

6. The authors, two specialists on the philosophy of social sciences, are defending the 'ontological turn' of anthropology, if one looks at it through the philosophy of Donald Davidson: 'At first look, one might think that [it] was nothing more than a puzzling, even confused fashion. On a closer look, it turns out to be interesting' (Paleček and Risjord 2013: 21). It is in fact a pity that few perspectival anthropologists seem to have ever read anything of the philosophical debate Davidson stands for. Nor had I ever taken notice of Paleček and Risjord's important article before Mona Suhrbier (Frankfurt) drew my attention to it.
7. Cf. Van Eynde 1999.
8. Viveiros quotes the Spanish translation.
9. This behaviour can be observed in Europe as well. On the outskirts of small towns in the rural region where I live, the destructions such hordes of wild boars (in this case: Old World) cause in gardens are frequent local news.

References

Baer, G. 1984. *Die Religion der Matsigenka, Ost-Peru*. Basel: Wepf & Co. AG Verlag.

Calavia Sáez, O. 2012. 'Do Perspectivismo Ameríndio ao Índio Real', *Campos, Revista de Antropologia Social* 13(2): 7–23.

Césaire, A. (1950) 1972. *Discourse on Colonialism*. New York: Monthly Review Press.

Cipolletti, M.S. 1992. 'El Espejo Deformante: El Mundo de los Muertos Secoya', in M.S. Cipolletti and E.J. Langdon (eds), *La Muerte y el Más Allá en las Culturas Indígenas Latinoamericanas*. Quito, Ecuador: Abya-Yala, pp. 157–78.

Halbmayer, E. 2012. 'Amerindian Mereology: Animism, Analogy, and the Multiverse', *Indiana* 29: 103–25.

Lévi-Strauss, C. 1964. *Le Cru et le Cuit*. Paris: Plon.

Lima, T.S. 1996. 'O Dois e Seu Múltiplo: Reflexões Sobre o Perspectivismo em uma Cosmologia Tupi', *Mana* 2(2): 21–47.

Obanda, S. 2002. *Re-création de la Philosophie Africaine: Rupture avec Tempels et Kagame*. Bern: Lang.

Paleček, M., and M. Risjord. 2013. 'Relativism and the Ontological Turn within Anthropology', *Philosophy of the Social Sciences* 43(1): 3–23.

Ramos, A.R. 2012. 'The Politics of Perspectivism', *Annual Review of Anthropology* 41: 481–94.

Rival, L. 2012. 'The Materiality of Life: Revisiting the Anthropology of Nature in Amazonia', *Indiana* 29: 127–43.

Stegmüller, W. 1969. *Probleme und Resultate der Wissenschaftstheorie und analytischen Philosophie*, 1, *Wissenschaftliche Erklärung und Begründung*. Berlin: Springer.

Tempels, P. (1945) 1949. *La Philosophie Bantoue*. Paris: Éditions Africaines.

Turner, T. 2009. 'The Crisis of Late Structuralism. Perspectivism and Animism: Rethinking Culture, Nature, Spirit, and Bodiliness', *Tipití. Journal of the Society for the Anthropology of Lowland South America* 7(1): 3–42.

Van Eynde, L. 1999. 'Husserl et la Reprise Génétique de la Méréologie', *Tijdschrift voor Filosofie* 61: 697–727.

Venkatesan, S., et al. 2010. 'Ontology is Just Another Word for Culture: Motion Tabled at the 2008 Meeting of the Group for Debates in Anthropological Theory, University of Manchester', *Critique of Anthropology* 30(2): 152–200.

Viveiros de Castro, E. 1986. *Araweté: os Deuses Canibais*. Rio de Janeiro: Jorge Zahar.

———. 1992. *From the Enemy's Point of View: Humanity and Divinity in an Amazonian Society*. Chicago, IL and London: The University of Chicago Press.

———. 1996. 'Os pronomes cosmológicos e o perspectivismo amerindio', *Mana* 2(2): 115–44.

———. 2000. *Araweté: O Povo do Ipixuna*. Lisbon: Museu Nacional de Etnologia.

———. 2002. *A Inconstância da Alma Selvagem, e Outros Ensaios de Antropologia*. São Paulo: Cosac Naify.

Index

EASA Series

Published in association with the European Association of Social Anthropologists (EASA)

Series Editor: Aleksandar Bošković, University of Belgrade

Social anthropology in Europe is growing, and the variety of work being done is expanding. This series is intended to present the best of the work produced by members of the EASA, both in monographs and in edited collections. The studies in this series describe societies, processes and institutions around the world, and are intended for both scholarly and student readership.

.

www.ingramcontent.com/pod-product-compliance
Lightning Source LLC
Chambersburg PA
CBHW070900030426
42336CB00014BA/2271